R Data Analysis Cookbook

Second Edition

A journey from data computation to data-driven insights

Kuntal Ganguly

BIRMINGHAM - MUMBAI

R Data Analysis Cookbook

Second Edition

Copyright © 2017 Packt Publishing

First published: May 2015

Second Edition: September 2017

Production reference: 1150917

Published by Packt Publishing Ltd.
Livery Place
35 Livery Street
Birmingham
B3 2PB, UK.
ISBN 978-1-78712-447-9

www.packtpub.com

Credits

Author
Kuntal Ganguly

Copy Editor
Manisha Sinha

Reviewers
Davor Lozić
Daniel Alvarez Rojas

Project Coordinator
Manthan Patel

Commissioning Editor
Amey Varangaonkar

Proofreader
Safis Editing

Acquisition Editor
Tushar Gupta

Indexer
Tejal Daruwale Soni

Content Development Editor
Tejas Limkar

Graphics
Tania Dutta

Technical Editor
Sagar Sawant

Production Coordinator
Deepika Naik

About the Author

Kuntal Ganguly is a big data analytics engineer focused on building large-scale data-driven systems using big data frameworks and machine learning. He has around 7 years of experience of building several big data and machine learning applications.

Kuntal provides solutions to AWS customers in building real-time analytics systems using AWS services and open source Hadoop ecosystem technologies such as Spark, Kafka, Storm, and Flink, along with machine learning and deep learning frameworks.

Kuntal enjoys hands-on software development, and has single-handedly conceived, architectured, developed, and deployed several large-scale distributed applications. Besides being an open source contributor, he is a machine learning and deep learning practitioner and is very passionate about building intelligent applications.

I am grateful to my mother, **Chitra Ganguly**, and father, **Gopal Ganguly**, for their love and support and for teaching me much about hard work, and even the little I have absorbed has helped me immensely throughout my life. I would also like to thank all my friends, colleagues, and mentors that I've had over the years.

You can reach Kuntal on LinkedIn at
`https://in.linkedin.com/in/kuntal-ganguly-59564088`

I believe that data science and artificial intelligence will give us superpowers.

About the Reviewers

Davor Lozić is a senior software engineer interested in various subjects, especially computer security, algorithms, and data structures. He manages teams of 15+ engineers and is a part-time assistant professor who lectures about database systems, Java, and interoperability. You can visit his website at `http://warriorkitty.com` and contact him from there. He likes cats! If you want to talk about any aspect of technology or if you have funny pictures of cats, feel free to contact him.

Daniel Alvarez Rojas is currently a data scientist at Hova Health, an IT/consulting company in the health sector. With experience in statistics, marketing, and BI, Daniel holds a BA in Business and Marketing and works in government consulting, helping health managers and directors to take data-driven decisions to solve industry challenges. He has spent years as an analyst in logistic companies, working on optimization and predictive models.

I extend my deepest gratitude to my family: my parents, Daniel and Sara, for always supporting me and my brothers; and Abdiel and Amy, for urging me to be the best example that I can be for them. To Alessandra, for all the love and wisdom. Hector, for being, more than a friend, a mentor. To Adrian, for opening the doors for a new stage.

www.PacktPub.com

For support files and downloads related to your book, please visit www.PacktPub.com. Did you know that Packt offers eBook versions of every book published, with PDF and ePub files available? You can upgrade to the eBook version at www.PacktPub.com and as a print book customer, you are entitled to a discount on the eBook copy. Get in touch with us at service@packtpub.com for more details. At www.PacktPub.com, you can also read a collection of free technical articles, sign up for a range of free newsletters and receive exclusive discounts and offers on Packt books and eBooks.

https://www.packtpub.com/mapt

Get the most in-demand software skills with Mapt. Mapt gives you full access to all Packt books and video courses, as well as industry-leading tools to help you plan your personal development and advance your career.

Why subscribe?

- Fully searchable across every book published by Packt
- Copy and paste, print, and bookmark content
- On demand and accessible via a web browser

About the Reviewers

Davor Lozić is a senior software engineer interested in various subjects, especially computer security, algorithms, and data structures. He manages teams of 15+ engineers and is a part-time assistant professor who lectures about database systems, Java, and interoperability. You can visit his website at `http://warriorkitty.com` and contact him from there. He likes cats! If you want to talk about any aspect of technology or if you have funny pictures of cats, feel free to contact him.

Daniel Alvarez Rojas is currently a data scientist at Hova Health, an IT/consulting company in the health sector. With experience in statistics, marketing, and BI, Daniel holds a BA in Business and Marketing and works in government consulting, helping health managers and directors to take data-driven decisions to solve industry challenges. He has spent years as an analyst in logistic companies, working on optimization and predictive models.

I extend my deepest gratitude to my family: my parents, Daniel and Sara, for always supporting me and my brothers; and Abdiel and Amy, for urging me to be the best example that I can be for them. To Alessandra, for all the love and wisdom. Hector, for being, more than a friend, a mentor. To Adrian, for opening the doors for a new stage.

www.PacktPub.com

For support files and downloads related to your book, please visit `www.PacktPub.com`. Did you know that Packt offers eBook versions of every book published, with PDF and ePub files available? You can upgrade to the eBook version at `www.PacktPub.com` and as a print book customer, you are entitled to a discount on the eBook copy. Get in touch with us at `service@packtpub.com` for more details. At `www.PacktPub.com`, you can also read a collection of free technical articles, sign up for a range of free newsletters and receive exclusive discounts and offers on Packt books and eBooks.

`https://www.packtpub.com/mapt`

Get the most in-demand software skills with Mapt. Mapt gives you full access to all Packt books and video courses, as well as industry-leading tools to help you plan your personal development and advance your career.

Why subscribe?

- Fully searchable across every book published by Packt
- Copy and paste, print, and bookmark content
- On demand and accessible via a web browser

Customer Feedback

Thanks for purchasing this Packt book. At Packt, quality is at the heart of our editorial process. To help us improve, please leave us an honest review on this book's Amazon page at https://www.amazon.in/dp/1787124479. If you'd like to join our team of regular reviewers, you can email us at customerreviews@packtpub.com. We award our regular reviewers with free eBooks and videos in exchange for their valuable feedback. Help us be relentless in improving our products!

Table of Contents

Preface

Data analytics with R has emerged as a very important topic for organizations of all kinds. R enables even those with only an intuitive grasp of the underlying concepts, without a deep mathematical background, to unleash powerful and detailed examinations of their data. This book empowers you by showing you ways to use R to generate professional analysis reports. The book also teaches you how to quickly adapt the example code for your own needs and save yourself the time needed to construct code from scratch.

What this book covers

Chapter 1, *Acquire and Prepare the Ingredients – Reading Your Data*, provides the recipes to acquire, format, and cleanse data from multiple formats. Handling missing values, standardizing datasets, and transforming between numerical and categorical data are also covered.

Chapter 2, *What's in There? – Exploratory Data Analysis*, shows you how to perform exploratory data analysis and find underlying patterns to understand our dataset before getting into the analysis process.

Chapter 3, *Where does it belong? - Classification*, covers several classification techniques from basic classification trees, logistic regression, and support vector machines to text classification using Naive Bayes to find sentiment analysis.

Chapter 4, *Give me a number - Regression*, covers several algorithms for data prediction, such as linear regression, random forests, neural networks, and regression trees.

Chapter 5, *Can you simplify that? – Data Reduction Techniques*, covers code recipes for data reduction and clustering. We explore the different clustering algorithms in a practical way.

Chapter 6, *Lessons from history - Time Series Analysis*, explores how to work with financial time series data, how to visualize it, and how to perform predictions using the ARIMA algorithms.

Chapter 7, *How does it look? - Advance data visualization*, explores how to make attractive visualizations, 3D graphs, and advanced maps.

Chapter 8, *This May also interest you – Building Recommendations Systems*, guides you step by step through applying machine learning and data mining techniques, building and optimizing recommender models, followed by a fraud system practical example.

Chapter 9, *It's all about Connections – Social Network Analysis*, explores how to acquire, visualize, and cluster social network data using public APIs.

Chapter 10, *Put your best foot forward – Document and present your Analysis*, shows you how to show and share the results of the data analysis. It includes recipes to use R markdown, KnitR, and Shiny to create reports and dynamic dashboards.

Chapter 11, *Work Smarter, not Harder – Efficient and elegant R code*, covers recipes to handle large datasets using the apply family of functions, the `plyr` package, and using data tables to slice and dice data.

Chapter 12, *Where in the world? – Geospatial Analysis*, teaches you how to perform a geospatial data analysis implementing tools such as Google Maps and QGIS using R implementations. It covers how to import maps and visualize your own data into the maps.

Chapter 13, *Playing nice – Working with external data sources*, shows you how to work with external data sources such as Excel, MySql, or MongoDB, and how to perform large data processing methods with in-memory processing using Apache Spark.

What you need for this book

The steps should be listed in a way that it prepares the system environment to be able to test the code examples in the book.

The following software is required:

- R base
- MS Office
- Apache Java (JDK)
- MySQL
- MongoDB

Although all the code should run on the R command line, I suggest you run the code in the book from R Studio instead of the R command line, as it is an IDE and is easy to use. Also, a few chapters specifically require the use of R Studio only.

Who this book is for

This book is for data science professionals or analysts who have performed machine learning tasks and now want to explore deep learning and want a quick reference that address the pain points that crop up while implementing deep learning. Those who wish to have an edge over other deep learning professionals will find this book quite useful.

Conventions

In this book, you will find a number of text styles that distinguish between different kinds of information. Here are some examples of these styles and an explanation of their meaning.

Code words in text, database table names, folder names, filenames, file extensions, pathnames, dummy URLs, user input, and Twitter handles are shown as follows: "We can include other contexts through the use of the include directive."

A block of code is set as follows:

```
[default]
exten => s,1,Dial(Zap/1|30)
exten => s,2,Voicemail(u100)
exten => s,102,Voicemail(b100)
exten => i,1,Voicemail(s0)
```

When we wish to draw your attention to a particular part of a code block, the relevant lines or items are set in bold:

```
[default]
exten => s,1,Dial(Zap/1|30)
exten => s,2,Voicemail(u100)
exten => s,102,Voicemail(b100)
exten => i,1,Voicemail(s0)
```

Any command-line input or output is written as follows:

```
# cp /usr/src/asterisk-addons/configs/cdr_mysql.conf.sample
/etc/asterisk/cdr_mysql.conf
```

New terms and **important** words are shown in bold. Words that you see on the screen, for example, in menus or dialog boxes, appear in the text like this: "Clicking the **Next** button moves you to the next screen."

Warnings or important notes appear in a box like this.

 Tips and tricks appear like this.

Reader feedback

Feedback from our readers is always welcome. Let us know what you think about this book--what you liked or disliked. Reader feedback is important for us as it helps us develop titles that you will really get the most out of.

To send us general feedback, simply email feedback@packtpub.com, and mention the book's title in the subject of your message.

If there is a topic that you have expertise in and you are interested in either writing or contributing to a book, see our author guide at www.packtpub.com/authors.

Customer support

Now that you are the proud owner of a Packt book, we have a number of things to help you to get the most from your purchase.

Downloading the example code

You can download the example code files for this book from your account at http://www.packtpub.com. If you purchased this book elsewhere, you can visit http://www.packtpub.com/support and register to have the files emailed directly to you.

You can download the code files by following these steps:

1. Log in or register to our website using your email address and password.
2. Hover the mouse pointer on the **SUPPORT** tab at the top.
3. Click on **Code Downloads** & **Errata**.
4. Enter the name of the book in the **Search** box.

5. Select the book for which you're looking to download the code files.
6. Choose from the drop-down menu where you purchased this book from.
7. Click on **Code Download**.

You can also download the code files by clicking on the Code Files button on the book's webpage at the Packt Publishing website. This page can be accessed by entering the book's name in the **Search** box. Please note that you need to be logged in to your Packt account.

Once the file is downloaded, please make sure that you unzip or extract the folder using the latest version of:

* WinRAR / 7-Zip for Windows
* Zipeg / iZip / UnRarX for Mac
* 7-Zip / PeaZip for Linux

The code bundle for the book is also hosted on GitHub at `https://github.com/PacktPublishing/R-Data-Analysis-Cookbook-Second-Edition`. We also have other code bundles from our rich catalog of books and videos available at `https://github.com/PacktPublishing/`. Check them out!

Downloading the color images of this book

We also provide you with a PDF file that has color images of the screenshots/diagrams used in this book. The color images will help you better understand the changes in the output. You can download this file from `https://www.packtpub.com/sites/default/files/downloads/RDataAnalysisCookbookSecondEdition_ColorImages.pdf`.

Errata

Although we have taken every care to ensure the accuracy of our content, mistakes do happen. If you find a mistake in one of our books--maybe a mistake in the text or the code-- we would be grateful if you could report this to us. By doing so, you can save other readers from frustration and help us improve subsequent versions of this book. If you find any errata, please report them by visiting `http://www.packtpub.com/submit-errata`, selecting your book, clicking on the Errata Submission Form link, and entering the details of your errata. Once your errata are verified, your submission will be accepted and the errata will be uploaded to our website or added to any list of existing errata under the Errata section of that title.

To view the previously submitted errata, go to
https://www.packtpub.com/books/content/support and enter the name of the book in the
search field. The required information will appear under the Errata section.

Piracy

Piracy of copyrighted material on the Internet is an ongoing problem across all media. At
Packt, we take the protection of our copyright and licenses very seriously. If you come
across any illegal copies of our works in any form on the Internet, please provide us with
the location address or website name immediately so that we can pursue a remedy.

Please contact us at copyright@packtpub.com with a link to the suspected pirated
material.

We appreciate your help in protecting our authors and our ability to bring you valuable
content.

Questions

If you have a problem with any aspect of this book, you can contact us at
questions@packtpub.com, and we will do our best to address the problem.

1
Acquire and Prepare the Ingredients - Your Data

In this chapter, we will cover:

- Working with data
- Reading data from CSV files
- Reading XML data
- Reading JSON data
- Reading data from fixed-width formatted files
- Reading data from R files and R libraries
- Removing cases with missing values
- Replacing missing values with the mean
- Removing duplicate cases
- Rescaling a variable to specified min-max range
- Normalizing or standardizing data in a data frame
- Binning numerical data
- Creating dummies for categorical variables
- Handling missing data
- Correcting data
- Imputing data
- Detecting outliers

Introduction

Data is everywhere and the amount of digital data that exists is growing rapidly, that is projected to grow to 180 zettabytes by 2025. **Data Science** is a field that tries to extract insights and meaningful information from structured and unstructured data through various stages such as asking questions, getting the data, exploring the data, modeling the data, and communicating result as shown in the following diagaram:

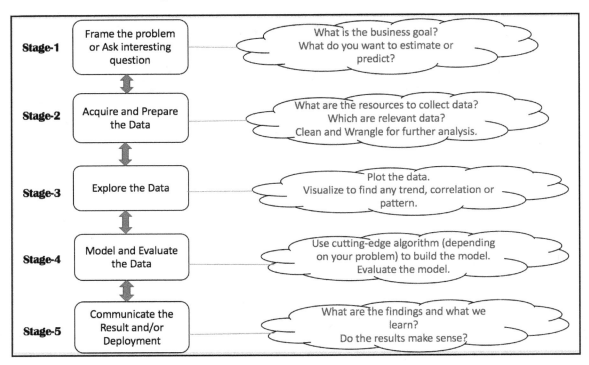

Data scientists or analysts often need to load or collect data from various resources having different input formats into R. Although R has its own native data format, data usually exists in text formats, such as **Comma Separated Values (CSV)**, **JavaScript Object Notation (JSON)**, and **Extensible Markup Language (XML)**. This chapter provides recipes to load such data into your R system for processing.

Raw, real-world datasets are often messy with missing values, unusable format, and outliers. Very rarely can we start analyzing data immediately after loading it. Often, we will need to preprocess the data to clean, impute, wrangle, and transform it before embarking on analysis. This chapter provides recipes for some common cleaning, missing value imputation, outlier detection, and preprocessing steps.

Working with data

In the wild, datasets come in many different formats, but each computer program expects your data to be organized in a well-defined structure.

As a result, every data science project begins with the same tasks: gather the data, view the data, clean the data, correct or change the layout of the data to make it tidy, handle missing values and outliers from the data, model the data, and evaluate the data.

With R, you can do everything from collecting your data (from the web or a database) to cleaning it, transforming it, visualizing it, modelling it, and running statistical tests on it.

Reading data from CSV files

CSV formats are best used to represent sets or sequences of records in which each record has an identical list of fields. This corresponds to a single relation in a relational database, or to data (though not calculations) in a typical spreadsheet.

Getting ready

If you have not already downloaded the files for this chapter, do it now and ensure that the `auto-mpg.csv` file is in your R working directory.

How to do it...

Reading data from `.csv` files can be done using the following commands:

1. Read the data from `auto-mpg.csv`, which includes a header row:

   ```
   > auto <- read.csv("auto-mpg.csv", header=TRUE, sep = ",")
   ```

2. Verify the results:

   ```
   > names(auto)
   ```

How it works...

The `read.csv()` function creates a data frame from the data in the `.csv` file. If we pass `header=TRUE`, then the function uses the very first row to name the variables in the resulting data frame:

```
> names(auto)

[1] "No"            "mpg"          "cylinders"
[4] "displacement" "horsepower"   "weight"
[7] "acceleration" "model_year"   "car_name"
```

The `header` and `sep` parameters allow us to specify whether the `.csv` file has headers and the character used in the file to separate fields. The `header=TRUE` and `sep=","` parameters are the defaults for the `read.csv()` function; we can omit these in the code example.

There's more...

The `read.csv()` function is a specialized form of `read.table()`. The latter uses whitespace as the default field separator. We will discuss a few important optional arguments to these functions.

Handling different column delimiters

In regions where a comma is used as the decimal separator, the `.csv` files use "`;`" as the field delimiter. While dealing with such data files, use `read.csv2()` to load data into R.

Alternatively, you can use the `read.csv("<file name>", sep=";", dec=",")` command.

Use `sep="t"` for tab-delimited files.

Handling column headers/variable names

If your data file does not have column headers, set `header=FALSE`.

The `auto-mpg-noheader.csv` file does not include a header row. The first command in the following snippet reads this file. In this case, R assigns default variable names `V1`, `V2`, and so on.

```
> auto   <- read.csv("auto-mpg-noheader.csv", header=FALSE)
> head(auto,2)

  V1 V2 V3  V4 V5   V6   V7 V8                     V9
1  1 28  4 140 90 2264 15.5 71 chevrolet vega 2300
2  2 19  3  70 97 2330 13.5 72       mazda rx2 coupe
```

If your file does not have a header row, and you omit the `header=FALSE` optional argument, the `read.csv()` function uses the first row for variable names and ends up constructing variable names by adding `X` to the actual data values in the first row. Note the meaningless variable names in the following fragment:

```
> auto   <- read.csv("auto-mpg-noheader.csv")
> head(auto,2)

  X1 X28 X4 X140 X90 X2264 X15.5 X71 chevrolet.vega.2300
1  2  19  3   70  97  2330  13.5  72       mazda rx2 coupe
2  3  36  4  107  75  2205  14.5  82          honda accord
```

We can use the optional `col.names` argument to specify the column names. If `col.names` is given explicitly, the names in the header row are ignored, even if `header=TRUE` is specified:

```
> auto <- read.csv("auto-mpg-noheader.csv",       header=FALSE, col.names =
c("No", "mpg", "cyl", "dis","hp",            "wt", "acc", "year", "car_name"))

> head(auto,2)
```

```
   No mpg cyl dis hp   wt   acc year          car_name
1  1   28   4 140 90 2264 15.5   71 chevrolet vega 2300
2  2   19   3  70 97 2330 13.5   72      mazda rx2 coupe
```

Handling missing values

When reading data from text files, R treats blanks in numerical variables as NA (signifying missing data). By default, it reads blanks in categorical attributes just as blanks and not as NA. To treat blanks as NA for categorical and character variables, set na.strings="":

```
> auto  <- read.csv("auto-mpg.csv", na.strings="")
```

If the data file uses a specified string (such as "N/A" or "NA" for example) to indicate the missing values, you can specify that string as the na.strings argument, as in na.strings= "N/A" or na.strings = "NA".

Reading strings as characters and not as factors

By default, R treats strings as factors (categorical variables). In some situations, you may want to leave them as character strings. Use stringsAsFactors=FALSE to achieve this:

```
> auto <- read.csv("auto-mpg.csv",stringsAsFactors=FALSE)
```

However, to selectively treat variables as characters, you can load the file with the defaults (that is, read all strings as factors) and then use as.character() to convert the requisite factor variables to characters.

Reading data directly from a website

If the data file is available on the web, you can load it directly into R, instead of downloading and saving it locally before loading it into R:

```
> dat <- read.csv("http://www.exploredata.net/ftp/WHO.csv")
```

Reading XML data

You may sometimes need to extract data from websites. Many providers also supply data in XML and JSON formats. In this recipe, we learn about reading XML data.

Getting ready

Make sure you have downloaded the files for this chapters and the files `cd_catalog.xml` and `WorldPopulation-wiki.htm` are in working directory of R. If the XML package is not already installed in your R environment, install the package now, as follows:

```
> install.packages("XML")
```

How to do it...

XML data can be read by following these steps:

1. Load the library and initialize:

```
> library(XML)
> url <- "cd_catalog.xml"
```

2. Parse the XML file and get the root node:

```
> xmldoc <- xmlParse(url)
> rootNode <- xmlRoot(xmldoc)
> rootNode[1]
```

3. Extract the XML data:

```
> data <- xmlSApply(rootNode,function(x) xmlSApply(x, xmlValue))
```

4. Convert the extracted data into a data frame:

```
> cd.catalog <- data.frame(t(data),row.names=NULL)
```

5. Verify the results:

```
> cd.catalog[1:2,]
```

How it works...

The `xmlParse` function returns an object of the `XMLInternalDocument` class, which is a C-level internal data structure.

The `xmlRoot()` function gets access to the root node and its elements. Let us check the first element of the root node:

```
> rootNode[1]

$CD
<CD>
  <TITLE>Empire Burlesque</TITLE>
  <ARTIST>Bob Dylan</ARTIST>
  <COUNTRY>USA</COUNTRY>
  <COMPANY>Columbia</COMPANY>
  <PRICE>10.90</PRICE>
  <YEAR>1985</YEAR>
</CD>
attr(,"class")
[1] "XMLInternalNodeList" "XMLNodeList"
```

To extract data from the root node, we use the `xmlSApply()` function iteratively over all the children of the root node. The `xmlSApply` function returns a matrix.

To convert the preceding matrix into a data frame, we transpose the matrix using the `t()` function and then extract the first two rows from the `cd.catalog` data frame:

```
> cd.catalog[1:2,]
             TITLE       ARTIST COUNTRY      COMPANY PRICE YEAR
1 Empire Burlesque    Bob Dylan     USA     Columbia 10.90 1985
2  Hide your heart  Bonnie Tyler      UK CBS Records  9.90 1988
```

There's more...

XML data can be deeply nested and hence can become complex to extract. Knowledge of XPath is helpful to access specific XML tags. R provides several functions, such as `xpathSApply` and `getNodeSet`, to locate specific elements.

Extracting HTML table data from a web page

Though it is possible to treat HTML data as a specialized form of XML, R provides specific functions to extract data from HTML tables, as follows:

```
> url <- "WorldPopulation-wiki.htm"
> tables <- readHTMLTable(url)
> world.pop <- tables[[6]]
```

The `readHTMLTable()` function parses the web page and returns a `list` of all the tables that are found on the page. For tables that have an `id` attribute, the function uses the `id` attribute as the name of that list element.

We are interested in extracting the "10 most populous countries", which is the fifth table, so we use `tables[[6]]`.

Extracting a single HTML table from a web page

A single table can be extracted using the following command:

```
> table <- readHTMLTable(url,which=5)
```

Specify `which` to get data from a specific table. R returns a data frame.

Reading JSON data

Several RESTful web services return data in JSON format, in some ways simpler and more efficient than XML. This recipe shows you how to read JSON data.

Getting ready

R provides several packages to read JSON data, but we will use the `jsonlite` package. Install the package in your R environment, as follows:

```
> install.packages("jsonlite")
```

If you have not already downloaded the files for this chapter, do it now and ensure that the `students.json` files and `student-courses.json` files are in your R working directory.

How to do it...

Once the files are ready, load the `jsonlite` package and read the files as follows:

1. Load the library:

```
> library(jsonlite)
```

2. Load the JSON data from the files:

```
> dat.1 <- fromJSON("students.json")
> dat.2 <- fromJSON("student-courses.json")
```

3. Load the JSON document from the web:

```
> url <-
"http://finance.yahoo.com/webservice/v1/symbols/allcurrencies/quote
?format=json"
> jsonDoc <- fromJSON(url)
```

4. Extract the data into data frames:

```
> dat <- jsonDoc$list$resources$resource$fields
> dat.1 <- jsonDoc$list$resources$resource$fields
> dat.2 <- jsonDoc$list$resources$resource$fields
```

5. Verify the results:

```
> dat[1:2,]
> dat.1[1:3,]
> dat.2[,c(1,2,4:5)]
```

How it works...

The `jsonlite` package provides two key functions: `fromJSON` and `toJSON`.

The `fromJSON` function can load data either directly from a file or from a web page, as the preceding steps 2 and 3 show. If you get errors in downloading content directly from the web, install and load the `httr` package.

Depending on the structure of the JSON document, loading the data can vary in complexity.

If given a URL, the `fromJSON` function returns a list object. In the preceding list, in step 4, we see how to extract the enclosed data frame.

Reading data from fixed-width formatted files

In fixed-width formatted files, columns have fixed widths; if a data element does not use up the entire allotted column width, then the element is padded with spaces to make up the specified width. To read fixed-width text files, specify the columns either by column widths or by starting positions.

Getting ready

Download the files for this chapter and store the `student-fwf.txt` file in your R working directory.

How to do it...

Read the fixed-width formatted file as follows:

```
> student  <- read.fwf("student-fwf.txt",     widths=c(4,15,20,15,4),
col.names=c("id","name","email","major","year"))
```

How it works...

In the `student-fwf.txt` file, the first column occupies 4 character positions, the second 15, and so on. The `c(4,15,20,15,4)` expression specifies the widths of the 5 columns in the data file.

We can use the optional `col.names` argument to supply our own variable names.

There's more...

The `read.fwf()` function has several optional arguments that come in handy. We discuss a few of these, as follows:

Files with headers

Files with headers use the following command:

```
> student  <- read.fwf("student-fwf-header.txt",
widths=c(4,15,20,15,4), header=TRUE, sep="t",skip=2)
```

If `header=TRUE`, the first row of the file is interpreted as having the column headers. Column headers, if present, need to be separated by the specified `sep` argument. The `sep` argument only applies to the header row.

The `skip` argument denotes the number of lines to skip; in this recipe, the first two lines are skipped.

Excluding columns from data

To exclude a column, make the column width negative. Thus, to exclude the email column, we will specify its width as −20 and also remove the column name from the col.names vector, as follows:

```
> student <- read.fwf("student-fwf.txt",widths=c(4,15,-20,15,4),
  col.names=c("id","name","major","year"))
```

Reading data from R files and R libraries

During data analysis, you will create several R objects. You can save these in the native R data format and retrieve them later as needed.

Getting ready

First, create and save the R objects interactively, as shown in the following code. Make sure you have write access to the R working directory.

```
> customer <- c("John", "Peter", "Jane")
> orderdate <- as.Date(c('2014-10-1','2014-1-2','2014-7-6'))
> orderamount <- c(280, 100.50, 40.25)
> order <- data.frame(customer,orderdate,orderamount)
> names <- c("John", "Joan")
> save(order, names, file="test.Rdata")
> saveRDS(order,file="order.rds")
> remove(order)
```

After saving the preceding code, the remove() function deletes the object from the current session.

How to do it...

To be able to read data from R files and libraries, follow these steps:

1. Load data from the R data files into memory:

    ```
    > load("test.Rdata")
    > ord <- readRDS("order.rds")
    ```

2. The `datasets` package is loaded in the R environment by default and contains the `iris` and `cars` datasets. To load these datasets data into memory, use the following code:

```
> data(iris)
> data(list(cars,iris))
```

The first command loads only the `iris` dataset, and the second loads both the `cars` and `iris` datasets.

How it works...

The `save()` function saves the serialized version of the objects supplied as arguments along with the object name. The subsequent `load()` function restores the saved objects, with the same object names that they were saved with, to the global environment by default. If there are existing objects with the same names in that environment, they will be replaced without any warnings.

The `saveRDS()` function saves only one object. It saves the serialized version of the object and not the object name. Hence, with the `readRDS()` function, the saved object can be restored into a variable with a different name from when it was saved.

There's more...

The preceding recipe has shown you how to read saved R objects. We see more options in this section.

Saving all objects in a session

The following command can be used to save all objects:

```
> save.image(file = "all.RData")
```

Saving objects selectively in a session

To save objects selectively, use the following commands:

```
> odd <- c(1,3,5,7)
> even <- c(2,4,6,8)
> save(list=c("odd","even"),file="OddEven.Rdata")
```

The `list` argument specifies a character vector containing the names of the objects to be saved. Subsequently, loading data from the `OddEven.Rdata` file creates both `odd` and `even` objects. The `saveRDS()` function can save only one object at a time.

Attaching/detaching R data files to an environment

While loading `Rdata` files, if we want to be notified whether objects with the same names already exist in the environment, we can use:

```
> attach("order.Rdata")
```

The `order.Rdata` file contains an object named `order`. If an object named `order` already exists in the environment, we will get the following error:

```
The following object is masked _by_ .GlobalEnv:

    order
```

Listing all datasets in loaded packages

All the loaded packages can be listed using the following command:

```
> data()
```

Removing cases with missing values

Datasets come with varying amounts of missing data. When we have abundant data, we sometimes (not always) want to eliminate the cases that have missing values for one or more variables. This recipe applies when we want to eliminate cases that have any missing values, as well as when we want to selectively eliminate cases that have missing values for a specific variable alone.

Getting ready

Download the `missing-data.csv` file from the code files for this chapter to your R working directory. Read the data from the `missing-data.csv` file, while taking care to identify the string used in the input file for missing values. In our file, missing values are shown with empty strings:

```
> dat <- read.csv("missing-data.csv", na.strings="")
```

How to do it...

To get a data frame that has only the cases with no missing values for any variable, use the `na.omit()` function:

```
> dat.cleaned <- na.omit(dat)
```

Now `dat.cleaned` contains only those cases from `dat` that have no missing values in any of the variables.

How it works...

The `na.omit()` function internally uses the `is.na()` function, that allows us to find whether its argument is `NA`. When applied to a single value, it returns a Boolean value. When applied to a collection, it returns a `vector`:

```
> is.na(dat[4,2])
[1] TRUE

> is.na(dat$Income)
 [1] FALSE FALSE FALSE FALSE FALSE  TRUE FALSE FALSE FALSE
[10] FALSE FALSE FALSE  TRUE FALSE FALSE FALSE FALSE FALSE
[19] FALSE FALSE FALSE FALSE FALSE FALSE FALSE FALSE FALSE
```

There's more...

You will sometimes need to do more than just eliminate the cases with any missing values. We discuss some options in this section.

Eliminating cases with NA for selected variables

We might sometimes want to selectively eliminate cases that have `NA` only for a specific variable. The example data frame has two missing values for `Income`. To get a data frame with only these two cases removed, use:

```
> dat.income.cleaned <- dat[!is.na(dat$Income),]
> nrow(dat.income.cleaned)
[1] 25
```

Finding cases that have no missing values

The `complete.cases()` function takes a data frame or table as its argument and returns a Boolean vector with TRUE for rows that have no missing values, and FALSE otherwise:

```
> complete.cases(dat)

 [1]  TRUE  TRUE  TRUE FALSE  TRUE FALSE  TRUE  TRUE  TRUE
[10]  TRUE  TRUE  TRUE FALSE  TRUE  TRUE  TRUE FALSE  TRUE
[19]  TRUE  TRUE  TRUE  TRUE  TRUE  TRUE  TRUE  TRUE  TRUE
```

Rows 4, 6, 13, and 17 have at least one missing value. Instead of using the `na.omit()` function, we can do the following as well:

```
> dat.cleaned <- dat[complete.cases(dat),]
> nrow(dat.cleaned)
[1] 23
```

Converting specific values to NA

Sometimes, we might know that a specific value in a data frame actually means that the data was not available. For example, in the `dat` data frame, a value of 0 for `Income` probably means that the data is missing. We can convert these to NA by a simple assignment:

```
> dat$Income[dat$Income==0] <- NA
```

Excluding NA values from computations

Many R functions return NA when some parts of the data they work on are NA. For example, computing the `mean` or `sd` on a vector with at least one NA value returns NA as the result. To remove NA from consideration, use the `na.rm` parameter:

```
> mean(dat$Income)
[1] NA

> mean(dat$Income, na.rm = TRUE)
[1] 65763.64
```

Replacing missing values with the mean

When you disregard cases with any missing variables, you lose useful information that the non-missing values in that case convey. You may sometimes want to impute reasonable values (those that will not skew the results of analysis very much) for the missing values.

Getting ready

Download the `missing-data.csv` file and store it in your R environment's working directory.

How to do it...

Read data and replace missing values:

```
> dat <- read.csv("missing-data.csv", na.strings = "")
> dat$Income.imp.mean <- ifelse(is.na(dat$Income),      mean(dat$Income,
na.rm=TRUE), dat$Income)
```

After this, all the NA values for Income will be the mean value prior to imputation.

How it works...

The preceding `ifelse()` function returns the imputed mean value if its first argument is NA. Otherwise, it returns the first argument.

There's more...

You cannot impute the mean when a categorical variable has missing values, so you need a different approach. Even for numeric variables, we might sometimes not want to impute the mean for missing values. We discuss an often-used approach here.

Imputing random values sampled from non-missing values

If you want to impute random values sampled from the non-missing values of the variable, you can use the following two functions:

```
rand.impute <- function(a) {
  missing <- is.na(a)
  n.missing <- sum(missing)
  a.obs <- a[!missing]
  imputed <- a
  imputed[missing] <- sample (a.obs, n.missing, replace=TRUE)
  return (imputed)
}

random.impute.data.frame <- function(dat, cols) {
  nms <- names(dat)
  for(col in cols) {
    name <- paste(nms[col],".imputed", sep = "")
    dat[name] <- rand.impute(dat[,col])
  }
  dat
}
```

With these two functions in place, you can use the following to impute random values for both `Income` and `Phone_type`:

```
> dat <- read.csv("missing-data.csv", na.strings="")
> random.impute.data.frame(dat, c(1,2))
```

Removing duplicate cases

We sometimes end up with duplicate cases in our datasets and want to retain only one among them.

Getting ready

Create a sample data frame:

```
> salary <- c(20000, 30000, 25000, 40000, 30000, 34000, 30000)
> family.size <- c(4,3,2,2,3,4,3)
> car <- c("Luxury", "Compact", "Midsize", "Luxury",    "Compact",
"Compact", "Compact")
```

```
> prospect <- data.frame(salary, family.size, car)
```

How to do it...

The `unique()` function can do the job. It takes a vector or data frame as an argument and returns an object of the same type as its argument, but with duplicates removed.

Remove duplicates to get unique values:

```
> prospect.cleaned <- unique(prospect)
> nrow(prospect)
[1] 7
> nrow(prospect.cleaned)
[1] 5
```

How it works...

The `unique()` function takes a vector or data frame as an argument and returns a similar object with the duplicate eliminated. It returns the non-duplicated cases as is. For repeated cases, the `unique()` function includes one copy in the returned result.

There's more...

Sometimes we just want to identify the duplicated values without necessarily removing them.

Identifying duplicates without deleting them

For this, use the `duplicated()` function:

```
> duplicated(prospect)
[1] FALSE FALSE FALSE FALSE  TRUE FALSE  TRUE
```

From the data, we know that cases 2, 5, and 7 are duplicates. Note that only cases 5 and 7 are shown as duplicates. In the first occurrence, case 2 is not flagged as a duplicate.

To list the duplicate cases, use the following code:

```
> prospect[duplicated(prospect), ]

   salary family.size     car
```

```
5   30000          3 Compact
7   30000          3 Compact
```

Rescaling a variable to specified min-max range

Distance computations play a big role in many data analytics techniques. We know that variables with higher values tend to dominate distance computations and you may want to rescale the values to be in the range of 0 - 1.

Getting ready

Install the scales package and read the data-conversion.csv file from the book's data for this chapter into your R environment's working directory:

```
> install.packages("scales")
> library(scales)
> students <- read.csv("data-conversion.csv")
```

How to do it...

To rescale the Income variable to the range *[0,1]*, use the following code snippet:

```
> students$Income.rescaled <- rescale(students$Income)
```

How it works...

By default, the rescale() function makes the lowest value(s) zero and the highest value(s) one. It rescales all the other values proportionately. The following two expressions provide identical results:

```
> rescale(students$Income)
> (students$Income - min(students$Income)) /      (max(students$Income) -
min(students$Income))
```

To rescale a different range than *[0,1]*, use the to argument. The following snippet rescales students$Income to the range (0,100):

```
> rescale(students$Income, to = c(1, 100))
```

There's more...

When using distance-based techniques, you may need to rescale several variables. You may find it tedious to scale one variable at a time.

Rescaling many variables at once

Use the following function to rescale variables:

```
rescale.many <- function(dat, column.nos) {
  nms <- names(dat)
  for(col in column.nos) {
    name <- paste(nms[col],".rescaled", sep = "")
    dat[name] <- rescale(dat[,col])
  }
  cat(paste("Rescaled ", length(column.nos),      " variable(s)n"))
  dat
}
```

With the preceding function defined, we can do the following to rescale the first and fourth variables in the data frame:

```
> rescale.many(students, c(1,4))
```

See also

- The *Normalizing or standardizing data in a data frame* recipe in this chapter.

Normalizing or standardizing data in a data frame

Distance computations play a big role in many data analytics techniques. We know that variables with higher values tend to dominate distance computations and you may want to use the standardized (or z) values.

Getting ready

Download the `BostonHousing.csv` data file and store it in your R environment's working directory. Then read the data:

```
> housing <- read.csv("BostonHousing.csv")
```

How to do it...

To standardize all the variables in a data frame containing only numeric variables, use:

```
> housing.z <- scale(housing)
```

You can only use the `scale()` function on data frames that contain all numeric variables. Otherwise, you will get an error.

How it works...

When invoked in the preceding example, the `scale()` function computes the standard z score for each value (ignoring NAs) of each variable. That is, from each value it subtracts the mean and divides the result by the standard deviation of the associated variable.

The `scale()` function takes two optional arguments, `center` and `scale`, whose default values are TRUE. The following table shows the effect of these arguments:

Argument	Effect
`center = TRUE, scale = TRUE`	Default behavior described earlier
`center = TRUE, scale = FALSE`	From each value, subtract the mean of the concerned variable
`center = FALSE, scale = TRUE`	Divide each value by the root mean square of the associated variable, where root mean square is $sqrt(sum(x^2)/(n-1))$
`center = FALSE, scale = FALSE`	Return the original values unchanged

There's more...

When using distance-based techniques, you may need to rescale several variables. You may find it tedious to standardize one variable at a time.

Standardizing several variables simultaneously

If you have a data frame with some numeric and some non-numeric variables, or want to standardize only some of the variables in a fully numeric data frame, then you can either handle each variable separately, which would be cumbersome, or use a function such as the following to handle a subset of variables:

```
scale.many <- function(dat, column.nos) {
  nms <- names(dat)
  for(col in column.nos) {
    name <- paste(nms[col],".z", sep = "")
    dat[name] <- scale(dat[,col])
  }
  cat(paste("Scaled ", length(column.nos), " variable(s)n"))
  dat
}
```

With this function, you can now do things like:

```
> housing <- read.csv("BostonHousing.csv")
> housing <- scale.many(housing, c(1,3,5:7))
```

This will add the z values for variables 1, 3, 5, 6, and 7, with .z appended to the original column names:

```
> names(housing)

[1] "CRIM"     "ZN"       "INDUS"   "CHAS"     "NOX"      "RM"
[7] "AGE"      "DIS"      "RAD"     "TAX"      "PTRATIO"  "B"
[13] "LSTAT"    "MEDV"     "CRIM.z"  "INDUS.z" "NOX.z"    "RM.z"
[19] "AGE.z"
```

See also

Rescaling a variable to [0,1] recipe in this chapter.

Binning numerical data

Sometimes, we need to convert numerical data to categorical data or a factor. For example, Naive Bayes classification requires all variables (independent and dependent) to be categorical. In other situations, we may want to apply a classification method to a problem where the dependent variable is numeric but needs to be categorical.

Getting ready

From the code files for this chapter, store the `data-conversion.csv` file in the working directory of your R environment. Then read the data:

```
> students <- read.csv("data-conversion.csv")
```

How to do it...

Income is a numeric variable, and you may want to create a categorical variable from it by creating bins. Suppose you want to label incomes of $10,000 or below as `Low`, incomes between $10,000 and $31,000 as `Medium`, and the rest as `High`. We can do the following:

1. Create a vector of break points:

   ```
   > b <- c(-Inf, 10000, 31000, Inf)
   ```

2. Create a vector of names for break points:

   ```
   > names <- c("Low", "Medium", "High")
   ```

3. Cut the vector using the break points:

   ```
   > students$Income.cat <- cut(students$Income, breaks = b, labels =
   names)
   > students
   ```

	Age	State	Gender	Height	Income	Income.cat
1	23	NJ	F	61	5000	Low
2	13	NY	M	55	1000	Low
3	36	NJ	M	66	3000	Low
4	31	VA	F	64	4000	Low
5	58	NY	F	70	30000	Medium
6	29	TX	F	63	10000	Low
7	39	NJ	M	67	50000	High
8	50	VA	M	70	55000	High

```
  9   23    TX     F    61    2000        Low
 10   36    VA     M    66   20000      Medium
```

How it works...

The cut() function uses the ranges implied by the breaks argument to infer the bins, and names them according to the strings provided in the labels argument. In our example, the function places incomes less than or equal to 10,000 in the first bin, incomes greater than 10,000 and less than or equal to 31,000 in the second bin, and incomes greater than 31,000 in the third bin. In other words, the first number in the interval is not included but the second one is. The number of bins will be one less than the number of elements in breaks. The strings in names become the factor levels of the bins.

If we leave out names, cut() uses the numbers in the second argument to construct interval names, as you can see here:

```
> b <- c(-Inf, 10000, 31000, Inf)
> students$Income.cat1 <- cut(students$Income, breaks = b)
> students
```

```
   Age State Gender Height Income Income.cat       Income.cat1
1   23    NJ     F      61   5000        Low      (-Inf,1e+04]
2   13    NY     M      55   1000        Low      (-Inf,1e+04]
3   36    NJ     M      66   3000        Low      (-Inf,1e+04]
4   31    VA     F      64   4000        Low      (-Inf,1e+04]
5   58    NY     F      70  30000     Medium (1e+04,3.1e+04]
6   29    TX     F      63  10000        Low      (-Inf,1e+04]
7   39    NJ     M      67  50000       High  (3.1e+04, Inf]
8   50    VA     M      70  55000       High  (3.1e+04, Inf]
9   23    TX     F      61   2000        Low      (-Inf,1e+04]
10  36    VA     M      66  20000     Medium (1e+04,3.1e+04]
```

There's more...

You might not always be in a position to identify the breaks manually and may instead want to rely on R to do this automatically.

Creating a specified number of intervals automatically

Rather than determining the breaks and hence the intervals manually, as mentioned earlier, we can specify the number of bins we want, say n, and let the `cut()` function handle the rest automatically. In this case, `cut()` creates n intervals of approximately equal width, as follows:

```
> students$Income.cat2 <- cut(students$Income,      breaks = 4, labels =
c("Level1", "Level2",       "Level3","Level4"))
```

Creating dummies for categorical variables

In situations where we have categorical variables (factors) but need to use them in analytical methods that require numbers (for example, **K nearest neighbors** (**KNN**), Linear Regression), we need to create dummy variables.

Getting ready

Read the `data-conversion.csv` file and store it in the working directory of your R environment. Install the `dummies` package. Then read the data:

```
> install.packages("dummies")
> library(dummies)
> students <- read.csv("data-conversion.csv")
```

How to do it...

Create dummies for all factors in the data frame:

```
> students.new <- dummy.data.frame(students, sep = ".")
> names(students.new)

[1] "Age"       "State.NJ" "State.NY" "State.TX" "State.VA"
[6] "Gender.F" "Gender.M" "Height"    "Income"
```

The `students.new` data frame now contains all the original variables and the newly added dummy variables. The `dummy.data.frame()` function has created dummy variables for all four levels of `State` and two levels of `Gender` factors. However, we will generally omit one of the dummy variables for `State` and one for `Gender` when we use machine learning techniques.

We can use the optional argument `all = FALSE` to specify that the resulting data frame should contain only the generated dummy variables and none of the original variables.

How it works...

The `dummy.data.frame()` function creates dummies for all the factors in the data frame supplied. Internally, it uses another `dummy()` function which creates dummy variables for a single factor. The `dummy()` function creates one new variable for every level of the factor for which we are creating dummies. It appends the variable name with the factor level name to generate names for the dummy variables. We can use the `sep` argument to specify the character that separates them; an empty string is the default:

```
> dummy(students$State, sep = ".")

     State.NJ State.NY State.TX State.VA
 [1,]       1        0        0        0
 [2,]       0        1        0        0
 [3,]       1        0        0        0
 [4,]       0        0        0        1
 [5,]       0        1        0        0
 [6,]       0        0        1        0
 [7,]       1        0        0        0
 [8,]       0        0        0        1
 [9,]       0        0        1        0
[10,]       0        0        0        1
```

There's more...

In situations where a data frame has several factors, and you plan on using only a subset of them, you create dummies only for the chosen subset.

Choosing which variables to create dummies for

To create a dummy only for one variable or a subset of variables, we can use the `names` argument to specify the column names of the variables we want dummies for:

```
> students.new1 <- dummy.data.frame(students,      names =
c("State","Gender") , sep = ".")
```

Handling missing data

In most real-world problems, data is likely to be incomplete because of incorrect data entry, faulty equipment, or improperly coded data. In R, missing values are represented by the symbol NA (not available) and are considered to be the first obstacle in predictive modeling. So, it's always a good idea to check for missing data in a dataset before proceeding for further predictive analysis. This recipe shows you how to handle missing data.

Getting ready

R provides three simple ways to handle missing values:

1. Deleting the observations.
2. Deleting the variables.
3. Replacing the values with mean, median, or mode.

Install the package in your R environment as follows:

```
> install.packages("Hmisc")
```

If you have not already downloaded the files for this chapter, do it now and ensure that the housing-with-missing-value.csv file is in your R working directory.

How to do it...

Once the files are ready, load the Hmisc package and read the files as follows:

1. Load the CSV data from the files:

   ```
   > housing.dat <- read.csv("housing-with-missing-value.csv",header = TRUE, stringsAsFactors = FALSE)
   ```

2. Check summary of the dataset:

   ```
   > summary(housing.dat)
   ```

The output would be as follows:

```
        X               crim               zn              indus            chas              nox               rm               age
Min.   :  1.0    Min.   : 0.00632   Min.   :  0.00   Min.   : 0.46   Min.   :0.00000   Min.   :0.3850   Min.   :3.561   Min.   :  2.90
1st Qu.:127.2    1st Qu.: 0.08204   1st Qu.:  0.00   1st Qu.: 5.19   1st Qu.:0.00000   1st Qu.:0.4490   1st Qu.:5.886   1st Qu.: 45.02
Median :253.5    Median : 0.25651   Median :  0.00   Median : 9.69   Median :0.00000   Median :0.5380   Median :6.208   Median : 77.50
Mean   :253.5    Mean   : 3.61352   Mean   : 11.36   Mean   :11.14   Mean   :0.06917   Mean   :0.5547   Mean   :6.285   Mean   : 68.57
3rd Qu.:379.8    3rd Qu.: 3.67708   3rd Qu.: 12.50   3rd Qu.:18.10   3rd Qu.:0.00000   3rd Qu.:0.6240   3rd Qu.:6.623   3rd Qu.: 94.08
Max.   :506.0    Max.   :88.97620   Max.   :100.00   Max.   :27.74   Max.   :1.00000   Max.   :0.8710   Max.   :8.780   Max.   :100.00

      dis              rad              tax             ptratio             b               lstat             medv
Min.   : 1.130   Min.   : 1.000   Min.   :187.0   Min.   :12.60   Min.   :  0.32   Min.   : 1.73   Min.   : 5.00
1st Qu.: 2.100   1st Qu.: 4.000   1st Qu.:279.0   1st Qu.:17.40   1st Qu.:375.38   1st Qu.: 6.95   1st Qu.:17.02
Median : 3.207   Median : 5.000   Median :330.0   Median :19.10   Median :391.44   Median :11.36   Median :21.20
Mean   : 3.795   Mean   : 9.515   Mean   :408.2   Mean   :18.47   Mean   :356.67   Mean   :12.65   Mean   :22.53
3rd Qu.: 5.188   3rd Qu.:24.000   3rd Qu.:666.0   3rd Qu.:20.20   3rd Qu.:396.23   3rd Qu.:16.95   3rd Qu.:25.00
Max.   :12.127   Max.   :24.000   Max.   :711.0   Max.   :22.00   Max.   :396.90   Max.   :37.97   Max.   :50.00
                 NA's   :40                       NA's   :40
```

3. Delete the missing observations from the dataset, removing all NAs with list-wise deletion:

```
> housing.dat.1 <- na.omit(housing.dat)
```

Remove NAs from certain columns:

```
> drop_na <- c("rad")
> housing.dat.2 <-housing.dat [complete.cases(housing.dat [ ,
!(names(housing.dat)) %in% drop_na]),]
```

4. Finally, verify the dataset with summary statistics:

```
> summary(housing.dat.1$rad)
 Min. 1st Qu. Median Mean 3rd Qu. Max.
 1.000 4.000 5.000 9.599 24.000 24.000

> summary(housing.dat.1$ptratio)
 Min. 1st Qu. Median Mean 3rd Qu. Max.
 12.60 17.40 19.10 18.47 20.20 22.00

> summary(housing.dat.2$rad)
 Min. 1st Qu. Median Mean 3rd Qu. Max. NA's
 1.000 4.000 5.000 9.599 24.000 24.000 35

> summary(housing.dat.2$ptratio)
 Min. 1st Qu. Median Mean 3rd Qu. Max.
 12.60 17.40 19.10 18.47 20.20 22.00
```

5. Delete the variables that have the most missing observations:

```
# Deleting a single column containing many NAs
> housing.dat.3 <- housing.dat$rad <- NULL

#Deleting multiple columns containing NAs:
> drops <- c("ptratio","rad")
>housing.dat.4 <- housing.dat[ , !(names(housing.dat) %in% drops)]
```

Finally, verify the dataset with summary statistics:

```
> summary(housing.dat.4)
```

```
        X             crim               zn             indus            chas              nox              rm               age
 Min.   :  1.0   Min.   : 0.00632   Min.   :  0.00   Min.   : 0.46   Min.   :0.00000   Min.   :0.3850   Min.   :3.561   Min.   :  2.90
 1st Qu.:127.2   1st Qu.: 0.08204   1st Qu.:  0.00   1st Qu.: 5.19   1st Qu.:0.00000   1st Qu.:0.4490   1st Qu.:5.886   1st Qu.: 45.02
 Median :253.5   Median : 0.25651   Median :  0.00   Median : 9.69   Median :0.00000   Median :0.5380   Median :6.208   Median : 77.50
 Mean   :253.5   Mean   : 3.61352   Mean   : 11.36   Mean   :11.14   Mean   :0.06917   Mean   :0.5547   Mean   :6.285   Mean   : 68.57
 3rd Qu.:379.8   3rd Qu.: 3.67708   3rd Qu.: 12.50   3rd Qu.:18.10   3rd Qu.:0.00000   3rd Qu.:0.6240   3rd Qu.:6.623   3rd Qu.: 94.08
 Max.   :506.0   Max.   :88.97620   Max.   :100.00   Max.   :27.74   Max.   :1.00000   Max.   :0.8710   Max.   :8.780   Max.   :100.00
      dis              tax              b              lstat             medv
 Min.   : 1.130   Min.   :187.0   Min.   :  0.32   Min.   : 1.73   Min.   : 5.00
 1st Qu.: 2.100   1st Qu.:279.0   1st Qu.:375.38   1st Qu.: 6.95   1st Qu.:17.02
 Median : 3.207   Median :330.0   Median :391.44   Median :11.36   Median :21.20
 Mean   : 3.795   Mean   :408.2   Mean   :356.67   Mean   :12.65   Mean   :22.53
 3rd Qu.: 5.188   3rd Qu.:666.0   3rd Qu.:396.23   3rd Qu.:16.95   3rd Qu.:25.00
 Max.   :12.127   Max.   :711.0   Max.   :396.90   Max.   :37.97   Max.   :50.00
```

6. Load the library:

```
> library(Hmisc)
```

7. Replace the missing values with mean, median, or mode:

```
#replace with mean
> housing.dat$ptratio <- impute(housing.dat$ptratio, mean)
> housing.dat$rad <- impute(housing.dat$rad, mean)

#replace with median
> housing.dat$ptratio <- impute(housing.dat$ptratio, median)
> housing.dat$rad <- impute(housing.dat$rad, median)

#replace with mode/constant value
> housing.dat$ptratio <- impute(housing.dat$ptratio, 18)
> housing.dat$rad <- impute(housing.dat$rad, 6)
```

Finally, verify the dataset with summary statistics:

```
> summary(housing.dat)
```

```
40 values imputed to 9.515021


40 values imputed to 18.4676

       X              crim               zn              indus            chas              nox               rm              age
Min.    :  1.0   Min.   : 0.00632   Min.   :  0.00   Min.   : 0.46   Min.    :0.00000   Min.   :0.3850   Min.    :3.561   Min.    :  2.90
1st Qu.:127.2   1st Qu.: 0.08204   1st Qu.:  0.00   1st Qu.: 5.19   1st Qu.:0.00000   1st Qu.:0.4490   1st Qu.:5.886   1st Qu.: 45.02
Median :253.5   Median : 0.25651   Median :  0.00   Median : 9.69   Median :0.00000   Median :0.5380   Median :6.208   Median : 77.50
Mean    :253.5   Mean   : 3.61352   Mean   : 11.36   Mean   :11.14   Mean    :0.06917   Mean   :0.5547   Mean    :6.285   Mean    : 68.57
3rd Qu.:379.8   3rd Qu.: 3.67708   3rd Qu.: 12.50   3rd Qu.:18.10   3rd Qu.:0.00000   3rd Qu.:0.6240   3rd Qu.:6.623   3rd Qu.: 94.08
Max.    :506.0   Max.   :88.97620   Max.   :100.00   Max.   :27.74   Max.    :1.00000   Max.   :0.8710   Max.    :8.780   Max.    :100.00
      dis              rad              tax            ptratio            b               lstat            medv
Min.    : 1.130   Min.   : 1.000   Min.   :187.0   Min.   :12.60   Min.    :  0.32   Min.   : 1.73   Min.    : 5.00
1st Qu.: 2.100   1st Qu.: 4.000   1st Qu.:279.0   1st Qu.:17.40   1st Qu.:375.38   1st Qu.: 6.95   1st Qu.:17.02
Median : 3.207   Median : 5.000   Median :330.0   Median :18.60   Median :391.44   Median :11.36   Median :21.20
Mean    : 3.795   Mean   : 9.515   Mean   :408.2   Mean   :18.47   Mean    :356.67   Mean   :12.65   Mean    :22.53
3rd Qu.: 5.188   3rd Qu.: 9.515   3rd Qu.:666.0   3rd Qu.:20.20   3rd Qu.:396.23   3rd Qu.:16.95   3rd Qu.:25.00
Max.    :12.127   Max.   :24.000   Max.   :711.0   Max.   :22.00   Max.    :396.90   Max.   :37.97   Max.    :50.00
```

How it works...

When you have large numbers of observations in your dataset and all the classes to be predicted are sufficiently represented by the data points, then deleting missing observations would not introduce bias or disproportionality of output classes.

In the `housing.dat` dataset, we saw from the summary statistics that the dataset has two columns, `ptratio` and `rad`, with missing values.

The `na.omit()` function lets you remove all the missing values from all the columns of your dataset, whereas the `complete.cases()` function lets you remove the missing values from some particular column/columns.

Sometimes, particular variable/variables might have more missing values than the rest of the variables in the dataset. Then it is better to remove that variable unless it is a really important predictor that makes a lot of business sense. Assigning `NULL` to a variable is an easy way of removing it from the dataset.

In both, the given way of handling missing values through the deletion approach reduces the total number of observations (or rows) from the dataset. Instead of removing missing observations or removing a variable with many missing values, replacing the missing values with the mean, median, or mode is often a crude way of treating the missing values. Depending on the context, such as if the variation is low or if the variable has low leverage over the response/target, such a naive approximation is acceptable and could possibly give satisfactory results. The `impute()` function in the `Hmisc` library provides an easy way to replace the missing value with the mean, median, or mode (constant).

There's more...

Sometime it is better to understand the missing pattern in the dataset through visualization before taking further decision about elimination or imputation of the missing values.

Understanding missing data pattern

Let us use the md.pattern() function from the mice package to get a better understanding of the pattern of missing data.

```
> library(mice)
> md.pattern(housing.dat)
```

	X	crim	zn	indus	chas	nox	rm	age	dis	tax	b	lstat	medv	ptratio	
466	1	1	1	1	1	1	1	1	1	1	1	1	1	1	0
40	1	1	1	1	1	1	1	1	1	1	1	1	1	0	1
	0	0	0	0	0	0	0	0	0	0	0	0	0	40	40

We can notice from the output above that 466 samples are complete, 40 samples miss only the ptratio value.

Next we will visualize the housing data to understand missing information using aggr_plot method from VIM package:

```
> library(VIM)
> aggr_plot <- aggr(housing.dat, col=c('blue','red'), numbers=TRUE,
sortVars=TRUE, labels=names(housing.dat), cex.axis=.7, gap=3,
ylab=c("Histogram of missing data","Pattern"))
```

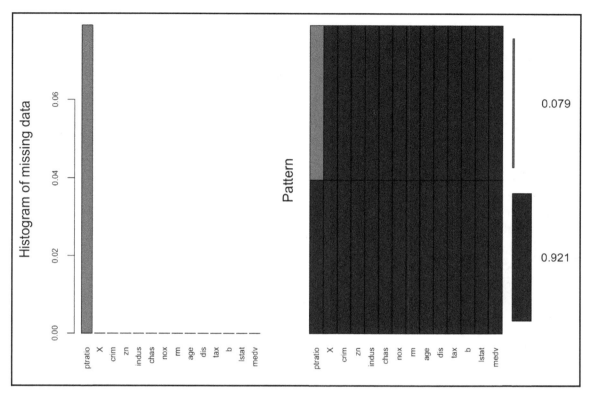

We can understand from the plot that almost 92.1% of the samples are complete and only 7.9% are missing information from the ptratio values.

Correcting data

In practice, raw data is rarely tidy, and is much harder to work with as a result. It is often said that 80 percent of data analysis is spent on the process of cleaning and correcting the data.

In this recipe, you will learn the best way to correctly layout your data to serve two major purposes:

- Making data suitable for software processing, whether that be mathematical functions, visualization, and others
- Revealing information and insights

Getting ready

Download the files for this chapter and store the `USArrests.csv` file in your R working directory. You should also install the `tidyr` package using the following command.

```
> install.packages("tidyr")
> library(tidyr)
> crimeData <- read.csv("USArrests.csv",stringsAsFactors = FALSE)
```

How to do it...

Follow these steps to correct the data from your dataset.

1. View some records of the dataset:

   ```
   > View(crimeData)
   ```

2. Add the column name `state` in the dataset:

   ```
   > crimeData <- cbind(state = rownames(crimeData), crimeData)
   ```

3. Gather all the variables between `Murder` and `UrbanPop`:

   ```
   > crimeData.1 <- gather(crimeData,
   key = "crime_type",
   value = "arrest_estimate",
   Murder:UrbanPop)

    > crimeData.1
   ```

4. Gather all the columns except the column `state`:

```
> crimeData.2 <- gather(crimeData,
key = "crime_type",
value = "arrest_estimate",
-state)

  > crimeData.2
```

5. Gather only the `Murder` and `Assault` columns:

```
> crimeData.3 <- gather(crimeData,
key = "crime_type",
value = "arrest_estimate",
Murder, Assault)

  > crimeData.3
```

6. Spread `crimeData.2` to turn a pair of `key:value`
(`crime_typ:arrest_estimate`) columns into a set of tidy columns

```
> crimeData.4 <- spread(crimeData.2,
key = "crime_type",
value = "arrest_estimate"
)
  > crimeData.4
```

How it works...

Correct data format is crucial for facilitating the tasks of data analysis, including data manipulation, modeling, and visualization. The tidy data arranges values so that the relationships in the data parallel the structure of the data frame. Every tidy dataset is based on two basic principles:

- Each variable is saved in its own column
- Each observation is saved in its own row

In the `crimeData` dataframe, the row names were `states`, hence we used the function `cbind()` to add a column named `state` in the dataframe. The function `gather()` collapses multiple columns into key-value pairs. It makes wide data longer. The `gather()` function basically takes four arguments, data (dataframe), key (column name representing new variable), value (column name representing variable values), and names of the columns to gather (or not gather).

In the `crimeData.2` data, all column names (except `state`) were collapsed into a single key column `crime_type` and their values were put into a value column `arrest_estimate`.

And, in the `crimeData.3` data, the two columns `Murder` and `Assault` were collapsed and the remaining columns (`state`, `UrbanPop`, and `Rape`) were duplicated.

The function `spread()` does the reverse of `gather()`. It takes two columns (key and value) and spreads them into multiple columns. It makes long data wider. The `spread()` function takes three arguments in general, data (dataframe), key (column values to convert to multiple columns), and value (single column value to convert to multiple columns' values).

There's more...

Beside the `spread()` and `gather()` functions, there are two more important functions in the `tidyr` package that help to make data tidy.

Combining multiple columns to single columns

The `unite()` function takes multiple columns and pastes them together into one column:

```
> crimeData.5 <- unite(crimeData,
              col = "Murder_Assault",
              Murder, Assault,
              sep = "_")
 > crimeData.5
```

We combine the columns `Murder` and `Assault` from the `crimeData` data-frame to generate a new column `Murder_Assault`, having the values separated by _.

Splitting single column to multiple columns

The `separate()` function is the reverse of `unite()`. It takes values inside a single character column and separates them into multiple columns:

```
> crimeData.6 <- separate_(crimeData.5,
         col = "Murder_Assault",
         into = c("Murder", "Assault"),
         sep = "_")
>crimeData.6
```

Imputing data

Missing values are considered to be the first obstacle in data analysis and predictive modeling. In most statistical analysis methods, list-wise deletion is the default method used to impute missing values, as shown in the earlier recipe. However, these methods are not quite good enough, since deletion could lead to information loss and replacement with simple mean or median, which doesn't take into account the uncertainty in missing values.

Hence, this recipe will show you the multivariate imputation techniques to handle missing values using prediction.

Getting ready

Make sure that the `housing-with-missing-value.csv` file from the code files of this chapter is in your R working directory.

You should also install the `mice` package using the following command:

```
> install.packages("mice")
> library(mice)
> housingData <- read.csv("housing-with-missing-value.csv",header = TRUE,
stringsAsFactors = FALSE)
```

How to do it...

Follow these steps to impute data:

1. Perform multivariate imputation:

```
#imputing only two columns having missing values
> columns=c("ptratio","rad")

> imputed_Data <- mice(housingData[,names(housingData) %in%
columns], m=5, maxit = 50, method = 'pmm', seed = 500)

>summary(imputed_Data)
```

2. Generate complete data:

```
> completeData <- complete(imputed_Data)
```

3. Replace the imputed column values with the `housing.csv` dataset:

    ```
    > housingData$ptratio <- completeData$ptratio
    > housingData$rad <- completeData$rad
    ```

4. Check for missing values:

    ```
    > anyNA(housingData)
    ```

How it works...

As we already know from our earlier recipe, the `housing.csv` dataset contains two columns, `ptratio` and `rad`, with missing values.

The `mice` library in R uses a predictive approach and assumes that the missing data is **Missing at Random (MAR)**, and creates multivariate imputations via chained equations to take care of uncertainty in the missing values. It implements the imputation in just two steps: using `mice()` to build the model and `complete()` to generate the completed data.

The `mice()` function takes the following parameters:

*   **m**: It refers to the number of imputed datasets it creates internally. Default is five.
*   **maxit**: It refers to the number of iterations taken to impute the missing values.
*   **method**: It refers to the method used in imputation. The default imputation method (when no argument is specified) depends on the measurement level of the target column and is specified by the `defaultMethod` argument, where `defaultMethod = c("pmm", "logreg", "polyreg", "polr")`.
*   **logreg**: Logistic regression (factor column, two levels).
*   **polyreg**: Polytomous logistic regression (factor column, greater than or equal to two levels).
*   **polr**: Proportional odds model (ordered column, greater than or equal to two levels).

We have used **predictive mean matching (pmm)** for this recipe to impute the missing values in the dataset.

The `anyNA()` function returns a Boolean value to indicate the presence or absence of missing values (NA) in the dataset.

There's more...

Previously, we used the impute() function from the Hmisc library to simply impute the missing value using defined statistical methods (mean, median, and mode). However, Hmisc also has the aregImpute() function that allows mean imputation using additive regression, bootstrapping, and predictive mean matching:

```
> impute_arg <- aregImpute(~ ptratio + rad , data = housingData, n.impute =
5)

> impute_arg
```

argImpute() automatically identifies the variable type and treats it accordingly, and the n.impute parameter indicates the number of multiple imputations, where five is recommended.

The output of impute_arg shows R^2 values for predicted missing values. The higher the value, the better the values predicted.

Check imputed variable values using the following command:

```
> impute_arg$imputed$rad
```

Detecting outliers

Outliers in data can distort predictions and affect the accuracy, if you don't detect and handle them appropriately, especially in the data preprocessing stage.

So, identifying the extreme values is important, as it can drastically introduce bias in the analytic pipeline and affect predictions. In this recipe, we will discuss the ways to detect outliers and how to handle them.

Getting ready

Download the files for this chapter and store the ozone.csv file in your R working directory. Read the file using the read.csv() command and save it in a variable:

```
> ozoneData <- read.csv("ozone.csv", stringsAsFactors=FALSE)
```

How to do it...

Perform the following steps to detect outliers in the dataset:

1. Detect outliers in the univariate continuous variable:

```
>outlier_values <- boxplot.stats(ozoneData$pressure_height)$out

>boxplot(ozoneData$pressure_height, main="Pressure Height",
boxwex=0.1)

>mtext(paste("Outliers: ", paste(outlier_values, collapse=", ")),
cex=0.6)
```

The output would be the following screenshot:

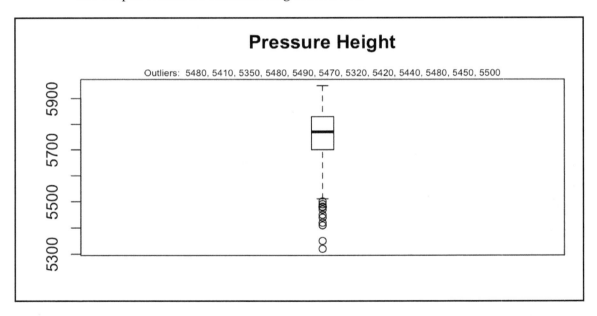

2. Detect outliers in bivariate categorical variables:

```
> boxplot(ozone_reading ~ Month, data=ozoneData, main="Ozone
reading across months")
```

The output would be the following screenshot:

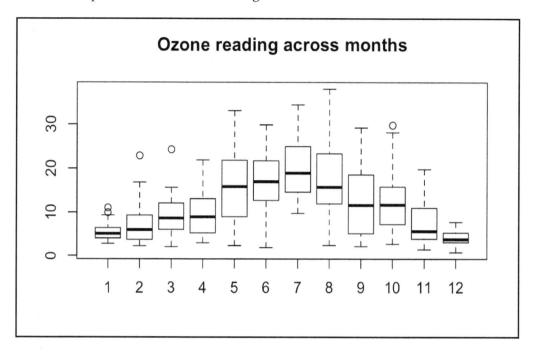

How it works...

The most commonly used method to detect outliers is visualization of the data, through boxplot, histogram, or scatterplot.

The `boxplot.stats()$out` function fetches the values of data points that lie beyond the extremes of the whiskers. The `boxwex` attribute is a scale factor that is applied to all the boxes; it improves the appearance of the plot by making the boxes narrower. The `mtext()` function places a text outside the plot area, but within the plot window.

In the case of continuous variables, outliers are those observations that lie outside `1.5 *` `IQR`, where **Inter Quartile Range** or **IQR**, is the difference between the 75th and 25th quartiles. The outliers in continuous variables show up as dots outside the whiskers of the boxplot.

In case of bivariate categorical variables, a clear pattern is noticeable and the change in the level of boxes suggests that `Month` seems to have an impact in `ozone_reading`. The outliers in respective categorical levels show up as dots outside the whiskers of the boxplot.

There's more...

Detecting and handling outliers depends mostly on your application. Once you have identified the outliers and you have decided to make amends as per the nature of the problem, you may consider one of the following approaches.

Treating the outliers with mean/median imputation

We can handle outliers with mean or median imputation by replacing the observations lower than the 5th percentile with mean and those higher than 95th percentile with median. We can use the same statistics, mean or median, to impute outliers in both directions:

```
> impute_outliers <- function(x,removeNA = TRUE){
    quantiles <- quantile( x, c(.05, .95 ),na.rm = removeNA )
    x[ x < quantiles[1] ] <- mean(x,na.rm = removeNA )
    x[ x > quantiles[2] ] <- median(x,na.rm = removeNA )
    x
}

> imputed_data <- impute_outliers(ozoneData$pressure_height)
```

Validate the imputed data through visualization:

```
> par(mfrow = c(1, 2))

> boxplot(ozoneData$pressure_height, main="Pressure Height having
Outliers", boxwex=0.3)

> boxplot(imputed_data, main="Pressure Height with imputed data",
boxwex=0.3)
```

The output would be the following screenshot:

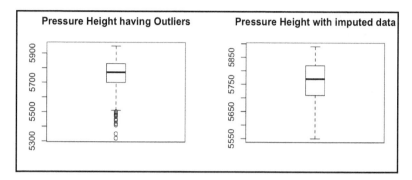

Handling extreme values with capping

To handle extreme values that lie outside the `1.5 * IQR`(Inter Quartile Range) limits, we could cap them by replacing those observations that lie below the lower limit, with the value of 5th percentile and those that lie above the upper limit, with the value of 95th percentile, as shown in the following code:

```
> replace_outliers <- function(x, removeNA = TRUE) {
    pressure_height <- x
    qnt <- quantile(pressure_height, probs=c(.25, .75), na.rm = removeNA)
    caps <- quantile(pressure_height, probs=c(.05, .95), na.rm = removeNA)
    H <- 1.5 * IQR(pressure_height, na.rm = removeNA)
    pressure_height[pressure_height < (qnt[1] - H)] <- caps[1]
    pressure_height[pressure_height > (qnt[2] + H)] <- caps[2]
    pressure_height
}

> capped_pressure_height <- replace_outliers(ozoneData$pressure_height)
```

Validate the capped variable `capped_pressure_height` through visualization:

```
> par(mfrow = c(1, 2))

> boxplot(ozoneData$pressure_height, main="Pressure Height with Outliers",
boxwex=0.1)

> boxplot(capped_pressure_height, main="Pressure Height without Outliers",
boxwex=0.1)
```

The output would be the following screenshot:

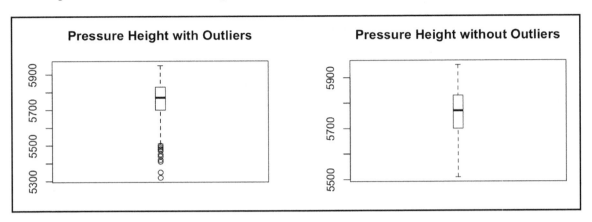

Transforming and binning values

Sometimes, transforming variables can also eliminate outliers. The natural log or square root of a value reduces the variation caused by extreme values. Some predictive analytics algorithms, such as decision trees, inherently deal with outliers by using binning techniques (a form of variable transformation).

Outlier detection with LOF

Local Outlier Factor or **LOF** is an algorithm implemented in DMwR package for identifying density-based local outliers, by comparing the local density of a point with that of its neighbors.

Now we will calculates the local outlier factors using the LOF algorithm using k number of neighbors:

```
> install.packages("DMwR")
> library(DMwR)
> outlier.scores <- lofactor(ozoneData, k=3)
```

Finally we will output the top 5 outlier by sorting the outlier score calculated above:

```
> outliers <- order(outlier.scores, decreasing=T)[1:5]
> print(outliers)
```

2
What's in There - Exploratory Data Analysis

In this chapter, you will cover:

- Creating standard data summaries
- Extracting a subset of a dataset
- Splitting a dataset
- Creating random data partitions
- Generating standard plots, such as histograms, boxplots, and scatterplots
- Generating multiple plots on a grid
- Creating plots with the lattice package
- Creating charts that facilitate comparisons
- Creating charts that help to visualize possible causality

Introduction

Exploratory analysis techniques are one part of the larger process of collecting data, learning from data, acting on data, and exploring data to uncover a meaningful pattern. The **Exploratory Data Analysis** (**EDA**) is a crucial step to take before diving into advanced analytics and machine learning, as it provides the context needed to develop an appropriate model for the problem at hand and to correctly interpret its results through visualization techniques to tease apart hidden patterns. In this chapter, we will discuss some of EDA's most common and essential practices, in order to summarize and visualize data so that the task of finding trends and patterns becomes causally easier.

Creating standard data summaries

In this recipe, we summarize the data using summary functions.

Getting ready

If you have not already downloaded the files for this chapter, do it now and ensure that the `auto-mpg.csv` file is in your R working directory.

How to do it...

Read the data from `auto-mpg.csv`, which includes a header row and columns separated by the default ", " symbol.

1. Read the data from `auto-mpg.csv` and convert `cylinders` to `factor`:

    ```
    > auto  <- read.csv("auto-mpg.csv", header = TRUE,
    stringsAsFactors = FALSE)
    > # Convert cylinders to factor
    > auto$cylinders <- factor(auto$cylinders, levels = c(3,4,5,6,8),
    labels = c("3cyl", "4cyl", "5cyl", "6cyl", "8cyl"))
    ```

2. Get the summary statistics:

    ```
    summary(auto)

            No              mpg           cylinders    displacement
     Min.   :  1.0    Min.   : 9.00    3cyl:  4    Min.   : 68.0
     1st Qu.:100.2    1st Qu.:17.50    4cyl:204    1st Qu.:104.2
     Median :199.5    Median :23.00    5cyl:  3    Median :148.5
     Mean   :199.5    Mean   :23.51    6cyl: 84    Mean   :193.4
     3rd Qu.:298.8    3rd Qu.:29.00    8cyl:103    3rd Qu.:262.0
     Max.   :398.0    Max.   :46.60                Max.   :455.0
       horsepower          weight        acceleration      model_year
     Min.   : 46.0    Min.   :1613    Min.   : 8.00    Min.   :70.00
     1st Qu.: 76.0    1st Qu.:2224    1st Qu.:13.82    1st Qu.:73.00
     Median : 92.0    Median :2804    Median :15.50    Median :76.00
     Mean   :104.1    Mean   :2970    Mean   :15.57    Mean   :76.01
     3rd Qu.:125.0    3rd Qu.:3608    3rd Qu.:17.18    3rd Qu.:79.00
     Max.   :230.0    Max.   :5140    Max.   :24.80    Max.   :82.00
       car_name
     Length:398
     Class :character
    ```

```
    Mode    :character
```

How it works...

The `summary()` function gives a six number summary for numerical variables: minimum, first quartile, median, mean, third quartile, and maximum. For factors (or categorical variables), the function shows the counts for each level; for character variables, it just shows the total number of available values.

There's more...

R offers several functions to take a quick peek at data, and we will discuss a few of these in this section.

Using the str() function for an overview of a data frame

The `str()` function gives a concise view of a data frame. In fact, we can use it to see the underlying structure of any arbitrary R object. The following commands and results show that the `str()` function tells us the type of the object whose structure we seek. It also tells us about the type of each of its component objects, along with an extract of some values. It can be very useful for getting an overview of a data frame.

```
> str(auto)

'data.frame': 398 obs. of  9 variables:
   $ No          : int   1 2 3 4 5 6 7 8 9 10 ...
   $ mpg         : num   28 19 36 28 21 23 15.5 32.9 16 13 ...
   $ cylinders   : Factor w/ 5 levels "3cyl","4cyl",..: 2 1 2 2 4     2 5
2 4 5 ...
   $ displacement: num   140 70 107 97 199 115 304 119 250 318 ...
   $ horsepower  : int   90 97 75 92 90 95 120 100 105 150 ...
   $ weight      : int   2264 2330 2205 2288 2648 2694 3962 2615     3897
3755 ...
   $ acceleration: num   15.5 13.5 14.5 17 15 15 13.9 14.8 18.5 14      ...
   $ model_year  : int   71 72 82 72 70 75 76 81 75 76 ...
   $ car_name    : chr   "chevrolet vega 2300" "mazda rx2 coupe"
"honda accord" "datsun 510 (sw)" ..
```

Computing the summary and the str() function for a single variable

When factor summaries are combined with those for numerical variables (as in the earlier example), `summary()` gives counts for a maximum of six levels and lumps the other counts under Other.

You can invoke `summary()` and the `str()` function for a single variable as well. In such a case, the summary you get for numerical variables remains as before, but for factors, you get counts for many more levels:

```
> summary(auto$cylinders)
> summary(auto$mpg)
> str(auto$cylinders)
```

Finding other measures

There are also other measures for data analysis that aren't found in `str()` and `summary()`. Many of them are in base packages, but some packages need to be installed for more unusual measures:

```
> install.packages(c("modeest","raster","moments"))
> library(modeest) #For mfv()
> library(raster)  #For quantile() and cv()
> library(moments) #For skewness() and kurtosis()
```

Here are some relevant functions:

Center measures:

```
> mean(auto$mpg)
[1] 23.51457
> median(auto$mpg)
[1] 23
> mfv(auto$mpg)
[1] 13
> quantile(auto$mpg)
   0% 25% 50% 75% 100%
  9.0 17.5 23.0 29.0 46.6
```

The `mfv()` function calculates the most frequent value or modes found in a vector. The 50 percent quantile is the same as the median.

Spread measures:

```
> sd(auto$mpg)
[1] 7.815984
> var(auto$mpg)
[1] 61.08961
> cv(auto$mpg)
[1] 33.2389
```

The coefficient of variation `cv()` function is a measure of relative variability and is calculated as `(sd/mean)*100`

Asymmetry measures:

```
> skewness(auto$mpg)
[1] 0.4553419
> kurtosis(auto$mpg)
[1] 2.480575
```

`skewness` here is `0.4553419`. This value implies that the distribution of the data is slightly skewed to the right or is positively skewed. Whereas, `kurtosis` describes the tail shape of the data distribution, and the value `2.480575` indicates positive `kurtosis` having fat-tailed distribution, and is said to be leptokurtic.

Extracting a subset of a dataset

In this recipe, we discuss two ways to subset data. The first approach uses the row and column indices/names and the other uses the `subset()` function.

Getting ready

Download the files for this chapter and store the `auto-mpg.csv` file in your R working directory. Read the data using the following command:

```
> auto <- read.csv("auto-mpg.csv", stringsAsFactors=FALSE)
```

The same subsetting principles apply for vectors, lists, arrays, matrices, and data frames. We illustrate with data frames.

How to do it...

The following steps extract a subset of a dataset:

1. Index by position. Get `model_year` and `car_name` for the first three cars by index position and index name:

    ```
    # Index by Position
    > auto[1:3, 8:9]
    > auto[1:3, c(8,9)]

    # Index by Name
    > auto[1:3,c("model_year", "car_name")]
    ```

2. Retrieve all details for the cars with the highest or lowest `mpg`, using the following code:

    ```
    > auto[auto$mpg == max(auto$mpg) | auto$mpg ==    min(auto$mpg),]
    ```

3. Get `mpg` and `car_name` for all the cars with `mpg > 30` and `cylinders == 6`:

    ```
    > auto[auto$mpg>30 & auto$cylinders==6, c("car_name","mpg")]
    ```

4. Get `mpg` and `car_name` for all the cars with `mpg > 30` and `cyl == 6`, using partial name match for cylinders:

    ```
    > auto[auto$mpg >30 & auto$cyl==6, c("car_name","mpg")]
    ```

5. Using the `subset()` function, get `mpg` and `car_name` for all the cars with `mpg > 30` and `cylinders == 6`:

    ```
    > subset(auto, mpg > 30 & cylinders == 6,
    select=c("car_name","mpg"))
    ```

How it works...

The first index in `auto[1:3, 8:9]` denotes the rows, and the second denotes the columns or variables. Instead of the column positions, we can also use the variable names. If using the variable names, enclose them in . . . .

If the required rows and columns are not contiguous, use a vector to indicate the needed rows and columns, as in `auto[c(1,3), c(3,5,7)]`.

Use column names instead of column positions, as column positions may change in the data file.

R uses the logical operators & (and), | (or), ! (negative unary), and == (equality check).

The `subset` function returns all the variables (columns) if you omit the `select` argument. Thus, `subset(auto, mpg > 30 & cylinders == 6)` retrieves all the cases that match the conditions `mpg > 30` and `cylinders = 6`.

However, while using the indices in a logical expression to select rows of a data frame, you always need to specify the variables needed or indicate all the variables with a comma following the logical expression:

```
> # incorrect
> auto[auto$mpg > 30]
Error in `[.data.frame`(auto, auto$mpg > 30) :    undefined columns
selected
>
> # correct
> auto[auto$mpg > 30, ]
```

 If we select a single variable, then subsetting returns a vector instead of a data frame.

There's more...

We mostly use the indices by name and position to subset data. Hence, we provide some additional details around using indices to subset data. The `subset()` function is used predominantly in cases when we need to repeatedly apply the subset operation for a set of arrays, lists, or vector elements.

Excluding columns

Use the minus sign for the variable positions that you want to exclude from the subset. Also, you cannot mix both positive and negative indices in the list. Both of the following approaches are correct:

```
> auto[,c(-1,-9)]
```

```
> auto[,-c(1,9)]
```

However, this subsetting approach does not work when specifying variables using names. For example, we cannot use `-c("No", "car_name")`. Instead, use `%in%` with `!` (negation) to exclude variables:

```
> auto[, !names(auto) %in% c("No", "car_name")]
```

Selecting based on multiple values

Select all the cars with `mpg = 15` or `mpg = 20`:

```
> auto[auto$mpg %in% c(15,20),c("car_name","mpg")]
```

Selecting using logical vector

You can specify the cases (rows) and variables you want to retrieve using Boolean vectors.

In the following example, R returns the first and second rows, and for each row, we only get the third variable column; we get the third variable alone. R returns the elements corresponding to `TRUE`:

```
> auto[1:2,c(FALSE,FALSE,TRUE)]
```

You can use the same approach for rows also.

If the lengths do not match, R recycles through the Boolean vector. However, it is always good practice to match the size.

Splitting a dataset

When we have categorical variables, we often want to create groups corresponding to each level and to analyze each group separately to reveal some significant similarities and differences between them.

The `split` function divides data into groups based on a factor or vector. The `unsplit()` function reverses the effect of `split`.

Getting ready

Download the files for this chapter and store the `auto-mpg.csv` file in your R working directory. Read the file using the `read.csv` command and save in the `auto` variable:

```
> auto <- read.csv("auto-mpg.csv", stringsAsFactors=FALSE)
```

How to do it...

Split `cylinders` using the following command:

```
> carslist <- split(auto, auto$cylinders)
```

How it works...

The `split(auto, auto$cylinders)` function returns a list of data frames, where each data frame belongs to particulars levels of `cylinders` variable. To reference a data frame from the list, use the `[` notation. Here, `carslist[1]` is a list of length *1* consisting of the first data frame that corresponds to three cylinder cars, and `carslist[[1]]` is the associated data frame for the three cylinder cars:

```
> str(carslist[1])
List of 1
 $ 3:'data.frame': 4 obs. of  9 variables:
  ..$ No          : int [1:4] 2 199 251 365
  ..$ mpg         : num [1:4] 19 18 23.7 21.5
  ..$ cylinders   : int [1:4] 3 3 3 3
  ..$ displacement: num [1:4] 70 70 70 80
  ..$ horsepower  : int [1:4] 97 90 100 110
  ..$ weight      : int [1:4] 2330 2124 2420 2720
  ..$ acceleration: num [1:4] 13.5 13.5 12.5 13.5
  ..$ model_year  : int [1:4] 72 73 80 77
  ..$ car_name    : chr [1:4] "mazda rx2 coupe" "maxda rx3"        "mazda
rx-7 gs" "mazda rx-4"

> names(carslist[[1]])

[1] "No"          "mpg"          "cylinders"     "displacement"
[5] "horsepower"  "weight"       "acceleration"  "model_year"
[9] "car_name"
```

Creating random data partitions

Analysts need an unbiased evaluation of the quality of their machine learning models. To get this, they partition the available data into two parts. They use one part to build the machine learning model and retain the remaining data as **hold out** data. After building the model, they evaluate the model's performance on the hold out data. This recipe shows you how to partition data. It separately addresses the situations when the target variable is numeric and when it is categorical. It also covers the process of creating two partitions or three.

Getting ready

If you have not already done so, make sure that the `BostonHousing.csv` and `boston-housing-classification.csv` files from the code files of this chapter are in your R working directory. You should also install the `caret` package using the following command:

```
> install.packages("caret")
> library(caret)
> bh <- read.csv("BostonHousing.csv")
```

How to do it...

You may want to develop a model using some machine learning technique (like linear regression or KNN) to predict the value of a house in a Boston neighborhood, using the data in the `BostonHousing.csv` file. The `MEDV` variable will serve as the target variable.

Case 1 - Numerical target variable and two partitions

To create a training partition with 80 percent of the cases and a validation partition with the rest, use the following code:

```
> trg.idx <- createDataPartition(bh$MEDV, p = 0.8, list = FALSE)
> trg.part <- bh[trg.idx, ]
> val.part <- bh[-trg.idx, ]
```

After this, the `trg.part` and `val.part` variables contain the training and validation partitions, respectively.

Case 2 - Numerical target variable and three partitions

Some machine learning techniques require three partitions, because they use two partitions just for building the model. Thus, the third (test) partition contains the hold out data for model evaluation.

Suppose we want a training partition with 70 percent of the cases, and the rest divided equally among validation and test partitions. We then use the following commands:

```
> trg.idx <- createDataPartition(bh$MEDV, p = 0.7, list = FALSE)
> trg.part <- bh[trg.idx, ]
> temp <- bh[-trg.idx, ]
> val.idx <- createDataPartition(temp$MEDV, p = 0.5, list = FALSE)
> val.part <- temp[val.idx, ]
> test.part <- temp[-val.idx, ]
```

Case 3 - Categorical target variable and two partitions

The `boston-housing-classification.csv` file has a `MEDV_CAT` variable that categorizes the median values into **HIGH** or **LOW**, and is suitable for a classification algorithm.

For partitioning the categorical response variable with 70-30 split, use the following commands:

```
> bh2 <- read.csv("boston-housing-classification.csv")
> trg.idx <- createDataPartition(bh2$MEDV_CAT, p=0.7, list =     FALSE)
> trg.part <- bh2[trg.idx, ]
> val.part <- bh2[-trg.idx, ]
```

Case 4 - Categorical target variable and three partitions

For a 70-15-15 split (training, validation, test), use the following commands:

```
> bh3 <- read.csv("boston-housing-classification.csv")
> trg.idx <- createDataPartition(bh3$MEDV_CAT, p=0.7, list =     FALSE)
> trg.part <- bh3[trg.idx, ]
> temp <- bh3[-trg.idx, ]
> val.idx <- createDataPartition(temp$MEDV_CAT, p=0.5,list =     FALSE)
> val.part <- temp[val.idx, ]
> test.part <- temp[-val.idx, ]
```

How it works...

The `createDataPartition()` function randomly selects row indices from the array supplied as its first argument. Rather than selecting randomly from the entire data frame, it does a more intelligent sampling, as we now describe.

If supplied with a numeric vector as the first argument, then `createDataPartition()` applies the random selection process by percentile groups, so as to get a good sampling of rows from the entire range of the target variable. By default, it considers five groups, but we can control this through the optional `groups` argument.

If supplied with a vector of factors, the function randomly samples for each value of the factor from the cases, thereby ensuring a good representation of all factor values in the training partition.

The `list` argument controls whether we want the output as a list or as a vector.

To avoid keeping duplicate data in both the original data frame as well as in the two data partitions, you can work with just the indices generated and refer to `bh[trg.idx,]` for the training partition and `bh[-trg.idx,]` for the validation partition.

When you have large data files, repeated subsetting may be inefficient and you may want to copy the data into the partitions up front.

There's more...

We discuss some additional information on data partitioning in this section.

Using a convenience function for partitioning

Rather than typing out the detailed steps each time, you can simplify the process by creating the following functions:

```
rda.cb.partition2 <- function(ds, target.index, prob) {
  library(caret)
  train.idx <- createDataPartition(y=ds[,target.index],        p = prob, list
= FALSE)
  list(train =  ds[train.idx, ], val = ds[-train.idx, ])
}

rda.cb.partition3 <- function(ds,
           target.index, prob.train, prob.val) {
```

```
library(caret)
train.idx <- createDataPartition(y=ds[,target.index],
        p = prob.train, list = FALSE)
train <- ds[train.idx, ]
temp <- ds[-train.idx, ]
val.idx <- createDataPartition(y=temp[,target.index],
        p = prob.val/(1-prob.train), list = FALSE)
list(train =  ds[train.idx, ],
        val = temp[val.idx, ], test = temp[-val.idx, ])
}
```

With the preceding two functions in place, you can write the following single line to create two partitions (80 percent, 20 percent) of a data frame:

```
dat1 <- rda.cb.partition2(bh, 14, 0.8)
```

You can do the following to get three partitions (70 percent, 15 percent, 15 percent):

```
dat2 <- rda.cb.partition3(bh, 14, 0.7, 0.15)
```

The rda.cb.partition2() and rda.cb.partition3() functions return a list with two and three components, respectively. To use the training and validation partitions from dat1, you can refer to dat1$train and dat1$val. The same applies to dat2; to get the test partition from dat2, use dat2$test.

Sampling from a set of values

To select a random sample size of 50 cases without replacement from the bh data frame, use the following command:

```
sam.idx <- sample(1:nrow(bh), 50, replace = FALSE)
```

Generating standard plots, such as histograms, boxplots, and scatterplots

Before even embarking on any numerical analyses, you may want to get a good idea about the data through a few quick plots. The base R system supports basic graphics, so for more advanced plots requirement, we generally use `lattice` and `ggplot` packages. In this recipe we will cover the simplest form of basic graphs.

Getting ready

If you have not already done so, download the data files for this chapter and ensure that they are available in your R environment's working directory, and run the following commands:

```
> auto <- read.csv("auto-mpg.csv")
>
> auto$cylinders <- factor(auto$cylinders, levels = c(3,4,5,6,8),
labels = c("3cyl", "4cyl", "5cyl", "6cyl", "8cyl"))
> attach(auto)
```

How to do it...

In this recipe, we cover histograms, boxplots, scatterplots, and scatterplot matrices.

Creating histograms

Generate a histogram for acceleration:

```
> hist(acceleration)
```

R determines the various properties of the generated graph (such as bin sizes, axes scales, axes titles, chart title, bar colors, and so on) automatically. The following diagram shows the output of the preceding command:

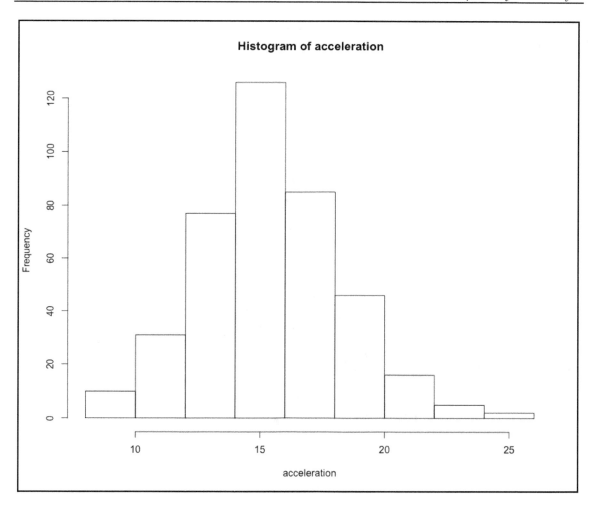

You can customize everything. The following code shows some options:

```
> hist(acceleration, col="blue", xlab = "acceleration",      main =
"Histogram of acceleration", breaks = 15)
```

The histogram of acceleration can be seen in the following diagram:

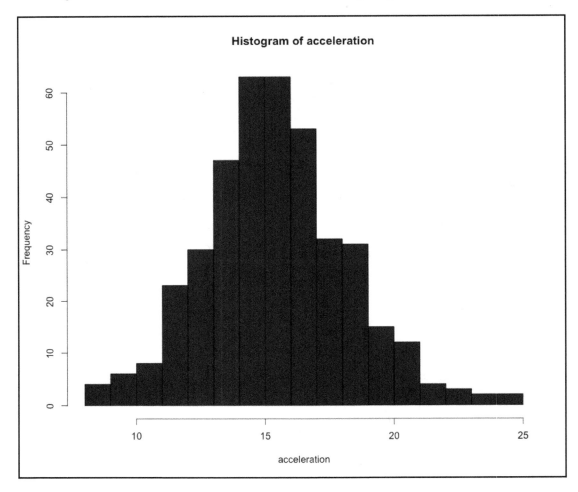

Creating boxplots

Create a boxplot for mpg, using the following command:

```
> boxplot(mpg, xlab = "Miles per gallon")
```

The following diagram is the boxplot:

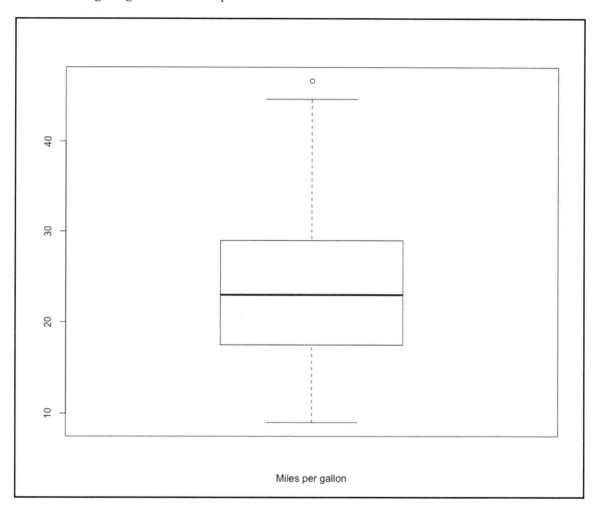

To generate `boxplots` for subsets within the whole dataset, you can use:

```
> boxplot(mpg ~ model_year, xlab = "Miles per gallon")
```

The following diagram is the boxplot:

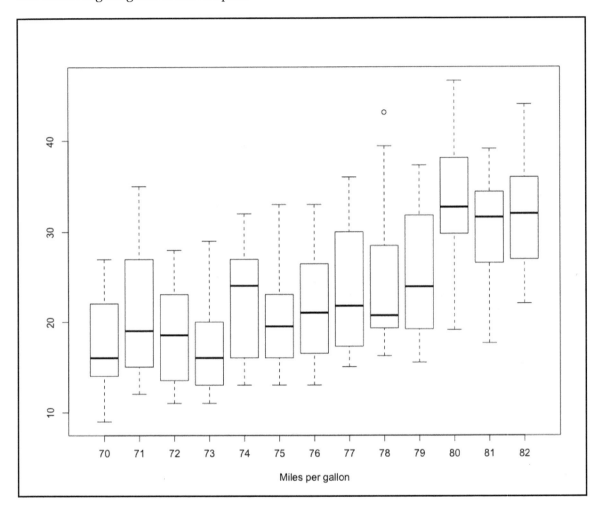

Miles per gallon

Now generate a `boxplot` of `mpg` by cylinders:

```
> boxplot(mpg ~ cylinders)
```

The following diagram is the boxplot:

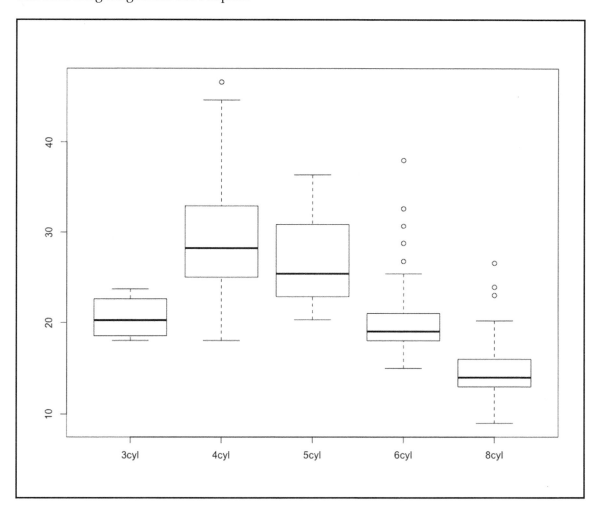

Creating scatterplots

Create a scatterplot for mpg by horsepower:

```
> plot(mpg ~ horsepower)
```

The following diagram is the scatterplot:

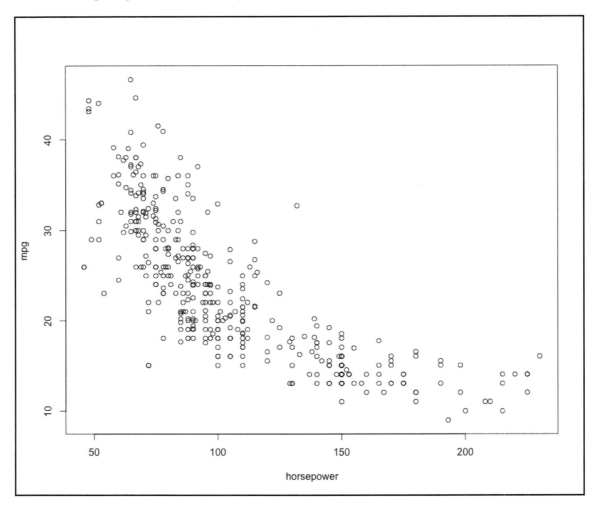

Creating scatterplot matrices

Create pairwise scatterplots for a set of variables:

```
> pairs(~mpg+displacement+horsepower+weight)
```

The following diagram is the scatterplot:

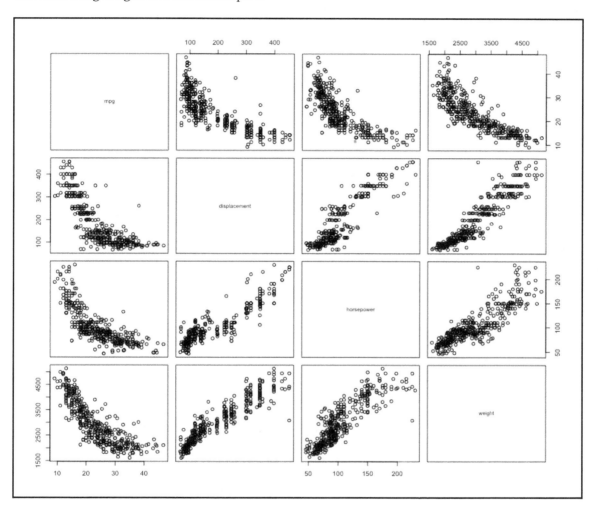

How it works...

Here, we describe how the preceding lines of code work.

Histograms

By default, the hist() function automatically determines the number of bars to display, based on the data. The breaks argument controls this.

You can also use a palette of colors instead of a single color, by using the following command:

```
> hist(mpg, col = rainbow(12))
```

The following diagram is the colored histogram:

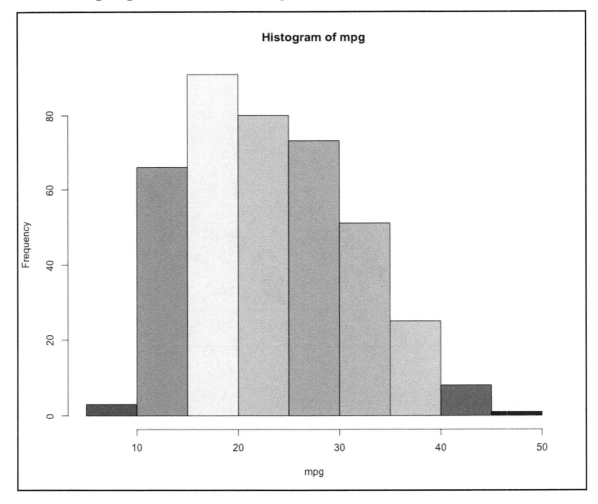

The `rainbow()` function returns a color palette with the color spectrum broken into the number of distinct colors specified, and the `hist()` function uses one color for each bar.

Boxplots

You can either give a simple vector or a formula (like `auto$mpg ~ auto$cylinders` in the preceding example) as the first argument to the `boxplot()` function. In the latter case, it creates separate boxplots for every distinct level of the right-hand side variable.

There's more...

You can overlay the plots and color specific points differently. We show some useful options in this section.

Overlay a density plot on a histogram

Histograms are very sensitive to the number of bins used. Kernel density plots give a smoother and more accurate picture of the distribution. Usually, we overlay a density plot on a histogram using the `density()` function to visualize data distribution.

If invoked by itself, the `density()` function only produces the density plot. To overlay it on the histogram, we use the `lines()` function, which does not erase the current chart and instead overlays the existing plot. Since the density plot plots relative frequencies (approximating a probability density function), we need to ensure that the histogram also shows the relative frequencies. The `prob=TRUE` argument achieves this:

```
hist(mpg, prob=TRUE)
lines(density(mpg))
```

The following diagram is the density plot:

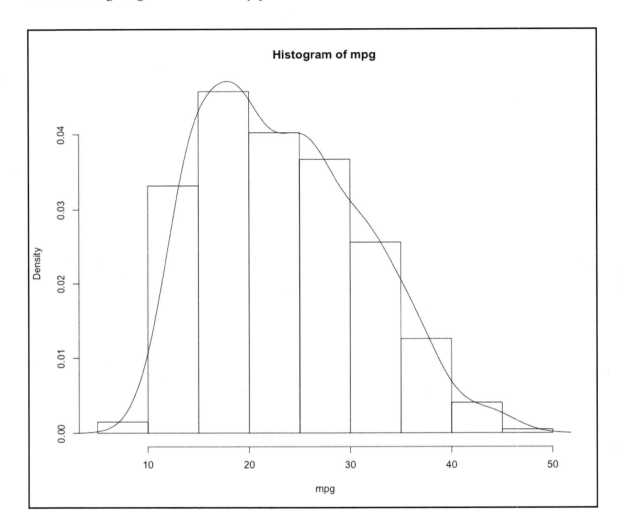

Overlay a regression line on a scatterplot

The following code first generates the scatterplot and then builds the regression model using lm. It then uses the abline() function to overlay the regression line on the existing scatterplot:

```
> plot(mpg ~ horsepower)
> reg <- lm(mpg ~ horsepower)
> abline(reg)
```

The following diagram is the scatterplot:

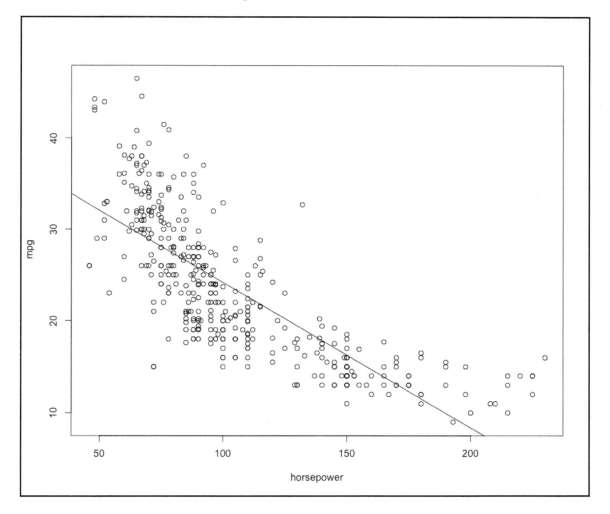

Color specific points on a scatterplot

Using the following code, you can first generate the scatterplot and then color the points with different colors corresponding to different values of cylinders. Note that mpg and weight are in different orders in the plot and points function invocations. This is because in plot, we ask the system to plot mpg as a function of weight, whereas in the points function, we just supply a set of (x,y) coordinates to plot.

```
> # first generate the empty plot
> # to get the axes for the whole dat
> plot(mpg ~ horsepower, type = "n")
> # Then plot the points in different colors
> with(subset(auto, cylinders == "8cyl"),        points(horsepower, mpg, col =
"blue"))
> with(subset(auto, cylinders == "6cyl"),        points(horsepower, mpg, col =
"red"))
> with(subset(auto, cylinders == "5cyl"),        points(horsepower, mpg, col =
"yellow"))
> with(subset(auto, cylinders == "4cyl"),        points(horsepower, mpg, col =
"green"))
> with(subset(auto, cylinders == "3cyl"),        points(horsepower, mpg))
```

The preceding commands produce the following output:

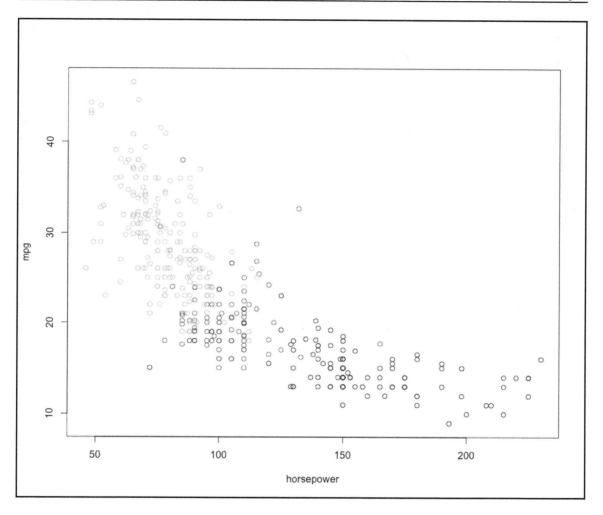

Generating multiple plots on a grid

We often want to see plots side by side for comparisons. This recipe shows how we can achieve this.

Getting ready

If you have not already done so, download the data files for this chapter and ensure that they are available in your R environment's working directory. Once this is done, run the following commands:

```
> auto <- read.csv("auto-mpg.csv")
> cylinders <- factor(cylinders,      levels = c(3,4,5,6,8),       labels =
c("3cyl", "4cyl", "5cyl", "6cyl", "8cyl"))
> attach(auto)
```

How to do it...

You may want to generate two side by side scatterplots from the data in `auto-mpg.csv`. Run the following commands to do so:

```
> # first get old graphical parameter settings
> old.par = par()
> # create a grid of one row and two columns
> par(mfrow = c(1,2))
> with(auto, {      plot(mpg ~ weight, main = "Weight vs. mpg")      plot(mpg
~ acceleration, main = "Acceleration vs. mpg")
  }
 )
> # reset par back to old value so that subsequent
> # graphic operations are unaffected by our settings
> par(old.par)
```

The following diagram shows the two scatterplots:

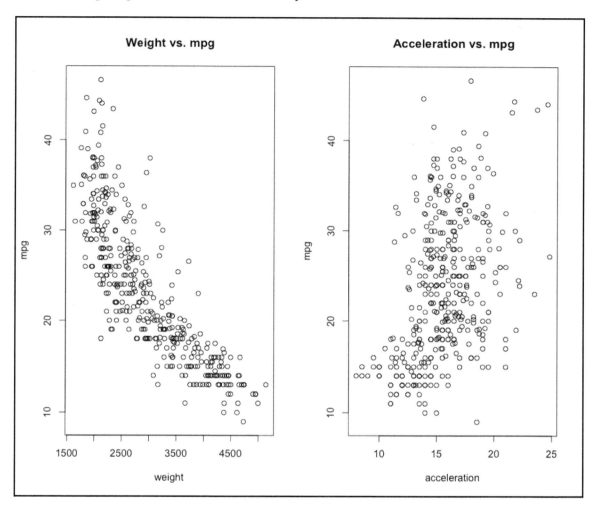

How it works...

The par(mfrow = c(1,2)) function call creates a grid with one row and two columns. The subsequent invocations of the plot() function fills the charts into these grid locations, row by row. Alternately, you can specify par(mfcol = ...) to specify the grid. In this case, the grid is created as in the case of mfrow, but the grid cells get filled in column by column.

Graphics parameters

In addition to creating a grid for graphics, you can use the par() function to specify numerous graphics parameters to control all aspects. Check the documentation if you need something specific.

Creating plots with the lattice package

The lattice package produces Trellis plots to capture multivariate relationships in the data. Lattice plots are useful for looking at complex relationships between the variables in a dataset. For example, we may want to see how y changes with x across various levels of z. Using the lattice package, we can draw histograms, boxplots, scatterplots, dot plots, and so on. Both plotting and annotation are done in one single call.

Getting ready

Download the files for this chapter and store the auto-mpg.csv file in your R working directory. Read the file using the read.csv function and save in the auto variable. Convert cylinders into a factor variable:

```
> auto <- read.csv("auto-mpg.csv", stringsAsFactors=FALSE)
> cyl.factor <- factor(auto$cylinders,labels=c("3cyl","4cyl",
"5cyl","6cyl","8cyl"))
```

How to do it...

To create plots with the `lattice` package, follow these steps:

1. Install and Load the `lattice` package:

    ```
    > library(lattice)
    ```

2. Draw a boxplot:

    ```
    > bwplot(~auto$mpg|cyl.factor, main="MPG by Number of
    Cylinders",xlab="Miles per Gallon")
    ```

3. Draw a scatterplot:

    ```
    > xyplot(mpg~weight|cyl.factor, data=auto,      main="Weight Vs MPG
    by Number of Cylinders",      ylab="Miles per Gallon", xlab="Car
    Weight")
    ```

How it works...

Lattice plot commands comprise the following four parts:

*   **Graph type**: This can be `bwplot`, `xyplot`, `densityplot`, `splom`, and so on
*   **Formula**: Variables and factor variables separated by |
*   **Data**: A data frame containing values
*   **Annotations**: These include caption, *x* axis label, and *y* axis label

In the boxplot, step 2, the `~auto$mpg|cyl.factor` formula instructs `lattice` to make the plot with `mpg` on the *x* axis, grouped by factors representing cylinders. Here, we have not specified any variable for the *y* axis. For boxplots and density plots, we need not specify the *y* axis. The output for boxplot resembles the following diagram:

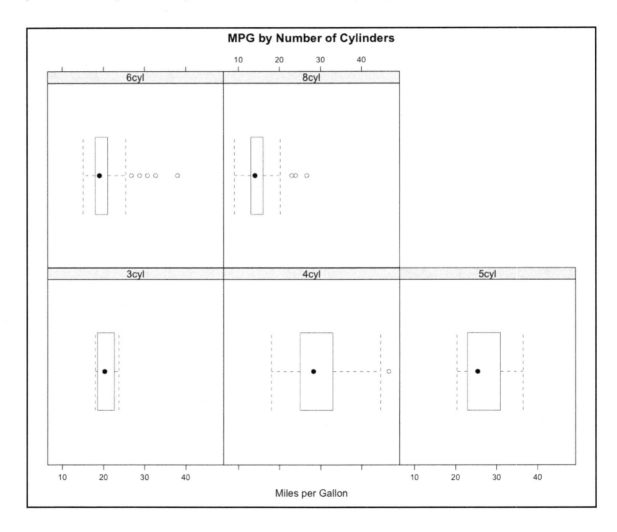

In the scatterplot, the xyplot function and the mpg~weight|cyl.factor formula instructs lattice to make the plot with weight on the *x* axis and mpg on the *y* axis, grouped by factors representing cylinders. For xyplot, we need to provide two variables; otherwise, R will produce an error. The scatterplot output is seen as follows:

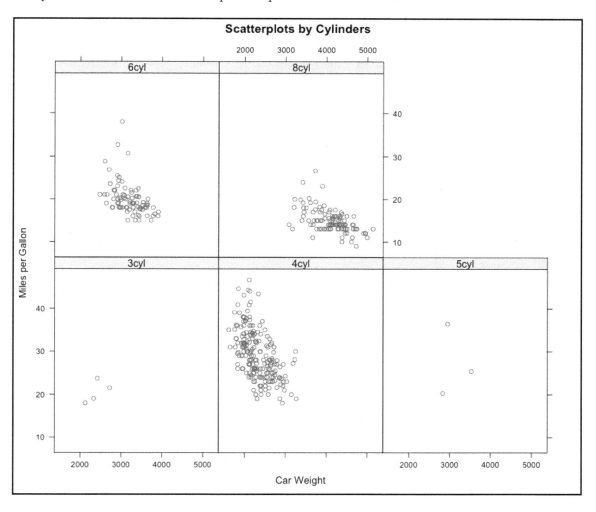

There's more...

Lattice plots provide default options to bring out the relationship between multiple variables. More options can be added to these plots to enhance the graphs.

Adding flair to your graphs

By default, `lattice` assigns the panel's height and width based on the screen device. Also, the plots use a default color scheme. However, these can be customized to your needs.

You should change the color scheme of all the `lattice` plots before executing the plot command. The color scheme affects all Trellis plots made with the `lattice` package:

```
> trellis.par.set(theme = col.whitebg())
```

Panels occupy the entire output window. This can be controlled with `aspect`. The layout determines the number of panels on the *x* axis and how they are stacked. Add these to the `plot` function call:

```
> bwplot(~mpg|cyl.factor, data=auto,main="MPG by Number Of Cylinders",
xlab="Miles per Gallon",layout=c(2,3),aspect=1)
```

See also

- *Generating standard plots, such as histograms, boxplots, and scatterplots*

Creating charts that facilitate comparisons

In large datasets, we often gain good insights by examining how different segments behave. The similarities and differences can reveal interesting patterns. This recipe shows how to create graphs that enable such comparisons with different variable types.

Getting ready

If you have not already done so, download the book's files for this chapter and save the `daily-bike-rentals.csv` file in your R working directory. Read the data into R using the following command and check the packages needed too:

```
> library(dplyr)
```

```
> bike <- read.csv("daily-bike-rentals.csv")
> bike$season <- factor(bike$season, levels = c(1,2,3,4),labels =
c("Spring", "Summer", "Fall", "Winter"))
> bike$workingday <- factor(bike$workingday, levels = c(0,1),labels =
c("Work day", "Free day"))
> bike$weathersit <- factor(bike$weathersit, levels = c(1,2,3),labels =
c("Clear", "Misty/cloudy", "Light snow"))
> attach(bike)
```

How to do it...

We base this recipe on the task of generating visualizations to facilitate the comparison of bike rentals by season.

Using base plotting system

Now we'll look at how to generate histograms of the count of daily bike rentals by season, using R's base plotting system:

1. Set up a 2 x 2 grid for plotting histograms for the four seasons:

   ```
   > par(mfrow = c(2,2))
   ```

2. Extract data for seasons:

   ```
   > spring <- subset(bike, season == "Spring")$cnt
   > summer <- subset(bike, season == "Summer")$cnt
   > fall <- subset(bike, season == "Fall")$cnt
   > winter <- subset(bike, season == "Winter")$cnt
   ```

3. Plot the histogram, density, mean, and median for each season:

   ```
   > hist(spring, prob=TRUE, xlab = "Spring daily rentals", main = "")
   > lines(density(spring))
   > abline(v = mean(spring), col = "red")
   > abline(v = median(spring), col = "blue")

   > hist(summer, prob=TRUE, xlab = "Summer daily rentals", main = "")
   > lines(density(summer))
   > abline(v = mean(summer), col = "red")
   > abline(v = median(summer), col = "blue")

   > hist(fall, prob=TRUE, xlab = "Fall daily rentals", main = "")
   > lines(density(fall))
   ```

```
> abline(v = mean(fall), col = "red")
> abline(v = median(fall), col = "blue")

> hist(winter, prob=TRUE, xlab = "Winter daily rentals", main = "")
> lines(density(winter))
> abline(v = mean(winter), col = "red")
> abline(v = median(winter), col = "blue")
```

You get the following output that facilitates comparisons across the seasons:

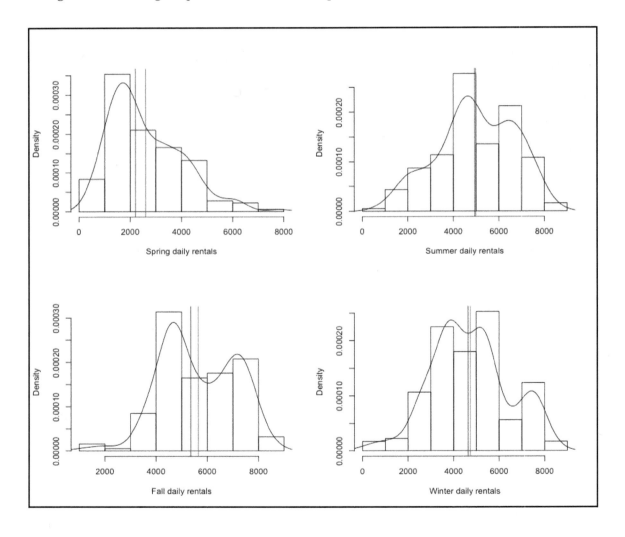

How it works...

We first created histogram based on different seasons, then added `density()` function over the distribution. Finally we used the `abline` method to show the mean and median of each distribution with color lines.

There's more...

There are other more useful visualizations besides boxplots and histograms.

Creating beanplots with the beanplot package

One of them is the beanplot, which can display the distribution with the visual structure of the boxplot and can also display the frequencies as a histogram. We will create one and assign colors with the `beanplot` package. The command is as follows:

```
> library(beanplot)
> beanplot(bike$cnt ~ bike$season, col = c("blue", "red", "yellow"))
```

The preceding code produces the following output:

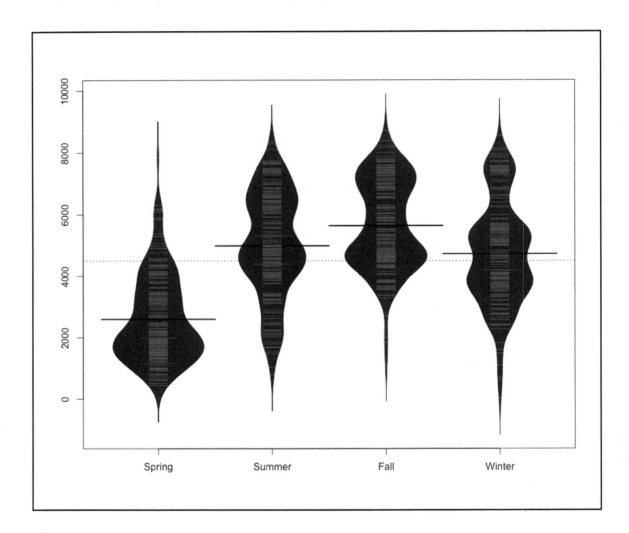

See also

- *Generating standard plots, such as histograms, boxplots, and scatterplots*
- Refer to `Chapter 7`, *How it looks - Advanced data visualization* for advance plots using the `ggplot` package.

Creating charts that help to visualize possible causality

When presenting data, rather than merely presenting information, we usually want to present an explanation of some phenomenon. Visualizing hypothesized causality helps to communicate our ideas clearly.

Getting ready

If you have not already done so, download the book's files for this chapter and save the `hourly-bike-rentals.csv` file in your R working directory. Read the data into R as follows:

```
> library(lattice)
> bike <- read.csv("daily-bike-rentals.csv")
> bike$season <- factor(bike$season, levels = c(1,2,3,4),
    labels = c("Spring", "Summer", "Fall", "Winter"))
> bike$weathersit <- factor(bike$weathersit, levels = c(1,2,3),
    labels = c("Clear", "Misty/cloudy", "Light snow"))
> bike$dteday = as.Date(bike$dteday, format = "%Y-%m-%d")
> attach(bike)
```

How to do it...

With the bike rentals data, you can show a hypothesized causality between the weather situation and the number of rentals by drawing boxplots of rentals under different weather conditions.

```
> bwplot(cnt ~ weathersit, data=bike, layout=c(1,1),xlab = "Weathersit",
ylab = "Frequency",
        par.settings = list(box.rectangle = list(fill=
rep(c('red','yellow','green'),2))))
```

The preceding command produces the following output:

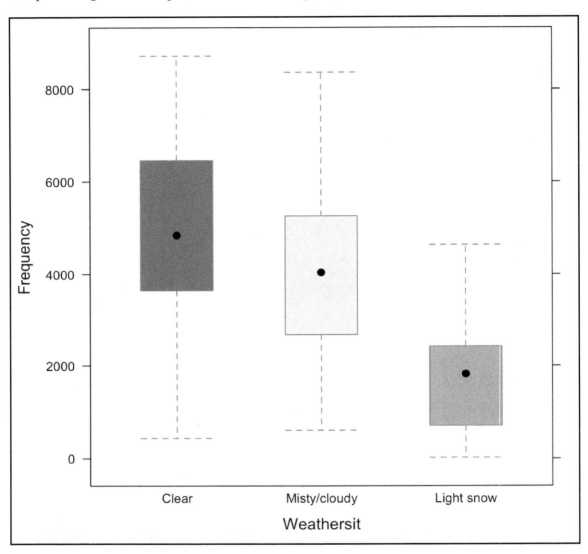

We can create other panels alongside our boxplot to have a clearer idea of data dispersion:

```
>   bwplot(cnt ~ weathersit,xlab = "Weathersit", ylab =
"Frequency",panel=function(x,y,...){
    panel.bwplot(x,y,...)
    panel.stripplot(x,y,jitter.data = TRUE,...)
  }, par.settings = list(box.rectangle = list(fill=
```

```
rep(c('red','yellow','green'),2))))
```

The preceding command produces the following plot:

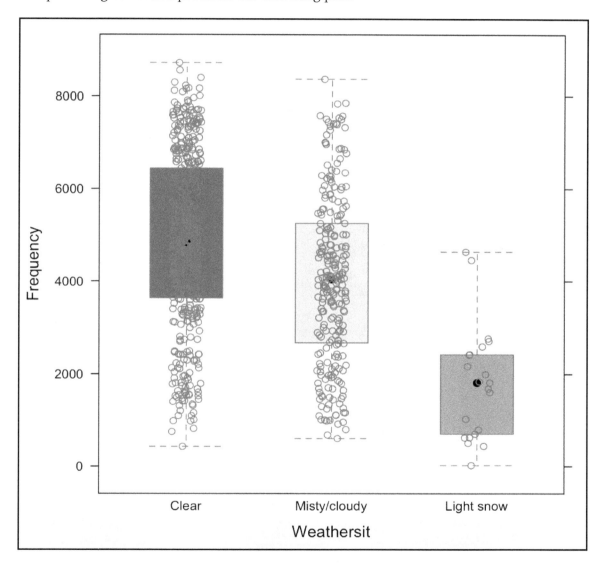

How it works...

We overlay the actual data points over the boxplot and add `jitter` by specifying `jitter.data = TRUE` in `stripplot` panel along side `bwplot`.

See also

- *Generating standard plots, such as histograms, boxplots, and scatterplots*
- Refer to `Chapter 7`, *How it looks - Advanced data visualization* for advance plots using the `ggplot` package.

3
Where Does It Belong? Classification

In this chapter, we will cover the following recipes:

- Generating error/classification confusion matrices
- Principal Component Analysis
- Generating receiver operating characteristic charts
- Building, plotting, and evaluating with classification trees
- Using random forest models for classification
- Classifying using the support vector machine approach
- Classifying using the Naive Bayes approach
- Classifying using the KNN approach
- Using neural networks for classification
- Classifying using linear discriminant function analysis
- Classifying using logistic regression
- Text classification for sentiment analysis

Introduction

Classification has massive application in real life. With the enormous growth of information datasets, data scientists or analysts often require high-performance classification algorithms to identify objects belonging to predefined categories; for example, predicting a customer as a potential buyer or not, classifying a product as defective or not, a customer as likely to default on a payment or not, and even analyzing sentiments in real time. This chapter covers recipes to use R to apply several classification techniques.

Generating error/classification confusion matrices

You might build a classification model and want to evaluate the model by comparing the model's predictions with the actual outcomes. You will typically do this on the holdout data. Getting an idea of how the model does in training data itself is also useful, but you should never use that as an objective measure.

Getting ready

If you have not already downloaded the files for this chapter, do so now and ensure that the `college-perf.csv` file is in your R working directory. The file has data about a set of college students. The `Perf` variable has their college performance classified as `High`, `Medium`, or `Low`. The `Pred` variable contains a classification model's predictions of the performance level. The following code reads the data and converts the factor levels to a meaningful order - by default, R orders factors alphabetically:

```
> cp <- read.csv("college-perf.csv")
> cp$Perf <- ordered(cp$Perf, levels =
+            c("Low", "Medium", "High"))

> cp$Pred <- ordered(cp$Pred, levels =
+            c("Low", "Medium", "High"))
```

How to do it...

To generate error/classification confusion matrices, follow these steps:

1. First, create and display a two-way table based on the `Actual` and `Predicted` values:

```
> tab <- table(cp$Perf, cp$Pred, dnn = c("Actual", "Predicted"))
> tab
        Predicted
Actual Low Medium High
  Low 1150 84 98
  Medium 166 1801 170
  High 35 38 458
```

2. Display the raw numbers as proportions or percentages. To get overall table-level proportions, use the following code:

```
> prop.table(tab)
        Predicted
Actual       Low  Medium    High
  Low    0.28750 0.02100 0.02450
  Medium 0.04150 0.45025 0.04250
  High   0.00875 0.00950 0.11450
```

3. We often find it more convenient to interpret row-wise or column-wise percentages. To get row-wise percentages rounded to one decimal place, you can pass a second argument as 1:

```
> round(prop.table(tab, 1)*100, 1)
        Predicted
Actual   Low Medium High
  Low    86.3    6.3  7.4
  Medium  7.8   84.3  8.0
  High    6.6    7.2 86.3
```

Passing 2 as the second argument yields column-wise proportions.

How it works...

The `table()` function performs a simple two-way cross-tabulation of values. For each unique value of the first variable, it counts the occurrences of different values of the second variable. It works for numeric, factor, and character variables.

There's more...

When dealing with more than two or three categories, seeing the error matrix as a chart could be useful to quickly assess the model's performance within various categories.

Visualizing the error/classification confusion matrix

You can create a `barplot` using the following command:

```
> barplot(tab, legend = TRUE)
```

The following output is the result of the preceding command:

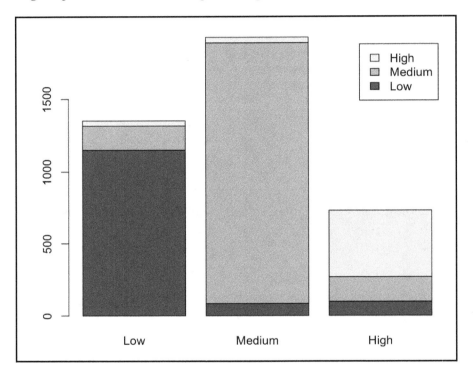

For a `mosaicplot`, the following command is used:

```
> mosaicplot(tab, main = "Prediction performance")
```

The following output is obtained on running the command:

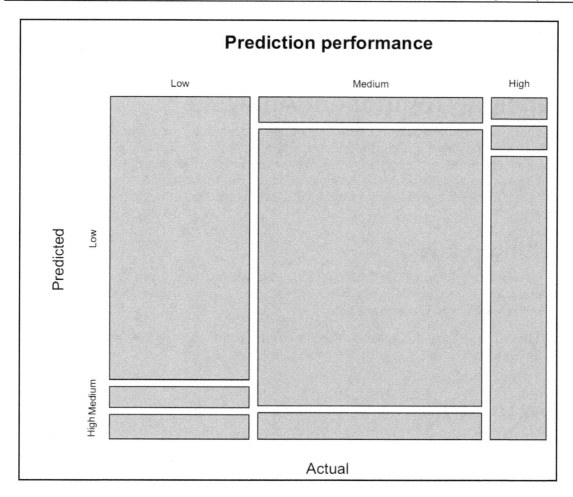

Comparing the model's performance for different classes

You can check whether the model's performance on different classes differs significantly with the summary function:

```
> summary(tab)
Number of cases in table: 4000
Number of factors: 2
Test for independence of all factors:
  Chisq = 4449, df = 4, p-value = 0
```

The low `p-value` tells us that the proportions for the different classes are significantly different.

Principal Component Analysis

Principal Component Analysis (PCA) is a statistical technique for dimensionality reduction that transforms data with high-dimensional space into low-dimensional space. Its goal is to replace a large number of correlated variables with a smaller number of uncorrelated variables while retaining as much information in the original variables as possible, hence playing a significant role in feature engineering tasks of the machine learning pipeline.

Getting ready

In this recipe, we will illustrate the technique of PCA using the `USArrests` dataset that contains crime-related statistics, such as `Assault`, `Murder`, `Rape`, and `UrbanPop`, per 100,000 residents in 50 states in the US.

If you have not already downloaded the files for this chapter, do so now and ensure that the `USArrests.csv` file is in your R working directory.

How to do it...

Perform the following steps to apply data reduction using PCA:

1. First, let's read the dataset, modify the row names to state names, and visualize its contents:

```
> usArrests=read.csv("USArrests.csv",stringsAsFactors = FALSE)
> rownames(usArrests)=usArrests$X
> usArrests$X=NULL
> head(usArrests)
           Murder Assault UrbanPop Rape
   Alabama   13.2    236      58   21.2
    Alaska   10.0    263      48   44.5
   Arizona    8.1    294      80   31.0
  Arkansas    8.8    190      50   19.5
California    9.0    276      91   40.6
  Colorado    7.9    204      78   38.7
```

2. Calculating the variance row-wise to see how each variable is varying, we can observe that `Assault` has the most variance:

```
> apply(usArrests , 2, var)
   Murder     Assault     UrbanPop Rape
  18.97047 6945.16571 209.51878 87.72916
```

3. To overcome the magnitude of the variables' influence on the result of PCA, scaling and centering the features is a very important step before applying PCA, using the `prcomp` method. The `print` method returns the standard deviation of each of the four **principal components** (**PCs**), and their rotations that are the coefficients of the linear combinations of the continuous variables:

```
> pca =prcomp(usArrests ,center = TRUE, scale =TRUE)
> print(pca)
Standard deviations:
[1] 1.5748783 0.9948694 0.5971291 0.4164494

Rotation:
               PC1         PC2         PC3        PC4
Murder   -0.5358995  0.4181809  -0.3412327 0.64922780
Assault  -0.5831836  0.1879856  -0.2681484 -0.74340748
UrbanPop -0.2781909 -0.8728062  -0.3780158 0.13387773
Rape     -0.5434321 -0.1673186   0.8177779 0.08902432
```

4. Next, we will use the `plot` method to decide how many PCs to retain for further analysis:

```
> plot(pca, type='l')
```

Here is the PCA represented graphically:

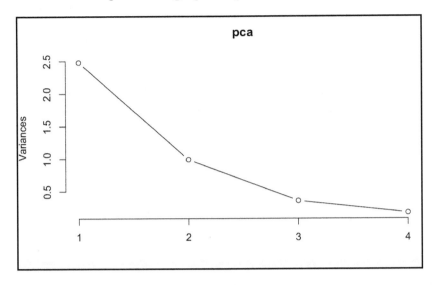

5. We will now use a `biplot` to understand the proportions of each variable along the two PCs (**PC1** and **PC2**):

```
> pca$rotation=-pca$rotation
> pca$x=-pca$x
> biplot (pca , scale =0)
```

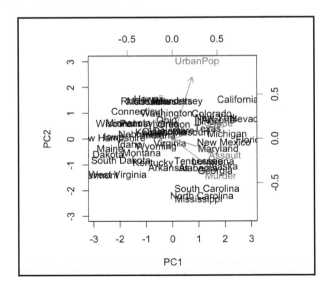

How it works...

The `Rotation` contains the PC loading matrix that explains the proportion of each variable along each principal component.

With the dataset having only four PCs, the `plot` function shows that the first two PCs explain most of the variability in the data.

From the preceding `biplot` image, we can see the two PCs (**PC1** and **PC2**) of the `USArrests` data, which represent how the feature space varies along the principal component vectors. The first principal component vector, **PC1**, more or less puts equal weight on three features, `Rape`, `Assault`, and `Murder`, indicating that these three features are more correlated with each other than the `UrbanPop` feature, whereas the second principal component, **PC2**, places extra weight on `UrbanPop` than the other three features that are less correlated with it.

Generating receiver operating characteristic charts

When using classification techniques, we can rely on the technique to classify cases automatically. Alternately, we can rely on the technique to only generate the probabilities of cases belonging to various classes and then determine the cutoff probabilities ourselves. A **receiver operating characteristic** (**ROC**) chart helps with the latter approach by giving a visual representation of the true and false positives at various cutoff levels. We will use the ROCR package to generate ROC charts.

Getting ready

If you have not already installed the ROCR package, install it now. Load the data files for this chapter from the book's website and ensure that the `rocr-example-1.csv` and `rocr-example-2.csv` files are in your R working directory.

How to do it...

To generate ROC charts, follow these steps:

1. Load the ROCR package:

```
> library(ROCR)
```

2. Read the data file and take a look:

```
> dat <- read.csv("roc-example-1.csv")
> head(dat)

       prob class
1 0.9917340     1
2 0.9768288     1
3 0.9763148     1
4 0.9601505     1
5 0.9351574     1
6 0.9335989     1
```

3. Create the prediction object:

```
> pred <- prediction(dat$prob, dat$class)
```

4. Create the performance object:

```
> perf <- performance(pred, "tpr", "fpr")
```

5. Plot the chart:

```
> plot(perf)
> lines( par()$usr[1:2], par()$usr[3:4] )
```

The following output is obtained:

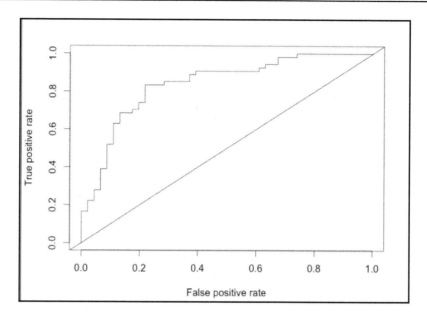

6. Find the cutoff values for various true positive rates. Extract the relevant data from the `perf` object into a data frame, `prob.cuts`:

```
> prob.cuts <- data.frame(cut=perf@alpha.values[[1]],
fpr=perf@x.values[[1]], tpr=perf@y.values[[1]])
> head(prob.cuts)
        cut fpr         tpr
1       Inf   0 0.00000000
2 0.9917340   0 0.01851852
3 0.9768288   0 0.03703704
4 0.9763148   0 0.05555556
5 0.9601505   0 0.07407407
6 0.9351574   0 0.09259259

> tail(prob.cuts)
            cut       fpr tpr
96  0.10426897 0.8913043   1
97  0.07292866 0.9130435   1
98  0.07154785 0.9347826   1
99  0.04703280 0.9565217   1
100 0.04652589 0.9782609   1
101 0.00112760 1.0000000   1
```

From the data frame, `cutoffs`, we can choose the cutoff corresponding to our desired true positive rate.

How it works...

Step 1 loads the package and step 2 reads in the data file.

Step 3 creates a prediction object based on the probabilities and class labels passed in as arguments. In the current examples, our class labels are 0 and 1, and by default, 0 becomes the *failure* class and 1 becomes the *success* class. We will see in the *There's more...* section of this recipe how to handle the case of arbitrary class labels.

Step 4 creates a performance object based on the data from the prediction object. We indicate that we want the true positive rate and false positive rate.

Step 5 plots the performance object. The `plot` function does not plot the diagonal line indicating the ROC threshold, and we add a second line of code to get that.

We generally use ROC charts to determine a good cutoff value for classification given the probabilities. Step 6 shows you how to extract the cutoff value corresponding to each point on the plot from the `performance` object. Armed with this, we can determine the cutoff that yields each of the true positive rates and, given a desired true positive rate, we can find the appropriate cutoff probability.

There's more...

We will discuss a few of ROCR's important features in the following sections.

Using arbitrary class labels

Unlike in the preceding example, we might have arbitrary class labels for success and failure. The `rocr-example-2.csv` file has `buyer` and `non-buyer` as the class labels, with `buyer` representing the success case.

In this case, we need to explicitly indicate the failure and success labels by passing in a vector with the failure case as the first element:

```
> dat <- read.csv("roc-example-2.csv")
> pred <- prediction(dat$prob, dat$class, label.ordering = c("non-buyer",
"buyer"))
> perf <- performance(pred, "tpr", "fpr")
> plot(perf)
> lines( par()$usr[1:2], par()$usr[3:4] )
```

Building, plotting, and evaluating with classification trees

You can use a couple of R packages to build classification trees. Under the hood, they all do the same thing.

Getting ready

If you do not already have the rpart, rpart.plot, and caret packages, install them now. Download the data files for this chapter from the book's website and place the banknote-authentication.csv file in your R working directory.

How to do it...

This recipe shows you how to use the rpart package to build classification trees and the rpart.plot package to generate nice-looking tree diagrams:

1. Load the rpart, rpart.plot, and caret packages:

```
> library(rpart)
> library(rpart.plot)
> library(caret)
```

2. Read the data:

```
> bn <- read.csv("banknote-authentication.csv")
```

3. Create data partitions. We need two partitions--training and validation. Rather than copying the data in the partitions, we will just keep the indices of the cases that represent the training cases and subset as and when needed:

```
> set.seed(1000)
> train.idx <- createDataPartition(bn$class, p = 0.7, list = FALSE)
```

4. Build the tree with the following code:

```
> mod <- rpart(class ~ ., data = bn[train.idx, ], method = "class",
control = rpart.control(minsplit = 20, cp = 0.01))
```

5. View the text output (your result could differ if you did not set the random seed as in step 3):

```
> mod
n= 961

node), split, n, loss, yval, (yprob)
      * denotes terminal node

 1) root 961 423 0 (0.55983351 0.44016649)
   2) variance>=0.321235 511   52 0 (0.89823875 0.10176125)
     4) curtosis>=-4.3856 482   29 0 (0.93983402 0.06016598)
       8) variance>=0.92009 413   10 0 (0.97578692 0.02421308) *
       9) variance< 0.92009 69   19 0 (0.72463768 0.27536232)
        18) entropy< -0.167685 52    6 0 (0.88461538 0.11538462) *
        19) entropy>=-0.167685 17    4 1 (0.23529412 0.76470588) *
     5) curtosis< -4.3856 29    6 1 (0.20689655 0.79310345)
      10) variance>=2.3098 7    1 0 (0.85714286 0.14285714) *
      11) variance< 2.3098 22    0 1 (0.00000000 1.00000000) *
   3) variance< 0.321235 450   79 1 (0.17555556 0.82444444)
     6) skew>=6.83375 76   18 0 (0.76315789 0.23684211)
      12) variance>=-3.4449 57    0 0 (1.00000000 0.00000000) *
      13) variance< -3.4449 19    1 1 (0.05263158 0.94736842) *
     7) skew< 6.83375 374   21 1 (0.05614973 0.94385027)
      14) curtosis>=6.21865 106   16 1 (0.15094340 0.84905660)
        28) skew>=-3.16705 16    0 0 (1.00000000 0.00000000) *
        29) skew< -3.16705 90    0 1 (0.00000000 1.00000000) *
      15) curtosis< 6.21865 268    5 1 (0.01865672 0.98134328) *
```

6. Generate a diagram of the tree (your tree might differ if you did not set the random seed as in step 3):

```
> prp(mod, type = 2, extra = 104, nn = TRUE, fallen.leaves = TRUE,
faclen = 4, varlen = 8, shadow.col = "gray")
```

The following output is obtained as a result of the preceding command:

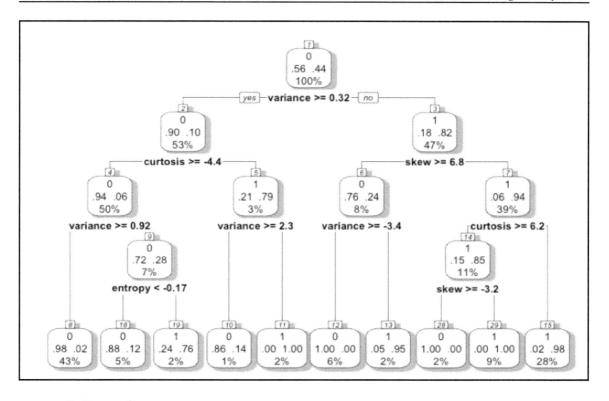

7. Prune the tree:

```
> # First see the cptable
> # !!Note!!: Your table can be different because of the
> # random aspect in cross-validation
> mod$cptable

        CP nsplit  rel error      xerror        xstd
1 0.69030733      0 1.00000000 1.0000000 0.03637971
2 0.09456265      1 0.30969267 0.3262411 0.02570025
3 0.04018913      2 0.21513002 0.2387707 0.02247542
4 0.01891253      4 0.13475177 0.1607565 0.01879222
5 0.01182033      6 0.09692671 0.1347518 0.01731090
6 0.01063830      7 0.08510638 0.1323877 0.01716786
7 0.01000000      9 0.06382979 0.1276596 0.01687712

> # Choose CP value as the highest value whose
> # xerror is not greater than minimum xerror + xstd
> # With the above data that happens to be
> # the fifth one, 0.01182033
> # Your values could be different because of random
```

```
> # sampling
> mod.pruned = prune(mod, mod$cptable[5, "CP"])
```

8. View the `pruned` tree (your tree will look different):

```
> prp(mod.pruned, type = 2, extra = 104, nn = TRUE, fallen.leaves =
TRUE, faclen = 4, varlen = 8, shadow.col = "gray")
```

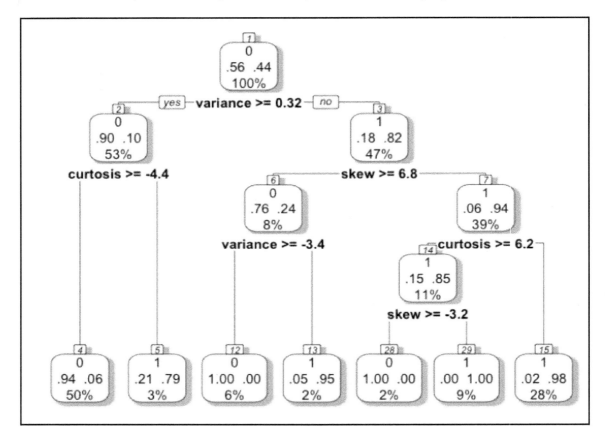

9. Use the `pruned` model to `predict` for a validation partition (note the minus sign before `train.idx` to consider the cases in the validation partition):

```
> pred.pruned <- predict(mod, bn[-train.idx,], type = "class")
```

10. Generate the error/classification confusion matrix:

```
> table(bn[-train.idx,]$class, pred.pruned, dnn = c("Actual",
"Predicted"))
```

```
        Predicted
Actual    0    1
     0  213   11
     1   11  176
```

How it works...

Steps 1 to 3 load the packages, read the data, and identify the cases in the training partition, respectively. See the *Creating random data partitions* recipe in `Chapter 2`, *What's in There? - Exploratory Data Analysis,* for more details on partitioning. In step 3, we set the random `seed` so that your results should match those that we display.

Step 4 builds the classification tree model:

```
> mod <- rpart(class ~ ., data = bn[train.idx, ], method = "class", control
= rpart.control(minsplit = 20, cp = 0.01))
```

The `rpart()` function builds the tree model based on the following:

- The formula specifying the dependent and independent variables
- The dataset to use
- A specification through `method="class"` that we want to build a classification tree (as opposed to a regression tree)
- Control parameters specified through the `control = rpart.control()` setting; here, we have indicated that the tree should only consider nodes with at least 20 cases for the splitting and use the complexity parameter value of 0.01-- these two values represent the defaults and we have included these just for illustration

Step 5 produces a textual display of the results. Step 6 uses the `prp()` function of the `rpart.plot` package to produce a nice-looking plot of the tree:

```
> prp(mod, type = 2, extra = 104, nn = TRUE, fallen.leaves = TRUE, faclen =
4, varlen = 8, shadow.col = "gray")
```

- Use `type=2` to get a plot with every node labeled and with the split label below the node

- Use `extra=4` to display the probability of each class in the node (conditioned on the node and hence summing to 1); add 100 (hence `extra=104`) to display the number of cases in the node as a percentage of the total number of cases
- Use `nn = TRUE` to display the node numbers; the root node is node number 1 and node n has child nodes numbered 2n and 2n+1
- Use `fallen.leaves=TRUE` to display all leaf nodes at the bottom of the graph
- Use `faclen` to abbreviate class names in the nodes to a specific maximum length
- Use `varlen` to abbreviate variable names
- Use `shadow.col` to specify the color of the shadow that each node casts

Step 7 prunes the tree to reduce the chance that the model too closely models the training data; that is, to reduce overfitting. Within this step, we first look at the complexity table generated through cross-validation. We then use the table to determine the cutoff complexity level as the largest `xerror` (cross-validation error) value that is not greater than one standard deviation above the minimum cross-validation error.

Steps 8 through 10 display the pruned tree, use the pruned tree to predict the class for the validation partition, and then generate the error matrix for the validation partition.

There's more...

We will discuss an important variation on predictions using classification trees in the following sections.

Computing raw probabilities

We can generate probabilities in place of classifications by specifying `type="prob"`:

```
> pred.pruned <- predict(mod, bn[-train.idx,], type = "prob")
```

Creating the ROC chart

Using the preceding raw probabilities and class labels, we can generate an ROC chart. See the *Generating ROC charts* recipe earlier in this chapter for more details:

```
> pred <- prediction(pred.pruned[,2], bn[-train.idx,"class"])
> perf <- performance(pred, "tpr", "fpr")
> plot(perf)
```

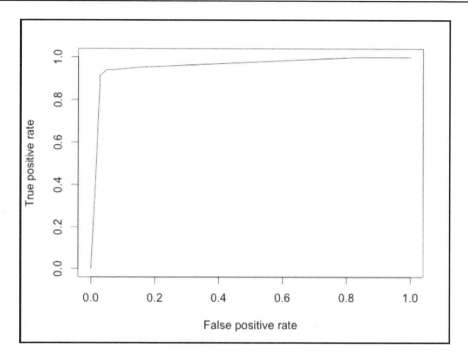

See also

- The *Creating random data partitions* recipe in Chapter 2, *What's in There? - Exploratory Data Analysis*
- The *Generating error/classification-confusion matrices* recipe in this chapter
- The *Building regression trees* recipe in Chapter 4, *Give Me a Number - Regression*

Using random forest models for classification

The randomForest package can help you to easily apply the very powerful (but computationally intensive) random forest classification technique.

Getting ready

If you have not already installed the `randomForest` and `caret` packages, install them now. Download the data files for this chapter from the book's website and place the `banknote-authentication.csv` file in your R working directory. We will build a `randomForest` model to predict class based on the other variables.

How to do it...

To use random forest models for classification, follow these steps:

1. Load the `randomForest` and `caret` packages:

   ```
   > library(randomForest)
   > library(caret)
   ```

2. Read the data and convert the response variable to a factor:

   ```
   > bn <- read.csv("banknote-authentication.csv")
   > bn$class <- factor(bn$class)
   ```

3. Select a subset of the data to build the model. In random forests, we do not need to actually partition the data for model evaluation as the tree construction process has partitioning inherent in every step. However, we keep aside some of the data here just to illustrate the process of using the model for prediction and also to get an idea of the model's performance:

   ```
   > set.seed(1000)
   > sub.idx <- createDataPartition(bn$class, p=0.7, list=FALSE)
   ```

4. Build the `randomForest` model. As it builds many classification trees, the following command can take a lot of processing time on even moderately large data:

   ```
   > mod <- randomForest(x = bn[sub.idx,1:4],
   y=bn[sub.idx,5],ntree=500, keep.forest=TRUE)
   ```

5. Use the model to `predict` for cases that we set aside in step 3:

   ```
   > pred <- predict(mod, bn[-sub.idx,])
   ```

6. Build the error matrix:

```
> table(bn[-sub.idx,"class"], pred, dnn = c("Actual", "Predicted"))
       Predicted
Actual   0   1
     0 227   1
     1   1 182
```

How it works...

Step 1 loads the necessary packages and step 2 reads the data and converts the response variable to a factor.

Step 3 sets aside some of the data for later use. Strictly speaking, we do not have to partition the data for random forests because, while building each tree, the method sets aside some of the cases for cross-validation. However, we set aside some of the cases just to illustrate the process of using the model for prediction. (We set the random `seed` to enable you to match your results with those that we display.)

Step 4 uses the `randomForest` function to build the model. As the predictor variables are in the first four variables of the data frame and we want to use only the selected subset for model building, we specify x= `bn[sub.idx,1:4]`. As the target variable is in the fifth column, we specify y= `bn[sub.idx,5]`. We specify the number of trees to build in the forest through the `ntree` argument (the default value is 500).

Step 5 illustrates how to predict using the model.

Step 6 uses the predictions and actual values to generate an error matrix.

> The model that the `randomForest` function produces does not keep information about the trees and hence we cannot use the model to predict future cases. To force the model to keep the generated forest, specify `keep.forest=TRUE`.

There's more...

We will discuss a few prominent options in the following sections.

Computing raw probabilities

As with simple classification tree models, we can generate probabilities in place of classifications by specifying `type="prob"`--the default value `response` generates classifications:

```
>   probs <- predict(mod, bn[-sub.idx,], type = "prob")
```

Generating the ROC chart

Using the preceding probabilities, we can generate the ROC chart. For details, refer to the *Generating ROC charts* earlier in this chapter:

```
> pred <- prediction(probs[,2], bn[-sub.idx,"class"])
> perf <- performance(pred, "tpr", "fpr")
> plot(perf)
```

The following output is the result of the preceding command:

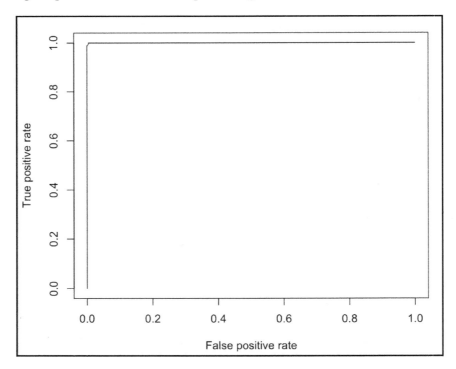

Specifying cutoffs for classification

Instead of using the default rule of simple majority for classification, we can specify cutoff probabilities as a vector of length equal to the number of classes. The proportion of the ratio of votes to the cutoff determines the winning class. We can specify this both at the time of tree construction and while using the model for predictions.

See also

- The *Creating random data partitions* recipe in `Chapter 2`, *What's in There? - Exploratory Data Analysis*
- The *Generating error/classification confusion matrices* recipe in this chapter
- The *Building random forest models for regression* recipe in `Chapter 4`, *Give Me a Number - Regression*

Classifying using the support vector machine approach

The `e1071` package can help you to easily apply the very powerful **support vector machine (SVM)** classification technique.

Getting ready

If you have not already installed the `e1071` and `caret` packages, install them now. Download the data files for this chapter from the book's website and place the `banknote-authentication.csv` file in your R working directory. We will build an SVM model to predict class based on the other variables.

How to do it...

To classify using SVM, follow these steps:

1. Load the `e1071` and `caret` packages:

```
> library(e1071)
> library(caret)
```

2. Read the data:

```
> bn <- read.csv("banknote-authentication.csv")
```

3. Convert the outcome variable `class` to a `factor`:

```
> bn$class <- factor(bn$class)
```

4. Partition the data:

```
> set.seed(1000)
> t.idx <- createDataPartition(bn$class, p=0.7, list=FALSE)
```

5. Build the model:

```
> mod <- svm(class ~ ., data = bn[t.idx,])
```

6. Check model performance on training data by generating an error/classification confusion matrix:

```
> table(bn[t.idx,"class"], fitted(mod), dnn = c("Actual",
"Predicted"))
       Predicted
Actual   0    1
     0 534    0
     1   0  427
```

7. Check model performance on the validation partition:

```
> pred <- predict(mod, bn[-t.idx,])
> table(bn[-t.idx, "class"], pred, dnn = c("Actual", "Predicted"))
       Predicted
Actual   0    1
     0 228    0
     1   0  183
```

8. Plot the model on the training partition. Our data has more than two predictors, but we can only show two in the plot. We have selected `skew` and `variance`:

```
> plot(mod, data=bn[t.idx,], skew ~ variance)
```

The following plot is the output of the preceding command:

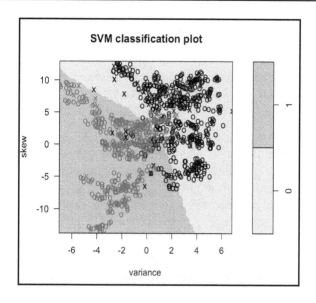

9. Plot the model on the validation partition. Our data has more than two predictors, but we can only show two in the plot. We have selected `skew` and `variance`:

```
> plot(mod, data=bn[-t.idx,], skew ~ variance)
```

The following plot is the result of the preceding command:

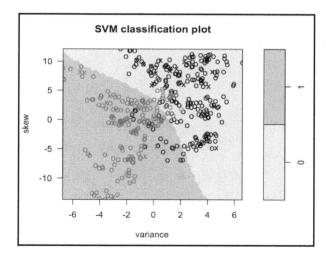

How it works...

The SVM builds a highly accurate model through `kernel trick`, by mapping nonlinear data to higher-dimension space, where the data can be more easily separated with a linear boundary or hyperplanes that maximize the margin width among different classes. It avoids overfitting by making use of regularization and in general does not suffer from local optima or **multicollinearity**.

The `svm` function determines the type of model (classification or regression) based on the nature of the outcome variable. When the outcome variable is a factor, `svm` builds a classification model. At a minimum, we need to pass the model formula and the dataset to use as arguments. (Alternately, we can pass the outcome variable and predictor variables separately as the `x` and `y` arguments.)

The resulting `svm` object, `mod`, contains the model to create an error/classification confusion matrix. The `svm` model retains the fitted values on the training partition, and hence we do not need to go through the step of creating the predictions. We access the fitted values through `fitted(mod)`. Refer to the *Generating error/classification confusion matrices* recipe in this chapter for details on the `table` function.

Then, we generate the model's predictions for the validation partition using the `predict` function. We pass as arguments the model and the data for which we need predictions. It then uses these predictions to generate the associated error/classification confusion matrix.

Finally, we use the `plot` function to plot the model's results. We pass as arguments the model and the data for which we need the plot. If the data has only two predictors, we can get the complete picture from such a plot. However, our example has four predictors and we have chosen two of them for the plot.

There's more...

The `svm` function has several additional arguments through which we can control its behavior.

Controlling the scaling of variables

By default, `svm` scales all the variables (predictor and outcome) to zero mean and unit variance before building a model as this generally produces better results. We can use the `scale` argument--a logical vector--to control this. If the length of the vector is 1, then it is recycled as many times as needed.

Determining the type of SVM model

By default, when the outcome variable is a factor, `svm` performs classification. When the outcome is numeric, it performs regression. We can override the default or select other options through these values for `type`:

- type = C-classification
- type = nu-classification
- type = one-classification
- type = eps-regression
- type = nu-.regression

Assigning weights to the classes

In cases where the sizes of the classes are highly skewed, the larger class could dominate. To balance this, we might want to weight the classes differently from the default equal weighting. We can use the `class.weights` argument for this:

```
> mod <- svm(class ~ ., data = bn[t.idx,], class.weights=c("0"=0.3, "1"=0.7
))
```

Choosing the cost of SVM

The `svm` function has a `cost` parameter that controls training errors and margins. For example, a small cost creates a large margin (a soft margin) and allows more misclassifications. On the other hand, a large cost creates a narrow margin (a hard margin) and permits fewer misclassifications:

```
# Large margin allowing more misclassification
> mod <- svm(class ~ ., data = bn[t.idx,], cost = 1)

# Narrow margin permitting few misclassification
> mod <- svm(class ~ ., data =bn[t.idx,], cost = 1000)
```

Tuning the SVM

The SVM provides a `tune.svm` function that allows us to tune its performance by adjusting the gamma and cost argument. After retrieving the best performance parameters from a summary of the tuned output, we can retrain the SVM with those parameters to enhance the model accuracy and efficiency:

```
> tuned = tune.svm(class ~ ., data = bn[t.idx,], gamma = 10^(-6:-1),cost =
10^(1:2))

> summary(tuned)
```

See also

- The *Creating random data partitions* recipe in `Chapter 2`, *What's in There? - Exploratory Data Analysis*
- The *Generating error/classification confusion matrices* recipe in this chapter

Classifying using the Naive Bayes approach

The `e1071` package contains the `naiveBayes` function for Naive Bayes classification.

Getting ready

If you do not already have the `e1071` and `caret` packages, install them now. Download the data files for this chapter from the book's website and place the `electronics-purchase.csv` file in your R working directory. Naive Bayes requires all the variables to be categorical. So, if needed, you should first convert all variables accordingly--refer to the *Binning numerical data* recipe in `Chapter 1`, *Acquiring and Preparing the Ingredients - Your Data*.

How to do it...

To classify using the Naive Bayes method, follow these steps:

1. Load the `e1071` and `caret` packages:

```
> library(e1071)
> library(caret)
```

2. Read the data:

```
> ep <- read.csv("electronics-purchase.csv")
```

3. Partition the data:

```
> set.seed(1000)
> train.idx <- createDataPartition(ep$Purchase, p = 0.67, list =
FALSE)
```

4. Build the model:

```
> epmod <- naiveBayes(Purchase ~ . , data = ep[train.idx,])
```

5. Look at the model:

```
> epmod
```

6. Predict for each case of the validation partition:

```
> pred <- predict(epmod, ep[-train.idx,])
```

7. Create the classification table for the validation partition and generate a confusion matrix from it:

```
> tab <- table(ep[-train.idx,]$Purchase, pred, dnn = c("Actual",
"Predicted"))

> confusionMatrix(tab)
Confusion Matrix and Statistics

       Predicted
Actual No Yes
   No   1  1
   Yes  0  2
              Accuracy : 0.75
                95% CI : (0.1941, 0.9937)
   No Information Rate : 0.75
```

```
      P-Value [Acc > NIR] : 0.7383
                    Kappa : 0.5
    Mcnemar's Test P-Value : 1.0000
              Sensitivity : 1.0000
              Specificity : 0.6667
            Pos Pred Value : 0.5000
            Neg Pred Value : 1.0000
                Prevalence : 0.2500
            Detection Rate : 0.2500
      Detection Prevalence : 0.5000
         Balanced Accuracy : 0.8333
           'Positive' Class : No
```

How it works...

Naïve Bayes assumes that all features are independent and equally important; that is, the effect of a predictor (*x*) to class (*c*) is independent of the effect of other predictors to class (*c*). Besides being simple to use, it is suitable when the training set is relatively small and may contain some noise and missing data.

In this recipe,we first load the required packages in step 1, read the data in step 2 , and identify the rows in the training partition (we set the random `seed` to enable you to match your results with ours) in step 3.

Step 4 builds the model using the `naiveBayes()` function and passing the formula and training partition as the arguments. Step 5 displays the conditional probabilities that the `naiveBayes()` function generates for use in making predictions.

Step 6 generates the model predictions for the validation partition and step 7 builds the error matrix as follows:

Step 6 generates the predictions for each case of the validation partition using the `predict()` function and passing the model and validation partition as arguments. Step 8 generates the error or classification confusion matrix using the `table()` and `confusionMatrix()` functions.

See also

- *Creating random data partitions* in `Chapter 2`, *What's in There? - Exploratory Data Analysis*

Classifying using the KNN approach

The `class` package contains the `knn` function for KNN classification.

Getting ready

If you have not already installed the `class` and `caret` packages, install them now. Download the data files for this chapter from the book's website and place the `vacation-trip-classification.csv` file in your R working directory. The `knn` function requires all the independent/predictor variables to be numeric and the dependent variable or target to be categorical. So, if needed, you should first convert variables accordingly--refer to the, *Creating dummies for categorical variables* and *Binning numerical data* recipes in `Chapter 1`, *Acquire and Prepare the Ingredients - Your Data*.

How to do it...

To classify using the **k-nearest neighbours** (**kNN**) method, follow these steps:

1. Load the `class` and `caret` packages:

```
> library(class)
> library(caret)
```

2. Read the data:

```
> vac <- read.csv("vacation-trip-classification.csv")
```

3. Standardize the predictor variables, `Income` and `Family_size`:

```
> vac$Income.z <- scale(vac$Income)
> vac$Family_size.z <- scale(vac$Family_size)
```

4. Partition the data. You need three partitions for KNN:

```
> set.seed(1000)
> train.idx <- createDataPartition(vac$Result, p = 0.5, list =
FALSE)
> train <- vac[train.idx, ]
> temp <- vac[-train.idx, ]
> val.idx <- createDataPartition(temp$Result, p = 0.5, list =
FALSE)
> val <- temp[val.idx, ]
```

```
> test <- temp[-val.idx, ]
```

5. Generate predictions for validation cases with k=1:

```
> pred1 <- knn(train[4:5], val[,4:5], train[,3], 1)
```

6. Generate an error matrix for k=1:

```
> errmat1 = table(val$Result, pred1, dnn = c("Actual",
"Predicted"))
```

7. Repeat the preceding process for many values of k and choose the best value for k. Look under the following *There's more...* section for a way to automate this process.

8. Use that value of k to generate predictions and the error matrix for the cases in the test partition (in the following code, we assume that k=1 was preferred):

```
> pred.test <- knn(train[4:5], test[,4:5], train[,3], 1)
> errmat.test = table(test$Result, pred.test, dnn = c("Actual",
"Predicted"))
```

How it works...

Steps 1 to 3 load the necessary packages and read the data file.

Step 4 creates three partitions (50 %, 25 %, and 25 %). We set the random seed to enable you to match your results with those that we display. Refer to the *Creating random data partitions* recipe in Chapter 2, *What's in There? - Exploratory Data Analysis,* for information on data partitioning.

Step 5 uses the knn function to generate predictions with k=1. It uses only the standardized values of the predictor variables and hence specifies train[,4:5] and val[,4:5].

Step 6 generates the error matrix for k=1.

There's more...

We now turn to some other ways in which you can use KNN classifications.

Automating the process of running KNN for many k values

The following convenience function frees you from the drudgery of repeatedly running nearly identical commands to run KNN for various values of `k`:

```
knn.automate <- function (trg_predictors, val_predictors, trg_target,
val_target, start_k, end_k)
{
  for (k in start_k:end_k) {
    pred <- knn(trg_predictors, val_predictors,
                        trg_target, k)
    tab <- table(val_target, pred, dnn = c("Actual", "Predicted"))
    cat(paste("Error matrix for k=", k,"\n"))
    cat("===========================\n")
    print(tab)
    cat("--------------------------\n\n\n")
  }
}
```

With the preceding function in place, you can use the following to run `knn` for `k=1` through `k=7` for the example in the main recipe:

```
> knn.automate(train[,4:5], val[,4:5], train[,3], val[,3], 1,7)
```

Selecting appropriate values of k using caret

Determining the number of nearest neighbors, that is, the value of `k`, plays a major role toward the efficacy of the model, thereby deciding how well the data can be utilized to generalize the results of the KNN algorithm. We will use the `caret` package to preprocess (center and scale) and train the data along with a validation mechanism to identify the best value of `k` automatically:

```
> trctrl <- trainControl(method = "repeatedcv", number = 10, repeats = 3)

> caret_knn_fit <- train(Result ~ Family_size + Income, data = train,
method = "knn",
                trControl=trctrl,
                preProcess = c("center", "scale"),
                tuneLength = 10)
```

The method parameter of the trainControl method holds the value for the resampling technique such as boot, cv, repeatedcv, LOOCV, LGOCV, and so on. For this illustration, we will use repeated cross-validation. The number parameter holds the number of resampling iterations and the repeats parameter contains the complete set of folds to compute the repeated cross-validation. The train method takes method as the KNN algorithm along with the preprocessing steps through the preProcess parameter:

```
> caret_knn_fit
k-Nearest Neighbors

21 samples
 2 predictor
 2 classes: 'Buyer', 'Non-buyer'

Pre-processing: centered (2), scaled (2)
Resampling: Cross-Validated (10 fold, repeated 3 times)
Summary of sample sizes: 19, 19, 19, 19, 19, 19, ...
Resampling results across tuning parameters:

   k   Accuracy  Kappa
   5  0.7500000  0.496666667
   7  0.6833333  0.363333333
   9  0.7333333  0.463333333
  11  0.6833333  0.373333333
  13  0.6833333  0.363333333
  15  0.7444444  0.483333333
  17  0.7944444  0.583333333
  19  0.5166667  0.040000000
  21  0.5166667  0.030000000
  23  0.5055556  -0.003333333

Accuracy was used to select the optimal model using the largest value.
The final value used for the model was k = 17.
```

Finally, we can see that the caret_knn_fit object generated by the train method automatically identifies the best value of k; here, k=17 as per the accuracy and kappa statistics.

Using KNN to compute raw probabilities instead of classifications

When we use KNN to classify cases, the underlying algorithm uses a simple majority vote to determine the class. In such a case, we implicitly consider all errors to be equally important. However, in situations with asymmetric costs--where we are prepared to make one kind of error more readily than another--we might not want to use a simple majority vote to determine the class. Instead, we might want to get the raw probabilities (proportions) for each class and choose a cutoff probability for classification. For example, it might be 10 times costlier to classify a buyer as a non-buyer than to classify a non-buyer as a buyer. In such cases, we might accept a probability far lower than 0.5 to classify a case as buyer, whereas a simple majority would require a probability slightly greater than 0.5.

To compute raw probabilities instead of classifications, use the `prob=TRUE` argument:

```
> pred5 <- knn(train[4:5], val[,4:5], train[,3], 5, prob=TRUE)
> pred5
[1] 1.0000000 0.8000000 1.0000000 0.6000000 0.8000000
[6] 0.6000000 0.6000000 0.8333333 0.6000000 0.8333333
Levels: Buyer Non-buyer
```

Using neural networks for classification

The `nnet` package contains the `nnet` function for classification using neural networks.

Getting ready

If you have not already installed the `nnet` and `caret` packages, install them now. Download the data files for this chapter from the book's website and place the `banknote-authentication.csv` file in your R working directory. We will use `class` as our target or outcome variable and all the remaining variables as predictors. Using neural networks requires all the independent/predictor variables to be numeric and the dependent variable or outcome to be *0 - 1*. However, the `nnet` function does all the work of generating dummies (contrasts) and correctly handles categorical outcome variables.

How to do it...

To use neural networks for classification, follow these steps:

1. Load the nnet and caret packages:

```
> library(nnet)
> library(caret)
```

2. Read the data:

```
> bn <- read.csv("banknote-authentication.csv")
```

3. Convert the outcome variable class to a factor:

```
> bn$class <- factor(bn$class)
```

4. Partition the data. The predictor variables are already numeric and the outcome variable class is already 0 - 1, so we do not have to do any data preparation. Refer to *Creating random data partitions* in Chapter 2, *What's In There? - Exploratory Data Analysis,* for details on how the following command works:

```
> train.idx <- createDataPartition(bn$class, p=0.7, list = FALSE)
```

5. Build the neural network model:

```
> mod <- nnet(class ~.,
data=bn[train.idx,],size=3,maxit=10000,decay=.001, rang = 0.05)
```

6. Use model to predict for validation partition:

```
> pred <- predict(mod, newdata=bn[-train.idx,], type="class")
```

7. Build and display the error/classification confusion matrix on the validation partition:

```
> table(bn[-train.idx,]$class, pred)
```

How it works...

Step 1 loads the packages needed and step 2 reads the data.

Step 3 converts the outcome variable class to a factor. For `nnet` to perform classification, we need the outcome variable to be a factor. If you have predictor variables that are really categorical but have numeric values, convert them to factors so that `nnet` can treat them appropriately. As we have only numeric predictor variables, we need not do anything for the predictor variables.

Step 4 partitions the data. See *Creating random data partitions* in `Chapter 2`, *What's In There? - Exploratory Data Analysis,* for more details on this step.

Step 5 builds the neural network model. We pass the formula and dataset as the first two arguments:

- The `size` argument specifies the number of units in the internal layer (`nnet` works with just one hidden layer). One rule of thumb is to set the number of units in the hidden layer close to the mean of the number of units in the input and output layers. Higher values can give slightly better results at the expense of computation time.
- `maxit` specifies the maximum number of iterations to perform to try for convergence. The algorithm stops if convergence is achieved earlier. If not, it stops after `maxit` iterations.
- `decay` controls overfitting.

Step 6 uses the model to generate predictions for the validation partition. We specified `type = "class"` to generate classifications.

Step 7 generates the error/classification confusion matrix.

There's more...

We will discuss some ideas to exercise greater control over the model building and prediction steps in the following sections.

Exercising greater control over nnet

Use the following additional options:

- By default, any missing values cause the function to fail. You can specify `na.action = na.omit` to exclude cases with any missing values.
- Use `skip = TRUE` to add skip layer connections from input nodes to the output nodes.

- Use the `rang` argument to specify the range for the initial random weights as `[-rang, rang]`; if the input values are large, select `rang` such that `rang*(max|variable|)` is close to 1.

Generating raw probabilities and plotting the ROC curve

Use the `type = "raw"` option to generate raw probabilities:

```
> pred <- predict(mod, newdata=bn[-train.idx,] type="raw")
```

Classifying using linear discriminant function analysis

The `MASS` package contains the `lda` function for classification using linear discriminant function analysis.

Getting ready

If you have not already installed the `MASS` and `caret` packages, install them now. Download the data files for this chapter from the book's website and place the `banknote-authentication.csv` file in your R working directory. We will use `class` as our target or outcome variable and all the remaining variables as predictors.

How to do it...

To classify using linear discriminant function analysis, follow these steps:

1. Load the `MASS` and `caret` packages:

   ```
   > library(MASS)
   > library(caret)
   ```

2. Read the data:

   ```
   > bn <- read.csv("banknote-authentication.csv")
   ```

3. Convert the outcome variable `class` to a `factor`:

```
> bn$class <- factor(bn$class)
```

4. Partition the data. The predictor variables are already numeric and the outcome variable `class` is already 0-1, so we do not have to do any data preparation. Refer to *Creating random data partitions* in `Chapter 2`, *What's In There? - Exploratory Data Analysis,* for details on how the following command works:

```
> set.seed(1000)
> t.idx <- createDataPartition(bn$class, p = 0.7, list=FALSE)
```

5. Build the **linear discriminant function** (LDF) model:

```
> ldamod <- lda(bn[t.idx, 1:4], bn[t.idx, 5])
```

6. Check how the model performs on the training partition (your results could differ because of random partitioning):

```
> bn[t.idx,"Pred"] <- predict(ldamod, bn[t.idx, 1:4])$class
> table(bn[t.idx, "class"], bn[t.idx, "Pred"], dnn = c("Actual",
"Predicted"))
        Predicted
Actual    0    1
     0  511   23
     1    0  427
```

7. Generate predictions on the validation partition and check performance (your results could differ):

```
> bn[-t.idx,"Pred"] <- predict(ldamod, bn[-t.idx, 1:4])$class
> table(bn[-t.idx, "class"], bn[-t.idx, "Pred"], dnn = c("Actual",
"Predicted"))
        Predicted
Actual    0    1
     0  219    9
     1    0  183
```

How it works...

Step 1 loads the `MASS` and `caret` packages and step 2 reads the data.

Step 3 converts our outcome variable to a factor.

Step 4 partitions the data. We set the random `seed` to enable you to match your results with those that we display.

Step 5 builds the LDF model. We pass the predictors as the first argument and the outcome values as the second argument to the `lda` function. We can also supply the details as a formula--see the following *There's more...* section.

Step 6 uses the `predict` function to generate the predictions for the training partition. We pass the model and predictor variables. The `class` component of the returned object from the `predict` function contains the predicted class values. We then use the `table` function to generate a two-way cross-table.

Step 7 evaluates the model on the validation partition by repeating the preceding two steps on that partition.

There's more...

The `lda` function has several optional arguments and we have shown the most commonly used ones earlier.

Using the formula interface for lda

Instead of specifying the predictors and outcome as two separate arguments, we could have written the preceding step 5 as follows:

```
> ldamod <- lda(class ~ ., data = bn[t.idx,])
```

See also

- The *Creating random data partitions* recipe in Chapter 2, *What's in There? - Exploratory Data Analysis*

Classifying using logistic regression

The `stats` package contains the `glm` function for classification using logistic regression.

Getting ready

If you have not already installed the `caret` package, install it now. Download the data files for this chapter from the book's website and place the `boston-housing-logistic.csv` file in your R working directory. We will use `CLASS` as our target or outcome variable and all the remaining variables as predictors. Our outcome variable has values of 0 or 1, with 0 representing neighborhoods with *Low* median home values and 1 representing neighborhoods with *High* median home values. Logistic regression requires all the independent/predictor variables to be numeric and the dependent variable or outcome to be categorical and binary. However, the `glm` function does all the work of generating dummies (contrasts) for categorical variables.

How to do it...

To classify using logistic regression, follow these steps:

1. Load the `caret` package:

   ```
   > library(caret)
   ```

2. Read the data:

   ```
   > bh <- read.csv("boston-housing-logistic.csv")
   ```

3. Convert the outcome variable `class` to a `factor`:

   ```
   > bh$CLASS <- factor(bh$CLASS, levels = c(0,1))
   ```

4. Partition the data. The predictor variables are already numeric and the outcome variable `CLASS` is already 0-1, so we do not have to do any data preparation. Refer to *Creating random data partitions* in `Chapter 2`, *What's In There? - Exploratory Data Analysis*, for details on how the following command works:

   ```
   > set.seed(1000)
   > train.idx <- createDataPartition(bh$CLASS, p=0.7, list = FALSE)
   ```

5. Build the logistic regression model:

   ```
   > logit <- glm(CLASS~., data = bh[train.idx,], family=binomial)
   ```

6. Examine the model (your results could differ because of random partitioning):

```
> summary(logit)
 Call:
glm(formula = CLASS ~ ., family = binomial, data = bh[train.idx,
    ])

Deviance Residuals:
    Min       1Q   Median       3Q      Max
-2.2629  -0.3431   0.0603   0.3251   3.3310

Coefficients:
             Estimate Std. Error z value Pr(>|z|)
(Intercept) 33.452508   4.947892   6.761 1.37e-11 ***
NOX        -31.377153   6.355135  -4.937 7.92e-07 ***
DIS         -0.634391   0.196799  -3.224  0.00127 **
RAD          0.259893   0.087275   2.978  0.00290 **
TAX         -0.007966   0.004476  -1.780  0.07513 .
PTRATIO     -0.827576   0.138782  -5.963 2.47e-09 ***
B            0.006798   0.003070   2.214  0.02680 *
---
Signif. codes:  0 '***' 0.001 '**' 0.01 '*' 0.05 '.' 0.1 ' ' 1

(Dispersion parameter for binomial family taken to be 1)

    Null deviance: 353.03  on 254  degrees of freedom
Residual deviance: 135.08  on 248  degrees of freedom
AIC: 149.08

Number of Fisher Scoring iterations: 6
```

7. Compute the probabilities of *success* for cases in the validation partition and store them in a variable called PROB_SUCC:

```
> bh[-train.idx,"PROB_SUCC"] <- predict(logit, newdata = bh[-
train.idx,], type="response")
```

8. Classify the cases using a cutoff probability of 0.5:

```
> bh[-train.idx,"PRED_50"] <- ifelse(bh[-train.idx, "PROB_SUCC"]>=
0.5, 1, 0)
```

9. Generate the error/classification confusion matrix (your results could differ):

```
> table(bh[-train.idx, "CLASS"], bh[-train.idx, "PRED_50"],
dnn=c("Actual", "Predicted"))
        Predicted
```

```
Actual   0   1
    0  42   9
    1  10  47
```

How it works...

Step 1 loads the `caret` package and step 2 reads the data file.

Step 3 converts the outcome variable to a factor. When the outcome variable is a factor, the `glm` function treats the first factor level as failure and the rest as *success*. In the present case, we wanted it to treat 0 as *failure* and 1 as *success*. To force 0 to be the first level (and hence *failure*), we specified `levels = c(0,1)`.

Step 4 creates the data partition (we set the random `seed` to enable you to match your results with those that we display).

Step 5 builds the logistic regression model and stores it in the `logit` variable. Note that we have specified the data to be only the cases in the training partition.

Step 6 displays important information about the model. The `Deviance Residuals:` section gives us an idea of the spread of the deviation of the log odds and not of the probability. The coefficients section shows us that all the coefficients used are statistically significant.

Step 7 uses `logit`, our logistic regression model, to generate probabilities for the cases in the validation partition. There is no direct function to make actual classifications using the model. This is why we first generate the probabilities by specifying `type = "response"`.

Step 8 uses a cutoff probability of `0.5` to classify the cases. You can use a different value depending on the relative costs of misclassification for the different classes.

Step 9 generates the error/classification confusion matrix for the preceding classification.

Text classification for sentiment analysis

Understanding the sentiments of your customers, what people are saying about your new product launch, or understanding latest trends in the market are vital for the success of your business and help you stay ahead of your competitors. In this recipe, we will perform real-time sentiment analysis from Twitter and classify it into various categories.

Getting ready

First, sign up for a Twitter developer account (https://apps.twitter.com) and create a sample application to generate API keys and credentials under the **Keys and Access Token** tab, which we will require later to fetch real-time data from Twitter.

Then install the following packages:

```
install.packages(c("twitteR","RColorBrewer","plyr","ggplot2","devtools","ht
tr"))
require(devtools)
```

The packages `sentiment`, `Rstem`, and `slam` are not available for direct installation in R (version 3.2 or higher), so you need to install it from source using the following command in the R console:

```
install_url("https://cran.r-project.org/src/contrib/Archive/Rstem/Rstem_0.4
-1.tar.gz")
install_url("https://cran.r-project.org/src/contrib/Archive/slam/slam_0.1-3
7.tar.gz")
install_url("https://cran.r-project.org/src/contrib/Archive/sentiment/senti
ment_0.2.tar.gz")
```

How to do it...

To use AdaBoost to combine classification tree models, follow these steps:

1. Load the `slam`, `sentiment`, and `twitterR` packages:

   ```
   > library(slam)
   > library(sentiment)
   > library(twitteR)
   ```

2. Set your API keys and secret keys information from the Twitter app and then authenticate using the `twitter oauth` method:

   ```
   > api_key <- <your consumer or api key>
   > api_secret <- <your api key secret>
   > access_token <- <your access token>
   > access_token_secret <- < your access token secret>

   > setup_twitter_oauth(api_key, api_secret, access_token,
   access_token_secret)
   [1] "Using direct authentication"
   ```

3. Now we will search Twitter based on the keyword `"machinelearning"`, and the number of tweets to be ingested can be increased/decreased by modifying the parameter value of n:

```
> MachineLearning_tweets = searchTwitter("machinelearning", n=1500,
lang="en")
```

4. Next, we will filter text from tweets and then create a `cleaning` function to remove punctuation, extra spaces, digits, and HTML links from `MachineLearning_text`:

```
> MachineLearning_text = sapply(MachineLearning_tweets, function(x)
x$getText())

>  clean.data = function(text) {

# delete re-tweet entries and remove @ word
text = gsub("(RT|via)((?:\\b\\W*@\\w+)+)", "", text)
text = gsub("@\\w+", "", text)
# delete punctuation and remove digits 0-9
text = gsub("[[:punct:]]", "", text )
text = gsub("[[:digit:]]", "", text)
# delete html links and unnecessary tabs,spaces
text = gsub("http\\w+", "", text)
text = gsub("[ \t]{2,}", "", text)
text = gsub("^\\s+|\\s+$", "", text)

return(text)
}

> MachineLearning_text= clean.data(MachineLearning_text)
```

5. Create an error handling function `handle.error` and then remove `NA` from the text:

```
> handle.error = function(x)
{
 # create missing value
 y = NA
 # tryCatch error
 try_error = tryCatch(tolower(x), error=function(e) e)
 # if not an error
 if (!inherits(try_error, "error"))
   y = tolower(x)
 # result
 return(y)
}
```

```
> MachineLearning_text = sapply(MachineLearning_text, handle.error)

# remove NAs and nullifying the column names
> MachineLearning_text = MachineLearning_text
[!is.na(MachineLearning_text)]

> names(MachineLearning_text) = NULL
```

6. Next, we will use the `classify_emotion` function from the `sentiment` package, applying the `naive bayes` algorithm to perform sentiment analysis:

```
> class_emo = classify_emotion(MachineLearning_text,
algorithm="bayes", prior=1.0)
```

7. Then we will extract the best fit from the `class_emo` object and replace the NAs with the `"unknown"` label:

```
> emotion = class_emo[,7]
> emotion[is.na(emotion)] = "unknown"
```

8. Now we will use the `classify_polarity` function from the `"sentiment"` package to classify some text as positive or negative and then extract the best fit from the `class_pol` object:

```
> class_pol = classify_polarity(MachineLearning_text,
algorithm="bayes")

> polarity = class_pol[,4]
```

9. Create a data frame with the results to obtain general statistics and finally sort the data frame:

```
> sent_df = data.frame(text= MachineLearning_text,
emotion=emotion,polarity=polarity, stringsAsFactors=FALSE)

> sent_df = within(sent_df,emotion <- factor(emotion,
levels=names(sort(table(emotion), decreasing=TRUE))))
```

10. Now let's plot the distribution of emotions:

```
> library(RColorBrewer)
> library(ggplot2)

> ggplot(sent_df, aes(x=emotion)) +

  geom_bar(aes(y=..count.., fill=emotion)) +
```

```
scale_fill_brewer(palette="Set2") +

labs(x="emotion categories", y="number of tweets") +

labs(title = "Sentiment Analysis about Machine Learning")
```

Here is the sentiment analysis shown graphically:

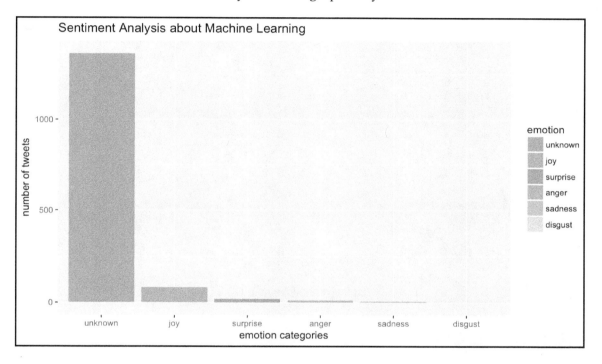

11. Now let's plot the distribution of polarity:

```
> ggplot(sent_df, aes(x=polarity)) +

geom_bar(aes(y=..count.., fill=polarity)) +

scale_fill_brewer(palette="Set3") +

labs(x="polarity categories", y="number of tweets") +

labs(title = "Sentiment Analysis about Machine Learning")
```

Here is the distribution of polarity:

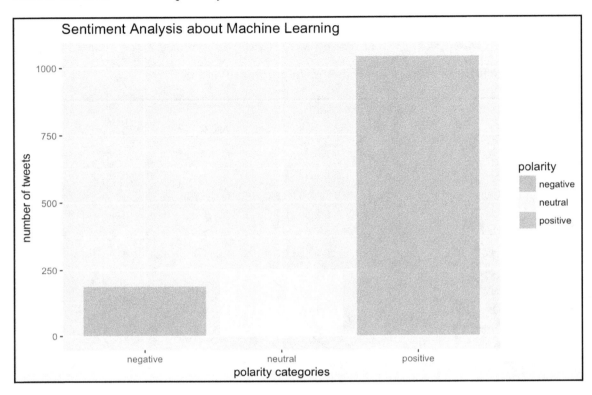

How it works...

The `classify_emotion` function helps us analyze the text and classify it into different categories of emotion--anger, disgust, fear, joy, sadness, and surprise - whereas the `classify_polarity` function helps us classify text as positive, negative, or neutral.

During the installation of the `slam` package, if you get *ERROR: compilation failed for package 'slam'*, then based on your operating system (macOS or Windows), you need to install the tools (`gcc/gfortran`) in order to compile the source package of slam. For Linux, the tools and compilers should be part of your installation.

Mac tools: `http://gcc.gnu.org/wiki/GFortranBinaries#MacOS`

Windows tools: `http://cran.r-project.org/bin/windows/Rtools/`
`. Also make sure that you are using latest version of R, as the slam package may not compile with R version below 3.3.0`

4
Give Me a Number - Regression

In this chapter, we will cover the following topics:

- Computing the root-mean-square error
- Building KNN models for regression
- Performing linear regression
- Performing variable selection in linear regression
- Building regression trees
- Building random forest models for regression
- Using neural networks for regression
- Performing k-fold cross-validation
- Performing leave-one-out cross-validation to limit overfitting

Introduction

Regression analysis is a form of predictive modeling technique that data analysts or data scientists use to investigate the relationship between a dependent variable (**target**) and an independent variables (**predictors**). This chapter covers recipes to apply various regression techniques for predicting future sales of a product, the amount of deposits that a bank will receive during the next month, the number of copies that a particular book will sell, and the expected selling price for a used car.

Computing the root-mean-square error

You may build a regression model and want to evaluate the model by comparing the model's predictions with the actual outcomes. You will generally evaluate a model's performance on the training data but will rely on the model's performance on the holdout data to get an objective measure.

Getting ready

If you have not already downloaded the files for this chapter, do so now and ensure that the rmse.csv file is in your R working directory. The file has data about a set of actual prices and the predicted values from some regression method. We will compute the **root-mean-square (RMS)** error of these predictions.

How to do it...

When using any regression technique, you will be able to generate predictions. This recipe shows you how to calculate the RMS error, given the predicted and actual numerical values of the outcome variable:

1. Compute the RMS error as follows:

```
> dat <- read.csv("rmse-example.csv")
> rmse <- sqrt(mean((dat$price-dat$pred)^2))
> rmse

[1] 2.934995
```

2. Plot the results, and show the 45-degree line:

```
> plot(dat$price, dat$pred, xlab = "Actual",  ylab = "Predicted")
> abline(0, 1)
```

How it works...

Step 1 computes the RMS error as defined--the square root of the mean squared errors. The dat$price - dat$pred parameter computes the vector of errors, and the code surrounding it computes the average of the squared errors and then finds the square root.

Step 2 generates the standard scatterplot and then adds on the 45-degree line.

There's more...

Since we compute RMS errors quite often, the following may be useful.

Using a convenience function to compute the RMS error

The following function may be handy when we need to compute the RMS error:

```
rdahb.rmse <- function(actual, predicted) {
  return (sqrt(mean((actual-predicted)^2)))
}
```

Armed with the function, we can compute the RMS error as follows:

```
> rmse <- rdahb.rmse(dat$price, dat$pred)
```

Building KNN models for regression

The FNN package provides the necessary functions to apply the KNN technique for regression. In this recipe, we look at the use of the knn.reg function to build the model and then the process of predicting with the model as well. We also show some additional convenience mechanisms to make the process easier.

Getting ready

Install the FNN, dummies, caret, and scales packages if you do not already have them installed. If you have not already downloaded the data files for this chapter, do so now and ensure that the education.csv file is in the R working directory. The file has data about several school districts in the US. The following table describes the variables:

Variable	Meaning
state	US state code
region	Region of the country (1 = NE, ...)
urban	Number of residents per thousand residing in urban areas in 1970

income	Per capita personal income in 1973
under 18	Number of residents per thousand under 18 years of age in 1974
expense	Per capita expenditure on public education in a state, projected for 1975

We will build a `knn` model to predict **expense** based on all other predictors except **state**.

How to do it...

To build KNN models for regressions, perform the following steps:

1. Load the `dummies`, `FNN`, `scales`, and `caret` packages as follows:

```
> library(dummies)
> library(FNN)
> library(scales)
> library(caret)
```

2. Read the data:

```
> educ <- read.csv("education.csv")
```

3. Generate dummies for the categorical variable `region`, and add them to `educ` as follows:

```
> dums <- dummy(educ$region, sep="_")
> educ <- cbind(educ, dums)
```

4. Because KNN performs distance computations, we should either `rescale` or standardize the predictors. In the present example, we have three numeric predictors and a categorical predictor in the form of three dummy variables. Standardizing dummy variables is tricky, and hence, we will scale the numeric ones to [0, 1] and leave the dummies alone because they are already in the 0-1 range:

```
> educ$urban.s <- rescale(educ$urban)
> educ$income.s <- rescale(educ$income)
> educ$under18.s <- rescale(educ$under18)
```

5. Create three partitions (because we are creating random partitions, your results can differ) as follows:

```
> set.seed(1000)
> t.idx <- createDataPartition(educ$expense, p = 0.6,  list =
```

```
FALSE)
> trg <- educ[t.idx,]
> rest <- educ[-t.idx,]
> set.seed(2000)
> v.idx <- createDataPartition(rest$expense, p=0.5,  list=FALSE)
> val <- rest[v.idx,]
> test <- rest[-v.idx,]
```

6. Build the model for several values of k. In the following code, we show how to
   compute the RMS error from scratch. You can also use the convenience
   rdahb.rmse function, which was shown in the *Computing the root mean squared*
   error recipe earlier in this chapter:

```
> # for k=1
> res1 <- knn.reg(trg[, 7:12], val[,7:12], trg[,6], 1,
algorithm="brute")
> rmse1 = sqrt(mean((res1$pred-val[,6])^2))
> rmse1

[1] 59.66909

> # Alternately you could use the following to
> # compute the RMS error. See the recipe
> # "Compute the Root Mean Squared error" earlier
> # in this chapter
> rmse1 = rdahb.rmse(res1$pred, val[,6])

> # for k=2
> res2 <- knn.reg(trg[, 7:12], val[,7:12], trg[,6], 2,
algorithm="brute")
> rmse2 = sqrt(mean((res2$pred-val[,6])^2))
> rmse2

[1] 38.09002

># for k=3
> res3 <- knn.reg(trg[, 7:12], val[,7:12], trg[,6], 3,
algorithm="brute")
> rmse3 = sqrt(mean((res3$pred-val[,6])^2))
> rmse3

[1] 44.21224

> # for k=4
> res4 <- knn.reg(trg[, 7:12], val[,7:12], trg[,6], 4,
algorithm="brute")
> rmse4 = sqrt(mean((res4$pred-val[,6])^2))
```

```
> rmse4

[1] 51.66557
```

7. We obtained the lowest RMS error for `k=2`. Evaluate the model on the test partition as follows:

```
> res.test <- knn.reg(trg[, 7:12], test[,7:12], trg[,6], 2,
algorithm="brute")
> rmse.test = sqrt(mean((res.test$pred-test[,6])^2))
rmse.test

[1] 35.05442
```

We obtain a much lower RMS error on the test partition than on the validation partition. Of course, this cannot be trusted too much since our dataset was so small.

How it works...

Step 1 loads the required packages, and step 2 reads the data.

Since KNN requires all the predictors to be numeric, step 3 uses the `dummy` function from the `dummies` package to generate dummies for the categorical variable region, and then adds the resulting dummy variables to the `educ` data frame.

Step 4 scales the numeric predictor variables to the [0, 1] range using the `rescale` function from the `scales` package. Standardizing the numerical predictors will be another option, but standardizing dummy variables will be tricky. Some analysts standardize numerical predictors and leave the dummy variables as they are. However, for consistency, we choose to have all of our predictors in the [0, 1] range. Since the dummies are already in that range, we rescale only the other predictors.

Step 5 creates the three partitions that KNN requires. We set the random seed to enable you to match your results with those that we display. Refer to the *Creating random data partitions* recipe in `Chapter 2`, *What's In There? - Exploratory Data Analysis* for more details. Since we have only 50 cases in our dataset, we have chosen to partition it roughly into 60%, 20%, and 20%. Instead of creating three partitions, we can manage with two and have the model building process use the leave-one-out cross-validation. We discuss this under the *There's more* section.

Step 6 builds the models for k=1 through k=4. We use only three of the four dummy variables. It invokes the knn.reg function and passes the following as arguments:

- Training predictors
- Validation predictors
- Outcome variable in the training partition.
- Value for k
- The algorithm to use for distance computations (we specified brute to use the brute-force method)

 If the dataset is large, one of the other options, kd_tree or cover_tree, may run faster.

Step 7 has highly repetitive code, and we show a convenience function under the *There's more* section to get all the results using a single command.

The model resulting from the call has several components. To compute the RMS error, we have used the pred component, which contains the predicted values.

Step 8 repeats the process for the test partition.

There's more...

Here we discuss some variations in running KNN.

Running KNN with cross-validation in place of a validation partition

We used three partitions in the preceding code. A different approach will be to use two partitions. In this case, knn.reg will use the leave-one-out cross-validation and predict for each case of the training partition itself. To use this mode, we pass only the training partition as argument and leave the other partition as NULL. After performing steps 1 through 4 from the main recipe, do the following:

```
> t.idx <- createDataPartition(educ$expense, p = 0.7,  list = FALSE)
> trg <- educ[t.idx,]
> val <- educ[-t.idx,]
> res1 <- knn.reg(trg[,7:12], test = NULL, y = trg[,6],  k=2,
```

```
    algorithm="brute")
> # When run in this mode, the result object contains
> # the residuals which we can use to compute rmse
> rmse <- sqrt(mean(res1$residuals^2))
> # and so on for other values of k
```

Using a convenience function to run KNN

We would normally run `knn` and compute the RMS error. The following convenience function can help:

```
rdacb.knn.reg <- function (trg_predictors, val_predictors,  trg_target,
val_target, k) {
  library(FNN)
  res <- knn.reg(trg_predictors, val_predictors, trg_target,        k,
algorithm = "brute")
  errors <- res$pred - val_target
  rmse <- sqrt(sum(errors * errors)/nrow(val_predictors))
  cat(paste("RMSE for k=", toString(k), ":", sep = ""), rmse,        "\n")
  rmse
}
```

With the preceding function, we can execute the following after reading the data, creating dummies, rescaling the predictors, and partitioning, that is, executing steps 1 through 4 of the main recipe:

```
> set.seed(1000)
> t.idx <- createDataPartition(educ$expense, p = 0.6, list = FALSE)
> trg <- educ[t.idx,]
> rest <- educ[-t.idx,]
>set.seed(2000)
> v.idx <- createDataPartition(rest$expense, p=0.5, list=FALSE)
> val <- rest[v.idx,]
> test <- rest[-v.idx,]
> rdacb.knn.reg(trg[,7:12], val[,7:12], trg[,6], val[,6], 1)

RMSE for k=1: 59.66909
[1] 59.66909
> rdacb.knn.reg(trg[,7:12], val[,7:12], trg[,6], val[,6], 2)

RMSE for k=2: 38.09002
[1] 38.09002

> # and so on
```

Using a convenience function to run KNN for multiple k values

Running `knn` for several values of k to choose the best one, involves repetitively executing similar lines of code several times. We can automate the process with the following convenience function that runs `knn` for multiple values of k, reports the RMS error for each, and also produces a scree plot of the RMS errors:

```
rdacb.knn.reg.multi <- function (trg_predictors, val_predictors,
trg_target, val_target, start_k, end_k)
{
  rms_errors <- vector()
  for (k in start_k:end_k) {
    rms_error <- rdacb.knn.reg(trg_predictors, val_predictors,
                               trg_target, val_target, k)
    rms_errors <- c(rms_errors, rms_error)
  }
  plot(rms_errors, type = "o", xlab = "k", ylab = "RMSE")
}
```

With the preceding function, we can execute the following after reading the data, creating dummies, rescaling the predictors, and partitioning, that is, executing steps 1 through 4 of the main recipe. The code runs `knn.reg` for values of k from 1 to 5:

```
> rdacb.knn.reg.multi(trg[,7:12], val[,7:12], trg[,6], val[,6], 1, 5)

RMSE for k=1: 59.66909
RMSE for k=2: 38.09002
RMSE for k=3: 44.21224
RMSE for k=4: 51.66557
RMSE for k=5: 50.33476
```

The preceding code also produces a plot of the RMS errors, as shown in the following:

See also

- The *Creating random data partitions* recipe in `Chapter 2`, *What's In There? - Exploratory Data Analysis*

- The *Computing the root mean squared error* recipe in this chapter
- The *Classifying using the KNN approach* recipe in `Chapter 3`, *Where Does It Belong? - Classification*

Performing linear regression

In this recipe, we discuss linear regression, arguably the most widely used technique. The `stats` package has the functionality for linear regression, and R loads it automatically at startup.

Getting ready

If you have not already done so, download the data files for this chapter and ensure that the `auto-mpg.csv` file is in your R working directory. Install the `caret` package if you have not already done so. We want to predict `mpg` based on `cylinders`, `displacement`, `horsepower`, `weight`, and `acceleration` variables.

How to do it...

To perform linear regression, follow these steps:

1. Load the `caret` package:

   ```
   > library(caret)
   ```

2. Read the data:

   ```
   > auto <- read.csv("auto-mpg.csv")
   ```

3. Convert the categorical variable `cylinders` into a factor with appropriate renaming of the levels:

   ```
   > auto$cylinders <- factor(auto$cylinders,  levels = c(3,4,5,6,8),
   labels = c("3cyl", "4cyl", "5cyl",  "6cyl", "8cyl"))
   ```

4. Create partitions:

```
> set.seed(1000)
> t.idx <- createDataPartition(auto$mpg, p = 0.7,  list = FALSE)
```

5. See `names` of the variables in the data frame:

```
> names(auto)

[1] "No"           "mpg"
[3] "cylinders"    "displacement"
[5] "horsepower"   "weight"
[7] "acceleration" "model_year"
[9] "car_name"
```

6. Build the linear regression model:

```
> mod <- lm(mpg ~ ., data = auto[t.idx, -c(1,8,9)])
```

7. View the basic results (your results may differ because of random sampling differences in creating the partitions):

```
> mod

Call:
lm(formula = mpg ~ ., data = auto[t.idx, -c(1, 8, 9)])

Coefficients:
  (Intercept)   cylinders4cyl   cylinders5cyl   cylinders6cyl
    39.450422        6.466511        4.769794        1.967411
 cylinders8cyl    displacement      horsepower          weight
     6.291938        0.004790       -0.081642       -0.004666
  acceleration
     0.003576
```

8. View more detailed results (your results may differ because of random sampling differences in creating the partitions):

```
> summary(mod)

Call:
lm(formula = mpg ~ ., data = auto[t.idx, -c(1, 8, 9)])

Residuals:
    Min      1Q  Median      3Q     Max
-9.8488 -2.4015 -0.5022  1.8422 15.3597
```

```
Coefficients:
                Estimate Std. Error t value Pr(>|t|)
(Intercept)   39.4504219  3.3806186  11.670  < 2e-16  ***
cylinders4cyl  6.4665111  2.1248876   3.043  0.00257  **
cylinders5cyl  4.7697941  3.5603033   1.340  0.18146
cylinders6cyl  1.9674114  2.4786061   0.794  0.42803
cylinders8cyl  6.2919383  2.9612774   2.125  0.03451  *
displacement   0.0047899  0.0109108   0.439  0.66100
horsepower    -0.0816418  0.0200237  -4.077  5.99e-05 ***
weight        -0.0046663  0.0009857  -4.734  3.55e-06 ***
acceleration   0.0035761  0.1426022   0.025  0.98001
---
Signif. codes:  0 '***' 0.001 '**' 0.01 '*' 0.05 '.' 0.1 ' ' 1

Residual standard error: 3.952 on 271 degrees of freedom
Multiple R-squared:  0.756,      Adjusted R-squared:  0.7488
F-statistic:   105 on 8 and 271 DF,  p-value: < 2.2e-16
```

9. Generate predictions for the test data:

```
> pred <- predict(mod, auto[-t.idx, -c(1,8,9)])
```

10. Compute the RMS error on the test data (your results can differ):

```
> sqrt(mean((pred - auto[-t.idx, 2])^2))
[1] 4.333631
```

11. View the diagnostic plots of the model:

```
> par(mfrow = c(2,2))
> plot(mod)
```

The following diagnostic plots are obtained as an output:

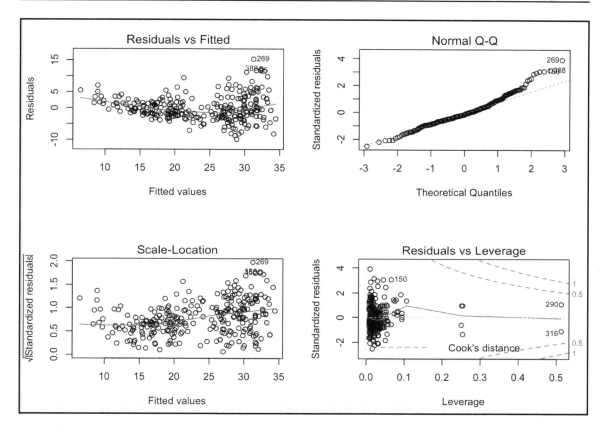

How it works...

Step 1 loads the `caret` package, step 2 reads the data, and step 3 converts the categorical variable cylinders (which have numeric values that R treats as numbers by default) into factors.

Step 4 creates the partitions (refer to the *Creating random data partitions* recipe in `Chapter 2`, *What's In There? - Exploratory Data Analysis* for more details). We set the random seed to enable you to match your results with what we have displayed.

Step 5 prints the variable names in the file so that we can use the appropriate variables in the linear regression model.

Step 6 uses the `lm` function that builds the linear regression model. We specified `data = auto[t.idx, -c(1,8,9)]` because we want the model to use only the training data and because we do not want to use `No`, `model_year`, and `car_name`, which correspond to variables 1, 8, and 9, respectively. We could instead have included all variables, but that would have meant having to explicitly specify only the required predictors in the formula expression. We choose the shorter version.

Although one of our predictors, `cylinders`, is a factor (categorical variable), we did not generate dummies for it because the `lm` function takes care of this automatically, and the regression coefficients in the output show this clearly.

Step 7 shows how we can simply print the value of the model variable to get the values of the regression coefficients.

Step 8 uses the summary function to get more information about the model.

In the detailed output, the `Residuals` section shows the distribution of the residuals on the training data through the quartiles. The `Coefficients` section gives details about the coefficients. The first column, `Estimate`, gives the estimates of the regression coefficients. The second column, `Std. Error`, gives the standard error of that estimate. The third column converts this standard error into a `t value` by dividing the coefficient by the standard error. The `Pr (> |t|)` column converts the `t value` into a probability of the coefficient being 0. The annotation after the last column symbolically shows the level of significance of the coefficient estimate by a dot, blank, or a few stars. The legends below the table explain what the annotation means. It is customary to consider a coefficient to be significant at a 95% level of significance (that is, probability being less than 0.05), which is represented by a `*`.

The next section gives information about how the regression performed as a whole. The `Residual standard error` is just the RMS adjusted for the degrees of freedom and is an excellent indicator of the average deviation of the predicted value from the actual value. The `Adjusted R-squared` value tells us what percentage of the variation in the outcome variable the regression model explains. The last line shows the `F-statistic` and the corresponding `p-value` for the whole regression.

Step 9 generates the predictions on the test data using the `predict` function.

Step 10 computes the RMS error.

Step 11 generates the diagnostic plots. Since the standard `plot` function for `lm` produces four plots, we set up a matrix of four plots up front before calling the function, and reset it after we finish plotting:

- **Residuals vs Fitted**: As its name suggests, this plots the residuals against the values fitted by the model to enable us to examine whether the residuals exhibit a trend. Ideally, we would like them to be trendless and almost a horizontal straight line at 0. In our example, we see a very slight trend.
- **Normal Q-Q**: This plot helps us check the extent to which the residuals are normally distributed by plotting the standardized residuals against the theoretical quartiles for the standard normal distribution. If the points all lie close to the 45-degree line, we will know that the normality condition is met. In our example, we note that, at the right extreme or at high values of the residuals, the standardized residuals are higher than expected and do not meet the normality requirement.
- **Scale Location**: This plot is very similar to the first plot, except that the square root of the standardized residuals is plotted against the fitted values. Once again, this is used to detect whether the residuals exhibit any trend.
- **Residuals vs Leverage**: You can use this plot to identify outlier cases that are exerting undue influence on the model. In our example, the labeled cases 330, 365, and 199 can be candidates for removal.

There's more...

We will discuss in the following sections a few options for using the lm function.

Forcing lm to use a specific factor level as the reference

By default, lm uses the lowest factor as the reference level. To use a different one as reference, we can use the relevel function. Our original model uses 3cyl as the reference level. Perform the following steps to force lm to use 4cyl as the reference:

```
> auto <- within(auto, cylinders <- relevel(cylinders,  ref = "4cyl") )
> mod <- lm(mpg ~., data = auto[t.idx, -c(1, 8, 9)])
```

The resulting model will not have a coefficient for 4cyl.

Using other options in the formula expression for linear models

Our example only showed the most common form of the formula for `lm`. The following table shows options to create models with interaction effects or to create models that apply arbitrary functions to predictor variables:

Formula expression	Corresponding regression model	Explanation
$Y \sim P$	$\hat{Y} \sim \beta_0 + \beta_1 P$	Straight line with Y intercept
$Y \sim P + Q$	$\hat{Y} \sim \beta_0 + \beta_1 P + \beta_2 Q$	Linear model with P and Q with no interaction terms
$Y \sim -1 + P$	$\hat{Y} \sim \beta_1 P$	Linear model with no intercept term
$Y \sim P : Q$	$\hat{Y} \sim \beta_0 + \beta_1 PQ$	Model with only the first order interaction terms for P and Q
$Y \sim P * Q$ or $Y \sim P + Q + P : Q$	$\hat{Y} \sim \beta_0 + \beta_1 P + \beta_2 Q + \beta_3 PQ$	Complete first order model with all interaction terms
$Y \sim P + I(\log(Q))$	$\hat{Y} \sim \beta_0 + \beta_1 P + \beta_2 \log(Q)$	Model with arbitrary function applied on predictor variable. The I or Identity function is used for this.
$Y \sim (P + Q + R)^\wedge 2$ or $Y \sim P * Q * R - P : Q : R$	$\hat{Y} \sim \beta_0 + \beta_1 P + \beta_2 Q + \beta_3 R + \beta_4 PQ + \beta_5 QR + \beta_6 PR$	Complete first order model and interaction terms for all orders up to the nth order where n is the exponent

See also

- The *Creating random data partitions* recipe in `Chapter 2`, *What's In There? - Exploratory Data Analysis*
- The *Performing variable selection in linear regression* recipe in this chapter

Performing variable selection in linear regression

The `MASS` package has the functionality for variable selection, and this recipe illustrates its use.

Getting ready

If you have not already done so, download the data files for this chapter and ensure that the `auto-mpg.csv` file is in your R working directory. We want to predict `mpg` based on `cylinders`, `displacement`, `horsepower`, `weight`, and `acceleration`.

How to do it...

To perform variable selection in linear regression, perform the following steps:

1. Load the `caret` and `MASS` packages:

```
> library(caret)
> library(MASS)
```

2. Read the data:

```
> auto <- read.csv("auto-mpg.csv")
```

3. Convert the categorical variable cylinders into a factor with appropriate renaming of the levels:

```
> auto$cylinders <- factor(auto$cylinders,  levels = c(3,4,5,6,8),
labels = c("3cyl", "4cyl", "5cyl", "6cyl", "8cyl"))
```

4. Create partitions:

```
> set.seed(1000)
> t.idx <- createDataPartition(auto$mpg, p = 0.7, list = FALSE)
```

5. See the names of the variables in the data frame:

```
> names(auto)
[1] "No"            "mpg"
[3] "cylinders"     "displacement"
[5] "horsepower"    "weight"
[7] "acceleration"  "model_year"
[9] "car_name"
```

6. Build the linear regression model:

```
> fit <- lm(mpg ~ ., data = auto[t.idx, -c(1,8,9)])
```

7. Run the variable selection procedure. This will produce quite a lot of output, which we will display and discuss later. Because of random partitioning, your actual numbers will vary:

```
> step.model <- stepAIC(fit, direction = "backward")
```

8. See the final model (your results may differ because of variations in your training sample):

```
> summary(step.model)
Call:
lm(formula = mpg ~ cylinders + horsepower + weight, data =
auto[t.idx,
    -c(1, 8, 9)])

Residuals:
    Min      1Q  Median      3Q     Max
-9.7987 -2.3676 -0.6214  1.8625 15.3231

Coefficients:
                 Estimate Std. Error t value Pr(>|t|)
(Intercept)    39.1290155  2.5434458  15.384  < 2e-16 ***
cylinders4cyl   6.7241124  2.0140804   3.339 0.000959 ***
cylinders5cyl   5.0579997  3.4762178   1.455 0.146810
cylinders6cyl   2.5090718  2.1315214   1.177 0.240170
cylinders8cyl   7.0991790  2.3133286   3.069 0.002365 **
horsepower     -0.0792425  0.0148396  -5.340 1.96e-07 ***
weight         -0.0044670  0.0007512  -5.947 8.34e-09 ***
---
```

```
Signif. codes:  0 '***' 0.001 '**' 0.01 '*' 0.05 '.' 0.1 ' ' 1

Residual standard error: 3.939 on 273 degrees of freedom
Multiple R-squared:  0.7558,    Adjusted R-squared:  0.7505
F-statistic: 140.9 on 6 and 273 DF,  p-value: < 2.2e-16
```

How it works...

For a description of steps 1 through 6, refer to the *How it works* section of the *Performing linear regression* recipe in this chapter (the previous recipe).

Step 7 runs the variable selection procedure. We have chosen to illustrate backward elimination in which the system first builds the model with all the predictors and eliminates predictors based on AIC scores. We show the sample output here:

```
Start:  AIC=778.38
mpg ~ cylinders + displacement + horsepower + weight + acceleration

                Df Sum of Sq    RSS    AIC
- acceleration   1      0.01 4232.1 776.38
- displacement   1      3.01 4235.1 776.58
<none>                       4232.1 778.38
- horsepower     1    259.61 4491.7 793.05
- weight         1    349.99 4582.1 798.63
- cylinders      4    859.84 5091.9 822.17

Step:  AIC=776.38
mpg ~ cylinders + displacement + horsepower + weight

                Df Sum of Sq    RSS    AIC
- displacement   1      3.02 4235.1 774.58
<none>                       4232.1 776.38
- horsepower     1    404.33 4636.4 799.93
- weight         1    451.22 4683.3 802.75
- cylinders      4    862.88 5094.9 820.34

Step:  AIC=774.58
mpg ~ cylinders + horsepower + weight

                Df Sum of Sq    RSS    AIC
<none>                       4235.1 774.58
- horsepower     1    442.36 4677.4 800.40
- weight         1    548.60 4783.7 806.69
- cylinders      4    862.50 5097.6 818.49
```

From the preceding output, you can see that the system first built the complete model. In that model, acceleration had the lowest AIC score of 776.38 and was, therefore, not included in the next one. In this process, the system eliminated displacement as well.

The complete model had five predictors, and the final one has three. In the process, the multiple R2 has remained almost unchanged, but we got a less complex model.

In the forward selection model, the system takes the reverse approach and adds predictors.

See also

- The *Creating random data partitions* recipe in Chapter 2, *What's In There? - Exploratory Data Analysis*
- The *Performing linear regression* recipe in this chapter

Building regression trees

This recipe covers the use of tree models for regression. The rpart package provides the necessary functions to build regression trees.

Getting ready

Install the rpart, caret, and rpart.plot packages if you do not already have them installed. If you have not already downloaded the data files for this chapter, do so now and ensure that the BostonHousing.csv and education.csv files are in the R working directory.

How to do it...

To build regression trees, perform the following steps:

1. Load the `rpart`, `rpart.plot`, and `caret` packages:

```
> library(rpart)
> library(rpart.plot)
> library(caret)
```

2. Read the data:

```
> bh <- read.csv("BostonHousing.csv")
```

3. Partition the data:

```
> set.seed(1000)
> t.idx <- createDataPartition(bh$MEDV, p=0.7, list = FALSE)
```

4. Build and view the regression tree model:

```
> bfit <- rpart(MEDV ~ ., data = bh[t.idx,])
> bfit
 n= 356

node), split, n, deviance, yval
      * denotes terminal node

 1) root 356 32071.8400 22.61461
   2) LSTAT>=7.865 242  8547.6860 18.22603
     4) LSTAT>=14.915 114  2451.4590 14.50351
       8) CRIM>=5.76921 56   796.5136 11.63929 *
       9) CRIM< 5.76921 58   751.9641 17.26897 *
     5) LSTAT< 14.915 128  3109.5710 21.54141
      10) DIS>=1.80105 121  1419.7510 21.12562 *
      11) DIS< 1.80105 7  1307.3140 28.72857 *
   3) LSTAT< 7.865 114  8969.3230 31.93070
     6) RM< 7.4525 93  3280.1050 28.70753
      12) RM< 6.659 46  1022.5320 25.24130 *
      13) RM>=6.659 47  1163.9800 32.10000
        26) LSTAT>=5.495 17   329.2494 28.59412 *
        27) LSTAT< 5.495 30   507.3747 34.08667 *
     7) RM>=7.4525 21   444.3295 46.20476 *
```

5. Plot the tree. Use the `prp` function from the `rpart.plot` package, and select the options shown in the following to get a good-looking plot. For convenience, the plot rounds off the `y` values.

```
> prp(bfit, type=2, nn=TRUE, fallen.leaves=TRUE, faclen=4,
varlen=8, shadow.col="gray")
```

The plot obtained appears as follows:

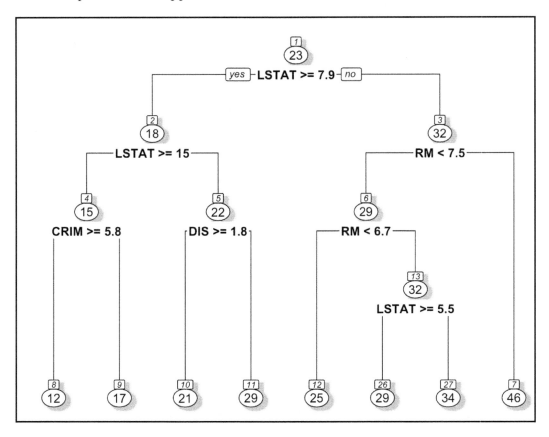

6. Look at the `cptable`. Your `cptable` may differ from that shown in the following output because of the random numbers used in the cross-validation process:

```
> bfit$cptable
```

```
          CP nsplit rel error    xerror       xstd
1 0.45381973      0 1.0000000 1.0068493 0.09724445
2 0.16353560      1 0.5461803 0.6403963 0.06737452
3 0.09312395      2 0.3826447 0.4402408 0.05838413
4 0.03409823      3 0.2895207 0.3566122 0.04889254
5 0.02815494      4 0.2554225 0.3314437 0.04828523
6 0.01192653      5 0.2272675 0.2891804 0.04306039
7 0.01020696      6 0.2153410 0.2810795 0.04286100
8 0.01000000      7 0.2051341 0.2791785 0.04281285
```

7. You can either choose the tree with the lowest cross-validation error (`xerror`) or use the 1 SD rule and choose the tree that comes to within 1 SD (`xstd`) of the minimum `xerror` and has fewer nodes. The former approach will cause us to select the tree with seven splits (in the last row). That tree will have eight nodes. To apply the latter approach, min `xerror` + *1 SE = 0.2791785 + 0.04281285 = 0.3219914*, which leads us to select the tree with five splits (on row 6).

8. You can simplify the process by just plotting the `cptree` command and using the resulting plot to select the cutoff value to use for pruning. The plot shows the size of the tree, which is one more than the number of splits. The table and the plot differ in another important way--the complexity or the `cp` values in these differ. The table shows the minimum `cp` value for which the corresponding split occurs. The plot shows the geometric means of the successive splits. As with the table, your plot may differ because of the random numbers used during cross-validation:

```
> plotcp(bfit)
```

To select the best `cp` value from the plot using the 1 SD rule, pick the leftmost `cp` value for which the cross-validation relative error (*y*-axis) lies below the dashed line. Using this value, we will pick a `cp` value of *0.018*:

9. Prune the tree with the chosen `cp` value, and plot it as follows:

```
> # In the command below, replace the cp value
> # based on your results
> bfitpruned <- prune(bfit, cp= 0.01192653)
> prp(bfitpruned, type=2, nn=TRUE, fallen.leaves=TRUE, faclen=4,
varlen=8, shadow.col="gray")
```

The following output is obtained:

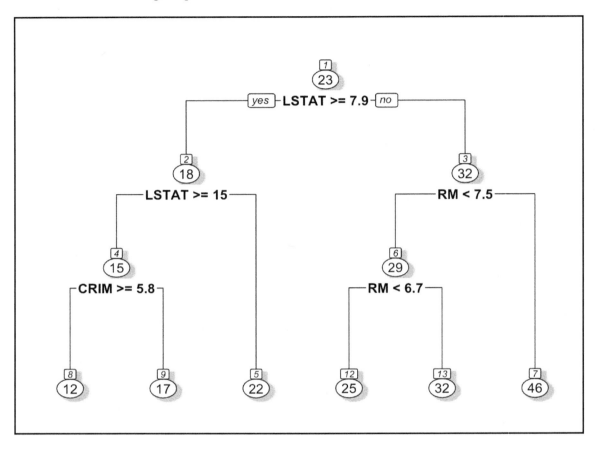

10. Use the chosen tree to compute the RMS error for the training partition:

```
> preds.t <- predict(bfitpruned, bh[t.idx,])
> sqrt(mean((preds.t-bh[t.idx,"MEDV"])^2))
[1] 4.524866
```

11. Generate predictions and the RMS error for the validation partition:

```
preds.v <- predict(bfitpruned, bh[-t.idx,])
> sqrt(mean((preds.v - bh[-t.idx,"MEDV"])^2))
[1] 4.535723
```

How it works...

Steps 1 and 2 load the required packages and read the data.

Step 3 partitions the data. Refer to the *Creating random data partitions* recipe in `Chapter 2, What's In There? - Exploratory Data Analysis* for more details. We set the random seed to enable you to match your results with those that we have displayed.

Step 4 uses the `rpart` function to build the tree model. It passes the formula as `MEDV ~ .` to indicate that `MEDV` is the outcome and that all the remaining variables will be predictors. It specifies `data = bh[t.idx, ]` to indicate that only the rows in the training partition should be used to build the model. It then prints the model details in textual form. The output shows information for the root node and subsequently for each split. Each row has the following information:

```
node), split, n, deviance, yval
```

- node number
- splitting condition that generated the node (for the root, it just says "root")
- number of cases at the node
- sum of squared errors at the node based on average value of outcome variable of the cases at the node
- average value of outcome variable of the cases at the node

We have many options to control how the `rpart` function works. It uses the following important defaults among others:

- *0.01* for the complexity factor, `cp`
- Minimum node size of 20 to split a node, `minsplit`
- The function does not split if a split will create a node with less than `round(minsplit/3)` cases, `minbucket`

You can control these by passing an `rpart.control` object while invoking `rpart`. The following code shows an example. Here we use values of `0.001`, `10`, and `5` for `cp`,`minsplit`, and `minbucket` respectively:

```
> fit <- rpart(MEDV ~ ., data = bh[t.idx,], control = 
rpart.control(minsplit = 10, cp = 0.001, minbucket = 5)
```

Step 5 plots the tree model using the `prp` function from the `rpart.print` package. The function provides several parameters through which we can control the plot's appearance. We describe a few options as follows; check the documentation for the other numerous options:

- `Type`: This refers to the amount of information and its placement
- `nn`: This refers to whether to display node numbers or not
- `fallen.leaves`: This refers to whether to display all the leaf nodes at the same level (bottom most), which results in a plot with only horizontal and vertical lines, making it easy on the eyes; otherwise, the plot has diagonal lines
- `faclen`: This refers to the length of factor level names in the splits--abbreviates if needed
- `varlen`: This refers to the length of variable names on the plot--truncates if needed
- `shadow.col`: This refers to the color of the shadow that each node casts

Step 6 prints the `cptable`, which is a component of the fitted tree model. The `cptable` shows comprehensive results of trees with differing number of nodes as well as the mean and standard deviation of the error on cross-validation for each tree size. This information helps us select our optimal tree. We explain the columns of the table as follows:

- `cp`: This refers to the complexity factor.
- `nsplit`: This refers to the number of splits in the best tree that the corresponding `cp` value yields.
- `rel error`: For the best tree with the specified number of splits, the overall squared classification error (on the data used to build the tree) is a proportion of the total squared error at the root node. The error at the root node is based on predicting every case as the average of the value of outcome variable across all cases.
- `xerror`: This refers to mean cross-validation error using the best tree with the specified number of splits.
- `Xstd`: This refers to standard deviation of the cross-validation error using the best tree with the specified number of splits.

Step 7 explains how we can use the information in `cptable` to prune the tree and prevent overfitting. We can choose either the tree with the lowest cross-validation error or the smallest one that comes within one SD of the cross-validation error. We can select the `cp` value corresponding to the selected tree and use that value to prune the tree.

Step 8 shows an easier way to select the best `cp` value by plotting the `cptable` with the `plotcp` function.

Step 9 prunes the tree with the chosen `cp` value.

Step 10 uses the `predict` function to generate predictions for the training partition and then computes the RMS error.

Step 11 does the same for the validation partition.

There's more...

Regression trees can also be built for categorical predictors as explained in this section.

Generating regression trees for data with categorical predictors

The `rpart` function works even when a dataset has categorical predictor variables. You just have to ensure that the variable is tagged as a factor. See the following example:

```
> ed <- read.csv("education.csv")
> ed$region <- factor(ed$region)
> set.seed(1000)
> t.idx <- createDataPartition(ed$expense, p = 0.7, list = FALSE)
> fit <- rpart(expense ~ region+urban+income+under18, data = ed[t.idx,])
> prp(fit, type=2, nn=TRUE, fallen.leaves=TRUE, faclen=4, varlen=8,
shadow.col="gray")
```

The following output is obtained:

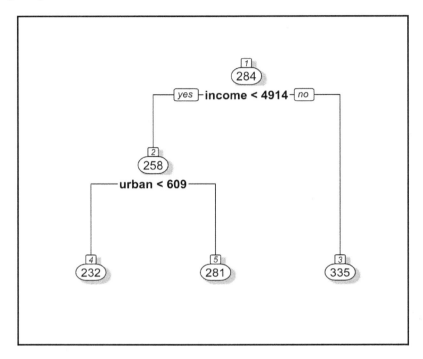

Regression trees can also be built for categorical predictors as explained in this section.

Generating regression trees using the ensemble method - Bagging and Boosting

Regression trees can also be built using the ensemble method that creates multiple models of the same type from different sub-samples of the same dataset.

Bootstrapped Aggregation (**Bagging**) is an ensemble method that combines together the predictions from separate tree models to provide superior results, and is also effective for high-variance methods such as decision trees.

Perform the following commands to apply bagging technique:

```
> install.packages("ipred")
> library(ipred)
> # using same BostonHousing.csv dataset used earlier
> fit <- bagging(MEDV ~., data= bh[t.idx,], control=
```

```
    rpart.control(minsplit=10))
> prediction.t <- predict(fit, bh[t.idx,]) # on training set

> sqrt(mean((prediction.t-bh[t.idx,"MEDV"])^2))# RMS for training
```

Boosting is another ensemble method developed for reducing bias where new models are built to learn the misclassification errors in the previous models. **Gradient Boosted Machines** (**GBM**) is generalized and adapted to use with CART decision trees for classification and regression.

Perform the following commands to apply boosting technique:

```
> install.packages("gbm")
> library(gbm)
> # using same BostonHousing.csv dataset used earlier
> gbmFit <- gbm(MEDV ~., data= bh, distribution="gaussian")

> prediction.t <- predict(gbmFit, bh) # on training set
> sqrt(mean((prediction.t-bh$MEDV)^2))# RMS for training
```

See also

- The *Creating random data partitions* recipe in `Chapter 2`, *What's In There? - Exploratory Data Analysis*
- The *Building, plotting, and evaluating classification trees* recipe in `Chapter 3`, *Where Does It Belong? - Classification*

Building random forest models for regression

Getting ready

If you have not already installed the `randomForest` and `caret` packages, install them now. Download the data files for this chapter from the book's website, and place the `BostonHousing.csv` file is in your R working directory. We will build a random forest model to predict `MEDV` based on the other variables.

How to do it...

To build random forest models for regression, perform the following steps:

1. Load the `randomForest` and `caret` packages:

```
> install.packages(c("caret","randomForest"))
> library(randomForest)
> library(caret)
```

2. Read the data:

```
> bn <- read.csv("BostonHousing.csv")
```

3. Partition the data:

```
> set.seed(1000)
> t.idx <- createDataPartition(bh$MEDV, p=0.7, list=FALSE)
```

4. Build the random forest model. Since this command builds many regression trees, it can take significant processing time on even moderate datasets:

```
> mod <- randomForest(x = bh[t.idx,1:13],
y=bh[t.idx,14],ntree=1000,  xtest = bh[-t.idx,1:13],  ytest = bh[-
t.idx,14], importance=TRUE, keep.forest=TRUE)
```

5. Examine the results (your results will most likely differ slightly because of the random factor):

```
> mod
Call:
 randomForest(x = bh[t.idx, 1:13], y = bh[t.idx, 14], xtest = bh[-
t.idx,      1:13], ytest = bh[-t.idx, 14], ntree = 1000, importance
= TRUE,      keep.forest = TRUE)
               Type of random forest: regression
                     Number of trees: 1000
No. of variables tried at each split: 4

          Mean of squared residuals: 12.61296
                    % Var explained: 86
                       Test set MSE: 6.94
                    % Var explained: 90.25
```

6. Examine the variable importance:

```
> mod$importance
            %IncMSE  IncNodePurity
CRIM      9.5803434    2271.5448
ZN        0.3410126     142.1191
INDUS     6.6838954    1840.7041
CHAS      0.6363144     193.7132
NOX       9.3106894    1922.5483
RM       36.2790912    8540.4644
AGE       3.7186444     820.7750
DIS       7.4519827    2012.8193
RAD       1.7799796     287.6282
TAX       4.5373887    1049.3716
PTRATIO   6.8372845    2030.2044
B         1.2240072     530.1201
LSTAT    67.0867117    9532.3054
```

7. Compare the predicted and actual values for the training partition:

```
> plot(bh[t.idx,14], predict( mod, newdata=bh[t.idx,]), xlab =
"Actual", ylab = "Predicted")
```

The following output is obtained on executing the preceding command:

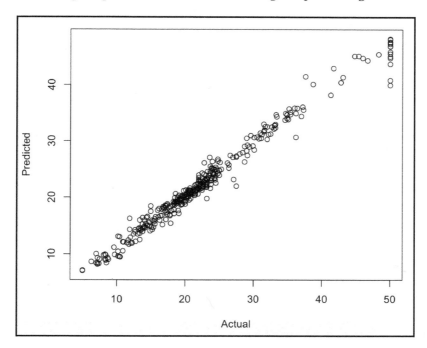

8. Compare the **out of bag** (**OOB**) predictions with actuals in the training partition:

```
> > plot(bh[t.idx,14], mod$predicted, xlab = "Actual", ylab =
"Predicted")
```

The preceding command produces the following output:

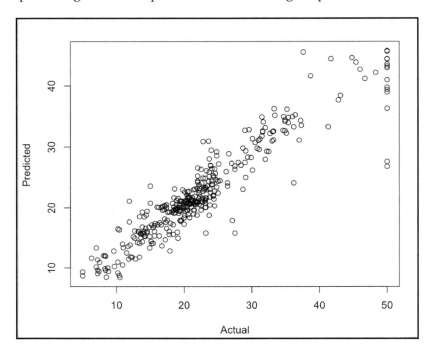

9. Compare the predicted and actual values for the test partition:

```
> plot(bh[-t.idx,14], mod$test$predicted, xlab = "Actual", ylab =
"Predicted")
```

The following plot is obtained as a result of the preceding command:

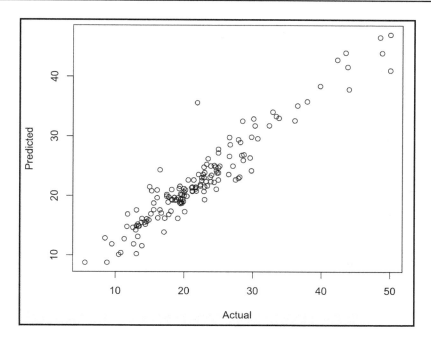

How it works...

Steps 1 and 2 load the necessary packages and read the data.

Step 3 partitions the data. Refer to the *Creating random data partitions* recipe in `Chapter 2,` *What's in There? - Exploratory Data Analysis,* for more details. We set the random seed to enable you to match your results with those that we have displayed. Technically speaking, we do not really need to partition the data for random forests because it builds many trees and uses only a subset of the data each time. Thus, each case is OOB for about a third of the trees built and can be used for validation. However, the method also allows us to provide a validation dataset separately, and we illustrate that process here.

Step 4 builds the random forest model. We show the command and describe the arguments as follows:

```
> mod <- randomForest(x = bh[t.idx,1:13],  y=bh[t.idx,14],ntree=1000,
xtest = bh[-t.idx,1:13],  ytest = bh[-t.idx,14], importance=TRUE,
keep.forest=TRUE)
```

- x: This denotes the predictors
- y: This denotes the outcome variables

- `Ntree`: This denotes the number of trees to build
- `Xtest`: These denote predictors in the validation partition
- `Ytest`: These denote outcome variables in the validation partition
- `Importance`: This refers to whether or not to compute the importance scores of the predictor variables
- `keep.forest`: This refers to whether or not to keep the trees built in the resulting model; only if we keep the trees can we generate predictions based on the model

Step 5 prints the model. This shows the mean squared error on the training and the validation partitions as well as the percentage of variability in the outcome variable that the model explains.

Step 6 uses the `importance` component of the model to print the computed importance level of each variable. For each tree generated, the method first generates the prediction. Then, for every variable (one at a time), it randomly permutes the values across the OOB cases and generates the predictions. The degradation in prediction with the variable permuted, indicates how important the variable is. For each predictor variable, the importance table reports the average value of importance across all trees. Higher values indicate higher importance.

Step 7 plots the predictions for the training partition against the actual values.

Step 8 plots the OOB predictions against the actual values using the `predicted` component of the `mod$predicted`model.

Step 9 uses `mod$test$predicted` to plot the performance of the model on the test cases against actuals.

There's more...

We discuss a few prominent options in this section.

Controlling forest generation

You can use the following additional options to control how the algorithm builds the forest:

- `mtry`: This is the number of predictors to randomly sample at each split; the default is `m/3`, where `m` is the number of predictors
- `nodesize`: This is the minimum size of terminal nodes; the default is 5, setting it higher causes smaller trees
- `maxnodes`: This is the maximum number of terminal nodes that a tree can have; if unspecified, the trees are grown to the maximum size possible, subject to `nodesize`

See also

- The *Creating random data partitions* recipe in `Chapter 2`, *What's in There? - Exploratory Data Analysis*
- The *Using random forest models for classification* recipe in `Chapter 3`, *Where Does It Belong? - Classification*

Using neural networks for regression

The `nnet` package contains functionality to build neural network models for classification as well as prediction. In this recipe, we cover the steps to build a neural network regression model using `nnet`.

Getting ready

If you do not already have the `nnet`, `caret`, and `devtools` packages installed, install them now. If you have not already downloaded the data files for this chapter, download them now and ensure that the `BostonHousing.csv` file is in your R working directory. We will build a model to predict `MEDV` based on all of the remaining variables.

How to do it...

To use neural networks for regression, follow these steps:

1. Load the `nnet` and `caret` packages:

```
> library(nnet)
> library(caret)
> library(devtools)
```

2. Read the data:

```
> bh <- read.csv("BostonHousing.csv")
```

3. Partition the data:

```
> set.seed(1000)
> t.idx <- createDataPartition(bh$MEDV, p=0.7, list=FALSE)
```

4. Find the range of the response variable to be able to scale it to [*0, 1*]:

```
> summary(bh$MEDV)
   Min. 1st Qu.  Median   Mean 3rd Qu.    Max.
   5.00   17.02   21.20  22.53   25.00   50.00
```

5. Build the model:

```
> fit <- nnet(MEDV/50 ~ ., data=bh[t.idx,], size=6, decay = 0.1,
maxit = 1000, linout = TRUE)
```

6. In preparation for plotting the network, get the code for the plotting function `plot.nnet` from *fawda123*'s GitHub page. The following GitHub page loads the function into R:

```
>
source_url('https://gist.githubusercontent.com/fawda123/7471137/raw
/466c1474d0a505ff044412703516c34f1a4684a5/nnet_plot_update.r')
```

7. Plot the network:

```
> plot(fit, max.sp = TRUE)
```

The following plot is obtained as a result of the preceding commands:

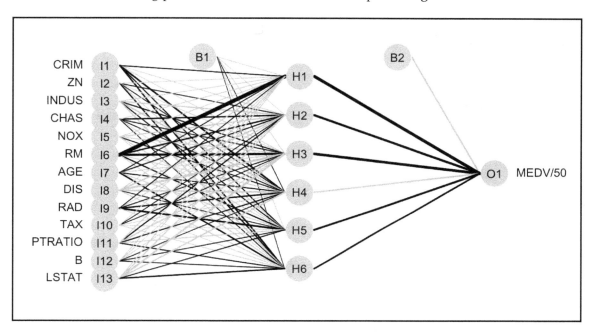

8. Compute the RMS error on the training data (your results can differ):

```
> t.rmse = sqrt(mean((fit$fitted.values * 50 - bh[t.idx,
"MEDV"])^2))
> t.rmse
[1] 2.797945
```

9. Generate predictions on the validation partition, and generate the RMS error (your results may differ):

```
> v.rmse <- sqrt(mean((predict(fit,bh[-t.idx,]*50 - bh[-t.idx,
"MEDV"])^2)))
> v.rmse
[1] 0.42959
```

How it works...

Step 1 loads the necessary packages--nnet for neural network modeling and `caret` for data partitioning. We also load `devtools` because we will be sourcing code using a web URL for printing the network.

Step 2 reads the file.

Step 3 partitions the data. Refer to the *Creating random data partitions* recipe from Chapter 2, *What's in There? - Exploratory Data Analysis* for more details. We have set the random seed to enable you to match your results with those that we have displayed.

Step 4 builds the neural net model using the `nnet` function of the `nnet` package:

```
> fit <- nnet(MEDV/50 ~ ., data=bh[t.idx,], size=6, decay = 0.1, maxit =
1000, linout = TRUE)
```

We divide our response variable by 50 to scale it to the range *[0, 1]*. We pass the following arguments:

- `size = 6`: This indicates the number of nodes in the hidden layer.
- `decay = 0.1`: This indicates the decay.
- `maxit = 1000`: This stops if the process does not converge in the `maxit` iterations. The default value for `maxit` is `100`. Provide a value based on trial and error.
- `linout = TRUE`: This specifies that we want a linear output unit and not logistic.

Step 6 loads code for the printing function from an eternal `url` using the `source_url` function of the `devtools` package.

Step 7 then plots the network. The thickness of the lines indicates the strength of the corresponding weights. We use `max.sp = TRUE` to cause the plot to have maximum possible spacing between the nodes.

Step 8 uses the `fitted` component of the model to compute the RMS error on the training partition.

Step 9 uses the `predict` function on the validation partition to generate predictions to compute the RMS error on the validation partition.

See also

- The *Creating random data partitions* recipe in `Chapter 2`, *What's in There? - Exploratory Data Analysis*
- The *Using neural networks for classification* recipe in `Chapter 3`, *Where Does It Belong? - Classification*

Performing k-fold cross-validation

The R implementation of some techniques, such as classification and regression trees, performs cross-validation out of the box to aid in model selection and to avoid overfitting. However, some others do not. When faced with several choices of machine learning methods for a particular problem, we can use the standard approach of partitioning the data into training and test sets and select them based on the results. However, cross-validation gives a more thorough evaluation of a model's performance on holdout data. Comparing the performance of methods using cross-validation can paint a truer picture of their relative performance.

Getting ready

We illustrate the approach with the Boston Housing data, and thus, you should download the code for this chapter and ensure that the `BostonHousing.csv` file is in your R working directory.

How to do it...

In this recipe, we show you basic code to perform k-fold cross-validation for linear regression. You can adapt the same code structure for all other regression methods. Although some packages such as caret, DAAG, and boot provide cross-validation functionality out of the box, they cover only a few machine learning techniques. You might find a generic framework to be useful and be able to adapt it to whatever machine learning technique you might want to apply it to. To do this, follow these steps:

1. Read the data:

```
> bh <- read.csv("BostonHousing.csv")
```

2. Create the two functions shown as follows; we show line numbers for discussion:

```
1 rdacb.kfold.crossval.reg <- function(df, nfolds) {
2   fold <- sample(1:nfolds, nrow(df), replace = TRUE)
3   mean.sqr.errs <- sapply(1:nfolds,
        rdacb.kfold.cval.reg.iter,
        df, fold)
4   list("mean_sqr_errs"= mean.sqr.errs,
        "overall_mean_sqr_err" = mean(mean.sqr.errs),
        "std_dev_mean_sqr_err" = sd(mean.sqr.errs))
5 }
```

```
6 rdacb.kfold.cval.reg.iter <- function(k, df, fold) {
7   trg.idx <- !fold %in% c(k)
8   test.idx <-  fold %in% c(k)
9   mod <- lm(MEDV ~ ., data = df[trg.idx, ] )
10  pred <- predict(mod, df[test.idx,])
11  sqr.errs <- (pred - df[test.idx, "MEDV"])^2
12  mean(sqr.errs)
13 }
```

3. With the preceding two functions in place, you can run k-fold cross-validation with k=5 as follows:

```
> res <- rdacb.kfold.crossval.reg(bh, 5)
> # get the mean squared errors from each fold
> res$mean_sqr_errs
> # get the overall mean squared errors
> res$overall_mean_sqr_err
> # get the standard deviation of the mean squared errors
> res$std_dev_mean_sqr_err
```

How it works...

Step 1 reads the data file.

In step 2, we define two functions to perform k-fold cross-validation. Rows 1-5 define the first function, and rows 6-13 define the second function.

The first function `rdacb.kfold.crossval.reg` sets up the k-folds and uses the second one to build the model and compute the errors for each fold.

Line 2 creates the folds by randomly sampling from 1 to k. Thus, if a data frame has 1,000 elements, this line will generate 1,000 random integers from 1 to k. The idea is that if the ith random number is, say, 3, then the ith case of the data frame belongs to the third fold.

Line 3 invokes the second function to compute the errors for each fold.

Line 4 creates a list with the raw values of the mean squared errors for each partition, the overall mean across all the folds, and the standard deviation of the mean squared errors.

The second function computes the error for a particular partition.

Lines 7 and 8 set up the training and test data. The fold number is passed in as the argument k and line 7 treats all data rows belonging to folds other than k as the training data. Line 8 sets up the data rows belonging to the kth fold as the test data.

Line 9 builds the linear regression model with the training data alone.

Line 10 generates the predictions on the test data.

Line 11 computes the squared errors.

Line 12 returns the mean of the squared errors.

See also

- The *Performing leave-one-out-cross-validation to limit overfitting* recipe in this chapter.

Performing leave-one-out cross-validation to limit overfitting

We provide the framework of the code to perform leave-one-out cross-validation for linear regression. You should be able to easily adapt this code to any other regression technique. The rationale and explanation presented under the previous recipe *Performing k-fold cross-validation* apply to this one as well.

How to do it...

To perform **leave-one-out cross-validation (LOOCV)** to limit overfitting, perform the following steps:

1. Read the data:

   ```
   > bh <- read.csv("BostonHousing.csv")
   ```

2. Create the two functions shown as follows; we show line numbers for discussion:

   ```
   1 rdacb.loocv.reg <- function(df) {
   2   mean.sqr.errs <- sapply(1:nrow(df),
               rdacb.loocv.reg.iter, df)
   3   list("mean_sqr_errs"= mean.sqr.errs,
               "overall_mean_sqr_err" = mean(mean.sqr.errs),
               "std_dev_mean_sqr_err" = sd(mean.sqr.errs))
   4 }

   5 rdacb.loocv.reg.iter <- function(k, df) {
   6   mod <- lm(MEDV ~ ., data = df[-k, ] )
   7   pred <- predict(mod, df[k,])
   8   sqr.err <- (pred - df[k, "MEDV"])^2
   9 }
   ```

3. With the preceding two functions in place, you can run LOOCV as follows (this runs 506 linear regression models and will take some time):

   ```
   > res <- rdacb.loocv.reg(bh)
   > # get the raw mean squared errors for each case
   > res$mean_sqr_errs
   > # get the overall mean squared error
   > res$overall_mean_sqr_err
   > # get the standard deviation of the mean squared errors
   > res$std_dev_mean_sqr_err
   ```

How it works...

Step 1 reads the data.

Step 2 creates two functions for performing LOOCV. Lines 1 to 4 define the first function `rdacb.loocv.reg` and lines 5 to 9 define the second one, `rdacb.loocv.reg.iter`:

- Line 2 of the first function `rdacb.loocv.reg` repeatedly calls the second function `rdacb.loocv.reg.iter` to build the regression model leaving one case out and compute the squared error
- Line 3 creates a list with the output elements
- Line 6 in the second function `rdacb.loocv.reg.iter` builds the regression model on the data frame leaving out one case
- Line 7 generates the prediction for the case that was left out
- Line 8 computes the squared error

Step 3 uses the preceding functions to perform LOOCV and displays the results.

See also

- The *Performing k-fold cross-validation* recipe in this chapter.

5

Can you Simplify That? Data Reduction Techniques

In this chapter, we will cover the following topics:

- Performing cluster analysis using hierarchical clustering
- Performing cluster analysis using partitioning clustering
- Image segmentation using mini-batch K-means
- Partitioning around medoids
- Clustering large applications
- Performing cluster validation
- Performing advance clustering
- Model-based clustering with the EM algorithm
- Reducing dimensionality with principal component analysis

Introduction

Data analysts often come across large datasets of unlabeled information with high dimensions/features and often seek to reduce the complexity of the data by applying **Clustering** or **PCA**.

Clustering is a data analysis technique used to discover groups of similar objects (close in terms of distance) or patterns in a dataset. Unlike supervised learning techniques (such as classification and regression), a clustering analysis does not use any labeled data, instead it uses the similarity between data features to group them into clusters. There are two standard clustering strategies: **partitioning methods** and **hierarchical clustering**.

PCA is a dimensionality reduction technique that transforms m-dimensional input space to n-dimensional ($n < m$) output space, with the objective to minimize the amount of information/variance lost by discarding ($m - n$) dimension.

This chapter will cover R recipes for cluster analysis and PCA to deal with the curse of dimensionality and unlabeled data.

Performing cluster analysis using hierarchical clustering

Hierarchical clustering builds a hierarchy of clusters either through the **agglomerative** or **divisive** method.

 Both these methods use a distance similarity measure to combine or split clusters. The recursive process continues until there is only one cluster left or you cannot split more clusters. Eventually, a **dendrogram** can be used to represent the hierarchy of clusters.

In this recipe, we will demonstrate how to cluster European protein consumption with hierarchical clustering.

Getting ready

If you have not already downloaded the files for this chapter, do so now and ensure that the `protein.csv` file is in your R working directory.

How to do it...

To perform hierarchical cluster analysis, follow these steps:

1. Read the data and normalize it to the same scale. We will ignore the `Country` variable during scaling (as it is a categorical variable):

   ```
   > proteinIntake <- read.csv("protein.csv")

   > head(proteinIntake)
   ```

   Here is how it will look:

	Country	RedMeat	WhiteMeat	Eggs	Milk	Fish	Cereals	Starch	Nuts	Fr.Veg
1	Albania	10.1	1.4	0.5	8.9	0.2	42.3	0.6	5.5	1.7
2	Austria	8.9	14.0	4.3	19.9	2.1	28.0	3.6	1.3	4.3
3	Belgium	13.5	9.3	4.1	17.5	4.5	26.6	5.7	2.1	4.0
4	Bulgaria	7.8	6.0	1.6	8.3	1.2	56.7	1.1	3.7	4.2
5	Czechoslovakia	9.7	11.4	2.8	12.5	2.0	34.3	5.0	1.1	4.0
6	Denmark	10.6	10.8	3.7	25.0	9.9	21.9	4.8	0.7	2.4

   ```
   > proteinIntakeScaled = as.data.frame(scale(proteinIntake[,-1]))
   > proteinIntakeScaled$Country =proteinIntake$Country
   ```

2. Now use agglomerative hierarchical clustering to cluster the scaled protein intake data:

   ```
   > hc = hclust(dist(proteinIntakeScaled, method="euclidean"),
   method="ward.D2")
   > hc
   Call:
   hclust(d = dist(proteinIntakeScaled, method = "euclidean"), method
   = "ward.D2")

   Cluster method : ward.D2
   Distance : euclidean
   Number of objects: 25
   ```

3. Lastly, use the `plot` function to plot the dendrogram:

   ```
   > plot(hc, hang = -0.01, cex = 0.7)
   ```

Here is how the **Cluster Dendrogram** will look:

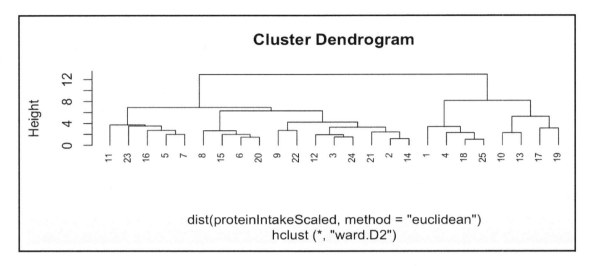

4. Additionally, we can use the `single` linkage method to perform hierarchical clustering and see how the generated dendrogram differs from the previous one:

```
> hc2 = hclust(dist(proteinIntakeScaled), method="single")
> plot(hc2, hang = -0.01, cex = 0.7)
```

Here is the dendrogram using the `single` linkage method:

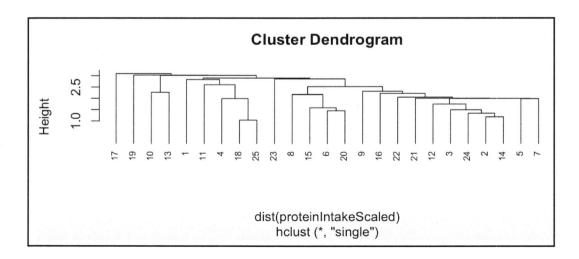

How it works...

The hierarchical clustering technique tries to build a hierarchy of clusters iteratively using either of the following two approaches:

- **Agglomerative hierarchical clustering**: This is a bottom-up approach. Each observation starts in its own cluster. We then compute the similarity (or the distance) between each cluster and then merge the two most similar ones at each iteration until there is only one cluster left.
- **Divisive hierarchical clustering**: This is a top-down approach. All observations start in one cluster, and we then split the cluster into the two least dissimilar clusters recursively until there is one cluster for each observation.

In this recipe, we perform hierarchical clustering on the European protein intake data. First, we load the data from `protein.csv` and then load it in the `proteinIntake` data frame. After scaling all the attributes (except the `Country` variable) to a normalized value, we perform hierarchical clustering using the `hclust` function and use the `euclidean` distance as distance metrics and `ward`'s minimum variance method to perform agglomerative clustering. You can also choose other distance metric such as `manhattan` or `hamming` in place of euclidean. Then, we use the `plot` function to plot the dendrogram of hierarchical clusters and specify `hang` to display labels at the bottom of the dendrogram, and also use the `cex` to shrink the label to 70 % of the normal size. Finally, we draw another dendrogram using single linkage to understand the effect of a different linkage strategy during cluster generation.

There's more...

So far in the recipe, we have used `hclust` to perform agglomerative hierarchical clustering, but if you would like to perform divisive hierarchical clustering, you can use the `diana` function from the `cluster` package.

1. Install and load the `cluster` package:

```
install.packages("cluster")
library(cluster)
```

2. Then, use `diana` to perform divisive hierarchical clustering:

```
dv = diana(proteinIntakeScaled, metric = "euclidean")
```

3. Lastly, plot a dendrogram and banner with the `plot` function:

```
plot(dv)
```

Here is the dendrogram using the `plot` function:

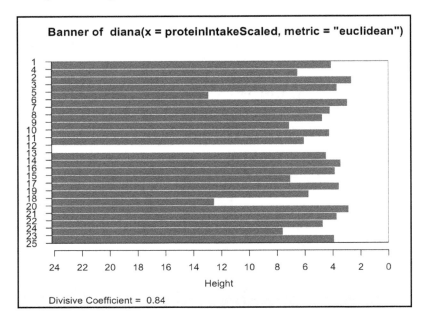

Cutting trees into clusters

Dendrograms only provide information about how data is grouped into various clusters. However, sometimes we need to determine how many clusters are within the dendrogram and cut the dendrogram at a certain tree height to separate the data into different groups. In this recipe, we illustrate how to separate the data into a given number of clusters using the `cutree` function.

Getting ready

To perform the `cutree` function, we need to have the previous recipe completed by generating the `hclust` object, `hc`.

How to do it...

Perform the following steps to cut the hierarchy of clusters into a given number of clusters:

1. First, categorize the data into four groups:

```
fit = cutree(hc, k = 4)
```

2. Then count the number of data within each cluster:

```
table(fit)
```

3. Finally, visualize how the data is clustered with the red rectangle border:

```
plot(hc)
rect.hclust(hc, k = 4 , border="red"
```

Here is the visualization with the red rectangle border:

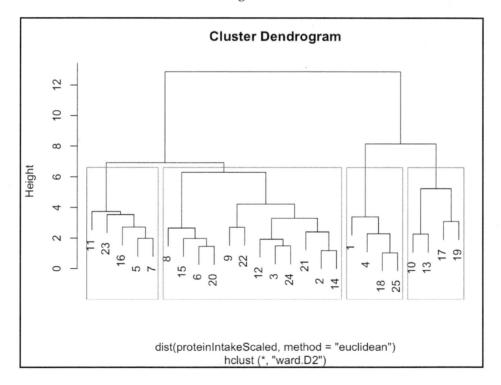

How it works...

We can determine the number of clusters from the dendrogram in the preceding figure. In the first step, we decided that there should be four clusters within the tree using the `k=4` attribute in the `cutree` function. Besides using the number of clusters to cut the tree, you can also specify the height as the cut tree parameter.

Next, we use the `table` function to count the number of data within each cluster and we find that most of the data is in `cluster 2`. Lastly, we draw red rectangles around the clusters to show how the data is categorized into the four clusters with the `rect.hclust` function.

Performing cluster analysis using partitioning clustering

K-means is a partitioning clustering technique that aims to partition n observations into k clusters in which each observation belongs to the cluster with the nearest mean, serving as a prototype of the cluster. The `K-means` method requires you to determine the number of clusters at the beginning, unlike hierarchical clustering. However, K-means clustering is much faster than hierarchical clustering as the construction of a hierarchical tree is very time-consuming.

Getting ready

In this recipe, we will continue to use the `protein.csv` dataset as the input data source to perform K-means clustering. Install and load the following package for cluster visualization:

```
if(!require(devtools)) install.packages("devtools")
devtools::install_github("kassambara/factoextra")
```

How to do it...

To perform cluster analysis using `kmeans` clustering, follow these steps:

1. First, load the `protein.csv` file and do some preprocessing to add row names as Country name and remove the `Country` variable before normalizing the data:

```
> proteinIntake <- read.csv("protein.csv")
> rownames(proteinIntake)=proteinIntake$Country
> proteinIntake$Country=NULL
> proteinIntakeScaled = as.data.frame(scale(proteinIntake))
```

2. Now use `kmeans` to cluster the scaled protein intake data:

```
> set.seed(22) ## To fix the random cluster initialization
> kmFit = kmeans(proteinIntakeScaled, 4)
> kmFit
```

Here is the K-means clustering indicative of the code:

```
K-means clustering with 4 clusters of sizes 4, 5, 10, 6

Cluster means:
      RedMeat  WhiteMeat       Eggs       Milk       Fish    Cereals
1  0.006572897 -0.2290150  0.1914789  1.34587480  1.1582546 -0.8722721
2  1.599006499  0.2988565  0.9341308  0.60911284 -0.1422470 -0.5948180
3 -0.677605893 -0.7595936 -0.8643394 -0.87567008 -0.1775148  0.9150064
4 -0.207544192  1.1696189  0.5344707  0.05460623 -0.3577726 -0.4478143
       Starch       Nuts     Fr.Veg
1   0.1676780 -0.9553392 -1.1148048
2   0.3451473 -0.3484949  0.1020010
3  -0.5299602  1.0565639  0.3292860
4   0.4838590 -0.8336346  0.1093924

Clustering vector:
        Albania         Austria         Belgium        Bulgaria
              3               4               2               3
  Czechoslovakia         Denmark       E Germany         Finland
              4               1               4               1
         France          Greece         Hungary         Ireland
              2               3               3               2
          Italy     Netherlands          Norway          Poland
              3               4               1               4
       Portugal         Romania           Spain          Sweden
              3               3               3               1
    Switzerland              UK            USSR       W Germany
              2               2               3               4
     Yugoslavia
              3

Within cluster sum of squares by cluster:
[1]  5.900318 12.069794 70.957748 12.692620
 (between_SS / total_SS =  53.0 %)

Available components:

[1] "cluster"      "centers"      "totss"        "withinss"
[5] "tot.withinss" "betweenss"    "size"         "iter"
[9] "ifault"
```

3. Let's compute the `mean` of each of the variables in the clusters:

```
aggregate(proteinIntakeScaled, by=list(cluster=kmFit$cluster),
mean)
```

cluster	RedMeat	WhiteMeat	Eggs	Milk	Fish	Cereals	Starch	Nuts	Fr.Veg
1	1	0.006572897	-0.2290150	0.1914789	1.34587480	1.1582546	-0.8722721	0.1676780	-0.9553392	-1.1148048
2	2	1.599006499	0.2988565	0.9341308	0.60911284	-0.1422470	-0.5948180	0.3451473	-0.3484949	0.1020010
3	3	-0.677605893	-0.7595936	-0.8643394	-0.87567008	-0.1775148	0.9150064	-0.5299602	1.0565639	0.3292860
4	4	-0.207544192	1.1696189	0.5344707	0.05460623	-0.3577726	-0.4478143	0.4838590	-0.8336346	0.1093924

4. Now let's visualize the result as a graph using a function from the `factoextra` package:

```
> library(factoextra)
> fviz_cluster(kmFit, data = proteinIntakeScaled)
```

The following image shows a visualization by means of a graph using the `factoextra` package:

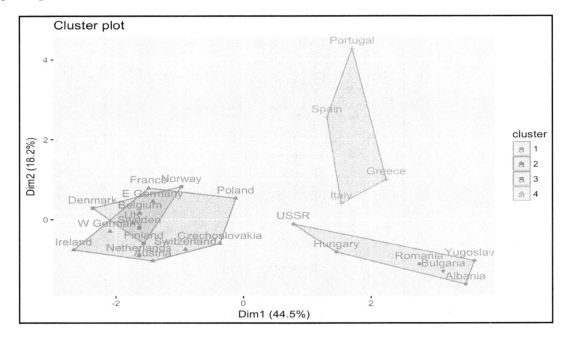

How it works...

In this recipe, we demonstrate how to use K-means clustering to cluster the protein intake data and we use `k=4` to set the number of clusters to be created as `4`. Then, the output of a fitted model shows the size of each cluster, the cluster means of four generated clusters, the cluster vectors with regard to each data point, the within-cluster sum of squares by the clusters, and other available components.

Before visualizing the clusters, we found that the data contains more than two variables (namely, **multidimension**) and we don't know what variables to choose for the *xy* coordinates of the scatter plot. A general solution in this scenario would be to perform PCA (discussed in the final recipe of this chapter) and plot data points according to the first two principal components, coordinates. The `fviz_cluster()` function in the `factoextra` package was used to visualize clusters, where observations are represented by points in the plot; using principal components when `ncol(proteinIntakeScaled) > 2`, an ellipse is drawn around each cluster.

There's more...

K-means clustering suffers when you have a large dataset (or lots of variables) and is also highly sensitive to outliers due to the use of the mean in the cluster centroid calculation. We will look at some other partitioning clustering algorithms to overcome the shortcomings of `kmeans` in the coming sections.

Image segmentation using mini-batch K-means

Mini-batch K-means is a variation of the classical K-means technique that we have used so far in this recipe. It is particularly useful to handle large datasets because, rather than using the whole data for each iteration (as K-means does), it uses mini-batches of random data samples to optimize the objective function. In this example, we will do image analysis and create a new image based on the clustered image features.

Getting ready

To perform the example using mini-batch `kmeans`, make sure you have downloaded the code for this chapter and `om.jpg` is in the working directory. Then install and load the following packages:

```
install.packages(c("OpenImageR","ClusterR"))
library(OpenImageR)
library(ClusterR)
```

How to do it...

1. First, read the image and then resize it to reduce the dimensions and then plot the image:

```
> img = readImage("bird.jpg")
> img_resize = resizeImage(img, 350, 350, method = 'bilinear')
> imageShow(img_resize)
```

Here is the sample image:

2. Now vectorize the image and check the image dimension:

```
> img_vector = apply(img_resize, 3, as.vector) # vectorize RGB
> dim(img_vector)
[1] 122500 3
```

3. Next, we will use `mini-batch-kmeans` clustering on the image vector and then predict the vectorized image using the cluster centroid. Finally, we will apply the prediction and cluster centroid to generate the following new segmented image, shown after the code:

```
> km_mb = MiniBatchKmeans(img_vector, clusters = 5, batch_size =
20, num_init = 5, max_iters = 100, init_fraction = 0.2, initializer
= 'kmeans++', early_stop_iter = 10, verbose = F)

> pr_mb = predict_MBatchKMeans(img_vector, km_mb$centroids)
> getcent_mb = km_mb$centroids
> new_im_mb = getcent_mb[pr_mb, ]

> dim(new_im_mb) = c(nrow(img_resize), ncol(img_resize), 3)
> imageShow(new_im_mb)
```

The following is the segmented image:

Partitioning around medoids

The **partitioning around medoids** (**PAM**) algorithm, which is also known as **k-medoids clustering,** is another partitioning clustering technique that is robust to outliers.

Getting ready

In this example, we will continue to use the `proteinIntakeScaled` data frame as the input data source to perform `pam` clustering. Load the following packages:

```
library(cluster)
library(factoextra)
```

How to do it...

Perform the following steps to partition using medoids approach:

1. First, compute `pam` with `k = 4` on the scaled data frame and check the `medoids`:

```
>pamFit <- pam(proteinIntakeScaled, 4)
> pamFit$medoids
```

The output of the preceding command:

	RedMeat	WhiteMeat	Eggs	Milk	Fish	Cereals	Starch	Nuts	Fr.Veg
Romania	-1.0839304	-0.43204252	-1.2848772	-0.8461152	-0.9651632	1.5810786	-0.7196689	1.1220326	-0.7406162
W Germany	0.4696633	1.24631815	1.0415022	0.2375653	-0.2598064	-1.2435778	0.5654541	-0.7916675	-0.1862628
Sweden	0.0215113	-0.02598752	0.5046454	1.0679178	0.9451781	-1.1615716	-0.3524909	-0.8420280	-1.1840990
Spain	-0.8150392	-1.21708219	0.1467409	-1.1979595	0.7982288	-0.2777275	0.8714358	1.4241958	1.6985391

2. Now plot the result:

```
> fviz_cluster(pamFit)
```

The following diagram gives a visualization of the results:

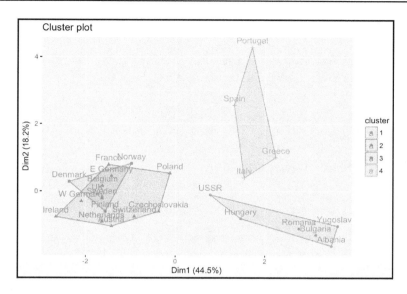

How it works...

The **PAM algorithm** is based on the search for k-medoids among the observations of the dataset. Unlike K-means clustering, where the calculation of cluster centroids could result in the centroid being outside the actual data points, `medoids` should always be represented from within the actual data points. After finding a set of k-medoids, k-clusters are constructed by assigning each observation to the nearest medoid.

In this example, we first apply the PAM algorithm using the `pam()` function from the `cluster` package on the scaled protein intake data frame. Next, we find the four cluster medoids (`Romania`, `W Germany`, `Sweden`, and `Spain`) from the fitted PAM model and finally visualize the cluster plot using `fviz_cluster()` from the `factoextra` package.

Clustering large application

Clustering large application (CLARA) is a partitioning technique that is well suited for larger datasets (more than several thousand observations) to reduce computing time and memory problems. CLARA draws multiple samples of the dataset, applies PAM to each sample to find the `medoids`, and then returns its best clustering as the output.

Getting ready

In this example, we will continue to use the `proteinIntakeScaled` data frame as the input data source to perform `clara` clustering.

How to do it...

1. First, load the following packages:

```
library(cluster)
library(factoextra)
```

2. Compute `clara` with `k = 4` and sample size (`samples=5`) on the scaled data frame and check the `medoids`:

```
> claraFit <- clara(proteinIntakeScaled, 4, samples=5)
> claraFit$medoids
```

Here is how the code will look with our computation:

	RedMeat	WhiteMeat	Eggs	Milk	Fish	Cereals	Starch	Nuts	Fr.Veg
Romania	-1.0839304	-0.43204252	-1.2848772	-0.8461152	-0.9651632	1.5810786	-0.7196689	1.1220326	-0.7406162
W Germany	0.4696633	1.24631815	1.0415022	0.2375653	-0.2598064	-1.2435778	0.5654541	-0.7916675	-0.1862628
Sweden	0.0215113	-0.02598752	0.5046454	1.0679178	0.9451781	-1.1615716	-0.3524909	-0.8420280	-1.1840990
Spain	-0.8150392	-1.21708219	0.1467409	-1.1979595	0.7982288	-0.2777275	0.8714358	1.4241958	1.6985391

3. Now visualize the result with a plot:

```
> fviz_cluster(claraFit)
```

The following figure shows the cluster plot of our computation:

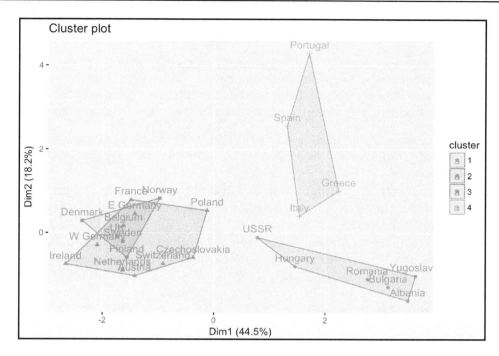

How it works...

Instead of taking the full dataset, the CLARA algorithm randomly chooses a small sample of the actual data as a representative of the data. Medoids are then calculated from this sample using PAM.

In this example, we first apply the CLARA algorithm using the `clara()` function from the `cluster` package on the scaled protein intake data frame. Then we check the four cluster medoids using the fitted CLARA model and finally visualize the cluster plot using `fviz_cluster()` from the `factoextra` package.

Performing cluster validation

Clustering is an unsupervised machine learning approach to partition a dataset into a set of groups or clusters, but sometimes it has a tendency to form clusters even though the data does not contain any clusters. Hence, it's essential to validate the quality of the clustering output. Broadly, clustering validation statistics can be categorized into four classes:

- **Relative clustering validation:** It evaluates the clustering structure by varying different parameter values for the same algorithm (namely, varying the **number of clusters k**).
- **Internal clustering validation:** It uses internal information such as (silhouette width, Dunn index) of the clustering process to evaluate the goodness of a clustering structure.
- **External cluster validation:** It uses ground truth information from the user about how the data should be grouped. As we know the *true* cluster number in advance, this approach is mainly used to select the right clustering algorithm for a specific dataset.
- **Clustering stability validation:** It is a special version of internal validation that evaluates the consistency of a clustering result by comparing it with the clusters obtained after each column is removed, one at a time.

Getting ready

In this recipe, we will use the R packages `cluster`, `fpc`, and `NbClust` to perform cluster validation on the `protein.csv` dataset.

Make sure you have downloaded the code for this chapter and the `protein.csv` file is in the R working directory. Then install and load the following packages:

```
> install.packages(c("factoextra","fpc","cluster","NbClust"))

> library(factoextra)
> library(cluster)
> library(fpc)
> library(NbClust)
```

How to do it...

Perform the following steps to perform cluster validation using the `proteinIntake` dataset:

1. First, load the `protein.csv` file and do some preprocessing to scale and alter the row names:

```
> proteinIntake <- read.csv("protein.csv")
> rownames(proteinIntake)=proteinIntake$Country
> proteinIntake$Country=NULL
> proteinIntakeScaled = as.data.frame(scale(proteinIntake))
```

2. Compute the optimal number of clusters and visualize the result:

```
> nb <- NbClust(proteinIntakeScaled, distance = "euclidean", min.nc
= 2,max.nc = 9, method = "ward.D2", index ="all")

> fviz_nbclust(nb) + theme_minimal()
```

The following figure gives us an idea of the computations:

```
Among all indices:
====================
* 2 proposed   0 as the best number of clusters
* 1 proposed   1 as the best number of clusters
* 6 proposed   2 as the best number of clusters
* 8 proposed   3 as the best number of clusters
* 2 proposed   5 as the best number of clusters
* 3 proposed   6 as the best number of clusters
* 1 proposed   7 as the best number of clusters
* 3 proposed   9 as the best number of clusters

Conclusion
=========================
* According to the majority rule, the best number of clusters is  3 .
```

The following image gives us a plot of the number of clusters versus frequency:

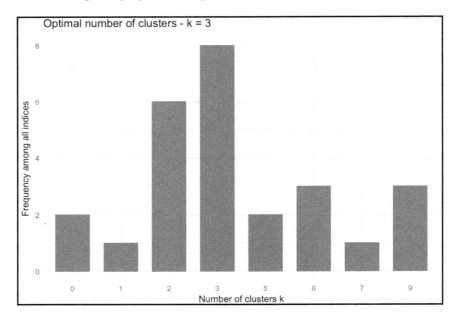

3. Next, let's compute the silhouette width for kmeans clustering and summarize the details:

```
> km.res = kmeans(proteinIntakeScaled, 3)
> sil.km <- silhouette(km.res$cluster,dist(proteinIntakeScaled))

# Summary of silhouette analysis
si.sum <- summary(sil.km )

# Average silhouette width of each cluster
si.sum$clus.avg.widths
        1         2         3
0.2063242 0.3062056 0.3811136

# The total average (mean of all individual silhouette widths)
si.sum$avg.width
[1] 0.3351694

# The size of each clusters
si.sum$clus.sizes
cl
 1 2 3
 4 6 15
```

4. Now visualize the silhouette plot for `kmeans`:

```
> fviz_silhouette(sil.km)
```

The following figure gives us the visualization of the silhouette for K-means:

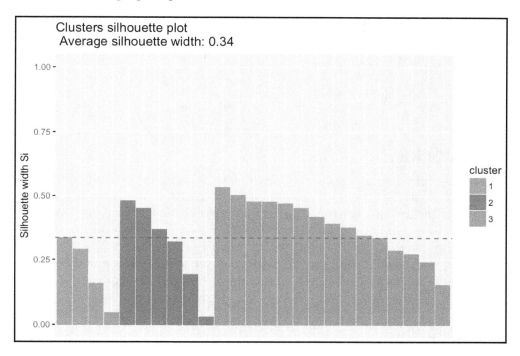

5. Next, we will calculate the within-cluster sum of squares, `dunns index` for `pam` clustering:

```
> dd <- dist(proteinIntakeScaled, method ="euclidean")
# Statistics for pam clustering
> install.packages("fpc")
> pam_stats <- cluster.stats(dd, pam.res$cluster)

# (pam) within clusters sum of squares
> pam_stats$within.cluster.ss
[1] 105.9863

# (pam) cluster average silhouette widths
> pam_stats$clus.avg.silwidths
        1         2         3
0.3062056 0.3811136 0.2063242
```

```
# (pam) cluster dunn  index
> pam_stats$dunn
[1] 0.5678917
```

6. Now we will compare the result of two clustering solutions:

    ```
    > res.stat <- cluster.stats(dd, km.res$cluster, pam.res$cluster)

    > res.stat$corrected.rand
    [1] 0.6837263

    > res.stat$vi
    [1] 0.3479491
    ```

How it works...

In this recipe, we demonstrate various state-of-the-art approaches to validate the generated clusters. First, we load the European protein intake dataset and normalize it. Then, we use the NbClust() function to identify the optimal number of clusters from the scaled protein data frame. The parameter of the NbClust function, max.nc, refers to the maximum number of clusters; min.nc refers to the minimum number of clusters. We then plot the optimal number of clusters for the protein intake dataset, which turns out to be k=3. More information about the parameters of the NbClust function can be found at https://www.rdocumentation.org/packages/NbClust/versions/3.0/topics/NbClust.

 You can try out different combination of parameters (distance, method, min.nc, and max.nc) from the NbClust function to achieve your optimal number of clusters and use this optimal number k information with other validation measures such as internal and external for further validation.

Next, we perform the internal clustering validation measure to identify the **compactness**, **connectedness**, and **separation** of the cluster partitions using silhouette width/coefficient and Dunn index. The main purpose of internal validation is to make sure that the average distance within clusters is as small as possible while the average distance between clusters is as large as possible.

More specifically, we apply **silhouette analysis** on `kmeans` cluster through the `summary` function; the `silhouette` plot displays a measure of how close each point in one cluster is to points in the neighboring clusters. It lies between -1 (poorly clustered observations) and 1 (well-clustered observations). It should be maximized.

Then, we calculate the Dunn index of the `pam` cluster. The Dunn index is the ratio between the smallest distance between observations not in the same cluster to the largest intra-cluster distance. It has a value between 0 and infinity and should be maximized.

Finally, we compare two cluster solutions, using the `cluster.stats()` function, and analyze the **corrected rand index** and **variation of information**. The corrected rand index is a measure to assess the similarity between two partitions, adjusted for chance, and has a range between -1 (no agreement) to 1 (perfect agreement). It should be **maximized**. The variation of information is a measure of the distance between two clusterings (partitions of elements) and should be **minimized**.

Performing Advance clustering

Both **hierarchical clustering** and **partitioning methods** (**K-means** and **PAM clustering**) are suitable to find spherical-shaped clusters or convex clusters and they use a heuristic approach to construct clusters, but they do not rely on a formal model and are severely affected by the presence of noise and outliers in the data. In this recipe, we will look at two advance clustering techniques to handle these shortcomings--**density-based clustering** and **model-based clustering**.

Density-based spatial clustering of applications with noise

Density-based spatial clustering of applications with noise (DBSCAN) is about classifying the data points in the dataset as core data points, border data points, and noise data points, with the use of density relations between points, such as directly density-reachable, density-reachable, and density-connected points. The major characteristics of DBSCAN are as follows:

- No need to specify the number of clusters to be generated
- Good at dealing with large datasets having noise
- Dealing with clusters of various shapes

In the following example, we will show you how to use DBSCAN to perform density-based clustering.

Getting ready

In this example, we will use the `multishapes` dataset from the `factoextra` package. Install and load the following packages if you haven't done so yet:

```
install.packages("fpc")
install.packages("factoextra")
```

How to do it...

To perform DBSCAN, follow the steps.

1. First, load the following packages:

    ```
    library(fpc)
    library(factoextra)
    ```

2. Let's now check and visualize the dataset:

    ```
    > data("multishapes", package = "factoextra")
    > dataPoints <- multishapes[, 1:2]
    > head(dataPoints)
           x          y
    1 -0.8037393 -0.8530526
    2  0.8528507  0.3676184
    3  0.9271795 -0.2749024
    4 -0.7526261 -0.5115652
    5  0.7068462  0.8106792
    6  1.0346985  0.3946550

    > plot(dataPoints)
    ```

    Here is an illustration of the dataset:

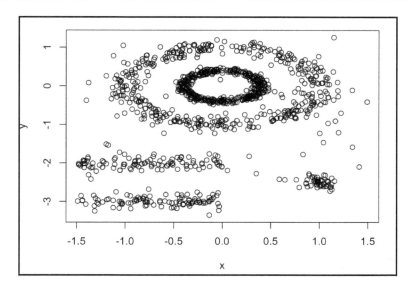

3. Now compute the dbscan, check its result, and plot the result:

```
> dsFit <- dbscan(dataPoints, eps = 0.15, MinPts = 5)
> print(dsFit)
```

This is the dbscan output:

```
dbscan Pts=1100 MinPts=5 eps=0.15
          0    1    2    3   4   5
border 31   24    1    5   7   1
seed    0  386  404   99  92  50
total  31  410  405  104  99  51
```

```
> fviz_cluster(dsFit, dataPoints, geom = "point")
```

The cluster plot is summed as follows:

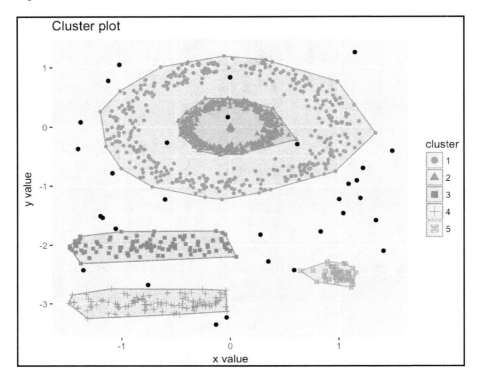

How it works...

Density-based clustering uses the idea of density reachability and density connectivity, which makes it very useful in discovering a cluster in nonlinear shapes. Density-based clustering takes two parameters into account--eps and MinPts. The eps parameter stands for the maximum radius of the neighborhood; MinPts denotes the minimum number of points within the eps neighborhood. Some of the common terminology associated with DBSCAN algorithm is as follows:

A point *A* in the dataset, with a neighbor count greater than or equal to MinPts, is referred to as a **core point**. The point *A* is called a **border point** if the number of its neighbors is less than MinPts, but belongs to the ∈-neighborhood of some core point *C*. Finally, if a point is neither a core nor border point, then it is called a **noise point** or an **outlier**.

- **Directly density-reachable**: If a point X is in the ϵ-neighborhood of Y and Y is a core point, then X is directly density reachable from point Y
- **Density-reachable**: If there are a set of core points leading from Y to X, then X is density reachable from Y
- **Density-connected**: If there exists a core point Z, such that both X and Y are density-reachable from Z, then two points X and Y are density-connected

In this example, we first load the multishapes dataset, then compute the DBSCAN using the `dbscan ()` function from the `fpc` package. The `print(dbscan())` function shows a statistic of the number of points belonging to the clusters that are seeds and border points and **cluster 0** represent outliers with black dots in the cluster plot. Finally, we can notice from the plot that DBSCAN automatically identifies the number of clusters in the dataset and is also capable of forming clusters of different shapes.

Model-based clustering with the EM algorithm

Model-based clustering techniques assume varieties of data models and apply an **expectation maximization** (**EM**) algorithm to obtain the most likely model, and then use that model to infer the most likely number of clusters. In this example, we will illustrate how to use the model-based technique to determine the most likely number of clusters.

Getting ready

In this example, we will continue to use the `multishapes` data frame as the input data source to perform model-based clustering.

How to do it...

Perform the following steps to perform model-based clustering:

1. First, install and load the following package:

```
install.packages("mclust")
library(mclust)
```

2. Then, perform model-based clustering on the multishapes dataset:

```
> mm = Mclust(dataPoints)
```

3. Now plot the result and press *1* to obtain the BIC against a number of components:

```
> plot(mm)
```

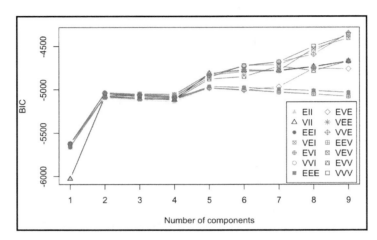

4. Next, press *2* to show the classification with respect to different combinations of features:

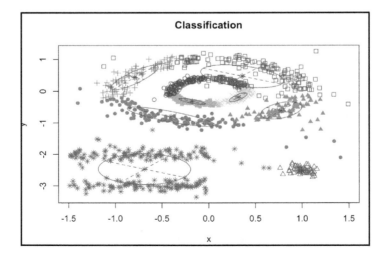

5. Then, press 3 to show the classification uncertainty with respect to different feature combinations:

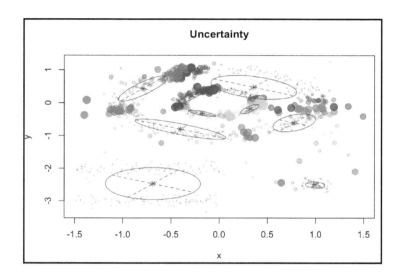

6. Next, press 4 to plot the density estimation:

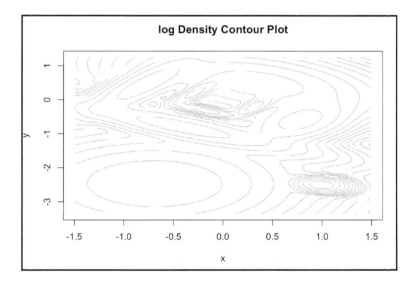

7. Finally, press *0* to exit the plotting menu. Lastly, use the `summary` function to obtain the most likely model and number of clusters:

```
> summary(mm)
```

```
------------------------------------------------------
Gaussian finite mixture model fitted by EM algorithm
------------------------------------------------------

Mclust VVE (ellipsoidal, equal orientation) model with 9 components:

 log.likelihood    n df       BIC       ICL
     -2015.328 1100 45 -4345.793 -4502.871

Clustering table:
   1   2   3   4   5   6   7   8   9
 125 215  83  90 103 101 118 215  50
```

How it works...

Model-based clustering tries to recover the distribution from the data assuming that the data is generated by an underlying probability distribution. One common model-based technique is using **finite mixture models**, which provide a modeling framework for the analysis of the probability distribution.

Model-based clustering process has several steps. First, the process selects the number and types of probability distribution component. Next, it fits a finite mixture model to calculate the posterior probabilities of a component membership. Lastly, it assigns the membership of each observation to the component with the maximum probability.

In this recipe, we first install and load the `Mclust` library and then fit the multishapes data into the model-based method using the `Mclust()` function. Next, we visualize the model based on clustering results with four different plots: **BIC**, **classification**, **uncertainty**, and **density plots**. Finally, we use the `summary` function to obtain the most likely model and the most possible number of clusters. For this example, the most possible number of clusters is **nine**, with a BIC value equal to *-4345.793*.

Reducing dimensionality with principal component analysis

The reduction of features can increase the efficiency of data processing and it is widely used in the fields of pattern recognition, text retrieval, and machine learning. PCA is the most widely used linear method in dealing with dimension reduction problems. It is useful when data contains lots of features and there is redundancy or correlation among these features

The `stats` package offers the `prcomp` function to perform PCA. This recipe shows you how to perform PCA using these capabilities.

Getting ready

If you have not already done so, download the data files for this chapter and ensure that the `BostonHousing.csv` file is in your R working directory. We want to predict MEDV based on the remaining 13 predictor variables. We will use PCA to reduce the dimensionality. Install and load the `corrplot` package to visualize correlation in the predictor variables:

```
install.packages("corrplot")
library(corrplot)
```

How to do it...

To reduce dimensionality with PCA, follow these steps:

1. Read the data:

   ```
   > bh <- read.csv("BostonHousing.csv")
   ```

2. View the correlation matrix to check whether some variables are highly correlated and whether PCA has the potential to yield some dimensionality reduction. As we are interested in reducing the dimensionality of the predictor variables, we leave out the outcome variable, MEDV:

   ```
   > corr <- cor(bh[,-14]) > corrplot(corr, method="color")
   ```

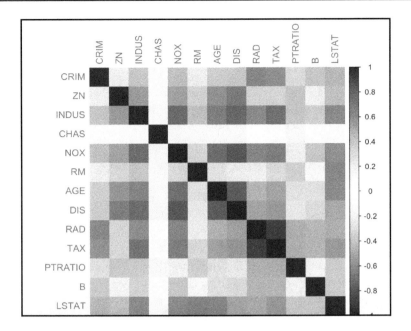

Positive correlations are displayed in blue and **negative correlations** in red. Color intensity and the size of the circle are proportional to the **correlation coefficients.** Ignoring the main diagonal, we see several correlations above 0.5 and a PCA can help reduce the dimensionality.

3. Build the PCA model:

```
> bh.pca <- prcomp(bh[,-14], scale = TRUE)
```

4. Examine the importance of the principal components:

```
summary(bh.pca)
```

```
Importance of components: PC1 PC2 PC3 PC4 Standard deviation 2.4752
1.1972 1.11473 0.92605 Proportion of Variance 0.4713 0.1103 0.09559
0.06597 Cumulative Proportion 0.4713 0.5816 0.67713 0.74310 PC5 PC6
PC7 PC8 Standard deviation 0.91368 0.81081 0.73168 0.62936
Proportion of Variance 0.06422 0.05057 0.04118 0.03047 Cumulative
Proportion 0.80732 0.85789 0.89907 0.92954 PC9 PC10 PC11 PC12
Standard deviation 0.5263 0.46930 0.43129 0.41146 Proportion of
Variance 0.0213 0.01694 0.01431 0.01302 Cumulative Proportion
0.9508 0.96778 0.98209 0.99511 PC13 Standard deviation 0.25201
Proportion of Variance 0.00489 Cumulative Proportion 1.00000
```

Note that from the reported cumulative proportions, the first seven principal components account for almost 90% of the variance.

5. Visualize the importance of the components through a scree plot or bar plot.

   For a `barplot`, use the following command:

   ```
   # barplot > plot(bh.pca)
   ```

   This is the resulting bar plot:

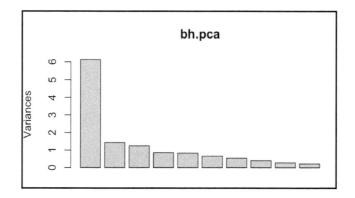

6. For a `scree plot`, the following command can be used:

   ```
   # scree plot > plot(bh.pca, type = "lines")
   ```

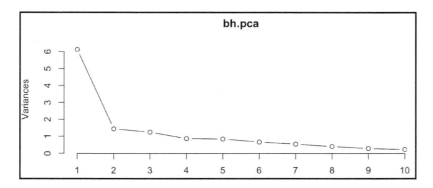

7. Create a `biplot` of the PCA results:

```
biplot(bh.pca, col = c("gray", "black"))
```

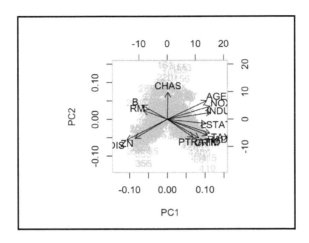

8. Use the x component of `bh.pca` to see the computed principal component values for each of these cases:

```
> head(bh.pca$x, 3)
```

9. See the rotations and standard deviations using the following command:

```
> bh.pca$rotation > bh.pca$sdev
```

How it works...

First, the data is read and then the correlation plot of the relevant dimensions is generated to examine whether there is scope for PCA to yield some dimensionality reduction. Next, the PCA model is generated using the `prcomp` function. We use `scale=TRUE` to generate the model based on the correlation matrix and not the covariance matrix. We then use the `summary` function to get different information on the model and then a `barplot` as well as a `scree plot` of the variances by PCA is generated using the `plot` function. Finally, we generate a biplot that uses the first two principal components as the main axes and shows how each variable loads on these two components. The top and right axes correspond to the scores of the data points on the two principal components.

6
Lessons from History - Time Series Analysis

In this chapter, we will cover the following recipes:

- Exploring finance datasets
- Creating and examining date objects
- Operating on date objects
- Performing preliminary analyses on time series data
- Using time series objects
- Decomposing time series
- Filtering time series data
- Smoothing and forecasting using the Holt-Winters method
- Building an automated ARIMA model

Introduction

Staying up to date with the pace of time is vital for the success of a business. A time series model is a collection of data items observed through repeated measurements over time. Most businesses or enterprises deal with time series data for analyzing website traffic, forecasting sales, studying inventory, and much more. In this recipe, we will look into time series analysis using various R packages.

Exploring finance datasets

In this recipe, we will explore the finance data downloaded from Yahoo! (`https://finance.yahoo.com/lookup`) using graphs or charts to understand the overall trends over the past few years. More specifically, we will explore the closing stock price of two organizations - **Amazon** and **Google** - for the last 10 years.

Getting ready

Download the code for this chapter, and make sure the files (`AMZN.csv` and `GOOG.csv`) are in the working directory of R.

How to do it...

Here is how we go about exploring the finance datasets:

1. Read the finance datasets `.csv` files. Also check the structure and first 5 rows of the datasets :

```
> AMZN=read.csv("AMZN.csv",stringsAsFactors = FALSE)
> str(AMZN)
'data.frame': 2518 obs. of 7 variables:
 $ Date : chr "2007-08-16" "2007-08-17" "2007-08-20" "2007-08-21"
...
 $ Open : num 72 74.5 75 74.2 78.2 ...
 $ High : num 73.2 75 75.3 77.8 79.5 ...
 $ Low : num 70.1 73.1 73.8 74.1 77.8 ...
 $ Close : num 72.8 75 74.7 77.5 78.5 ...
 $ Adj.Close: num 72.8 75 74.7 77.5 78.5 ...
 $ Volume : int 10787300 7240600 5916100 8429100 6848100 5665000
5665700 6951300 5767000 5076800 ...

> GOOG=read.csv("GOOG.csv",stringsAsFactors = FALSE)
> head(GOOG, 5)
```

The first 5 rows of the google finance dataset.

	Date	Open	High	Low	Close	Adj.Close	Volume
1	2007-08-16	245.0913	247.2881	239.3329	244.8423	244.8423	17355900
2	2007-08-17	247.7912	249.5646	244.9070	249.0864	249.0864	10999800
3	2007-08-20	250.2918	250.3417	247.0739	248.0303	248.0303	5414700
4	2007-08-21	248.5384	253.1312	247.9556	252.3591	252.3591	7248200
5	2007-08-22	254.0278	257.1611	253.6742	255.4176	255.4176	6529700

2. Convert the date column of each dataset:

```
> AMZN$Date=as.Date(AMZN$Date)
> GOOG$Date=as.Date(GOOG$Date)
```

3. Now let's plot the closing stock price with respect to date, for comparing both `Google` and `Amazon` side by side:

```
> library(ggplot2)

> ggplot(AMZN,aes(Date,Close)) +
  geom_line(aes(color="amazon")) +
  geom_line(data=GOOG,aes(color="google")) +
  labs(color="Legend") +
  scale_colour_manual("", breaks = c("amazon","google"),
                      values = c("blue", "brown")) +
  ggtitle("Closing Stock Prices: Amazon and Google ") +
  theme(plot.title = element_text(lineheight=.7, face="bold"))
```

The following is the comparison of closing stocks of **Amazon** and **Google**:

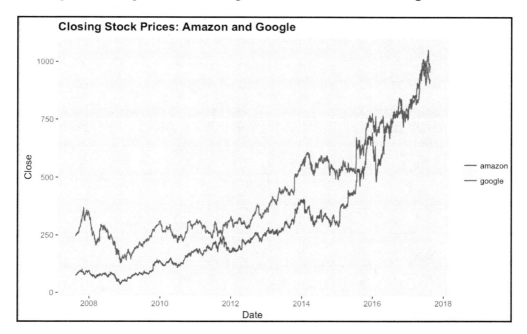

How it works...

Step 1 shows how to load the stock price data of both Google and Amazon.

Step 2 shows how to convert the date column into proper R date format using the `as.date()` function.

Step 3 shows how to visualize the stock price of both these organizations for the last 10 years (from 2007 to 2017). We can notice from the graph that Google has higher closing stock price from mid-2007 to early 2016 compared to Amazon, but from mid-2016, both these organizations have almost similar stock prices till now.

There's more...

R provides an easy way of pulling near-real-time stock data directly through API using the `quantmod` package:

```
install.packages("quantmod")
library("quantmod")
```

With the `quantmod` package, it is really easy to pull historical data from Yahoo or Google finance with a single line of code:

```
getSymbols('AMZN')
```

Besides pulling historical stock data, `quantmod` also provides various visualization functions for exploring the data. The following command creates a bar chart and chart series for the Amazon stocks:

```
barChart(AMZN)
```

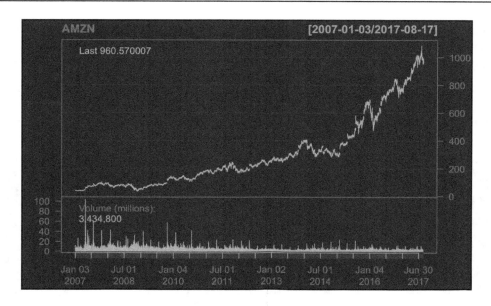

```
chartSeries(AMZN, TA="NULL")
```

Here, TA="Null" indicates not to use any technical indicator.

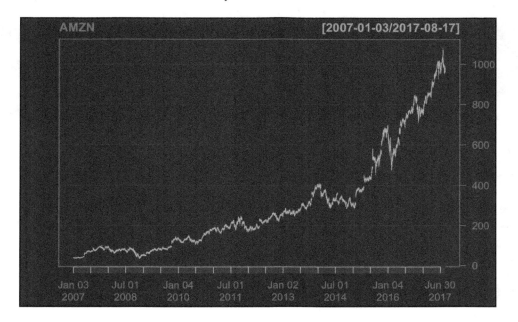

This package also provides **moving average convergence divergence** (**MACD**) with the chart series. In a moving average crossover strategy, a slow-moving average and a fast moving-average are computed separately, and the difference between the two averages is called the MACD line. The following command plots the chart for the closing price of AMZN along with the MACD parameters:

```
data=AMZN[,4]
chartSeries(data, TA='addMACD()')
```

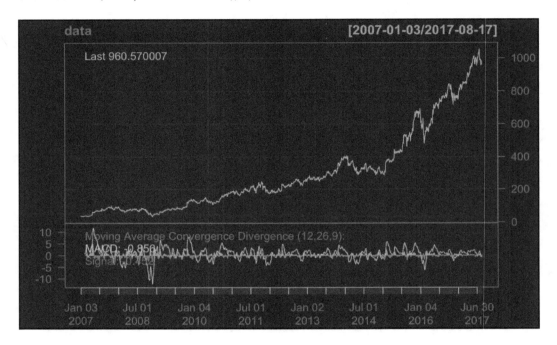

Creating and examining date objects

The base R package provides date functionality. This grab-bag recipe shows you several date-related operations in R. R internally represents dates as the number of days from January 1, 1970.

Getting ready

In this recipe, we will only be using features from the base package and not from any external data. Therefore, you do not need to perform any preparatory steps.

How to do it...

Internally, R represents dates as the number of days from January 1, 1970:

1. Get today's date:

   ```
   > Sys.Date()
   ```

2. Create a date object from a string:

   ```
   > # Supply year as two digits
   > # Note correspondence between separators in the date string and
   the format string
   > as.Date("1/1/80", format = "%m/%d/%y")
   [1] "1980-01-01"

   > # Supply year as 4 digits
   > # Note uppercase Y below instead of lowercase y as above
   > as.Date("1/1/1980", format = "%m/%d/%Y")
   [1] "1980-01-01"

   > # If you omit format string, you must give date as "yyyy/mm/dd"
   or as "yyyy-mm-dd"
   > as.Date("1970/1/1")
   [1] "1970-01-01"

   > as.Date("70/1/1")
   [1] "0070-01-01"
   ```

3. Use other options for separators (this example uses hyphens) in the format string, and also see the underlying numeric value:

   ```
   > dt <- as.Date("1-1-70", format = "%m-%d-%y")
   > as.numeric(dt)
   [1] 0
   ```

4. Explore other format string options:

   ```
   > as.Date("Jan 15, 2015", format = "%b %d, %Y")
   [1] "2015-01-15"

   > as.Date("January 15, 15", format = "%B %d, %y")
   [1] "2015-01-15"
   ```

5. Create dates from numbers by typecasting:

   ```
   > dt <- 1000
   ```

```
> class(dt) <- "Date"
> dt                      # 1000 days from 1/1/70
[1] "1972-09-27"

> dt <- -1000
> class(dt) <- "Date"
> dt                      # 1000 days before 1/1/70
[1] "1967-04-07"
```

6. Create dates directly from numbers by setting the origin date:

```
> as.Date(1000, origin = as.Date("1980-03-31"))
[1] "1982-12-26"

> as.Date(-1000, origin = as.Date("1980-03-31"))
[1] "1977-07-05"
```

7. Examine the date components:

```
> dt <- as.Date(1000, origin = as.Date("1980-03-31/"))
> dt
[1] "1982-12-26"

> # Get year as four digits
> format(dt, "%Y")
[1] "1982"

> # Get the year as a number rather than as character string
> as.numeric(format(dt, "%Y"))
[1] 1982

> # Get year as two digits
> format(dt, "%y")
[1] "82"

> # Get month
> format(dt, "%m")
[1] "12"

> as.numeric(format(dt, "%m"))
[1] 12

> # Get month as string
> format(dt, "%b")
[1] "Dec"

> format(dt, "%B")
[1] "December"
```

```
> months(dt)
[1] "December"

> weekdays(dt)
[1] "Sunday"

> quarters(dt)
[1] "Q4"

> julian(dt)
[1] 4742
attr(,"origin")
[1] "1970-01-01"

> julian(dt, origin = as.Date("1980-03-31/"))
[1] 1000
attr(,"origin")
[1] "1980-03-31"
```

How it works...

Step 1 shows how to get the system date.

Steps 2 through 4 show how to create dates from strings. You can see that by specifying the format string appropriately, we can read dates from almost any string representation. We can use any separator as long as we mimic them in the format string. The following table summarizes the formatting options for the components of the date:

Format specifier	Description
%d	Day of month as a number, for example, 15
%m	Month as a number, for example, 10
%b	Abbreviated string representation of month, for example, Jan
%B	Complete string representation of month, for example, January
%y	Year as two digits, for example, 87
%Y	Year as four digits, for example, 2001

Step 5 shows how an integer can be typecast as a date.

Internally, R represents dates as Unix time or epoch time which is defined as the number of seconds that have elapsed since 00:00:00 Coordinated Universal Time (UTC), Thursday, 1 January 1970, hence, zero corresponds to January 1, 1970. We can convert positive and negative numbers to dates. Negative numbers give dates before January 1, 1970.

Step 6 shows how to find the date with a specific offset from a given date (origin).

Step 7 shows how to examine the individual components of a date object using the `format` function along with the appropriate format specification (refer to the preceding table) for the desired component. Step 6 also shows the use of the `months`, `weekdays`, and `julian` functions for getting the month, day of the week, and the Julian date corresponding to a date. If we omit the origin in the `julian` function, R assumes January 1, 1970 as the origin.

Operating on date objects

R supports many useful manipulations with date objects, such as date addition and subtraction, and the creation of date sequences. This recipe shows many of these operations in action. For details on creating and examining date objects, refer to the *Creating and examining date objects*, recipe earlier in this chapter.

Getting ready

The `base` R package provides date functionality, and you do not need any preparatory steps.

How to do it...

1. Perform addition and subtraction of days from date objects:

```
> dt <- as.Date("1/1/2001", format = "%m/%d/%Y")
> dt
[1] "2001-01-01"

> dt + 100                    # Date 100 days from dt
[1] "2001-04-11"

> dt + 31
[1] "2001-02-01"
```

2. Subtract date objects to find the number of days between two dates:

```
> dt1 <- as.Date("1/1/2001", format = "%m/%d/%Y")
> dt2 <- as.Date("2/1/2001", format = "%m/%d/%Y")
> dt1-dt1

Time difference of 0 days
> dt2-dt1

Time difference of 31 days
> dt1-dt2

Time difference of -31 days
> as.numeric(dt2-dt1)
[1] 31
```

3. Compare the date objects:

```
> dt2 > dt1
[1] TRUE

> dt2 == dt1
[1] FALSE
```

4. Create date sequences:

```
> d1 <- as.Date("1980/1/1")
> d2 <- as.Date("1982/1/1")
> # Specify start date, end date and interval
> seq(d1, d2, "month")
 [1] "1980-01-01" "1980-02-01" "1980-03-01" "1980-04-01"
 [5] "1980-05-01" "1980-06-01" "1980-07-01" "1980-08-01"
 [9] "1980-09-01" "1980-10-01" "1980-11-01" "1980-12-01"
[13] "1981-01-01" "1981-02-01" "1981-03-01" "1981-04-01"
[17] "1981-05-01" "1981-06-01" "1981-07-01" "1981-08-01"
[21] "1981-09-01" "1981-10-01" "1981-11-01" "1981-12-01"
[25] "1982-01-01"

> d3 <- as.Date("1980/1/5")
> seq(d1, d3, "day")
[1] "1980-01-01" "1980-01-02" "1980-01-03" "1980-01-04"
[5] "1980-01-05"

> # more interval options
> seq(d1, d2, "2 months")
 [1] "1980-01-01" "1980-03-01" "1980-05-01" "1980-07-01"
 [5] "1980-09-01" "1980-11-01" "1981-01-01" "1981-03-01"
 [9] "1981-05-01" "1981-07-01" "1981-09-01" "1981-11-01"
```

```
[13] "1982-01-01"

> # Specify start date, interval and sequence length
> seq(from = d1, by = "4 months", length.out = 4 )
[1] "1980-01-01" "1980-05-01" "1980-09-01" "1981-01-01"
```

5. Find a future or past date from a given date, based on an interval:

```
> seq(from = d1, by = "3 weeks", length.out = 2)[2]
[1] "1980-01-22"
```

How it works...

Step 1 shows how you can add and subtract days from a date to get the resulting date.

Step 2 shows how you can find the number of days between two dates through subtraction. The result is a `difftime` object that you can convert into a number if needed.

Step 3 shows the logical comparison of dates.

Step 4 shows two different ways to create sequences of dates. In one, you specify the `from` date, the `to` date, and the fixed interval `by` between the sequence elements as a string. In the other, you specify the `from` date, the interval, and the number of sequence elements you want. If you're using the latter approach, you have to name the arguments.

Step 5 shows how you can create sequences by specifying the intervals more flexibly.

See also

- The *Creating and examining date objects* recipe in this chapter

Performing preliminary analyses on time series data

Before creating proper time series objects, we may want to do some preliminary analyses. This recipe shows you how.

Getting ready

The base R package provides all the necessary functionality. If you have not already downloaded the data files for this chapter, please do it now, and ensure that they are located in your R working directory.

How to do it...

1. Read the file. We will use a data file that has the share prices of Walmart (downloaded from Yahoo Finance) between March 11, 1999 and January 15, 2015:

   ```
   > wm <- read.csv("walmart.csv")
   ```

2. View the data as a line chart:

   ```
   > plot(wm$Adj.Close, type = "l")
   ```

   The data can be viewed as a line chart as follows:

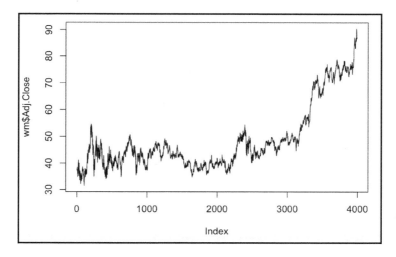

3. Compute and plot daily price movements:

   ```
   > d <- diff(wm$Adj.Close)
   > plot(d, type = "l")
   ```

The plotted daily price movements appear as follows:

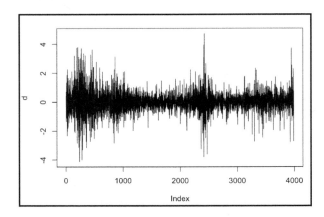

4. Generate a histogram of the daily price changes along with a density plot:

```
> hist(d, prob = TRUE, ylim = c(0,0.8), main = "Walmart stock", col
= "blue")
> lines(density(d), lwd = 3)
```

The following histogram shows the daily price change:

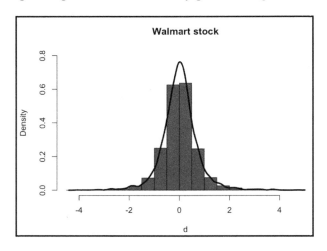

5. Compute one-period returns:

```
> wmm <- read.csv("walmart-monthly.csv")
> wmm.ts <- ts(wmm$Adj.Close)
> d <- diff(wmm.ts)
```

```
> wmm.return <- d/lag(wmm.ts, k=-1)
> hist(wmm.return, prob = TRUE, col = "blue")
```

The following histogram shows the output of the preceding command:

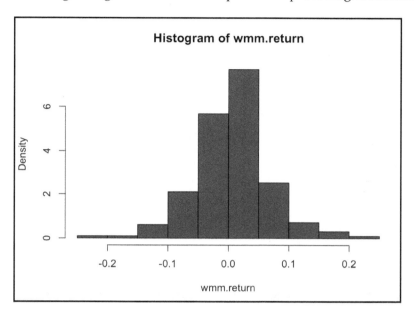

How it works...

Step 1 reads the data, and step 2 plots it as a line chart.

Step 3 uses the `diff` function to generate single-period differences. It then uses the `plot` function to plot the differences. By default, the `diff` function computes single-period differences. You can use the `lag` argument to compute differences for greater lags. For example, the following calculates two-period lagged differences:

```
> diff(wmm$Adj.Close, lag = 2)
```

Step 4 generates a histogram of one-period price changes. It uses `prob=TRUE` to generate a histogram based on proportions and then adds on a density plot as well to give a higher-granularity view of the shape of the distribution.

Step 5 computes one-period returns for the stock by dividing the one-period differences by the stock value at the first of the two periods that the difference is based on. It then generates a histogram of the returns.

See also

- The *Using time series objects* recipe in this chapter

Using time series objects

In this recipe, we look at various features to create and plot time series objects. We will consider data with both a single and multiple time series.

Getting ready

If you have not already downloaded the data files for this chapter, do it now, and ensure that the files are in your R working directory.

How to do it...

1. Read the data. The file has 100 rows and a single column named `sales`:

```
> s <- read.csv("ts-example.csv")
```

2. Convert the data to a simplistic time series object without any explicit notion of time:

```
> s.ts <- ts(s)
> class(s.ts)
[1] "ts"
```

3. Plot the time series:

```
> plot(s.ts)
```

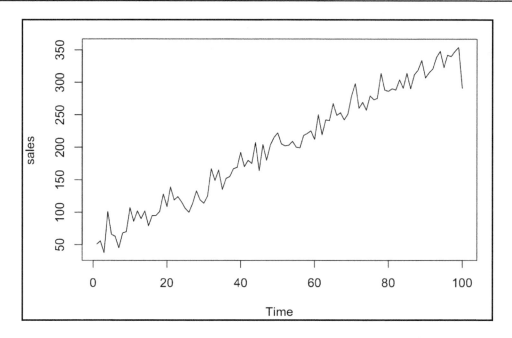

4. Create a proper time series object with proper time points:

```
> s.ts.a <- ts(s, start = 2002)
> s.ts.a
Time Series:
Start = 2002
End = 2101
Frequency = 1
        sales
  [1,]     51
  [2,]     56
  [3,]     37
  [4,]    101
  [5,]     66
  (output truncated)
> plot(s.ts.a)
> # results show that R treated this as an annual
> # time series with 2002 as the starting year
```

The result of the preceding commands is seen in the following graph:

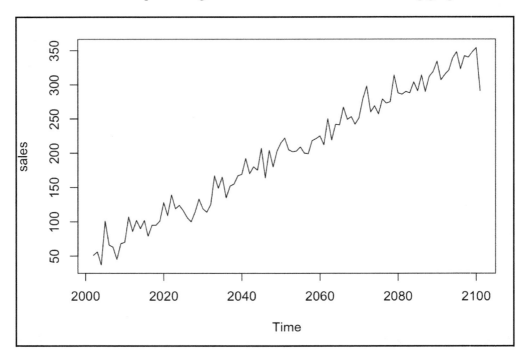

To create a monthly time series, run the following command:

```
> # Create a monthly time series
> s.ts.m <- ts(s, start = c(2002,1), frequency = 12)
> s.ts.m
```

```
      Jan Feb Mar Apr May Jun Jul Aug Sep Oct Nov Dec
2002   51  56  37 101  66  63  45  68  70 107  86 102
2003   90 102  79  95  95 101 128 109 139 119 124 116
2004  106 100 114 133 119 114 125 167 149 165 135 152
2005  155 167 169 192 170 180 175 207 164 204 180 203
2006  215 222 205 202 203 209 200 199 218 221 225 212
2007  250 219 242 241 267 249 253 242 251 279 298 260
2008  269 257 279 273 275 314 288 286 290 288 304 291
2009  314 290 312 319 334 307 315 321 339 348 323 342
2010  340 348 354 291
> plot(s.ts.m)  # note x axis on plot
```

The following plot can be seen as a result of the preceding commands:

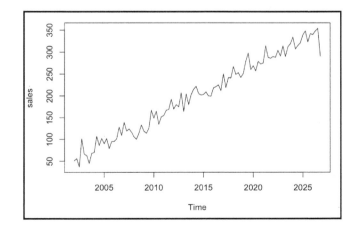

```
# Specify frequency = 4 for quarterly data
> s.ts.q <- ts(s, start = 2002, frequency = 4)
> s.ts.q

     Qtr1 Qtr2 Qtr3 Qtr4
2002   51   56   37  101
2003   66   63   45   68
2004   70  107   86  102
2005   90  102   79   95
2006   95  101  128  109
(output truncated)
> plot(s.ts.q)
```

5. Query the time series objects (we use the `s.ts.m` object we created in the previous step):

```
> # When does the series start?
> start(s.ts.m)
[1] 2002    1
> # When does it end?
> end(s.ts.m)
[1] 2010    4
> # What is the frequency?
> frequency(s.ts.m)
[1] 12
```

6. Create a time series object with multiple time series. This data file contains US monthly consumer prices for white flour and unleaded gas for the years 1980 through 2014 (downloaded from the website of the US Bureau of Labor Statistics):

```
> prices <- read.csv("prices.csv")
> prices.ts <- ts(prices, start=c(1980,1), frequency = 12)
```

7. Plot a time series object with multiple time series:

```
> plot(prices.ts)
```

The plot in two separate panels appears as follows:

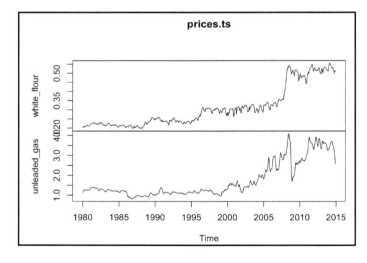

```
> # Plot both series in one panel with suitable legend
> plot(prices.ts, plot.type = "single", col = 1:2)
> legend("topleft", colnames(prices.ts), col = 1:2, lty = 1)
```

The two series plotted in one panel appear as follows:

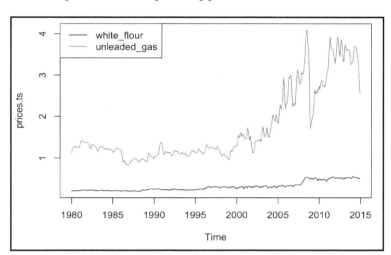

How it works...

Step 1 reads the data.

Step 2 uses the `ts` function to generate a time series object based on the raw data.

Step 3 uses the `plot` function to generate a line plot of the time series. We see that the time axis does not provide much information. Time series objects can represent time in more friendly terms.

Step 4 shows how to create time series objects with a better notion of time. It shows how we can treat a data series as an annual, monthly, or quarterly time series. The `start` and `frequency` parameters help us control these data series.

Although the time series we provide is just a list of sequential values, in reality, our data can have an implicit notion of time attached to it. For example, the data can be annual numbers, monthly numbers, or quarterly ones (or something else, such as 10-second observations of something). Given just the raw numbers (as in our data file, `ts-example.csv`), the `ts` function cannot figure out the time aspect and, by default, assumes no secondary time interval at all.

We can use the `frequency` parameter to tell `ts` how to interpret the time aspect of the data. The `frequency` parameter controls how many secondary time intervals there are in one major time interval. If we do not explicitly specify it, by default, `frequency` takes on a value of 1. Thus, the following code treats the data as an annual sequence, starting in 2002:

```
> s.ts.a <- ts(s, start = 2002)
```

The following code, on the other hand, treats the data as a monthly time series, starting in January 2002. If we specify the `start` parameter as a number, then R treats it as starting at the first sub period, if any, of the specified `start` period. When we specify `frequency` as different from 1, then the `start` parameter can be a vector such as `c(2002,1)` to specify the series, the major period, and the sub period where the series starts. `c(2002,1)` represents January 2002:

```
> s.ts.m <- ts(s, start = c(2002,1), frequency = 12)
```

Similarly, the following code treats the data as a quarterly sequence, starting in the first quarter of 2002:

```
> s.ts.q <- ts(s, start = 2002, frequency = 4)
```

The `frequency` values of 12 and 4 have a special meaning--they represent monthly and quarterly time sequences.

We can supply `start` and `end`, just one of them, or none. If we do not specify either, then R treats `start` as 1 and figures out `end` based on the number of data points. If we supply one, then R figures out the other based on the number of data points.

While `start` and `end` do not play a role in computations, `frequency` plays a big role in determining seasonality, which captures periodic fluctuations.

If we have some other specialized time series, we can specify the `frequency` parameter appropriately. Here are two examples:

- With measurements taken every 10 minutes and seasonality pegged to the hour, we should specify `frequency` as 6
- With measurements taken every 10 minutes and seasonality pegged to the day, we use `frequency = 24*6` (6 measurements per hour times 24 hours per day)

Step 5 shows the use of the `start`, `end`, and `frequency` functions to query time series objects.

Steps 6 and 7 show that R can handle data files that contain multiple time series.

See also

- The *Performing preliminary analyses on time series objects* recipe in this chapter

Decomposing time series

The `stats` package provides many functions to process the time series. This recipe covers the use of the `decompose` and `stl` functions to extract the seasonal, trend, and random components of time series.

Getting ready

If you have not already downloaded the data files for this chapter, do it now, and ensure that the files are in your R working directory.

How to do it...

The following steps decompose the time series:

1. Read the data. The file has the Bureau of Labor Statistics monthly price data for unleaded gas and white flour for 1980 through 2014:

   ```
   > prices <- read.csv("prices.csv")
   ```

2. Create and plot the time series of gas prices:

   ```
   prices.ts = ts(prices, start = c(1980,1), frequency = 12)
   > plot(prices.ts)
   ```

The following is the plot of time versus prices as per our command:

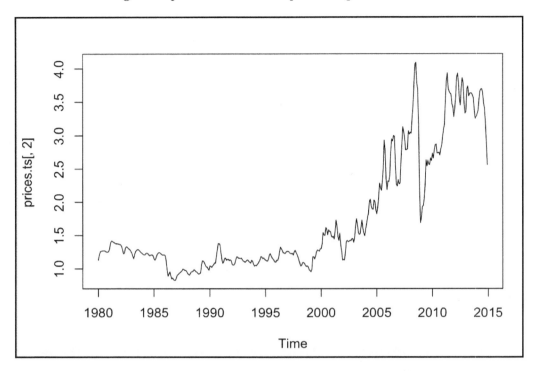

3. The preceding plot shows seasonality in gas prices. The amplitude of fluctuations seems to increase with time, and hence this looks like a multiplicative time series. Thus, we will use the log of the prices to make it additive. Use the `stl` function to perform a Loess decomposition of the gas prices:

    ```
    > prices.stl <- stl(log(prices.ts[,1]), s.window ="period")
    ```

4. Plot the results of `stl`:

    ```
    > plot(prices.stl)
    ```

The following plot is the result of the preceding command:

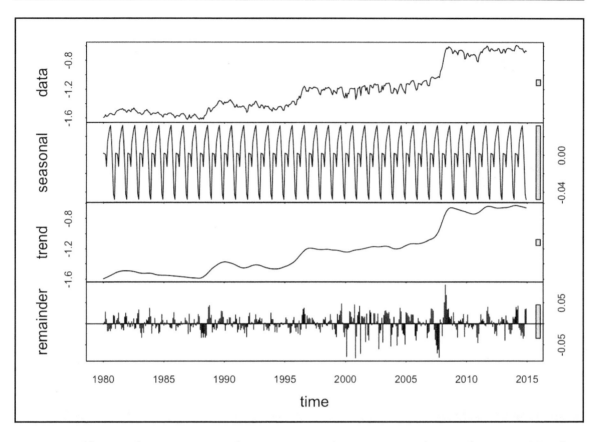

5. Alternately, you can use the `decompose` function to perform a decomposition by moving averages:

```
> prices.dec <- decompose(log(prices.ts[,2]))
> plot(prices.dec)
```

The following graph shows the output of the preceding command:

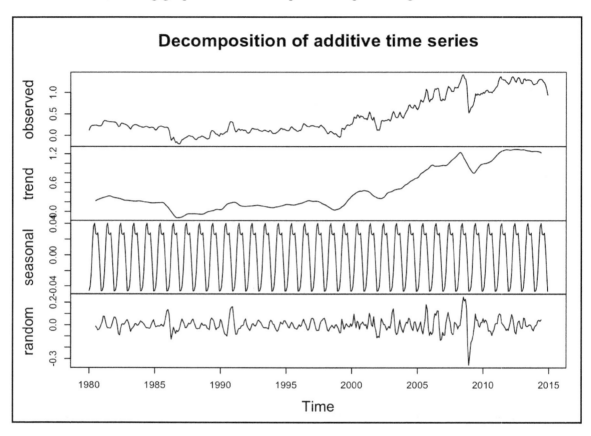

6. Adjust the gas prices for seasonality, and plot it:

```
gas.seasonally.adjusted <- prices.ts[,2] -     prices.dec$seasonal
> plot(gas.seasonally.adjusted)
```

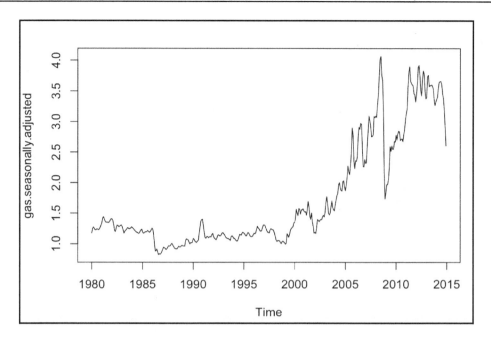

How it works...

Step 1 reads the data, and Step 2 creates and plots the time series. For more details, refer to the *Using time series objects* recipe earlier in this chapter.

Step 3 shows the use of the `stl` function to decompose an additive time series. Since our earlier plot indicated that the amplitude of the fluctuations increased with time, thereby suggesting a multiplicative time series, we applied the `log` function to convert it into an additive time series and then decomposed it.

Step 4 uses the `plot` function to plot the results.

Step 5 uses the `decompose` function to perform a decomposition through moving averages and then plots it.

Step 6 adjusts gas prices for seasonality by subtracting the seasonal component from the original time series of the gas prices and then plots the resulting time series.

See also

- The *Using time series objects* recipe in this chapter
- The *Filtering time series data* recipe in this chapter
- The *Smoothing and forecasting using the Holt-Winters method* recipe in this chapter

Filtering time series data

This recipe shows how we can use the `filter` function from the `stats` package to compute moving averages.

Getting ready

If you have not already done so, download the data files for this chapter, and ensure that they are available in your R working directory.

How to do it...

To filter time series data, follow these steps:

1. Read the data. The file has fictitious weekly sales data for some product:

   ```
   > s <- read.csv("ts-example.csv")
   ```

2. Create the filtering vector. We assume a seven-period filter:

   ```
   > n <- 7
   > wts <- rep(1/n, n)
   ```

3. Compute the symmetrically filtered values (three past values, one current value, and three future values) and one-sided values (one current and six past values):

   ```
   > s.filter1 <- filter(s$sales, filter = wts, sides = 2)
   > s.filter2 <- filter(s$sales, filter = wts, sides = 1)
   ```

4. Plot the filtered values:

   ```
   > plot(s$sales, type = "l")
   > lines(s.filter1, col = "blue", lwd = 3)
   > lines(s.filter2, col = "red", lwd = 3)
   ```

The plotted filtered values appear as follows:

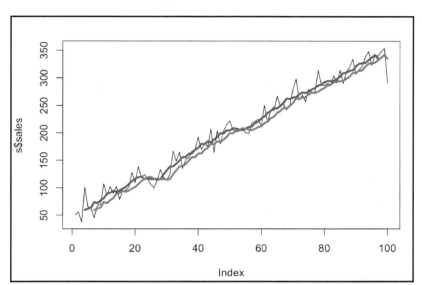

How it works...

Step 1 reads the data.

Step 2 creates the filtering weights. We used a window of seven periods. This means that the weighted average of the current value and six others will comprise the filtered value at the current position.

Step 3 computes the two-sided filter (the weighted average of the current value and three prior and three succeeding values) and a one-sided filter based on the current value and six prior ones.

Step 4 plots the original data and the symmetric and one-sided filters. We can see that the two-sided filter tracks the changes earlier.

See also

- The *Using time series objects* recipe in this chapter
- The *Decomposing time series* recipe in this chapter
- The *Smoothing and forecasting using the Holt-Winters method* recipe in this chapter

Smoothing and forecasting using the Holt-Winters method

The `stats` package contains functionality for applying the `HoltWinters` method for exponential smoothing in the presence of trends and seasonality, and the `forecast` package extends this to forecasting. This recipe addresses these topics.

Getting ready

If you have not already downloaded the files for this chapter, do it now, and place them in your R working directory. Install and load the `forecast` package.

How to do it...

To apply the `HoltWinters` method for exponential smoothing and forecasting, follow these steps:

1. Read the data. The file has monthly stock prices from Yahoo! Finance for Infosys between March 1999 and January 2015:

    ```
    > infy <- read.csv("infy-monthly.csv")
    ```

2. Create the time series object:

    ```
    > infy.ts <- ts(infy$Adj.Close, start = c(1999,3),     frequency =
    12)
    ```

3. Perform Holt-Winters exponential smoothing:

    ```
    > infy.hw <- HoltWinters(infy.ts)
    ```

4. Plot the results:

```
> plot(infy.hw, col = "blue", col.predicted = "red")
```

The plotted result can be seen as follows:

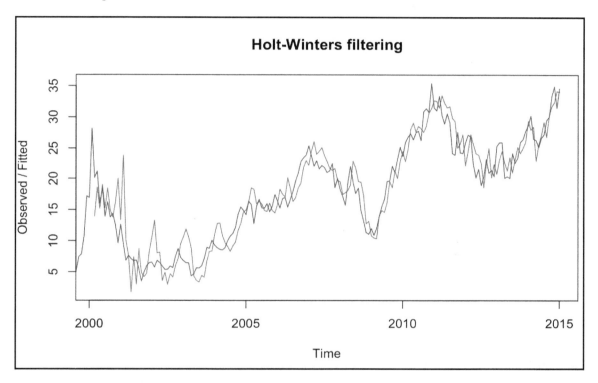

5. Examine the results:

```
> # See the squared errors
> infy.hw$SSE
[1] 1446.232
> # The alpha beta and gamma used for filtering
> infy.hw$alpha
    alpha
0.5658932
> infy.hw$beta
       beta
0.009999868
> infy.hw$gamma
gamma
    1
```

```
> # the fitted values
> head(infy.hw$fitted)
         xhat     level     trend        season
[1,] 13.91267 11.00710 0.5904618   2.31510417
[2,] 18.56803 15.11025 0.6255882   2.83218750
[3,] 15.17744 17.20828 0.6403124  -2.67114583
[4,] 19.01611 18.31973 0.6450237   0.05135417
[5,] 15.23710 18.66703 0.6420466  -4.07197917
[6,] 18.45236 18.53545 0.6343104  -0.71739583
```

6. Generate and plot forecasts with the Holt-Winters model:

```
> library(forecast)
> infy.forecast <- forecast(infy.hw, h=20)
> plot(infy.forecast)
```

The following is the resulting forecasted plot:

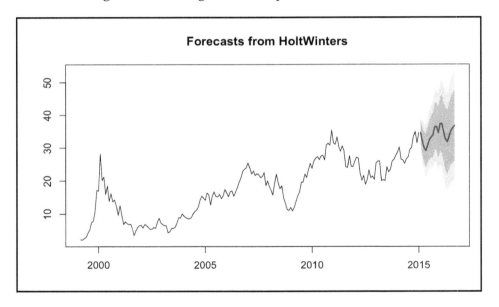

How it works...

Step 1 reads the data, and in step 2, the time series object `ts` is created. For more details, refer to *Using time series objects* recipe earlier in this chapter.

In step 3, the `HoltWinters` function is used to smooth the data.

In step 4, the resulting `HoltWinters` object is plotted. It shows the original time series as well as the smoothed values.

Step 5 shows the functions available to extract information from the Holt-Winters model object.

In step 6, the `predict.HoltWinters` function is used to predict future values. The colored bands show the 85% and 95% confidence intervals.

See also

- The *Using time series objects* recipe in this chapter
- The *Decomposing time series* recipe in this chapter
- The *Filtering time series data* recipe in this chapter

Building an automated ARIMA model

The `forecast` package provides the `auto.arima` function to fit the best **AutoRegressive Integrated Moving Average (ARIMA)** models for a univariate time series.

Getting ready

If you have not already downloaded the files for this chapter, do it now, and place them in your R working directory. Install and load the `forecast` package.

How to do it...

To build an automated ARIMA model, follow these steps:

1. Read the data. The file has monthly stock prices from Yahoo! Finance for Infosys between March 1999 and January 2015:

    ```
    > infy <- read.csv("infy-monthly.csv")
    ```

2. Create the time series object:

```
> infy.ts <- ts(infy$Adj.Close, start = c(1999,3),      frequency =
12)
```

3. Run the ARIMA model:

```
> infy.arima <- auto.arima(infy.ts)
```

4. Summary of the ARIMA model is obtained as follows:

```
> summary(infy.arima)
Series: infy.ts
ARIMA(2,1,1)(1,0,1)[12]

Coefficients:
        ar1 ar2 ma1 sar1 sma1
    -0.7513 -0.0368 0.5580 -0.3977 0.4678
s.e. 0.3945 0.1304 0.3881 0.8703 0.8476

sigma^2 estimated as 4.687: log likelihood=-413.89
AIC=839.79 AICc=840.25 BIC=859.27

Training set error measures:
                ME RMSE MAE MPE MAPE
Training set 0.1830564 2.130592 1.598993 0.5759281 10.50643
                MASE ACF1
Training set 0.2974547 -0.006531631
```

5. Generate the `forecast` using the ARIMA model:

```
> infy.forecast <- forecast(infy.arima, h=10)
```

6. Plot the results:

```
> plot(infy.forecast)
```

The plotted result can be seen as follows:

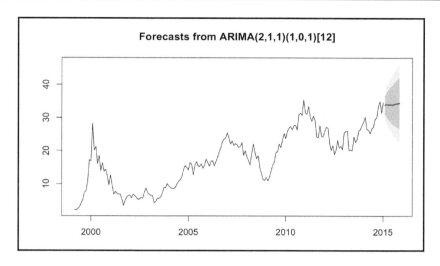

How it works...

Step 1 reads the data.

In step 2, the time series object `ts` is created. For more details, refer to the *Using time series objects* recipe earlier in this chapter.

In step 3, the `auto.arima` function in the `forecast` package is used to generate the ARIMA model. This function conducts an orderly search to generate the best ARIMA model according to the `AIC`, `AICc`, or the `BIC` value. The idea is to choose a model with minimum `AIC` and `BIC` values. We control the criterion used through the `ic` parameter (for example, `ic = "aicc"`). If we provide no value, the function uses `AICc`.

In step 4, the forecast for the specified time horizon (the `h` parameter) is generated.

Step 5 plots the results. The two bands show the 85 % and the 95 % confidence intervals. You can control the color of the data line through the `col` parameter and the color of the forecast line through `fcol`.

See also

- The *Using time series objects* recipe in this chapter

7
How does it look? - Advanced data visualization

In this chapter, we will cover the following topics:

- Creating scatter plots
- Creating line graphs
- Creating bar graphs
- Making distributions plots
- Creating mosaic graphs
- Making treemaps
- Plotting a correlations matrix
- Creating heatmaps
- Plotting network graphs
- Labeling and legends
- Coloring and themes
- Multivariate chart
- Creating 3D graphs and animation
- Selecting a graphics device

Introduction

Base R's graphics provide plots to feed ranges of data as x and y elements. They manipulate colors, scale dimensions, and present other parts of the graph as graphical elements or options. However, they lack advanced plotting or visualization features. The `ggplot2` library implements the grammar of graphics, a coherent system for describing and building graphs. The grammar of graphics is designed to help you in separating and identifying each step of the charting process to better decide on the best way to visualize data. A `ggplot2` graph is built up from a few basic elements:

- **Data**: The raw data for visualization
- **Geometries** (`geom_`): The geometric shapes that will represent the data
- **Aethetics** (`aes`): The aesthetics of the geometric and statistical objects, such as color, size, shape, and position
- **Scales** (`scale_`): This what lies defines the mapping between the data and aesthetic dimensions, such as data range to plot width or factor values to colors

In short, you feed data into `ggplot2`, then apply a series of mappings and transformations to create a visual representation of that data.

This chapter will teach you how to visualize your data using `ggplot2`--one of the most elegant, versatile plotting packages in R, along with some other useful packages.

Creating scatter plots

Scatter plots are one of the most popular graphs for data analysis; they are used to display the relationship between two quantitative variables, and are similar to line graphs in that they use horizontal and vertical axes to plot data points. Simply put, scatter plots show the relationship between two variables and how much one variable is affected by another.

Getting ready

Make sure that the `auto-mpg.csv` file is in the working directory of R. Read the file using the `read.csv` command and save in the `auto` variable. Convert `cylinders` to a `factor` variable. If you have not done so already, install the `ggplot2` package as follows:

```
> install.packages("ggplot2")
> library(ggplot2)
> auto <- read.csv("auto-mpg.csv", stringsAsFactors=FALSE)
> auto$cylinders <- factor(auto$cylinders,labels=c("3cyl","4cyl",
"5cyl","6cyl","8cyl"))
```

How to do it...

To create plots with the `ggplot2` package, follow these steps:

1. Draw the initial plot:

    ```
    > plot <- ggplot(auto, aes(weight, mpg))
    ```

2. Add layers:

    ```
    > plot + geom_point()
    > plot + geom_point(alpha=1/2, size=5,
    aes(color=factor(cylinders))) + geom_smooth(method="lm", se=FALSE,
    col="green") + facet_grid(cylinders~.) + theme_bw(base_family =
    "Calibri", base_size = 10) + labs(x = "Weight") + labs(y = "Miles
    Per Gallon") + labs(title = "MPG Vs Weight")
    ```

How it works...

Let's start from the top:

1. We will first discuss some variations:

    ```
    > plot <- ggplot(auto, aes(weight, mpg))
    ```

2. First, we draw the plot. At this point, the graph is not printed as we have not added layers to it. The plot object need at least one layer to display the graph:

    ```
    > plot + geom_point()
    ```

This plots the points to produce the following scatter plot:

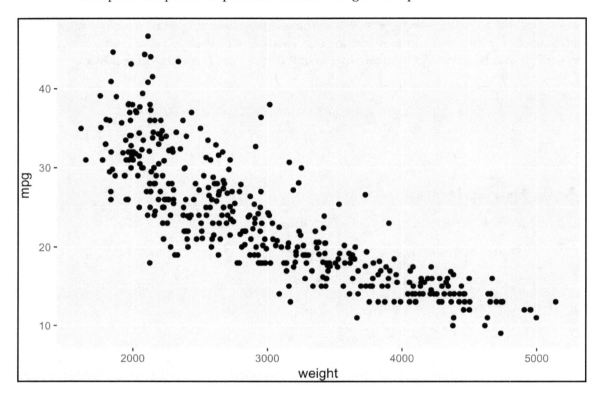

3. We can use various arguments to control how the points appear, for example, alpha, for the intensity of the dots, the color of the dots, and the size and shape of the dots. We can also use the `aes` argument to add aesthetics to this layer which produces the plot as follows:

```
> plot + geom_point(alpha=1/2, size=5,
aes(color=factor(cylinders)))
```

4. Append the following code to the preceding command:

```
+ geom_smooth(method="lm", se=FALSE, col="green")
```

Adding `geom_smooth` helps you see a pattern. The `method=lm` argument uses a linear model as the smoothing method. The `se` argument is set to `TRUE` by default and hence displays the confidence interval around the smoothed line. This supports aesthetics similar to `geom_point`. In addition, we can also set the `linetype`. The output obtained resembles the following diagram:

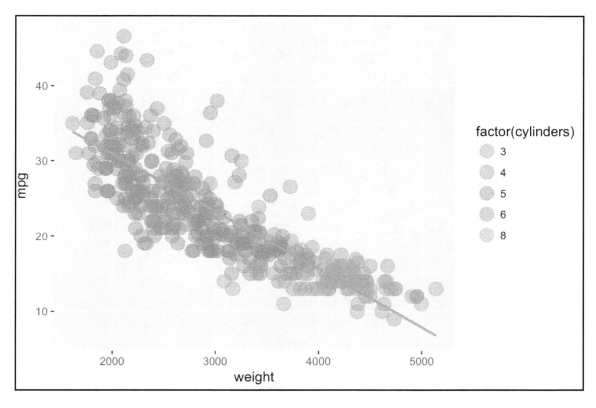

By default, the `geom_smooth` function uses two different smoothing approaches based on the number of observations. If the number of observations exceeds 1,000, it uses gam smoothing; otherwise, it uses loess. Given the familiarity with linear models, people mostly use the `lm` smoothing.

5. Append the following code to the preceding command:

```
+ facet_grid(cylinders~.)
```

This adds additional dimensions to the graph using `facets`. We can add cylinders as a new dimension to the graph. Here, we use the simple `facet_grid` function. If we want to add more dimensions, we can use `facet_wrap` and specify how to wrap the rows and columns as follows:

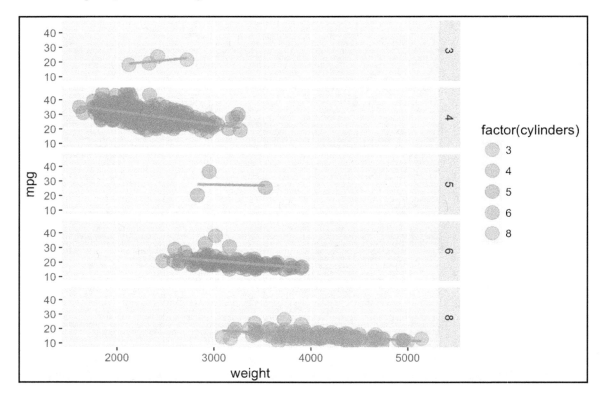

If we change to `facet_grid(~.cylinders)`, the plots for each level of the cylinder are arranged horizontally.

6. Appending the following code adds labels to get the final plot:

```
+ labs(x = "Weight") + labs(y = "Miles Per Gallon") + labs(title =
"MPG Vs Weight")
```

Here is the result of the preceding code:

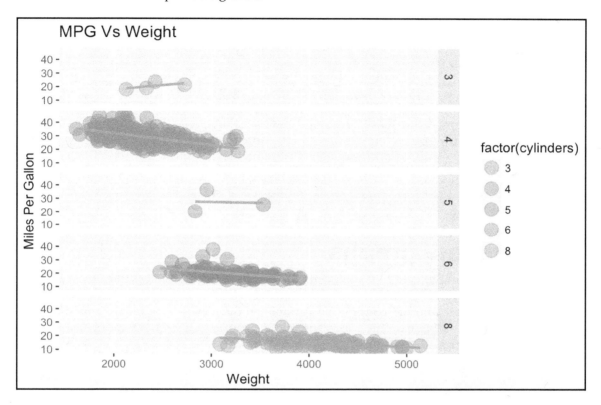

There's more...

The best way to learn `ggplot` is to try out different options to see how they impact the graph. Here, we describe a few additional variations of `ggplot`.

Graph using qplot

A simplistic version of ggplot is qplot and it uses the same ggplot2 package. qplot can also be chained with + to add additional layers in the plot. The generic form of qplot is as follows:

```
> qplot(x, y, data=, color=, shape=, size=, alpha=, geom=, method=,
formula=, facets=, xlim=, ylim= xlab=, ylab=, main=, sub=)
```

For certain types of graphs such as histograms and bar charts, we need to supply only *x* (and can therefore omit *y*):

```
> # Regression of mpg by weight for each type of cylinders
> qplot(weight, mpg, data=auto, geom=c("point", "smooth"), method="lm",
formula=y~x, color=cylinders, main="Regression of MPG on Weight")
```

Creating line graphs

Line graphs are normally used to visualize relationships between two continuous variables along the *x* axis and *y* axis; that is, how the continuous variable on the *x* axis changes its relation with respect to another continuous variable on the *y* axis. Line graphs can also be used with a discrete variable on the *x* axis and are appropriate when the variable is ordered as such (small, medium, and large).

Getting ready

Download the book's files for this chapter and save the mtcars.csv file in your R working directory. Install and load the ggplot2 library and then read the data into R using the read.csv() command:

```
> install.packages("ggplot2")
> library(ggplot2)
> mtcars <- read.csv("mtcars.csv", stringsAsFactors=FALSE)
```

How to do it...

To create a line graph, follow these steps:

1. Create a line plot:

```
> plot <- ggplot(mtcars, aes(wt, mpg))
Add layers:
> plot + geom_line()
> plot + geom_line(linetype = "dashed")
> plot + geom_line(color="red")
```

How it works...

Let's start from the top:

1. We will first discuss some variations of the line graph:

```
> plot <- ggplot(mtcars, aes(wt, mpg))
```

2. First, we draw the plot. At this point, the graph is not printed as we have not added layers to it. The ggplot needs at least one layer to display the graph:

```
> plot + geom_line()
```

3. This plots the lines to produce the following line graph:

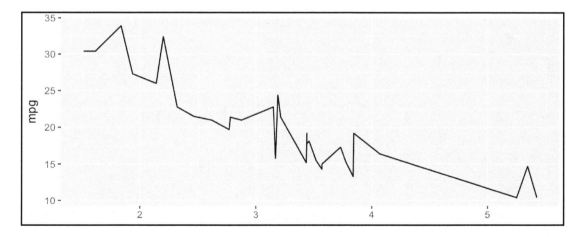

We can use various arguments to control how the line appears, such as linetype, for the type of line (solid, dashed, and so on), color of the line, and size of the line. We can also provide multiple arguments to this layer and this produces the following plot:

```
> plot + geom_line(linetype = "dashed",color="red")
```

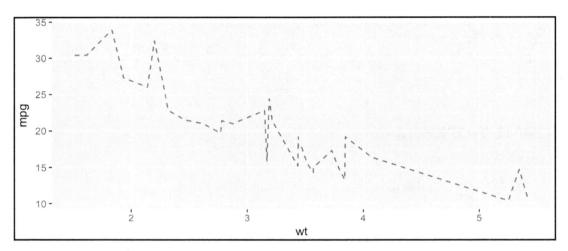

We can also add aesthetics to this layer, such as grouping line type by color:

```
> plot + geom_line(aes(color=as.factor(carb)))
```

This plots shows the line graph generated grouped by color based on carburettors (carb) type:

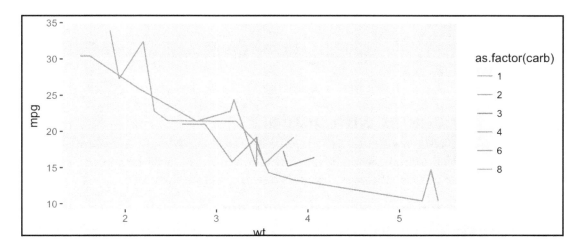

Creating bar graphs

Bar charts are usually used to explore how one (or more) categorical variables are distributed. In ggplot, the geom_bar geometry counts the number of occurrences of each factor variable that appears in the data. This recipe shows you how to create bar graphs that enable segment-wise comparisons with different variable types.

Getting ready

If you have not already done so, download the book's files for this chapter and save the daily-bike-rentals.csv file in your R working directory. Read the data into R using the following command, and also check the packages needed:

```
> library(ggplot2)
> library(dplyr)

> bike <- read.csv("daily-bike-rentals.csv")
> bike$season <- factor(bike$season, levels = c(1,2,3,4),labels =
c("Spring", "Summer", "Fall", "Winter"))
> bike$workingday <- factor(bike$workingday, levels = c(0,1),labels =
c("Work day", "Free day"))
> bike$weathersit <- factor(bike$weathersit, levels = c(1,2,3),labels =
c("Clear", "Misty/cloudy", "Light snow"))
> attach(bike)
```

How to do it...

We base this recipe on the task of generating visualizations to facilitate the comparison of bike rentals by season.

Creating bar charts with ggplot2

First, we will visualize the total number of bicycle rentals per station by means of a bar chart. For this, we need to make a small transformation to the data with the dplyr package and then we will use the ggplot2 package to generate the plot:

1. Create a data frame to summarize and transform the station, workingday, and cnt variables with dplyr:

```
> bike.sum =bike %>%
  group_by(season, workingday) %>%
  summarize(rental = sum(cnt))
```

2. Plot the bar graph for each station:

```
> ggplot(bike.sum, aes(x= season, y= rental)) +
geom_bar(show.legend = TRUE, stat = "identity") + labs(title =
"Rentals for Season and Day")
```

The following diagram is the ggplot:

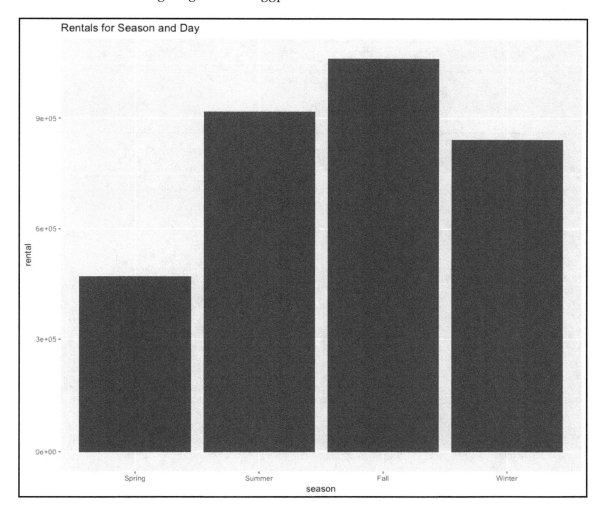

3. Now plot a bar graph by each station segmented by the `workingday` variable:

```
> ggplot(bike.sum, aes(x= season, y= rental, fill = workingday,
label = scales::comma(rental))) + geom_bar(show.legend = TRUE, stat
= "identity") + labs(title = "Rentals for Season and Day") +
scale_y_continuous(labels = scales::comma) + geom_text(size = 3,
position = position_stack(vjust = 0.5))
```

The following diagram is the ggplot:

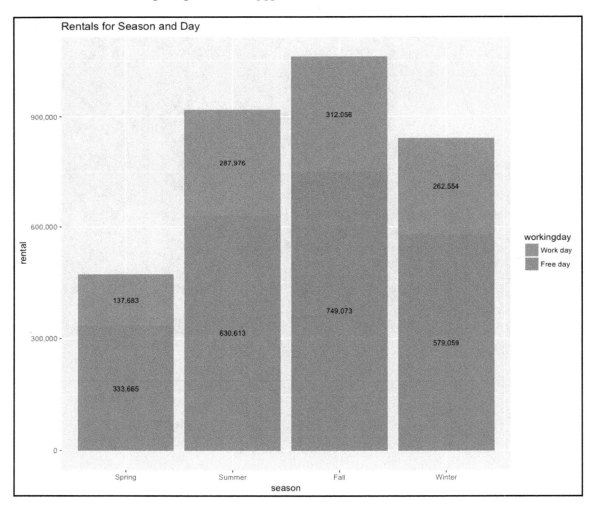

How it works...

Bar graphs are perhaps the most commonly used kind of data visualization. They're typically used to display numeric values (on the y axis) for various categories (on the x axis). By default, bar graphs use a very dark grey color for the bars. To color the bars, use fill. Also, by default, there is no outline around the fill. To add an outline, use color.

We use `stat= "identity"` to denote that the `y` variable is a column in the dataset, whereas `stat = "bin"` is used when the variable is not a column in the dataset. Default is count data when you set `stat = "bin"`.

```
geom_bar(show.legend = TRUE, stat = "identity", fill="lightblue",
colour="black)
```

In large datasets, we often gain good insights by examining how different segments behave. The similarities and differences can reveal interesting patterns in the dataset.

Making distributions plots

Histograms are plots used to explore the distribution of one or more quantitative variables. Another very useful way of representing distributions is to look at the kernel density function, which represents an approximation of the distribution of the data as a continuous function, instead of different bins, by estimating the probability density function.

Getting ready

If you have not already done so, download the book's files for this chapter and save the `faithful.csv` file in your R working directory. Read the data into R using the following command and also check the packages needed:

```
> library(ggplot2)

> faithful <- read.csv("faithful.csv")
```

How to do it...

Perform the following steps to generate a histogram plot:

1. First, generate histograms of the count of daily bike rentals by season:

```
hist_plot <- ggplot(faithful, aes(x=waiting)) + geom_histogram()
```

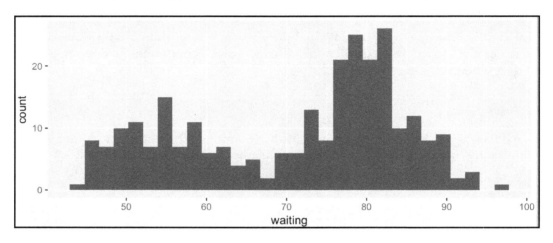

2. Next, create a histogram plot changing `binwidth`:

```
> hist_plot + geom_histogram(binwidth=5, fill="white",
colour="black")
```

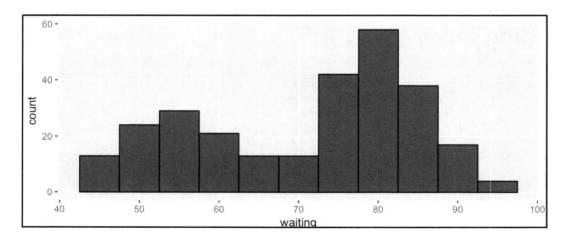

3. Finally, layout the density curve over the histogram:

```
> ggplot(faithful, aes(x=waiting, y=..density..))
+geom_histogram(fill="cornsilk", colour="grey60", size=.2) +
geom_density() +
xlim(35, 105)
```

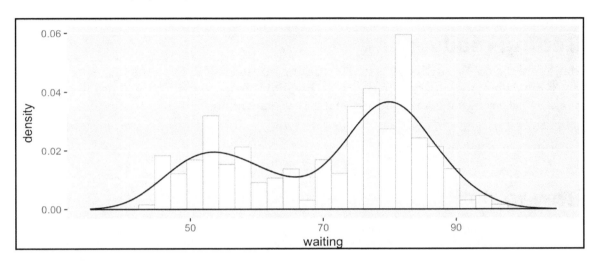

How it works...

Step 1: All `geom_histogram()` geometry requires is a single quantitative column from a data frame or a single vector of data. In this recipe, we use the faithful dataset, which contains data about the Old Faithful geyser in two columns: eruptions, referring to the length of each eruption, and waiting, referring to the length of time until the next eruption.

Step 2: The `geom_histogram()`, by default, groups data into 30 bins and it may be too fine or too coarse for your data. We can change the size of the bins using the `binwidth` parameter.

Step 3: We used the density curve to compare the theoretical and observed distributions by overlaying it with the histogram. The area under the density curve always sums to 1. Histogram result can vary widely based on bin width, number of bins or simply changing the start and end of a bin, whereas you can practically get similar plot using density curve and have better understanding of your data distribution.

Creating mosaic graphs

A mosaic plot is a multidimensional extension of a spine plot that summarizes the conditional probabilities of co-occurrence of the categorical values in a list of records of the same length, and is used to visualize data from two or more qualitative variables.

Getting ready

Make sure the file mtcars.csv is in the working directory of R. Read the file using the read.csv command and save in the mtcars variable respectively. We will use the mosaicplot from the base R package stats for visualization.

```
> library(stats)
> mtcars=read.csv("mtcars.csv")
```

How to do it...

To create a mosaic plot, use the following steps:

1. First, define a formula interface for raw data to visualize cross-tabulation of the numbers of gears and carburetors in Motor Trend car data, along with labeling and color information:

```
> mosaicplot(~ gear + carb, data = mtcars, color = 2:5, las = 1)
```

The following mosaic plot is generated from the preceding command:

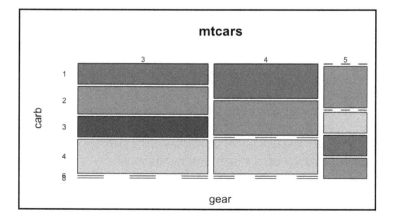

How it works...

First, we create a formula based on the number of gears and carburetors. Then we apply the style of axis labels (`las`) or (recycling) vector of colors (`color`) for color shading. By default, grey boxes are drawn. The `color = TRUE` command uses a gamma-corrected grey palette. The `color = FALSE` command gives empty boxes with no shading.

Making treemaps

The `treemap` package is an area-based visualization for displaying hierarchical data using nested figures, where the size of each rectangle represents a numerical metric.

Getting ready

Make sure that the `post-data.csv` file is in the working directory of R. Now install and load the `treemap` library:

```
> install.packages("treemap")
> library(treemap)
```

How to do it...

To create treemap, follow these steps:

1. First, create a dataframe that has three branches, each branch containing several subbranches and each subbranch with a value that we map to an area:

```
> branch=c(rep("branch-1",4),rep("branch-2",2),rep("brach-3",3))
> subbranch=paste("subbranch" , c(1,2,3,4,1,2,1,2,3), sep="-")
> value=c(13,5,22,12,11,7,3,1,23)
> data=data.frame(branch,subbranch,value)
```

2. Next, draw the plot and specify the levels in the order of importance- branch >
   subbranch > sub-subbranch through the index argument:

```
> treemap(data,
index=c("branch","subbranch"),
vSize="value",
type="index" )
```

How it works...

In the preceding treemap, we passed both categorical variables through the index attribute, but sometimes you need require to pass both categorical and numerical variables to gather better information about the hierarchical structure of the plot:

```
> post_data=read.csv("post-data.csv")
> treemap(post_data,
index=c("category", "comments"),
vSize="views",
type="index" )
```

The following is the treemap plot generated from the preceding command:

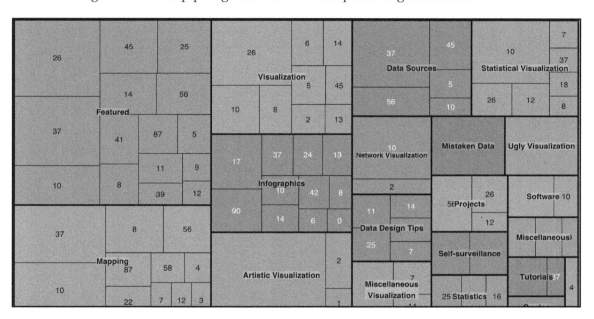

Plotting a correlations matrix

A correlation matrix is used to investigate the dependence between multiple variables at the same time. The result is a table containing the correlation coefficients between each variable and the others. Plotting the correlation matrix helps us understand the relationship among different variables, and often provides us with good information about feature/variable selection or about eliminating redundant features before doing further data analysis.

Getting ready

If you have not already done so, download the book's files for this chapter and save the `mtcars.csv` file in your R working directory. Read the data into R using the following command and also check the packages needed:

```
> library(ggplot2)
> install.packages("corrplot")
> library(corrplot)
```

How to do it...

To load the correlation matrix, run the `mtcars` file as shown in the following points:

1. First, load the `mtcars` dataset and prepocess to rename row names and non-numeric columns:

   ```
   > mtcars=read.csv("mtcars.csv")
   > rownames(mtcars) <- mtcars$X
   > mtcars$X=NULL
   ```

2. Then generate the numerical correlation matrix, using the `cor()` function from the `stats` package, which will create correlation coefficients for each pair of columns. There are different methods for correlation analysis--pearson, spearman, and kendall--that you can pass as arguments to the method attribute of the `cor` function:

   ```
   > mtcars_cor <- cor(mtcars, method="pearson")
   ```

3. Next, print the value of the correlation matrix rounded up to 2 digits(`digits=2`):

   ```
   > round(mtcars_cor, digits=2)
   ```

	mpg	cyl	disp	hp	drat	wt	qsec	vs	am	gear	carb
mpg	1.00	-0.85	-0.85	-0.78	0.68	-0.87	0.42	0.66	0.60	0.48	-0.55
cyl	-0.85	1.00	0.90	0.83	-0.70	0.78	-0.59	-0.81	-0.52	-0.49	0.53
disp	-0.85	0.90	1.00	0.79	-0.71	0.89	-0.43	-0.71	-0.59	-0.56	0.39
hp	-0.78	0.83	0.79	1.00	-0.45	0.66	-0.71	-0.72	-0.24	-0.13	0.75
drat	0.68	-0.70	-0.71	-0.45	1.00	-0.71	0.09	0.44	0.71	0.70	-0.09
wt	-0.87	0.78	0.89	0.66	-0.71	1.00	-0.17	-0.55	-0.69	-0.58	0.43
qsec	0.42	-0.59	-0.43	-0.71	0.09	-0.17	1.00	0.74	-0.23	-0.21	-0.66
vs	0.66	-0.81	-0.71	-0.72	0.44	-0.55	0.74	1.00	0.17	0.21	-0.57
am	0.60	-0.52	-0.59	-0.24	0.71	-0.69	-0.23	0.17	1.00	0.79	0.06
gear	0.48	-0.49	-0.56	-0.13	0.70	-0.58	-0.21	0.21	0.79	1.00	0.27
carb	-0.55	0.53	0.39	0.75	-0.09	0.43	-0.66	-0.57	0.06	0.27	1.00

4. Now generate the correlation plot using the `corrplot()` function:

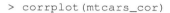

```
> corrplot(mtcars_cor)
```

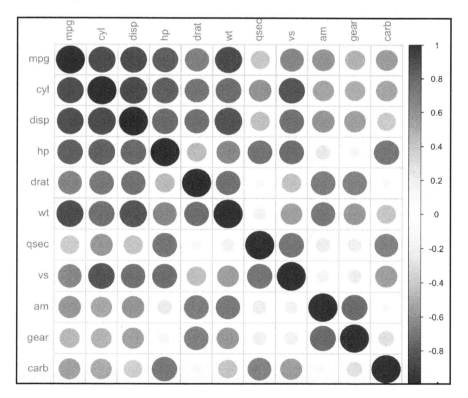

Positive correlations are displayed in blue and negative correlations in red color. Color intensity and the size of the circle are proportional to the correlation coefficients.

5. Finally, create a correlation matrix with colored squares and black labels, rotated 45 degrees along the top:

```
> corrplot(mtcars_cor, method="shade", shade.col=NA,
tl.col="black", tl.srt=45)
```

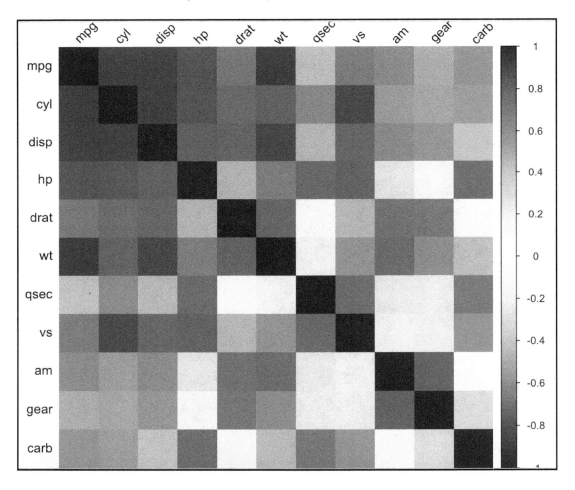

How it works...

The `corrplot()` function has lots of options. You can create a lighter palette so that the text is readable by removing the color legend and ordering the correlated items closer together, using the `order="AOE"` option:

```
> col <- colorRampPalette(c("#BB4444", "#EE9988", "#FFFFFF", "#77AADD",
"#4477AA"))
> corrplot(mtcars_cor, method="shade", shade.col=NA, tl.col="black",
tl.srt=45, col=col(200), addCoef.col="black", addcolorlabel="no",
order="AOE")
```

	gear	am	drat	mpg	vs	qsec	wt	disp	cyl	hp	carb
gear	1	0.79	0.7	0.48	0.21	-0.21	-0.58	-0.56	-0.49	-0.13	0.27
am	0.79	1	0.71	0.6	0.17	-0.23	-0.69	-0.59	-0.52	-0.24	0.06
drat	0.7	0.71	1	0.68	0.44	0.09	-0.71	-0.71	-0.7	-0.45	-0.09
mpg	0.48	0.6	0.68	1	0.66	0.42	-0.87	-0.85	-0.85	-0.78	-0.55
vs	0.21	0.17	0.44	0.66	1	0.74	-0.55	-0.71	-0.81	-0.72	-0.57
qsec	-0.21	-0.23	0.09	0.42	0.74	1	-0.17	-0.43	-0.59	-0.71	-0.66
wt	-0.58	-0.69	-0.71	-0.87	-0.55	-0.17	1	0.89	0.78	0.66	0.43
disp	-0.56	-0.59	-0.71	-0.85	-0.71	-0.43	0.89	1	0.9	0.79	0.39
cyl	-0.49	-0.52	-0.7	-0.85	-0.81	-0.59	0.78	0.9	1	0.83	0.53
hp	-0.13	-0.24	-0.45	-0.78	-0.72	-0.71	0.66	0.79	0.83	1	0.75
carb	0.27	0.06	-0.09	-0.55	-0.57	-0.66	0.43	0.39	0.53	0.75	1

To deal with NA values present in the correlation matrix, you can probably use the `use="complete.obs"` or `use="pairwise.complete.obs"` option before plotting. Like many other standalone graphing functions, the `corrplot()` function has its own set of useful options, as follows:

Option	Description
`type={"lower"|"upper"}`	Only use the lower or upper triangle
`diag=FALSE`	Don't show values on the diagonal
`addshade="all"`	Add lines indicating the direction of the correlation
`shade.col=NA`	Hide correlation direction lines
`method="shade"`	Use colored squares
`method="ellipse"`	Use ellipses
`addCoef.col="color"`	Add correlation coefficients, in *color*
`tl.srt="number"`	Specify the rotation angle for top labels
`tl.col="color"`	Specify the label color
`order={"AOE"|"FPC"|"hclust"}`	Sort labels using angular order of eigenvectors, first principle component, or hierarchical clustering

There's more...

We can also use ggplot to visualize a correlation matrix through `geom_tile` or `geom_raster` geometry.

Visualizing a correlation matrix with ggplot2

We will use the `reshape` package to melt the correlation matrix and then use the `geom_tile()` function from the `ggplot2` package to visualize the correlation matrix. In the case of large data, the `geom_raster()` function can be used in place of the `geom_tile` function.

```
> library(reshape2)
> melted_cormat <- melt(mtcars_cor)
> head(melted_cormat)
> ggplot(data = melted_cormat, aes(x=Var1, y=Var2, fill=value)) +
geom_tile()
```

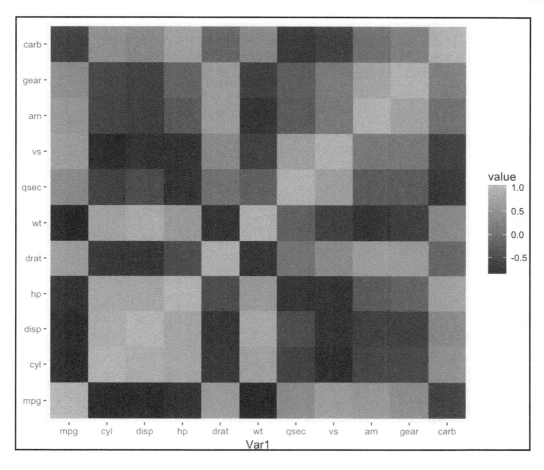

This default plot is not visually appealing; hence, in the next recipe, we will show you the advanced feature of visualizing a correlation matrix through a heatmap.

Creating heatmaps

A heatmap uses color to communicate relationships between data values. A simple heatmap provides an immediate visual summary of information and allows the user to understand complex datasets. In this recipe, we will continue to use the mtcars_cor matrix from the previous recipe and use ggplot2 for visualization along with plotting a heatmap over geospatial data.

Getting ready

Define helper functions to reorder the correlation matrix and identify hidden patterns in the matrix using hierarchical clustering:

```
> get_lower_triangle<-function(cormat){
cormat[upper.tri(cormat)] <- NA
return(cormat)
}
get_upper_triangle <- function(cormat){
cormat[lower.tri(cormat)]<- NA
return(cormat)
}
> reorder_cormat <- function(cormat){
# Use correlation between variables as distance
dd <- as.dist((1-cormat)/2)
hc <- hclust(dd)
cormat <-cormat[hc$order, hc$order]
}
```

How to do it...

For creating heatmaps, follow these steps:

1. First, reorder the correlation matrix and melt it:

```
> cormat <- reorder_cormat(mtcars_cor)
> upper_tri <- get_upper_triangle(cormat)
> melted_cormat <- melt(upper_tri, na.rm = TRUE)
```

2. Next, use the reordered correlation data and plot for the visualization of a heatmap plot:

```
> ggplot(melted_cormat, aes(Var2, Var1, fill = value))+
geom_tile(color = "white")+
scale_fill_gradient2(low = "blue", high = "red", mid = "white",
midpoint = 0, limit = c(-1,1), space = "Lab",
="Pearson\nCorrelation") +
theme_minimal()+
theme(axis.text.x = element_text(angle = 45, vjust = 1, size = 12,
hjust = 1))+
coord_fixed()
```

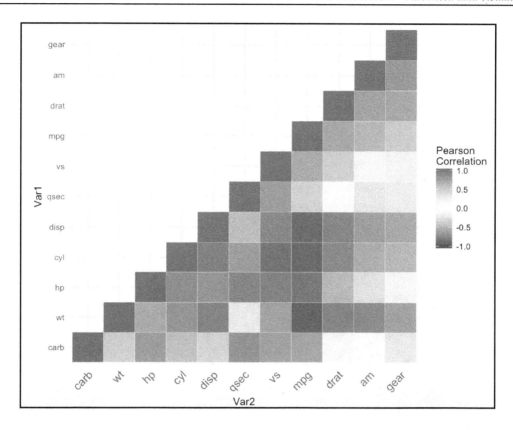

How it works...

In the preceding visualization plot, the negative correlations are shown in blue color and the positive correlations in red color.

The scale_fill_gradient2 function is used with the *limit = c(-1,1)* argument as correlation coefficients range from *-1* to *1* , whereas the coord_fixed() function ensures that units on the *x* axis are of the same length as the units on the *y* axis.

There's more...

Heatmaps are also useful to overlay spatial data over geographical regions.

Plotting a heatmap over geospatial data

In this example, we will plot a heatmap over the map of Tartu, a city in eastern Estonia, to overlay housing distribution using the latitude and longitude of houses provided in the dataset. First, install and load the require package:

```
> install.packages(c("ggmap","maps"))
> library(ggmap)
Next load the housing data containing latitude and longitiude information.
Then load the google map of tartu city:
> tartu_housing_data <- read.csv("tartu_housing.csv", sep=";")
> tartu_map <- get_map(location="tartu", maptype="satellite", zoom = 12)
Then overlay the spatial (lat,lon) information over the map:
> ggmap(tartu_map, extent='device') +
> geom_point(aes(x=lon, y=lat), colour="yellow", alpha=0.1, size=2,
data=tartu_housing_data)
```

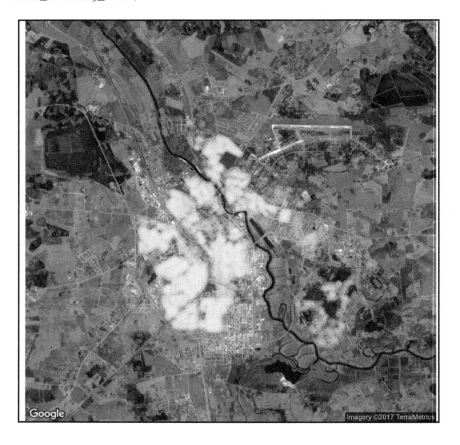

Instead of only plotting the spatial point, we can overlay the density distribution of the heatmap as follows:

```
> tartu_map_g <- get_map(location="tartu", zoom = 13)
> ggmap(tartu_map_g, extent='device') +
geom_density2d(data=tartu_housing_data, aes(x=lon, y=lat), size=.3) +
stat_density2d(data=tartu_housing_data, aes(x=lon, y=lat, fill = ..level..,
alpha = ..level..), size = 0.01, bins = 16, geom = 'polygon')+
scale_fill_gradient(low = "green", high = "red") + scale_alpha(range = c(0,
0.30), guide = FALSE)
```

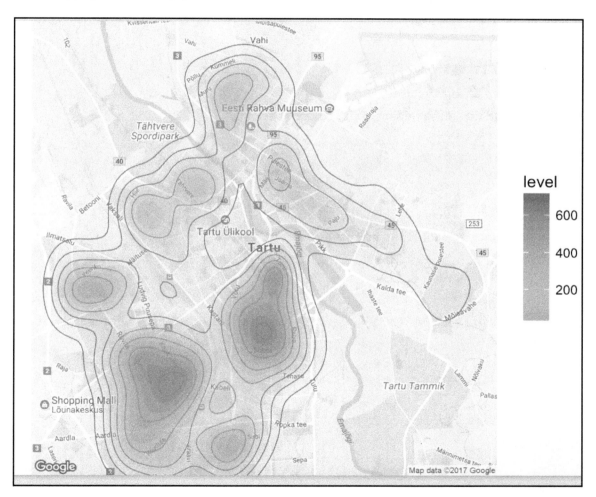

See also

For more information about maps and spatial data visualization or analysis, refer to `Chapter 12`, *Where in the world? - Geospatial Analysis*.

Plotting network graphs

In order to create a graph, we need to pass a vector containing pairs of items to the `graph()` function, and then plot the graph object. In this recipe, we will create a network of directed and undirected graphs and plot them using the `igraph` package.

Getting ready

Install and load the latest version of the `igraph` package:

```
> install.packages("igraph")
> library(igraph)
```

How to do it...

To plot the network graph, the steps are as follows:

1. First, specify the edges for a directed graph:

```
> graph_directed <- graph(edges=c(1,2, 2,3, 2,4, 1,4, 5,5, 3,6,
5,6),n=6)
Next specify the edges for an undirected graph using directed=FALSE
parameter:
> graph_undirected <- graph(edges=c(1,2, 2,3, 2,4, 1,4, 5,5, 3,6,
5,6),n=6, directed=FALSE)
Now plot both the directed and undirected graph side by side:
> par(mfrow=c(1,2))
> plot(graph_directed)
> plot(graph_undirected)
```

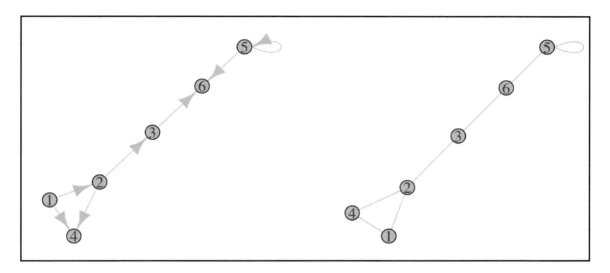

2. Next, specify an edge list that has vertex names, and also mention the isolated list of names:

```
> graph_isolation <- graph( c( "Kuntal", "Maulim", "Maulim",
"Yana","Yana","Kuntal", "Ranadeep", "Rabindrika","Ranadeep",
"Kuntal"),isolates=c("Sonam", "Arunava", "Gina",
"Prakriti","Nainika") )
```

3. Finally, plot the directed names graph with isolated nodes:

```
> plot(graph_isolation, edge.arrow.size=.5, vertex.color="gold",
vertex.size=15, vertex.frame.color="gray",
vertex.label.color="black", vertex.label.cex=0.8,
vertex.label.dist=2, edge.curved=0.2)
```

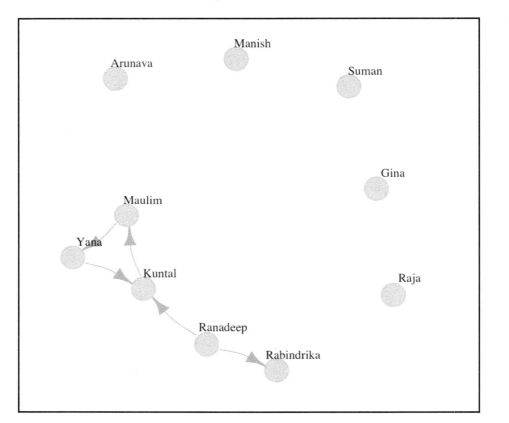

How it works...

In a network graph, the position of the nodes is random and unspecified by the data. You need to set the random seed before plotting the graph to make it repeatable and you can also try different random numbers until you get the desired output:

```
> set.seed(100)
> plot(gu)
```

See also

For information about Network Graph Analysis, refer to `Chapter 9`, *It's All About Your Connections - Social Network Analysis*.

Labeling and legends

Labeling your graph is an important aspect of visualization, as the default variable names will not add clarity to the graph. ggplot has two ways to add labels and legends:

```
ggtitle(label): for adding the main title
xlab(label): for adding the x axis label
ylab(label): for adding the y axis label
```

You can also use the `labs(...)` method to add all of these--the main title, axis labels, and even legend titles. In this recipe, you will learn about adding labels and legends to your plot by adding extra layers to it.

Getting ready

If you have not done so already, make sure that the `ToothGrowth.csv` file is in the working directory of R. Then load the dataset and required packages:

```
> library(ggplot2)
> toothgrowth=read.csv("ToothGrowth.csv")
```

How to do it...

To add labels and legends, perform the following steps:

1. Create the box plot:

```
> p <- ggplot(toothgrowth, aes(x=dose, y=len)) + geom_boxplot()
```

2. Add the main title and labels to the x and y axes:

```
> p + ggtitle("Tooth growth Length vs Dose(mg/day) ") + xlab("Dose
of Vitamin C(mg/day)") + ylab("Tooth Length")
```

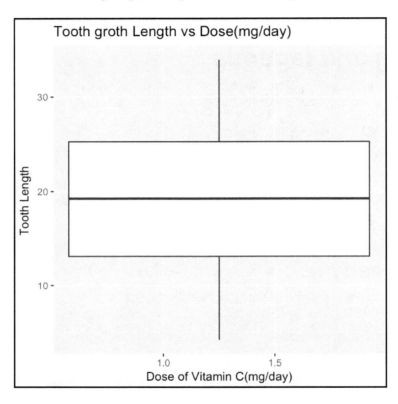

3. Add legends and a title to the plot:

```
> p_leg <- ggplot(toothgrowth, aes(x=dose, y=len,
fill=as.factor(dose))) + geom_boxplot()
> p_leg + labs(fill = "Dose (mg)")
```

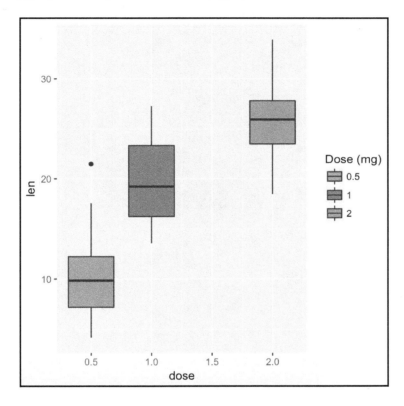

4. To move the legend from the default place:

```
> p_leg + labs(fill = "Dose (mg)")+ theme(legend.position="top")
```

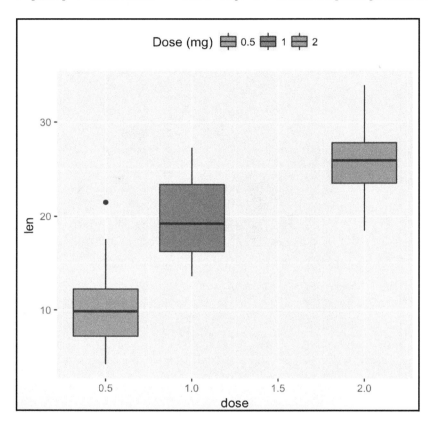

5. Remove the legend:

```
> p_leg + guides(fill=FALSE)
```

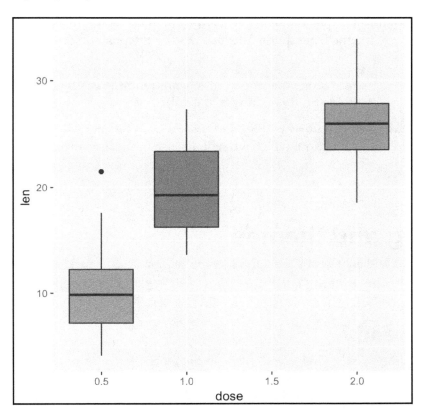

How it works...

First, we create a box plot and then add the title and *x* axis and *y* axis labels respectively.

Then we add legends, by specifying an extra attribute filled within the aesthetic, and use the `labs` method to define the legend title. We also modify the position of the legend in the plot.

Finally, we show how to remove the legend (if it is not required) using `guides()` and specifying the scale variable (in this example, it is fill).

 Note: Appearance of labels and title can also be modified through the `theme()` function, which we will discuss in the next recipe.

Coloring and themes

In this recipe we will change the look and feel of the plot (background color, panel background color and grid lines) using `theme()` function of the `ggplot2` package.

Getting ready

Make sure that the `ToothGrowth.csv` file is in the working directory of R. Read the file using the `read.csv` command and save in the `toothgrowth` variable respectively.

Load the `ggplot2` package:

```
> library(ggplot2)
> toothgrowth=read.csv("ToothGrowth.csv")
```

How to do it...

To add labels and legends, perform the following steps:

1. Create the box plot:

```
> p <- ggplot(toothgrowth, aes(x=dose, y=len)) + geom_boxplot()
```

2. Add a theme of your choice:

```
> p + theme_bw()
> p + theme_dark()
> p + theme_grey()# Grey back ground and white lines
```

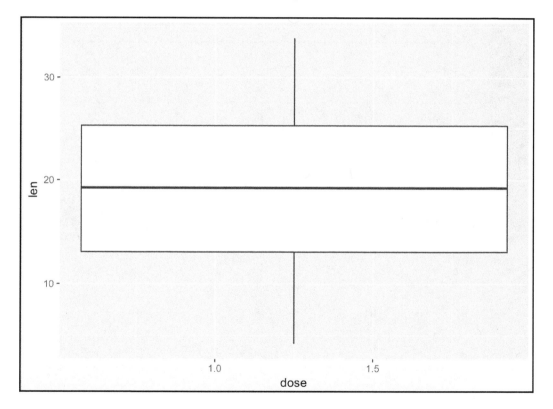

3. Change the plot background color (not the panel):

```
> p + theme(plot.background = element_rect(fill = "darkblue"))
```

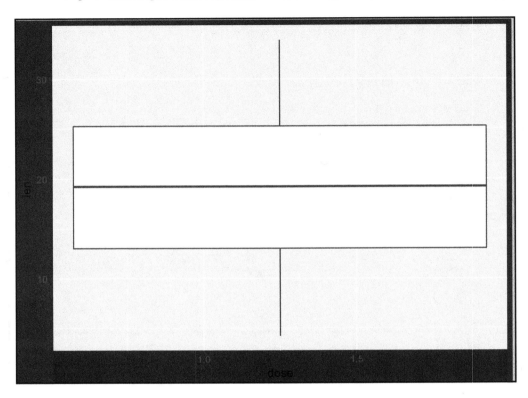

4. Modify the appearance of the axis tick mark, labels, size, and orientation:

```
> p + theme(axis.text.x = element_text(face="bold",
color="#993333", size=14, angle=45), axis.text.y =
element_text(face="bold", color="#993333", size=14, angle=45))
```

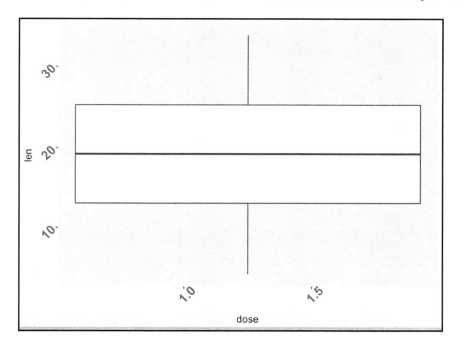

5. Remove panel borders and grid lines:

```
> p + theme(panel.border = element_blank(),
panel.grid.major = element_blank(),
panel.grid.minor = element_blank())
```

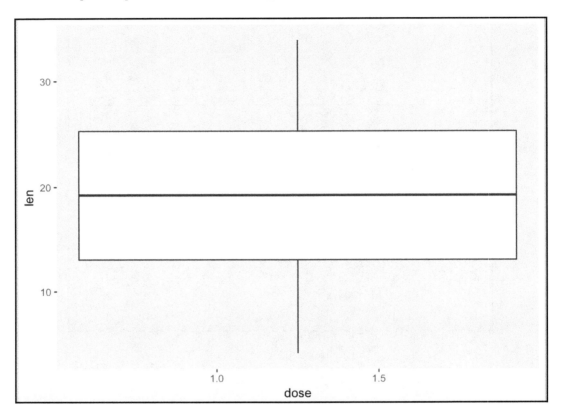

How it works...

First, we create a box plot using the ToothGrowth data, then add a theme to the plot based on our choice and clarity. Then we update the background color of the plot using the `plot.background` attribute of the `theme()` function. We modify the appearance (color, size, and orientation angle) of the axis ticks and labels. Finally, we remove the border and grid from the plot with the `element_blank()` value.

Creating multivariate plots

When exploring data, we want to get a feel for the interaction of as many variables as possible. Although our display and print media can display only two dimensions, by creatively using R's plotting features we can bring many more dimensions into play. In this recipe, we show you how you can bring up to five variables into play.

Getting ready

Read the data from the file and create factors. We also attach the data to save on keystrokes as follows. Download the GGally and ggplot2 package, if you have not already done so:

```
> library(ggplot2)
> library(GGally)
> bike <- read.csv("daily-bike-rentals.csv")
> bike$season <- factor(bike$season, levels = c(1,2,3,4),
labels = c("Spring", "Summer", "Fall", "Winter"))
> bike$weathersit <- factor(bike$weathersit, levels = c(1,2,3),
labels = c("Clear", "Misty/cloudy", "Light snow"))
> bike$windspeed.fac <- cut(bike$windspeed, breaks=3,
labels=c("Low", "Medium", "High"))
> bike$weekday <- factor(bike$weekday, levels = c(0:6),
labels = c("Sun", "Mon", "Tue", "Wed", "Thur", "Fri", "Sat"))
> attach(bike)
```

How to do it...

To create the plot, follow these steps.

1. Create a multivariate plot using the following commands:

```
> plot <- ggplot(bike,aes(temp,cnt))
> plot + geom_point(size=3, aes(color=factor(windspeed))) +
geom_smooth(method="lm", se=FALSE, col="red") +
facet_grid(weekday ~ season) + theme(legend.position="bottom")
```

The preceding commands produce the following output:

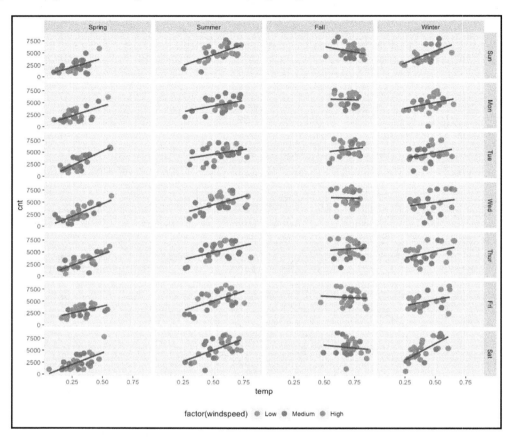

How it works...

Let's start from the top and discuss various parts of the plot:

```
> plot <- ggplot(bike,aes(temp,cnt))
```

First, we draw the plot. At this point, the graph is not printed as we have not added layers to it. ggplot needs at least one layer to display the graph. Next we add points to produce the scatter plot using the `geom_point` geometry:

```
plot + geom_point(size=3, aes(color=factor(windspeed)))
```

We can use various arguments to control how the points appear--the color of the dots and the size and shape of the dots. We can also use the `aes` argument to add aesthetics to this layer as well:

```
geom_smooth(method="lm", se=FALSE, col="red")
```

Adding `geom_smooth` helps you see a pattern. The `method=lm` argument uses a linear model as the smoothing method. The `se` argument is set to `TRUE` by default and hence displays the confidence interval around the smoothed line. This supports aesthetics similar to `geom_point`. In addition, we can set the linetype. By default, the `geom_smooth` function uses two different smoothing approaches based on the number of observations. If the number of observations exceeds 1,000, it uses gam smoothing; otherwise, it uses loess. Given the familiarity with linear models, people mostly use the `lm` smoothing.

The following code adds additional dimensions to the graph using facets:

```
facet_grid(weekday ~ season)
```

It divide by levels of `weekday` in the vertical direction and `season` in horizontal direction. The theme here is used to generate the legend feature in the graph theme (`legend.position="bottom"`)

There's more...

The following discussions are very pertinent to this recipe.

Multivariate plots with the GGally package

With the `GGally` package, we can create a multivariate plot of an entire data frame. It's pretty useful to have the big picture of a dataset. Ggpairs integrates with the other `ggplot` functions and automatically selects a visualization for each segment of the grid. We will create one with the previously viewed auto dataset. If you have not imported it, perform the following commands:

```
> auto <- read.csv("auto-mpg.csv", stringsAsFactors=FALSE)
 > auto$cylinders <- factor(auto$cylinders,labels=c("3cyl","4cyl",
"5cyl","6cyl","8cyl"))
```

Now use the `ggpairs()` function to create the plot; we will only select mpg, cylinders, displacement, and horsepower:

```
> ggpairs(auto[,2:5])
```

Look at the results in the following image:

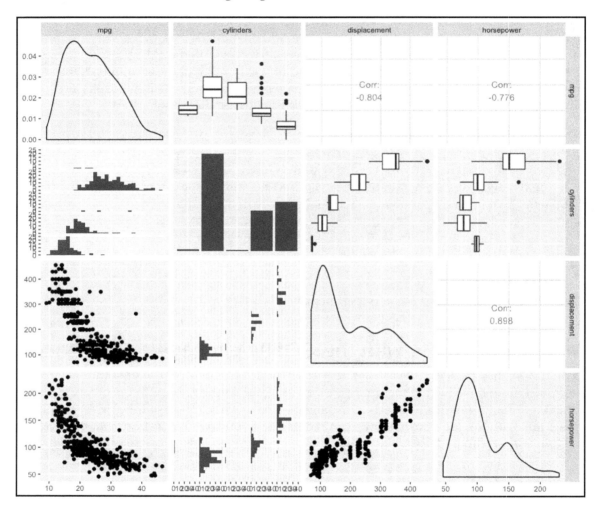

Now add formatting and make a comparison by seasons within each view:

```
> ggpairs(auto[,2:5], aes(colour = cylinders, alpha = 0.4 ), title =
"Multivariate Analysis") + theme(plot.title = element_text(hjust = 0.5))
```

The preceding commands produce the following output:

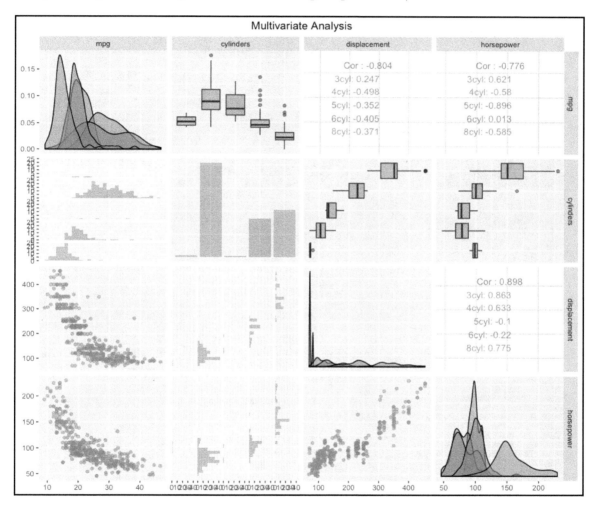

Finally, we can change the form of the visualizations according to the types of variables and their position:

```
> ggpairs(auto[,2:5], aes(colour = cylinders, alpha = 0.4 ), title =
"Multivariate Analysis", upper = list(continuous = "density"), lower =
list(combo = "denstrip")) + theme(plot.title = element_text(hjust = 0.5))
```

The preceding commands produce the following output:

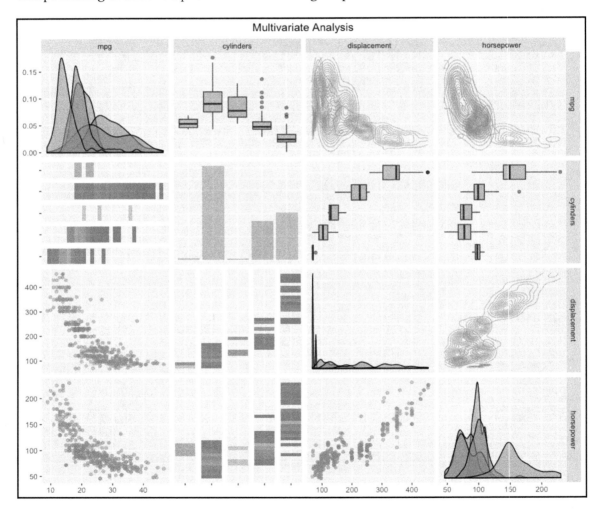

Creating 3D graphs and animation

Sometimes, a two-dimensional view is not sufficient to understand and analyze the data; hence, besides the *x*, *y* variable, an additional data dimension can be represented by a color variable. In this recipe, we will use the `plot3D` package in R to visualize three-dimensional graphs.

Getting ready

Make sure that you have downloaded the code for this chapter and the `mtcars.csv` file is located in the working directory of R.

Install and load the latest version of the `plot3D` package:

```
> install.packages("plot3D")
> library(plot3D)
```

How to do it...

1. Load the `mtcars` dataset and preprocess it to add row names and remove the model name column:

```
> mtcars=read.csv("mtcars.csv")
> rownames(mtcars) <- mtcars$X
> mtcars$X=NULL
> head(mtcars)
```

	mpg	cyl	disp	hp	drat	wt	qsec	vs	am	gear	carb
Mazda RX4	21.0	6	160	110	3.90	2.620	16.46	0	1	4	4
Mazda RX4 Wag	21.0	6	160	110	3.90	2.875	17.02	0	1	4	4
Datsun 710	22.8	4	108	93	3.85	2.320	18.61	1	1	4	1
Hornet 4 Drive	21.4	6	258	110	3.08	3.215	19.44	1	0	3	1
Hornet Sportabout	18.7	8	360	175	3.15	3.440	17.02	0	0	3	2
Valiant	18.1	6	225	105	2.76	3.460	20.22	1	0	3	1

2. Next, create a three-dimensional scatter plot:

```
> scatter3D(x=mtcars$wt, y=mtcars$disp, z=mtcars$mpg, clab =
c("Miles/(US) gallon"))
```

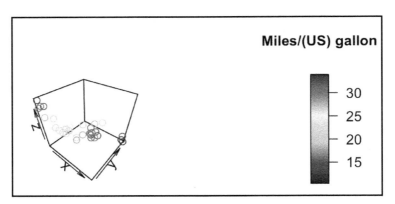

3. Next, add title and axis labels to the scatter plot:

```
> scatter3D(x=mtcars$wt, y=mtcars$disp, z=mtcars$mpg, pch = 18,
theta = 20, phi = 20, main = "Motor Trend Car Road Tests", xlab =
"Weight lbs",ylab ="Displacement (cu.in.)", zlab = "Miles gallon")
```

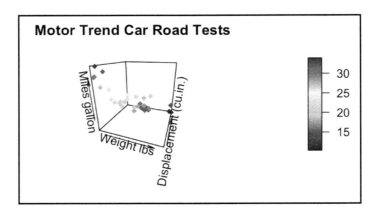

Rotating a 3D plot can provide a more complete view of the data. Now view the plot in different directions by altering the values of two attributes--theta and phi:

```
> scatter3D(x=mtcars$wt, y=mtcars$disp, z=mtcars$mpg,clab = c("Cars
Mileage"),theta = 15, phi = 0, bty ="g")
```

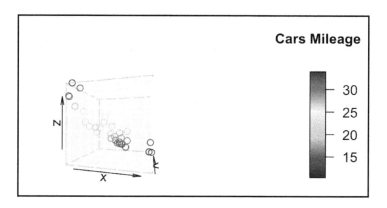

How it works...

The `scatter3D()` function from the `plot3D` package has the following parameters:

- **x, y, z**: Vectors of point coordinates
- **colvar**: A variable used for the coloring
- **col**: A color palette to color the `colvar` variable
- **labels**: Refers to the text to be written
- **add**: Logical; if `TRUE`, then the points will be added to the current plot, and if `FALSE`, a new plot is started
- **pch**: Shape of the points
- **cex**: Size of the points
- **theta**: The azimuthal direction
- **phi**: Co-latitude; both `theta` and `phi` can be used to define the angles for the viewing direction
- **Bty**: Refers to the type of enclosing box and can take various values such as f-full box, b-default value (back panels only), g- grey background with white grid lines, and bl- black background

There's more...

The following concepts are very important for this recipe.

Adding text to an existing 3D plot

We can use the `text3D()` function to add text based on the car model name, alongside the data points:

```
> scatter3D(x=mtcars$wt, y=mtcars$disp, z=mtcars$mpg, phi = 0, bty = "g",
pch = 20, cex = 0.5)
> text3D(x=mtcars$wt, y=mtcars$disp, z=mtcars$mpg, labels =
rownames(mtcars), add = TRUE, colkey = FALSE, cex = 0.5)
```

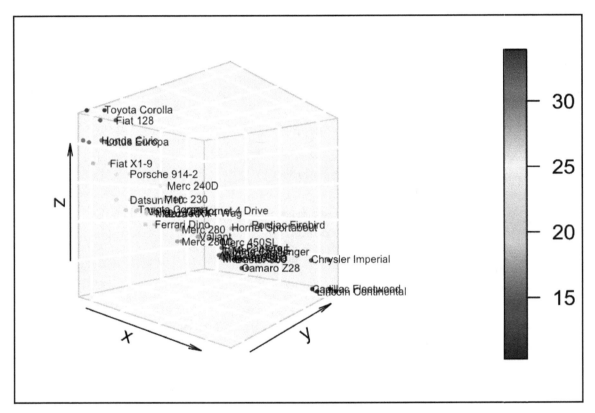

Using a 3D histogram

The three-dimensional histogram function, `hist3D()`, has the following attributes:

- **z**: Values contained within a matrix.
- **x, y:** Vectors, where length of *x* should be equal to nrow(z) and length of *y* should be equal to ncol(z).
- **colvar**: Variable used for the coloring and has the same dimension as z.
- **col**: Color palette used for the `colvar` variable. By default, a *red-yellow-blue* color scheme.
- **add**: Logical variable. If `TRUE`, adds surfaces to the current plot. If `FALSE`, starts a new plot.

Let's plot the Death rate of Virgina using a 3D histogram:

```
data(VADeaths)
hist3D(z = VADeaths, scale = FALSE, expand = 0.01, bty = "g", phi = 20, col
= "#0085C2", border = "black", shade = 0.2, ltheta = 80, space = 0.3,
ticktype = "detailed", d = 2)
```

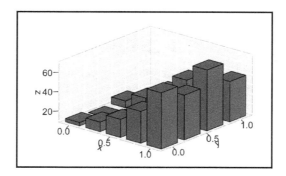

Using a line graph

To visualize the plot with a line graph, add the type parameter to the `scatter3D()` function. The type parameter can take the values l(only line), b(both line and point), and h(horizontal line and points both).

The 3D plot with a horizontal line and plot:

```
> scatter3D(x=mtcars$wt, y=mtcars$disp, z=mtcars$mpg,type="h", clab =
c("Miles/(US) gallon"))
```

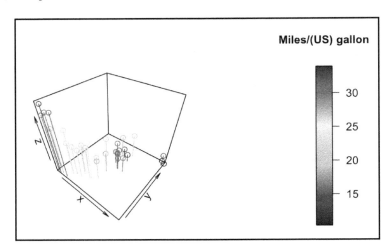

Selecting a graphics device

R can send its output to several different graphic devices to display graphics in different formats. By default, R prints to the screen. However, we can save graphs in the following file formats as well: PostScript, PDF, PNG, JPEG, Windows metafile, Windows BMP, and so on.

Getting ready

If you have not already done so, download the data files for this chapter, ensure that the auto-mpg.csv file is available in your R environment's working directory, and run the following commands:

```
> auto <- read.csv("auto-mpg.csv")
> cylinders <- factor(cylinders, levels = c(3,4,5,6,8), labels = c("3cyl",
"4cyl", "5cyl", "6cyl", "8cyl"))
> attach(auto)
```

How to do it...

To send the graphic output to the computer screen, you have to do nothing special. For other devices, you first open the device, send your graphical output to it, and then close the device to close the corresponding file.

To create a PostScript file, see the following code:

```
> postscript(file = "auto-scatter.ps")
> boxplot(mpg)
> dev.off()
> pdf(file = "auto-scatter.pdf")
> boxplot(mpg)
> dev.off()
> png(file="mpg-boxplot.png",width=400,height=350,res=72)
> boxplot(mpg)
> dev.off()
```

How it works...

Invoking the function appropriate for the graphics device, such as `postscript()` and `pdf()`, opens the file for output. The actual plotting operation writes to the device (file), and the `dev.off()` function closes the device (file).

The best practice is to create a script file that begins with a call to the device driver (postscript, `.pdf`, `.jpeg`, or `.png`), runs the graphics commands, and then finishes with a call to `dev.off()`.

When exploring data, we want to get a feel for the interaction of as many variables as possible. Although our display and print media can display only two dimensions, by creatively using R's plotting features we can bring many more dimensions into play. In this recipe, we show you how you can bring up to five variables into play.

8

This may also interest you - Building Recommendations

In this chapter, we will cover the following topics:

- Building collaborative filtering systems
- Performing content-based systems
- Building hybrid systems
- Performing similarity measures
- Application of ML algorithms - image recognition system
- Evaluating models and optimization
- A practical example - fraud detection system

Introduction

With gigantic growth of information worldwide and the significant rise of users, companies nowadays are analyzing the past behavior of users to build intelligent applications to provide recommendations and choices of interest in terms of *Relevant Job postings*, *Movies of Interest*, *Suggested Videos*, *Friends*, or *People You May Know*, and so on. A **Recommender System** provides information or items that are likely to be of interest to a user in an automated fashion.

In this chapter, we will build, evaluate, and optimize three different categories of recommender systems: **Content-based Recommenders**, **Collaborative Filtering**, and **Hybrid Recommenders**.

The following illustration is indicative of their relations:

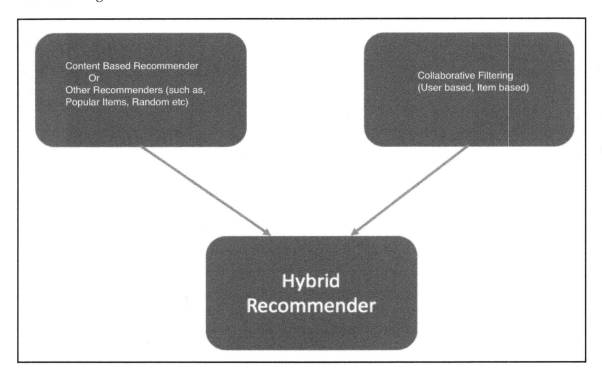

This chapter provides recipes for you to exploit all of these capabilities.

We will also build an **image recognition system** using deep learning and, finally, you will learn how to handle a skewed or imbalanced dataset through a practical example of a **fraud detection system**.

Building collaborative filtering systems

The basic idea of collaborative filtering is that if user A and user B shared the same interests in the past (have a similar purchase history or they liked the same book/movie), then they will also have similar tastes in the future, such as a recently viewed movie by user A that user B has not yet seen which could be proposed to user B. Netflix movie recommendations are one good example of this type of recommender system.

Getting ready

Install the latest version of the `recommenderlab` packages and load the following package:

```
> install.packages("recommenderlab")
> library(recommenderlab)
> data(MovieLense)
```

How to do it...

Here is how we proceed with collaborating filtering systems:

1. First, define `ratings_movies`, the matrix containing users who have rated at least 50 movies and the movies that have been watched at least 100 times:

   ```
   > ratings_movies <- MovieLense[rowCounts(MovieLense) > 50,
   colCounts(MovieLense) > 100]
   ```

2. Now split the `ratings_movies` matrix into training and test sets using an 80/20 ratio:

   ```
   > which_train <- sample(x = c(TRUE, FALSE), size =
   nrow(ratings_movies),
   replace = TRUE, prob = c(0.8, 0.2))
   > recc_data_train <- ratings_movies[which_train, ]
   > recc_data_test <- ratings_movies[!which_train, ]
   ```

 The `Recommenderlab` package provides you with the `evaluationScheme` function to perform advance splitting of datasets. Refer to the *Evaluation of model and optimization* recipe of this chapter.

Item-based collaborative filtering (IBCF) calculates the similarities between items in a dataset using similarity measures, such as cosine or pearson, and then uses these similarity values to predict ratings for user-item pairs not present in the dataset.

3. Now let's build the IBCF model and extract some information about the model:

   ```
   > ibcf_recc_model <- Recommender(data = recc_data_train, method =
   "IBCF", parameter = list(k = 30))
   > ibcf_model_details <- getModel(ibcf_recc_model)
   > ibcf_model_details
   ```

4. Now, identify the top n recommended movies to the users in the test set. We define n_recommended as the number of items to recommend to each user:

```
> n_recommended <- 6
> ibcf_recc_predicted <- predict(object = recc_ ibcf_recc_model,
newdata = recc_data_test, n = n_recommended)
> ibcf_recc_predicted
Recommendations as 'topNList' with n = 6 for 104 users.
```

5. Next, define a matrix to give the recommendations for each user and finally, visualize the recommendations for the first three users:

```
> ibcf_recc_matrix <- sapply(ibcf_recc_predicted@items,
function(x){ colnames(ratings_movies)[x]
})
> View(ibcf_recc_matrix[, 1:3])
```

Here is the output of our code:

	1	16	21
1	G.I. Jane (1997)	Ed Wood (1994)	Sound of Music, The (1965)
2	Grumpier Old Men (1995)	Natural Born Killers (1994)	Brazil (1985)
3	English Patient, The (1996)	Firm, The (1993)	Miracle on 34th Street (1994)
4	Close Shave, A (1995)	Nightmare Before Christmas, The (1993)	Ghost (1990)
5	Leaving Las Vegas (1995)	Swingers (1996)	Dr. Strangelove or: How I Learned to Stop Worrying an...
6	Casablanca (1942)	Return of the Jedi (1983)	Some Like It Hot (1959)

User-based collaborative filtering (UBCF) calculates the similarities between users in a dataset using similarity measures and uses these similarity values to predict how user U will rate an item I based on other users having similar taste.

6. Let's build the UBCF model and extract some information about the model:

```
> ubcf_recc_model <- Recommender(data = recc_data_train, method =
"UBCF")
> ubcf_model_details <- getModel(ubcf_recc_model)
> ubcf_model_details
```

7. Similar to IBCF, determine the top five recommendations for each new user:

```
> n_recommended <- 5
> ubcf_recc_predicted <- predict(object = ubcf_recc_model, newdata
= recc_data_test, n = n_recommended)
> ubcf_recc_predicted
Recommendations as 'topNList' with n = 5 for 104 users.
```

8. Next, define a matrix to give the recommendations for each user and, finally, visualize the recommendations for the first four users:

```
> ubcf_recc_matrix <- sapply(ubcf_recc_predicted@items,
function(x){ colnames(ratings_movies)[x]
})
> View(ubcf_recc_matrix[, 1:4])
```

The output of the code is as follows:

	1	16	21	37
1	Close Shave, A (1995)	Star Wars (1977)	Shawshank Redemption, The (1994)	Princess Bride, The (1987)
2	Glory (1989)	Titanic (1997)	Usual Suspects, The (1995)	Silence of the Lambs, The (1991)
3	Lawrence of Arabia (1962)	Wizard of Oz, The (1939)	L.A. Confidential (1997)	It's a Wonderful Life (1946)
4	Casablanca (1942)	Casablanca (1942)	Raiders of the Lost Ark (1981)	Usual Suspects, The (1995)
5	L.A. Confidential (1997)	Princess Bride, The (1987)	Schindler's List (1993)	Shawshank Redemption, The (1994)

How it works...

The basic intuition of IBCF is that, given a new user, the algorithm considers the user's purchases and recommends similar items through the following steps:

1. For two given items, measure how similar they are in terms of having received similar ratings by similar users.
2. Next, find the k-most similar items for each given item.
3. Finally, for each user, identify the items that are most similar to the user's purchases.

The basic idea of UBCF is that, given a new user, we will identify its similar users and then recommend the top-rated items purchased by similar users through the following steps:

1. Measure how similar each user is to the new one using popular similarity measures such as correlation and cosine.
2. Next, identify the most similar users with the following options:

   - Calculate the top k users using `k-nearest_neighbors`
   - Then take account of the users whose similarity is above a defined threshold

3. Items purchased by the most similar users are rated with two approaches:

- Average rating
- Weighted average rating, using the similarities as weights

4. Finally, pick the top-rated items.

There's more...

The `recommenderlab` package provides options for the recommendation algorithm and we can display the models applicable to the `realRatingMatrix` using `recommenderRegistry$get_entries`:

```
> recommender_models <- recommenderRegistry$get_entries(dataType =
"realRatingMatrix")
> names(recommender_models)
```

```
[1] "ALS_realRatingMatrix"
[2] "ALS_implicit_realRatingMatrix"
[3] "IBCF_realRatingMatrix"
[4] "POPULAR_realRatingMatrix"
[5] "RANDOM_realRatingMatrix"
[6] "RERECOMMEND_realRatingMatrix"
[7] "SVD_realRatingMatrix"
[8] "SVDF_realRatingMatrix"
[9] "UBCF_realRatingMatrix"
```

Visualizing Rating Matrix: Rating matrix can be visualized by building a heat map whose colors represent the ratings. Each row of the matrix corresponds to a user, each column to a movie, and each cell to its rating. Perform the following steps to build heatmap using `image` function of recommenderlab package:

1. Build a heatmap of MovieLense matrix data.

```
> image(MovieLense, main = "Heatmap of the rating matrix")
```

A white area in the top-right region can be noticed from the following chart indicating that the row and columns are sorted:

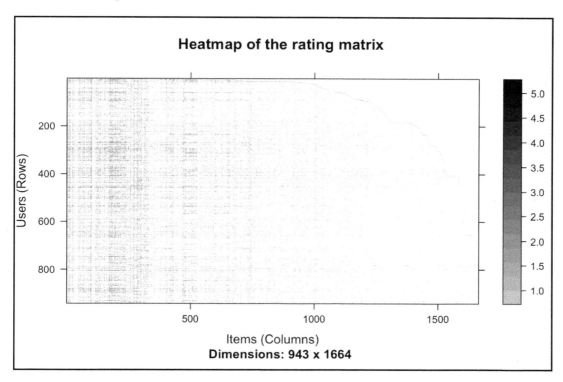

2. Since the MovieLense matrix has too many users and items, the chart is hard to read. So we will now visualize the top percentile of users and movies using quantile function.

```
> min_n_movies <- quantile(rowCounts(MovieLense), 0.99)
> min_n_users <- quantile(colCounts(MovieLense), 0.99)

> image(MovieLense[rowCounts(MovieLense) >
min_n_movies,colCounts(MovieLense) > min_n_users], main ="Heatmap
of the top users and movies")
```

From the following chart, you can notice that most of the users have seen all the top movies,indicated by darker columns(as these darker columns represent the highest-rated movies). Conversely, darker rows represent users giving higher ratings.

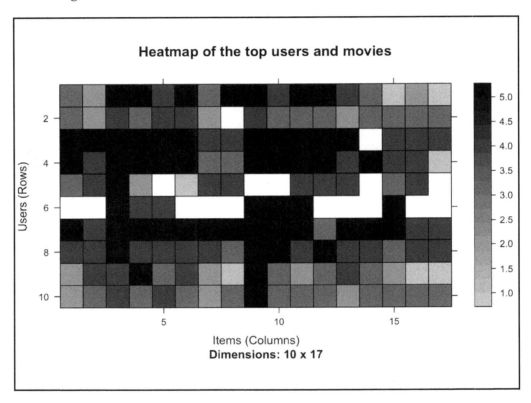

3. Now we will visualize the top 2 percent of users and movies in the new rating matrix:

```
> ratings_movies <- MovieLense[rowCounts(MovieLense) >
50,colCounts(MovieLense) > 100]
> min_movies <- quantile(rowCounts(ratings_movies), 0.98)
> min_users <- quantile(colCounts(ratings_movies), 0.98)

> image(ratings_movies[rowCounts(ratings_movies) >
min_movies,colCounts(ratings_movies) > min_users], main = "Heatmap
of the top users and movies")
```

We can notice from the following chart that some rows are darker than the others, meaning that some users has given higher ratings to all the movies.

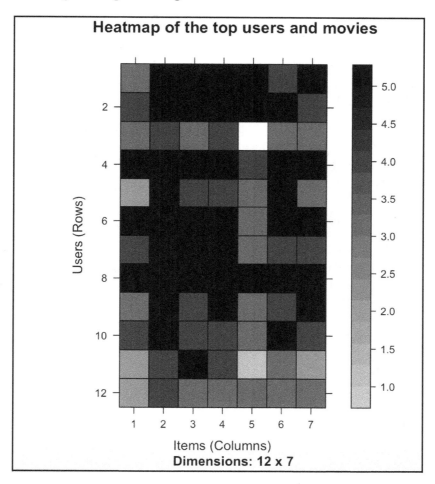

Using collaborative filtering on binary data

In the previous two sections, we built recommendation models based on item or user preferences with the data displaying the rating for each purchase. However, in some real-world scenarios, the following two things can take place:

- We know the items that have been purchased but not their ratings
- For each user, we don't know which items were purchased but we know which items were liked

In these contexts, we can build a user-item matrix whose values would be 1 if the user purchased (or liked) the item and 0 otherwise. In our case, starting from `ratings_movies`, we can build a `rating_movies_viewed` matrix whose values will be 1 if the user viewed the movie and 0 otherwise.

Perform the following steps to binarize the data and apply collaborative filtering on it:

1. Build a `ratings_movies_viewed` matrix using the `binarize` function:

    ```
    > ratings_movies_viewed <- binarize(ratings_movies,minRating = 1)
    ```

2. Split the viewed matrix into training and test sets:

    ```
    > which_train <- sample(x = c(TRUE, FALSE), size =
    nrow(ratings_movies_viewed),replace = TRUE, prob = c(0.8, 0.2))
    > recc_data_train <- ratings_movies_viewed [which_train, ]
    > recc_data_test <- ratings_movies_viewed [!which_train, ]
    ```

In the case of binary data, distance measurement such as correlation and cosine don't work properly. Instead, we use the **Jaccard** index--the number of elements in the intersection between the two sets divided by the number of elements in their union:

$$distance\left(item_1,item_2\right) = \frac{item_1 \cap item_2}{item_1 \cup item_2}$$

Next, build item-based collaborative filtering on the binarized data (you can use user-based filtering as well):

```
> recc_model <- Recommender(data = recc_data_train, method = "IBCF",
parameter = list(method = "Jaccard"))
> model_details <- getModel(recc_model)
```

Just like the previous two sections, let's see the recommendations for the first four users:

```
> n_recommended <- 6
> recc_predicted <- predict(object = recc_model, newdata = recc_data_test,
n = n_recommended)
> recc_matrix <- sapply(recc_predicted@items, function(x){
  colnames(ratings_movies)[x]
})
> View(recc_matrix[, 1:4])
```

	24	26	37	38
1	Raiders of the Lost Ark (1981)	Raiders of the Lost Ark (1981)	Back to the Future (1985)	Raiders of the Lost Ark (1981)
2	Back to the Future (1985)	Empire Strikes Back, The (1980)	Return of the Jedi (1983)	Back to the Future (1985)
3	Empire Strikes Back, The (1980)	Back to the Future (1985)	Silence of the Lambs, The (1991)	Indiana Jones and the Last Crusade (1989)
4	Indiana Jones and the Last Crusade (1989)	Indiana Jones and the Last Crusade (1989)	Princess Bride, The (1987)	Empire Strikes Back, The (1980)
5	Star Wars (1977)	Silence of the Lambs, The (1991)	Monty Python and the Holy Grail (1974)	Silence of the Lambs, The (1991)
6	Terminator, The (1984)	Princess Bride, The (1987)	Forrest Gump (1994)	Star Wars (1977)

Performing content-based systems

Content-based filtering, also known as cognitive filtering, recommends items based on a comparison between the content/feature of the items and a user profile. In this recipe, we will develop a content-based recommender for movie recommendations using a clustering-based approach.

Getting ready

We will be using the ml-100k dataset from the MovieLens website (https://grouplens.org/datasets/movielens/) in this recipe.

1. First, download the movieTitle data:

```
> movie_URL <-
"http://files.grouplens.org/datasets/movielens/ml-100k/u.item"
> movieTitleDF <- read.table(movie_URL, header = F, sep = "|",
quote = "\"")
```

2. Next, download the user-rating data:

```
> users_URL <-
"http://files.grouplens.org/datasets/movielens/ml-100k/u.data"
> userDF <- read.table(users_URL, header = F, sep = "\t", quote =
"\"")
```

How to do it...

Perform the following steps to build a content-based recommender system using **K-means** clustering:

1. First, rename the column names of both the datasets and remove the unwanted columns:

```
> names(movieTitleDF) <- c("MovieID", "Title", "ReleaseDate",
"VideoReleaseDate", "IMDB", "Unknown", "Action", "Adventure",
"Animation", "Childrens", "Comedy", "Crime", "Documentary",
"Drama", "Fantasy", "FilmNoir", "Horror", "Musical", "Mystery",
"Romance", "SciFi", "Thriller", "War", "Western")
> movieTitleDF$ReleaseDate <- NULL;
> movieTitleDF$VideoReleaseDate <- NULL
> movieTitleDF$IMDB <- NULL
> movieTitleDF <- unique(movieTitleDF)

> names(userDF) <- c("UserID", "ItemID", "Rating")
> userDF <- userDF[,1:3]
```

2. Next, check the structure of the datasets:

```
> str(movieTitleDF)
'data.frame': 1682 obs. of  21 variables:
 $ MovieID    : int  1 2 3 4 5 6 7 8 9 10 ...
 $ Title      : Factor w/ 1664 levels "'Til There Was You
(1997)",..: 1525 618 555 594 344 1318 1545 111 391 1240 ...
 $ Unknown    : int  0 0 0 0 0 0 0 0 0 0 ...
 $ Action     : int  0 1 0 1 0 0 0 0 0 0 ...
 $ Adventure  : int  0 1 0 0 0 0 0 0 0 0 ...
 $ Animation  : int  1 0 0 0 0 0 0 0 0 0 ...
 $ Childrens  : int  1 0 0 0 0 0 0 1 0 0 ...
 $ Comedy     : int  1 0 0 1 0 0 0 1 0 0 ...
 $ Crime      : int  0 0 0 0 1 0 0 0 0 0 ...
 $ Documentary: int  0 0 0 0 0 0 0 0 0 0 ...
 $ Drama      : int  0 0 0 1 1 1 1 1 1 1 ...
 $ Fantasy    : int  0 0 0 0 0 0 0 0 0 0 ...
 $ FilmNoir   : int  0 0 0 0 0 0 0 0 0 0 ...
 $ Horror     : int  0 0 0 0 0 0 0 0 0 0 ...
 $ Musical    : int  0 0 0 0 0 0 0 0 0 0 ...
 $ Mystery    : int  0 0 0 0 0 0 0 0 0 0 ...
 $ Romance    : int  0 0 0 0 0 0 0 0 0 0 ...
 $ SciFi      : int  0 0 0 0 0 1 0 0 0 0 ...
 $ Thriller   : int  0 1 1 0 1 0 0 0 0 0 ...
 $ War        : int  0 0 0 0 0 0 0 0 1 ...
 $ Western    : int  0 0 0 0 0 0 0 0 0 ...
```

```
> str(userDF)
'data.frame':  100000 obs. of  3 variables:
 $ UserID: int  196 186 22 244 166 298 115 253 305 6 ...
 $ ItemID: int  242 302 377 51 346 474 265 465 451 86 ...
 $ Rating: int  3 3 1 2 1 4 2 5 3 3 ...
```

3. Define a function to cluster the movies based on their genre affiliation using k-means:

```
> clusterMovies<-function(movieTitleDF){
  set.seed(123)
  i<-1
  #get rid of movie ids and titles
  movieTitleDF<-movieTitleDF[,c(-1,-2)]
  movieCluster <- kmeans(movieTitleDF, 10, nstart = 20)
  return(movieCluster)
}
```

4. Define a function to find all the movies already watched and rated by the selected user:

```
> getUserInfo<-function(dat,id){
  a<-subset(dat, UserID==id,select=c(ItemID, Rating))
  # allocate 0 to the cluster column
  cluster<-0
  activeUser <- data.frame( a[order(a$ItemID),] ,cluster)
  return(activeUser)
}
```

5. Create a function to assign cluster numbers to each movie:

```
> setUserMovieCluster<-function(movieCluster, activeUser){
 df1<- data.frame(cbind(movieTitleDF$MovieID, clusterNum =
movieCluster$cluster))
  names(df1)<-c("movie_id", "cluster")
  activeUser$cluster<-df1[match(activeUser$ItemID,df1$movie_id),2]
  return(activeUser)}
```

6. Next, calculate the average movie rating for each cluster:

```
> getAverageClusterRating<-function(movieCluster, activeUser){
  like<-aggregate(activeUser$Rating,
by=list(cluster=activeUser$cluster), mean)
  if(max(like$x)<3){
    like<-as.vector(0)
  } else{
    like<-as.vector(t(max(subset(like, x>=3, select=cluster))))
```

```
  }
  return(like)
}
```

7. Define a function to select movies from a cluster:

```
> getGoodMovies<-function(like, movieCluster, movieTitleDF){
  df1<- data.frame(cbind(movieTitleDF$MovieID, clusterNum =
movieCluster$cluster))
  names(df1)<-c("movie_id", "cluster")
  if(like==0){
    recommend<-movieTitleDF[sample.int(n = dim(titleFilmDF)[1],
size = 100), 1]
  }
  else{
    recommend<-as.vector(t(subset(df1, cluster==like,
select=movie_id)))
  }
  return(recommend)
}
```

8. Now we will define a function using all the preceding defined functions to find all the movies that the user has not yet seen:

```
> getRecommendedMovies<-function(movieTitleDF, userDF, userid){
  movieCluster<-clusterMovies(movieTitleDF)
  activeUser<-getUserInfo(userDF, userid)
  activeUser<-setUserMovieCluster(movieCluster, activeUser)
  like<-getAverageClusterRating(movieCluster, activeUser)
  recommend<-getGoodMovies(like, movieCluster, movieTitleDF)
  # only select not yet watched movies
  recommend<-recommend[-activeUser$ItemID]
  # add movietitle
  mov_title<-movieTitleDF[match(recommend,movieTitleDF$MovieID),2]
  recommend<-data.frame(recommend,mov_title)
  return(recommend)
}
```

9. Now, we define the function to suggest a certain number of movies to a particular user:

```
> suggestMovies<-function(movieTitleDF, userDF, userid,
num_movies){
  #get suggestions
  suggestions = getRecommendedMovies(movieTitleDF, userDF, userid)
  #select stated number of selections
  suggestions = suggestions[1:num_movies,]
  writeLines("You may like these movies:")
```

```
#print suggestions without column headers or row indices
write.table(suggestions[2], row.names = FALSE, col.names = FALSE)
}
```

10. Finally, choose any UserID from the user dataframe (`userDF`) and use the `suggestMovies()` method to find some (that is, num_movies =5) recommended movies for the user:

```
> suggestMovies(movieTitleDF, userDF, 196, 5)

You may like these movies:
"French Twist (Gazon maudit) (1995)"
"I.Q. (1994)"
"While You Were Sleeping (1995)"
"Forrest Gump (1994)"
"Four Weddings and a Funeral (1994)"
```

How it works...

The basic idea of content-based filtering algorithms starts with a description of items and for each user, the algorithms recommend items that are similar to its past purchases through the following steps:

1. Define item descriptions.
2. Define user profiles based on purchases.
3. Recommend to each user the items matching their profile.

User profiles are calculated from their purchases, so the algorithms recommend items similar to past purchases.

Step 1: We rename the column names and remove unwanted columns from the datasets.

Step 2: We verify the structure of the datasets to check the number of variables and its type.

Step 3: In the `clusterMovies()` function, we have used the k-means approach to cluster and choose the number of clusters as 10, but you can try an alternate clustering algorithm along with a different number of clusters.

Refer to `Chapter 5`, *Can you simplify that- Data Reduction Technique*, to find out more about other clustering techniques and choosing an optimal number of clusters.

Step 4: We are finding all the movies that are watched and rated by each user using userID.

Step 5: We are assigning cluster number to each movies.

Step 6: Next we calculate average rating of each cluster.

Step 7: In the `getGoodMovies()` function, we select random 100 movies if there is no cluster with a baseline rating of 3 or above. Otherwise, we select all movies that the user has watched and not yet seen.

Step 8: In the `getRecommendedMovies()` function, we first create a movie cluster and then find the relevant information about our selected user. After this, we calculate the average rating per cluster and find the movies belonging to that cluster that the user likes the most. Finally, select all the movies that the user has not yet seen.

Building hybrid systems

In this recipe, we will continue to use the MovieLense dataset and develop a hybrid recommender system by combining two other recommender systems, namely, UBCF and Random Selection.

Getting ready

Install and load the `recommenderlab` package:

```
> install.packages("recommenderlab")
> library(recommenderlab)
```

How to do it...

The hybrid system can be built as follows:

1. First, load the dataset:

   ```
   > data("MovieLense")
   ```

2. Filter out the dataset with relevant users (namely, users who have rated above 50 movies):

   ```
   > MovieLense50 <- MovieLense[rowCounts(MovieLense) >50,]
   ```

3. Split the data into training and test sets:

```
> train <- MovieLense50[1:100]
> test <- MovieLense50[101:105]
```

4. Build the hybrid recommender system using multiple models together and check the model:

```
> hybrid_recom <- HybridRecommender(
  Recommender(train, method = "UBCF"),
  Recommender(train, method = "RANDOM"),
  weights = c(.7,.3)
)

> getModel(hybrid_recom)
```

5. Next, `predict` the hybrid model on test data to show the top 10 (using `n=10`) movies for five users:

```
> as(predict(hybrid_recom, test, n=10), "list")

[[1]]
 [1] "Jaws (1975)"
 [2] "Shallow Grave (1994)"
 [3] "Dr. Strangelove or: How I Learned to Stop Worrying and Love
the Bomb (1963)"
 [4] "Harold and Maude (1971)"
 [5] "Postino, Il (1994)"
 [6] "Wizard of Oz, The (1939)"
 [7] "Amadeus (1984)"
 [8] "Cinema Paradiso (1988)"
 [9] "Titanic (1997)"
[10] "Cool Hand Luke (1967)"

[[2]]
 [1] "Mrs. Doubtfire (1993)"
 [2] "Cinema Paradiso (1988)"
 [3] "Fried Green Tomatoes (1991)"
 [4] "Secret of Roan Inish, The (1994)"
 [5] "Spitfire Grill, The (1996)"
 [6] "Big Night (1996)"
 [7] "Quiet Man, The (1952)"
 [8] "Bananas (1971)"
 [9] "Shadowlands (1993)"
[10] "Rosewood (1997)"

[[3]]
```

```
[1] "Star Wars (1977)"
[2] "Shawshank Redemption, The (1994)"
[3] "Raising Arizona (1987)"
[4] "Blade Runner (1982)"
[5] "Close Shave, A (1995)"
[6] "Toy Story (1995)"
[7] "Dr. Strangelove or: How I Learned to Stop Worrying and Love
the Bomb (1963)"
[8] "My Fair Lady (1964)"
[9] "Monty Python and the Holy Grail (1974)"
[10] "Graduate, The (1967)"

[[4]]
[1] "Chairman of the Board (1998)"
[2] "Santa Clause, The (1994)"
[3] "Star Wars (1977)"
[4] "Dr. Strangelove or: How I Learned to Stop Worrying and Love
the Bomb (1963)"
[5] "Red Rock West (1992)"
[6] "Twisted (1996)"
[7] "Operation Dumbo Drop (1995)"
[8] "Remains of the Day, The (1993)"
[9] "William Shakespeare's Romeo and Juliet (1996)"
[10] "Die Hard: With a Vengeance (1995)"

[[5]]
[1] "Fargo (1996)"
[2] "2001: A Space Odyssey (1968)"
[3] "Raiders of the Lost Ark (1981)"
[4] "Wallace & Gromit: The Best of Aardman Animation (1996)"
[5] "Harold and Maude (1971)"
[6] "Fantasia (1940)"
[7] "Close Shave, A (1995)"
[8] "Taxi Driver (1976)"
[9] "Brassed Off (1996)"
[10] "Deconstructing Harry (1997)"
```

How it works...

Hybrid recommender systems combine various recommender systems and replace the disadvantages of one system with the advantages of another system to build a more robust final system. For example, by combining collaborative filtering methods, where the model fails when new items don't have ratings, with content-based systems, where feature information about the items is available, new items can be recommended more accurately and efficiently.

In the previous example, we mixed similar user-liked movies (UBCF) with Random recommendation for diversity. The `weights` attribute of the `HybridRecommender()` function refers to the priority of various selected models.

Performing similarity measures

Almost every recommender system works on the concept of similarity between items or users. In this recipe, we will explore some common similarity measurement techniques such as Euclidean distance, Cosine distance, and Pearson correlation, which are widely used in recommender systems.

Getting ready

Make sure that you have downloaded the `mtcars.csv` file for this chapter and kept it in your R working directory. Also, if you have not yet installed the following package, do so before you proceed any further.

Install the latest version of the `lsa` package:

```
> install.packages("lsa")
```

How to do it...

We proceed as follows with the similarity measures:

1. First, calculate the similarity between two items using Euclidean distance:

```
> x1 <- rnorm(30)
> x2 <- rnorm(30)
> Euclidean_dist = dist(rbind(x1,x2) ,method="euclidean")
> Euclidean_dist

         x1
x2 6.427449
```

2. Next, calculate the `cosine` similarity between two vectors. Load the `lsa` package:

```
> library(lsa)
> vector1 = c( 1, 1, 1, 0, 0, 0, 0, 0, 0, 0, 0, 0 )
> vector2 = c( 0, 0, 1, 1, 1, 1, 1, 0, 1, 0, 0, 0 )
> cosine(vector1, vector2)

          [,1]
[1,] 0.2357023
```

3. Finally, calculate the Pearson correlation between two variables using the `mtcars` dataset:

```
> mtcars_data <- read.csv("mtcars.csv")
> rownames(mtcars_data) <- mtcars_data$X
> mtcars_data$X <- NULL
> coeff <- cor(mtcars_data, method="pearson")
> coeff
```

	mpg	cyl	disp	hp	drat	wt	qsec	vs	am	gear	carb
mpg	1.0000000	-0.8521620	-0.8475514	-0.7761684	0.68117191	-0.8676594	0.41868403	0.6640389	0.59983243	0.4802848	-0.55092507
cyl	-0.8521620	1.0000000	0.9020329	0.8324475	-0.69993811	0.7824958	-0.59124207	-0.8108118	-0.52260705	-0.4926866	0.52698829
disp	-0.8475514	0.9020329	1.0000000	0.7909486	-0.71021393	0.8879799	-0.43369788	-0.7104159	-0.59122704	-0.5555692	0.39497686
hp	-0.7761684	0.8324475	0.7909486	1.0000000	-0.44875912	0.6587479	-0.70822339	-0.7230967	-0.24320426	-0.1257043	0.74981247
drat	0.6811719	-0.6999381	-0.7102139	-0.4487591	1.00000000	-0.7124406	0.09120476	0.4402785	0.71271113	0.6996101	-0.09078980
wt	-0.8676594	0.7824958	0.8879799	0.6587479	-0.71244065	1.0000000	-0.17471588	-0.5549157	-0.69249526	-0.5832870	0.42760594
qsec	0.4186840	-0.5912421	-0.4336979	-0.7082234	0.09120476	-0.1747159	1.00000000	0.7445354	-0.22986086	-0.2126822	-0.65624923
vs	0.6640389	-0.8108118	-0.7104159	-0.7230967	0.44027846	-0.5549157	0.74453544	1.0000000	0.16834512	0.2060233	-0.56960714
am	0.5998324	-0.5226070	-0.5912270	-0.2432043	0.71271113	-0.6924953	-0.22986086	0.1683451	1.00000000	0.7940588	0.05753435
gear	0.4802848	-0.4926866	-0.5555692	-0.1257043	0.69961013	-0.5832870	-0.21268223	0.2060233	0.79405876	1.0000000	0.27407284
carb	-0.5509251	0.5269883	0.3949769	0.7498125	-0.09078980	0.4276059	-0.65624923	-0.5696071	0.05753435	0.2740728	1.00000000

How it works...

First, we calculate the Euclidean distance between two objects with the `dist()` function provided in the R `base` package. The Euclidean distance between two points with coordinates *(x, y)* and *(a, b)* is calculated as follows:

$$dist\left(\left(x,y\right),\left(a,b\right)\right)=\sqrt{\left(x-a\right)^{2}+\left(y-b\right)^{2}}$$

The cosine similarity metric between two vectors is a measure that calculates the cosine of the angle between them and is a measurement of orientation and not magnitude, as represented in the following equation:

$$\cos \theta = \frac{\vec{a} \cdot \vec{b}}{\|\vec{a}\| \|\vec{b}\|}$$

Pearson's correlation coefficient is a popular correlation coefficient calculated between two variables as the covariance of the two variables divided by the product of their standard deviations. The Pearson correlation coefficient r gives the measure of strength of a linear association between two variables, where $r = 1$ means a perfect positive correlation and the value $r = -1$ means a perfect negative correlation.

The diagonal element of the `corr()` matrix calculated earlier are all 1, indicating the variable has perfect positive correlation with itself:

$$r = \frac{\sum_i (x_i - \overline{x})(y_i - \overline{y})}{\sqrt{\sum_i (x_i - \overline{x})^2} \sqrt{\sum_i (y_i - \overline{y})^2}}$$

Empirical studies have shown that Pearson coefficient outperforms other similarity measures for user-based collaborative filtering recommender systems, whereas the Cosine similarity consistently performs well in item-based collaborative filtering.

Application of ML algorithms - image recognition system

Machine learning or ML algorithms are widely used in various domains and are generally a way of fine-tuning systems with tunable parameters, thereby making the system better with examples in a supervised or unsupervised way. Nowadays, researchers are pushing machine learning with the help of deep neural networks to perform outstanding tasks, which only humans were capable of doing before.

Though it is impossible to list every use case or example of machine learning, we will list some of the most prominent applications:

- Identification of unwanted spam messages in emails
- Segmentation of customer behavior for targeted advertising

- Forecast of weather behavior and long-term climate changes
- Detection of fraudulent credit card transactions
- Actuarial estimates of financial damage of storms and natural disasters
- Recommendation of correct products or items
- Autonomous and self-driving cars
- Optimization of energy use in homes and office buildings
- Projection of areas where criminal activity is most likely
- Discovery of genetic sequences linked to diseases
- Face recognition, image categorization, speech recognition, and many more

In this recipe, we will develop an **image classification system** using pretrained deep neural networks in R.

Getting ready

We will use a popular deep learning framework `mxnet` for image categorization.

Install the latest version of the following packages:

```
> cran <- getOption("repos")
> cran["dmlc"] <- "https://s3.amazonaws.com/mxnet-r/"
> options(repos = cran)
> install.packages("mxnet")

> install.packages("jpeg")
> install.packages("png")

> library(devtools)
> devtools::install_github('rich-iannone/DiagrammeR')
> source("http://bioconductor.org/biocLite.R")
> biocLite()
> biocLite("EBImage")
```

How to do it...

1. First, load the libraries and download the pretrained Inception model, then extract it:

```
> library(mxnet)
> library(EBImage)
```

```
> library(jpeg)
> library(png)

> if (!file.exists("synset.txt"))
{download.file("http://data.dmlc.ml/mxnet/models/imagenet/inception
-bn.tar.gz", destfile = "inception-bn.tar.gz")
  untar("inception-bn.tar.gz")
}
```

2. Use the model loading function to load the unzipped pretrained model into R:

```
> model <<- mx.model.load("./Inception-BN", iteration = 126)
> synsets <<- readLines("synset.txt")
```

3. Load the image of an elephant using the readImage function of the EBImage package (you can use another image if you want):

```
> image <- readImage("elephant.jpg")
```

4. Preprocess the image (resizing and subtracting the mean) before feeding into a deep network:

```
> preproc.image <- function(image) {
  # resize to 224 x 224, needed by input of the model.
  resized <- resize(image, 224, 224)
  # convert to array (x, y, channel)
  arr <- as.array(resized) * 255
  dim(arr) <- c(224, 224, 3)
  # substract the mean
  normed <- arr - 117
  # Reshape to format needed by mxnet (width, height, channel, num)
  dim(normed) <- c(224, 224, 3, 1)
  return(normed)
}
```

5. Normalize the image using the preproc function defined in the preceding code:

```
> normed <- preproc.image(image)
```

6. Next, classify the image using the predict function to get the probability over different output classes:

```
> prob <- predict(model, X = normed)
> max.idx <- order(prob[,1], decreasing = TRUE)[1:5]
> result <- synsets[max.idx]
> display(image)
> result
```

7. The image and its predicted labels (top 3) along with their probability are shown here:

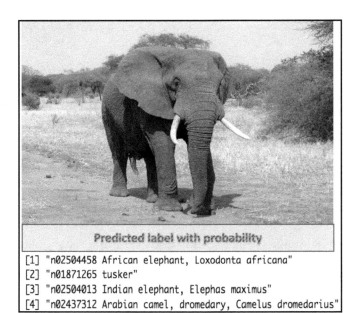

Predicted label with probability

```
[1] "n02504458 African elephant, Loxodonta africana"
[2] "n01871265 tusker"
[3] "n02504013 Indian elephant, Elephas maximus"
[4] "n02437312 Arabian camel, dromedary, Camelus dromedarius"
```

How it works...

MXNet is a fast and efficient library for deep learning tasks. The Inception model is trained on the ImageNet (Large Visual Recognition Challenge) dataset, where models try to classify entire images into 1,000 classes, such as Zebra, Dalmatian, and Dishwasher.

Evaluating models and optimization

After we build the models, we must decide which model to use and its parameters. First, we can test the performance of some models and/or parameter configurations and then choose the one that performs best with the dataset under consideration.

This recipe will show you how to evaluate recommender models and compare their performances to choose the most appropriate model with optimized parameters.

Getting ready

We will use the MovieLense dataset from the `recommenderlab` package for evaluation.

Install the latest version of the `recommenderlab` and `ggplot2` packages:

```
> install.packages("recommenderlab")
> install.packages("ggplot2 ")
```

How to do it...

1. First, load the library and dataset:

    ```
    > library(recommenderlab)
    > library(ggplot2)
    > data(MovieLense)
    ```

2. Next, preprocess the dataset to create a new dataset containing relevant users and movies:

    ```
    > ratings_movies <- MovieLense[rowCounts(MovieLense) > 50,
    colCounts(MovieLense)>100]
    > ratings_movies
    ```

    There are 560 users and 332 ratings with 560 x 332 dimensional rating matrix of class `realRatingMatrix` with 55298 ratings.

3. Prepare the data for validation using the k-fold approach:

    ```
    > n_fold <- 4
    > items_to_keep <- 15
    > rating_threshold <- 3
    > eval_sets <- evaluationScheme(data = ratings_movies, method =
    "cross-validation",k = n_fold, given = items_to_keep, goodRating =
    rating_threshold)
    ```

4. Count the number of items that we have in each set:

    ```
    > size_sets <- sapply(eval_sets@runsTrain, length)
    > size_sets
    [1] 420 420 420 420
    ```

    Now we will show two ways of evaluating the recommendation technique-- evaluating the ratings and evaluating the recommendations model.

Evaluating the Ratings: It evaluates the model by comparing the estimated ratings with the real ones

1. First, define an item-based recommendation model along with its parameters for evaluation:

```
> model_to_evaluate <- "IBCF"
> model_parameters <- NULL
> eval_recommender <- Recommender(data = getData(eval_sets,
"train"),method = model_to_evaluate, parameter = model_parameters)
```

2. The IBCF can recommend new items and predict their ratings. Specify the number of items that we want to recommend so that we can build the matrix with the predicted ratings using the `predict` function:

```
> items_to_recommend <- 10

> eval_prediction <- predict(object = eval_recommender, newdata
=getData(eval_sets, "known"), n = > items_to_recommend, type =
"ratings")

> class(eval_prediction)

[1] "realRatingMatrix"
attr(,"package")
[1] "recommenderlab"
```

3. Next, visualize the distribution of the number of movies per user:

```
> qplot(rowCounts(eval_prediction)) + geom_histogram(binwidth = 20)
+ ggtitle("Distribution of movies per user")
```

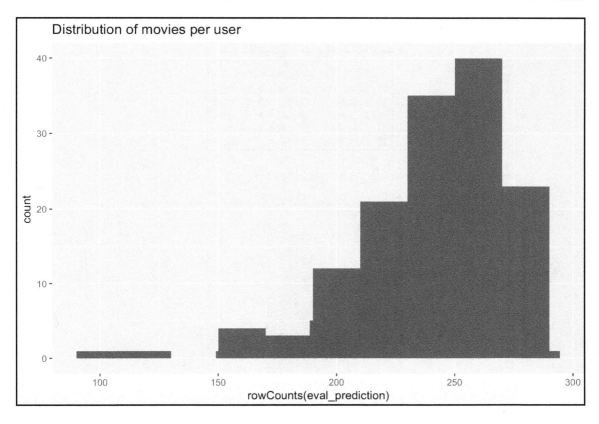

The number of movies per user is roughly between 150 and 300.

4. Now let's measure the accuracy about each user predicted by the model:

```
> eval_accuracy <- calcPredictionAccuracy(
  x = eval_prediction, data = getData(eval_sets, "unknown"), byUser
=TRUE)

> head(eval_accuracy)
```

The following is the result of the code:

	RMSE	MSE	MAE
7	1.125763	1.267343	0.8281174
11	1.163445	1.353603	0.9460402
18	1.086492	1.180465	0.8696023
21	1.684008	2.835884	1.3155852
22	1.445691	2.090022	1.1084598
23	1.188968	1.413644	0.8866241

5. Finally, visualize the RMSE distribution by user:

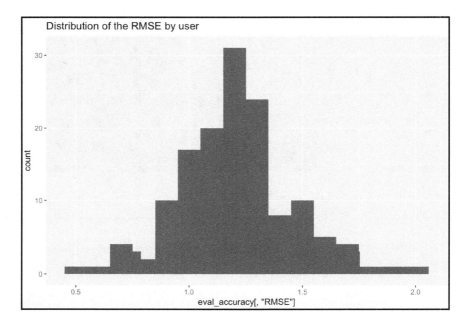

Most of the RMSEs are in the range of 0.8 to 1.4.

Evaluating the recommendations: This measures the accuracy by comparing the recommendations with the purchases having a positive rating.

1. The `rating_threshold` is already defined for positive ratings and is contained in the `eval_set`. We will use the `evaluate` function to evaluate the IBCF model:

```
> results <- evaluate(x = eval_sets, method = model_to_evaluate, n
=seq(10, 100, 10))
```

2. Next, extract a list of confusion matrices using the `getConfusionMatrix` method of the `recommender` package, where each element of the list corresponds to a different split of the k-fold (defined under `eval_sets`):

```
> head(getConfusionMatrix(results)[[1]])
```

The following is the result of the previous code:

	TP	FP	FN	TN	precision	recall	TPR	FPR
10	3.000000	7.00000	75.10714	231.8929	0.3000000	0.03861904	0.03861904	0.02897558
20	5.850000	14.15000	72.25714	224.7429	0.2925000	0.07396527	0.07396527	0.05852941
30	8.714286	21.28571	69.39286	217.6071	0.2904762	0.11376990	0.11376990	0.08804772
40	11.378571	28.62143	66.72857	210.2714	0.2844643	0.15061808	0.15061808	0.11871507
50	13.785714	36.21429	64.32143	202.6786	0.2757143	0.18121755	0.18121755	0.15050525
60	16.142857	43.85714	61.96429	195.0357	0.2690476	0.21328375	0.21328375	0.18265956

3. Finally, visualize the evaluation result with a precision recall curve:

```
> plot(results, "prec/rec", annotate = TRUE, main = "Precision-recall")
```

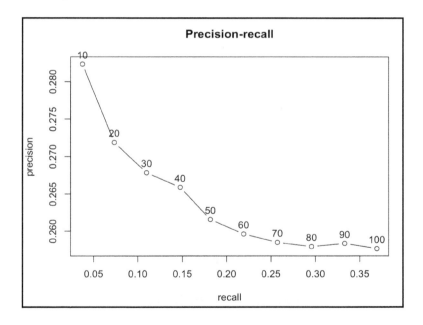

How it works...

Evaluating a model consists of comparing the recommendations with the unknown purchases. We have used three functions in this recipe to split the dataset, evaluate the recommendation model, and measure the accuracy of the model.

The `evaluationScheme` function of the `recommenderlab` package is used to split the dataset into training and test sets and has the following parameters:

- **data**: This is the initial dataset.
- **method**: This is the way to split the data. In this case, it's split.
- **train**: This is the percentage of data in the training set.
- **given**: This is the number of items to keep.
- **goodRating**: This is the rating threshold.
- **k**: This is the number of times to run the evaluation.

The `calcPredictionAccuracy` function is used to measure the accuracy and it computes the following aspects:

- **Root mean square error (RMSE)**: This is the standard deviation of the difference between the real and predicted ratings.
- **Mean squared error (MSE)**: This is the mean of the squared difference between the real and predicted ratings. It's the square of RMSE, so it contains the same information.
- **Mean absolute error (MAE)**: This is the mean of the absolute difference between the real and predicted ratings.

The `evaluate` function is used to measure accuracy by comparing the recommendations with the purchases having a positive rating. Its parameters are as follows:

- **x**: This is the object containing the evaluation scheme.
- **method**: This is the recommendation technique.
- **n**: This is the number of items to recommend to each user. If we can specify a vector of *n*, the function will evaluate the recommender performance depending on *n*.

There's more...

Applying different models on the same data, we can compare the performance metrics to pick the most appropriate recommender.

Identifying a suitable model

In order to evaluate various models properly, we need to test them by varying the number of items or movies:

1. Store each model in a list with its name and parameters and then define the number of recommendation items for each user:

```
> models_to_evaluate <- list( IBCF_cos = list(name = "IBCF", param
= list(method = "cosine")), IBCF_cor = list(name = "IBCF", param =
list(method = "pearson")), UBCF_cos = list(name = "UBCF", param =
list(method = "cosine")), UBCF_cor = list(name = "UBCF", param =
list(method = "pearson")), random = list(name = "RANDOM",
param=NULL) )
> n_recommendations <- c(1, 5, seq(10, 100, 10))
```

2. Run and evaluate the models:

```
> list_results <- evaluate(x = eval_sets, method =
models_to_evaluate, n = n_recommendations)
```

3. Next, identify the most suitable model with **Area Under Curve (AUC)** and precision recall curve:

```
> plot(list_results, annotate = 1, legend = "topleft")+ title("ROC
curve")
```

The following is the result of the code:

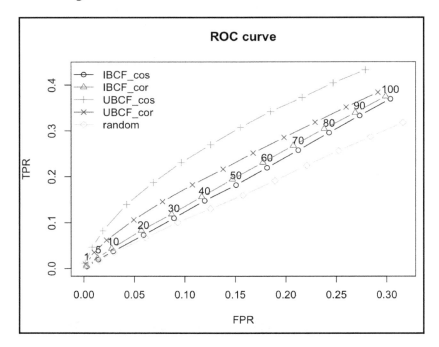

4. You will notice from the preceding graph that the UBCF model has the highest AUC with cosine distance, so it's the best-performing model among others.

```
> plot(list_results, "prec/rec", annotate = 1, legend =
"bottomright")+ title("Precision-recall")
```

The preceding code gives us the following illustration of the result:

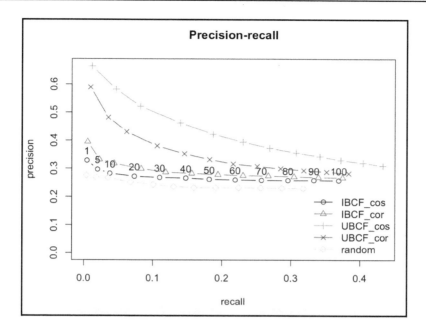

The UBCF with cosine distance is still the top model as seen from the precision recall curve as well.

Optimizing parameters

Once we have identified our best model, the next step would be to optimize this model. Every recommendation model contains some parameters--numeric or categorical. For instance, IBCF takes account of the k-closest items, but how can we optimize the value of k?

1. Instead of specifying a single value while evaluating the model, we can specify a range of values for the parameter and then evaluate the model to find out the optimal value for this parameter:

```
> vector_k <- c(5, 10, 20, 30, 40)
> models_to_evaluate <- lapply(vector_k, function(k){
  list(name = "IBCF", param = list(method = "cosine", k = k))
})
> names(models_to_evaluate) <- paste0("IBCF_k_", vector_k)
```

2. Now visualize the best performing k with ROC curve:

```
> plot(list_results, annotate = 1, legend = "topleft")+ title("ROC
curve")
```

The following result gives the visualization of the best performing K with **ROC curve**:

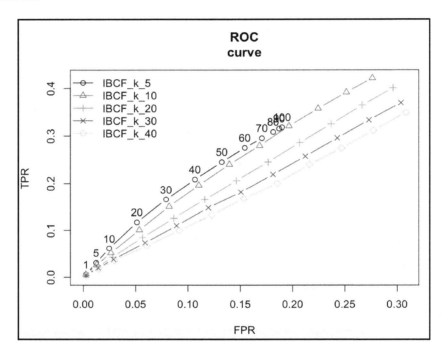

As seen from the ROC curve, *k=10* has the biggest AUC. Another good candidate is 5, but it doesn't have a high TPR.

3. Finally, visualize the precision-recall curve:

```
> plot(list_results, "prec/rec", annotate = 1, legend =
"bottomright")+ title("Precision-recall")
```

The **Precision-recall** curve gives us the following result:

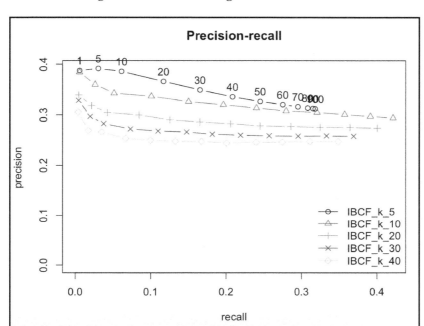

From the precision-recall curve, you can see that *k=10* achieved the highest recall, but if you are more interested in the precision, *k = 5* would be a better choice.

A practical example - fraud detection system

Machine learning algorithms tend to tremble when faced with imbalanced classification datasets due to the lack of necessary information about the minority class to make an accurate prediction. Imbalanced classification refers to a supervised learning problem where one class outnumbers another class by a large proportion.

Luckily, there are some useful techniques to treat imbalanced datasets before applying the dataset for ML prediction:

- **Undersampling**: This approach reduces the number of observations from the majority class to make the dataset balanced and is well suited for large datasets by eliminating some training examples of the majority class.
- **Oversampling**: This approach randomly replicates the observations from the minority class to balance the data. It is also known as **Upsampling**.

- **Synthetic Minority Oversampling** (**SMOTE**): This approach generates a random set of artificial data based on feature space (rather than data space) similarities from minority samples to shift the classifier's learning bias toward the minority class.

> In this recipe, we will analyze the credit card transaction dataset from Kaggle (`https://www.kaggle.com/dalpozz/creditcardfraud`) and develop a fraud detection algorithm using the SMOTE technique discussed in the preceding section.

Getting ready

Make sure that you have downloaded the code for this chapter and that the `creditcard.csv` file is in your working directory of R.

Install the latest version of the following packages:

```
> install.packages("caret")
> install.packages("pROC")
> install.packages("DMwR")
> install.packages("caTools")
```

How to do it...

1. First, load the packages and read the credit card dataset:

   ```
   > library(caret)
   > library(pROC)
   > library(DMwR)
   > library(caTools)

   > creditCardData <- read.csv("creditcard.csv")
   ```

2. Next, change the type of response variable `Class` from `int` to `factor` and then check the number of fraud (1) or normal (0) transaction examples:

   ```
   > creditCardData$Class<-
   factor(ifelse(creditCardData$Class==0,"0","1"))
   > table(data$Class)
        0      1
   284315    492
   ```

3. Now split the dataset into training and test sets and check the dataset target variable proportion:

```
> splitIndex <- createDataPartition(creditCardData$Class, p = .70,
list = FALSE, times = 1)
> trainSplit <- creditCardData[ splitIndex,]
> table(trainSplit$Class)
     0       1
199025     340
> testSplit <- creditCardData[-splitIndex,]
> table(testSplit$Class)
     0       1
 85290     152
```

4. Apply the SMOTE algorithm to balance the training set:

```
> trainSplit <- SMOTE(Class ~ ., trainSplit, perc.over = 200,
perc.under=100)

> table(trainSplit$Class)
   0    1
 690 1035
```

5. Next, convert the target variable to int and train the balanced dataset using the bagging approach with cross-validation:

```
> trainSplit$Class<- as.numeric(trainSplit$Class)
> trCtrl <- trainControl(method = "cv", number = 10)
> tbmodel <- train(Class ~ ., data = trainSplit, method =
"treebag",
                   trControl = trCtrl)
> tbmodel

Bagged CART

1725 samples
30 predictor

No pre-processing
Resampling: Cross-Validated (10 fold)
Summary of sample sizes: 1553, 1552, 1552, 1552, 1553, 1553, ...
Resampling results:

RMSE       Rsquared
0.2076757  0.8201645
```

6. Convert the response variable `Class` to a factor before doing the prediction:

```
> predictors <- names(trainSplit)[names(trainSplit) != 'Class']
> pred <- predict(tbmodel$finalModel, testSplit[,predictors])
```

7. Calculate the value of `auc` to measure accuracy:

```
> auc <- roc(testSplit$Class, pred)

> print(auc)

Call:
roc.default(response = testSplit$Class, predictor = pred)

Data: pred in 85294 controls (testSplit$Class 0) < 147 cases
(testSplit$Class 1).
```

Area under the curve: 0.9889.

8. Finally, visualize the AUC curve:

```
> plot(auc, ylim=c(0,1), print.thres=TRUE, main=paste('AUC with
SMOTE:',round(auc$auc[[1]],2)))
> abline(h=1,col='blue',lwd=2)
> abline(h=0,col='red',lwd=2)
```

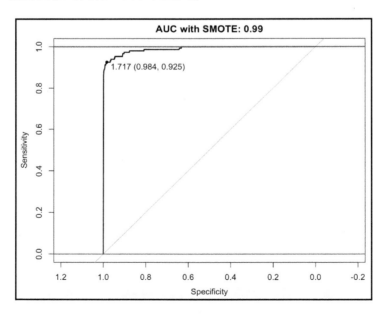

How it works...

First, we read the credit card dataset and verify the number of fraud (492) versus normal (284315) transactions.

After splitting the dataset into training and test sets with a 70/30 ratio using the `createDataPartition ()` method from the `caret` package, we then apply the `SMOTE()` method from the `DMwR` package to generate synthetic data for the minority class (fraud denoted by 1) in the dataset. The `perc.over` and `perc.under` attributes of the `SMOTE` function determine the generation of the number of oversampled and under-sampled data respectively.

Next, we apply a tree-based bagging (`treebag`) algorithm with 10-fold cross validation to train the model using an artificially created balanced dataset with the SMOTE approach seen earlier. We use the train method of the `caret` package to train the model and the `trainControl()` method to define the cross-validation with the number of folds (in our case, 10). Bagging is an ensemble technique that combines the predictions from multiple machine learning models together to make more accurate predictions than any individual model.

Finally, the trained model is used to predict on the test data and, as confusion matrix accuracy is not meaningful for unbalanced classification, AUC is calculated using the `roc()` method of the `pROC` package and plotted to visualize the accuracy of the model.

9
It's All About Your Connections - Social Network Analysis

In this chapter, we will cover the following topics:

- Downloading social network data using public APIs
- Creating adjacency matrices and edge lists
- Plotting social network data
- Computing important network metrics
- Cluster analysis
- Force layout
- YiFan Hu layout

Introduction

When we think of the term **social network**, sites such as Twitter, Facebook, Google+, LinkedIn, and Meetup immediately come to mind. However, data analysts have applied the concepts of social network analysis in domains as varied as co-authorship networks, human networks, the spread of disease, migratory birds, and interlocking corporate board memberships, just to name a few. While working with graph and network visualizations, a good tool provides the data analyst with the capability to restructure the network in order to visualize the required parts of the graph in an enhanced way.

R provides various packages containing ready-to-use efficient layout algorithms to manipulate and analyze network data. In this chapter, we will cover recipes to make sense of real-world social network data (from Meetup and Twitter) with R.

Downloading social network data using public APIs

Social networking websites provide public APIs to enable us to download their data. In this recipe, we cover the process of downloading data from `Meetup.com` using their public API. You can adapt this basic approach to download data from other websites. In this recipe, we get the data in JSON format and then import it to an R data frame.

Getting ready

In this recipe, you will download data from `Meetup.com`. To gain access to the data, you need to be a member:

- If you do not have an account in `http://www.meetup.com`, sign up and become a member of a couple of groups.
- You need your own API key to download data through scripts. Get your own by clicking on the **API Key** link on `http://www.meetup.com/meetup_api/`. Save the key.

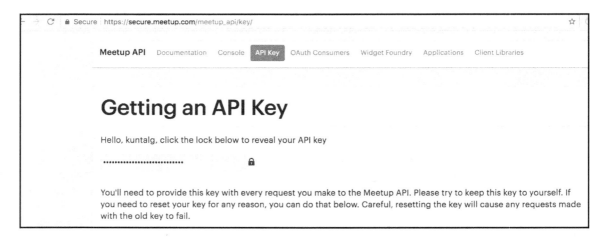

You can replicate the steps in this recipe without additional information. However, if you would like more details, you can read about the API at `http://www.meetup.com/meetup_api/`.

Download the `groups.json` file from chapters code and place it in your R working directory.

How to do it...

In this recipe, we see how to get data from the console and how R scripts are used.

1. Download information about Meetup groups that satisfy certain criteria. http://www.meetup.com allows you to download data from their **Console** by filling up fields to define your criteria. Alternately, you can also construct a suitable URL to directly get the data. The former approach has some limitations when downloading large volumes of data.

2. In this recipe, we first show you how to get data from the console. We then show you how to use R scripts that use URLs for larger data volumes. We will first get a list of groups. Use your browser to visit http://www.meetup.com/meetup_api/. Click on **Console** and then click on the first link under **v2 groups** on the right (**GET /2/groups**). Enter the **topic** you are interested in and enter your two-character ISO country code (see http://en.wikipedia.org/wiki/ISO_3166-1 for country codes) and **city** or **zip** (that is, zip code). You can specify **radius** to restrict the number of groups returned. We used hiking for **topic**, US for **country**, 08816 for **zip**, and 25 for **radius**. Click on **Show Response** to see the results. If you get an error, try with different values. If you used different selection criteria, you may see many groups. From the earlier results, you will notice information on many attributes for each group. You can use the **only** field to get some of these attributes, for example, to get only the group ID, name, and number of members, enter id, name, members in the **only** textbox (note that there is no space after the commas).

3. You can also get information using a URL directly, but you will need to use your API key for this. For example, the following URL gets the ID, name, and number of members for all hiking-related groups in Amsterdam, NL (replace <<yourapikey>> with the API key you downloaded earlier in the *Getting started* part of this recipe; no angle braces are needed):
   http://api.meetup.com/2/groupstopic=hiking&country=NL&city=Amst erdam&only=id,name,members&key=<<yourapikey>>

You will note that the results look different in the console when using the URL directly, but this is just a formatting issue. The console pretty-prints the JSON, whereas we see unformatted JSON when we use a URL.

4. We will now save the downloaded data; the process depends on whether you used the console approach in *step 2* or the URL approach in *step 3*. If you used the console approach, you should select the block of text starting with the { before `results` and ending with the very last }. Paste the copied text into a text editor and save the file as `groups.json`. On the other hand, if you used the URL approach of step 3, right-click and select **Save As** to save the displayed results as a file named `groups.json` in your R working directory. You can use online json formatter (`http://jsoneditoronline.org/`) to print the JSON properly and then select the appropriate part of the JSON.

5. Or simply you can also use the `groups.json` file that you downloaded earlier.

6. We will now load the data from the saved JSON file into an R data frame. For details, refer to the *Reading JSON data* recipe in Chapter 1, *Acquire and Prepare the Ingredients - Your Data*:

```
> library(jsonlite)
> g <- fromJSON("groups.json") '
> groups <- g$results
> head(groups)
```

7. For each group, we will now use the `Meetup.com` API to download member information to a data frame called `users`. Among the code files that you downloaded for this chapter is a file called `rdacb.getusers.R`. Source this file into your R environment now and run the following code. For each group from our list of groups, this code uses the `Meetup.com` API to get the group's members. It generates a data frame with a set of `group_id` and `user_id` pairs.
   In the following command, replace `<<apikey>>` with your actual API key from the *Getting ready* section. Be sure to enclose the key in double quotes and also be sure that you do not have any angle brackets in the command. This command can take a while to execute because of the sheer number of web requests and the volume of data involved. If you get an error message, see *How it works* in the following section:

```
> source("rdacb.getusers.R")
> # in command below, substitute your api key for
> # <<apikey>> and enclose it in double-quotes
> members <- rdacb.getusers(groups, <<apikey>>)
```

This creates a data frame with the variables, (`group_id`, `user_id`).

8. The `members` data frame now has information about the social network, and normally we will use it for all further processing. However, as it is very large, many of the steps in subsequent recipes will take a lot of processing time. For convenience, we reduce the size of the social network by retaining only members who belong to more than 16 groups. This step uses data tables; see Chapter 9, *Work Smarter, Not harder - Efficient and Elegant R code*, for more details. If you like to work with the complete network, you can skip this step:

```
> library(data.table)
> users <- setDT(members)[,.SD[.N > 16], by = user_id]
```

9. Save the members data before further processing:

```
> save(users,file="meetup_users.Rdata")
```

How it works...

Steps 2 and 3 get data from `Meetup.com` using their console.

By default, Meetup APIs return 20 results (JSON documents) for each call. However, by adding `page=n` to the console or the URL (where *n* is a number), we can get more documents (up to a maximum of 200). The API response contains metadata information including the number of documents returned (in the `count` element), the total documents available (the `total_count` element), the URL used to get the response, and the URL to get the next set of results (the `next` element).

Step 4 saves the results displayed in the browser as `groups.json` in your R working directory.

Step 5 loads the JSON data file into an R data frame using the `from JSON` function in the `jsonlite` package. For more details on this, refer to the *Reading JSON data* recipe in `Chapter 1`, *Acquire and Prepare the Ingredients - Your Data*.

The returned object `g` contains the results in the `results` element, and we assign `g$results` (a data frame) to the `groups` variable.

Step 6 uses the `rdacb.getusers` convenience function to iterate through each group and get its members. The function constructs the appropriate API URL using `group` and `id`. As each call returns only a fixed number of users, the `while` loop of the function iterates till it gets all the users. The `next` element of the result returned tells us if the group has more members.

There can be groups with no members and hence we check whether `temp$results` returns a data frame. The API returns group and user IDs as they are in `Meetup.com`.

If the `Meetup.com` site is overloaded with several API requests during the time of your invocation, you may get an error message:

```
Errorinfunction(type,msg,asError=TRUE):Emptyreplyfromserver.
```

Retry the same step. Depending on the number of groups and the number of members in each group, this step can take a long time.

At this point, we have the data for a very large social network. Subsequent recipes in this chapter use the social network that we create in this recipe. Some of the steps in subsequent recipes can take a lot of processing time if run on the complete network. Using a smaller network will suffice for illustration. Therefore, step 7 uses data.table to retain only members who belong to more than 16 groups.

Step 8 saves the member data in a file for possible future use. We now have a two-mode network, where the first mode is a set of groups and the second mode is the list of members. From this, we can either create a network of users based on common group memberships or a network of groups based on common members. In the rest of this chapter, we do the former.

We created a data frame in which each row represents a membership of an individual user in a group. From this information, we can create representations of social networks.

See also

- *Reading JSON data* in Chapter 1, *Acquire and Prepare the Ingredients - Your Data*
- *Slicing, dicing, and combining data with data tables* in Chapter 9, *Work Smarter, Not Harder - Efficient and Elegant R Code*

Creating adjacency matrices and edge lists

We can represent social network data in different formats. We cover two common representations:

- Sparse adjacency matrices
- Edge lists

Taking data from the Meetup.com social networking site (from the previous recipe in this chapter--*Downloading social network data using public APIs*), this recipe shows how you can convert a data frame with membership information to a sparse adjacency matrix and then to an edge list.

In this application, nodes represent users of Meetup.com and an edge connects two nodes if they are members of at least one common group. The number of common groups for a pair of people will represent the weight of the connection.

Getting ready

If you have not yet installed the `Matrix` packages, you should do so now using the following code:

```
> install.packages("Matrix")
```

If you completed the prior recipe, *Downloading social network data using public APIs*, and have the `meetup_users.Rdata` file, you can use it. Otherwise, you can download that data file from the book's website and place it in your R working directory.

How to do it...

To create adjacency matrices and edge lists, follow these steps:

1. Load `Meetup.com` user information from the `meetup_users.Rdata` file. This creates a data frame called `users` which has the variables, (`user_id` and `group_id`):

   ```
   > load("meetup_users.Rdata")
   ```

2. Create a sparse matrix with groups on the rows and users on the columns with TRUE on each (`group_id`, `user_id`) position, where the group has the user as a member. If you have a large number of users, this step will take a long time. It also needs a lot of memory to create a sparse matrix. If your R session freezes, you will have to either find a computer with more RAM or reduce the number of users and try again:

   ```
   > library(Matrix)
   > grp.membership = sparseMatrix(users$group_id, users$user_id, x =
   TRUE)
   ```

3. Use the sparse matrix to create an `adjacency` matrix with users on both rows and columns with the number of common groups between a pair of users as the matrix element:

   ```
   > adjacency = t(grp.membership) %*% grp.membership
   ```

4. We can use the group membership matrix, that is, (`grp.membership`), to create a network of groups instead of users with groups as the nodes and edges representing common memberships across groups. In this example, we will consider only a network of users.

5. Use the `adjacency` matrix to create an `edgelist`:

```
> users.edgelist <- as.data.frame(summary(adjacency))
> names(users.edgelist)
[1] "i" "j" "x"
```

6. The relationship between any two users is reciprocal. That is, if users 25 and 326 have 32 groups in common, then the `edgelist` currently duplicates that information as (25, 362, 32) and (362, 25, 32). We need to keep only one of these. Also, our `adjacency` matrix has non-zero diagonal elements and the edge list has edges corresponding to those. We can eliminate these by keeping only the edges corresponding to the upper or lower triangle of the `adjacency` matrix:

```
# Extract upper triangle of the edgelist
> users.edgelist.upper <- users.edgelist[users.edgelist$i <
users.edgelist$j,]
```

7. Save the data, just in case:

```
> save(users.edgelist.upper, file = "users_edgelist_upper.Rdata")
```

How it works...

Step 1 loads the `users` group membership data from a `meetup_users.Rdata` saved file. This creates a `users` data frame with the `(user_id, group_id)` structure. From this, we want to create a network in which the nodes are users and a pair of users has an edge if they are members of at least one common group. We want to have the number of common group memberships as the weight of an edge.

Step 2 converts the information in the group membership data frame to a sparse matrix with groups on the rows and users on the columns. To clarify, the following table shows a sample matrix with four groups and nine users. The first group has users 1, 4, and 7 as members, while the second has users 1, 3, 4, and 6 as members, and so on. We have shown the complete matrix here, but step 2 creates a much more space efficient sparse representation of this information:

			Users						
	1	**2**	**3**	**4**	**5**	**6**	**7**	**8**	**9**
1	1	.	.	1	.	.	1	.	.
2	1	.	1	1	.	1	.	.	.
3	1	1	.	1	.	1	1	.	1
4	.	1	1	.	.	1	.	.	1

(Groups labels the rows)

While the sparse matrix has all the network information, several social network analysis functions work with the data represented as an **adjacency matrix** or as an **edge list**. We want to create a social network of `Meetup.com` users. The adjacency matrix will have the shape of a square matrix with users on both rows and columns and the number of shared groups as the matrix element. For the sample data in the preceding figure, the adjacency matrix will look like this:

Users	1	2	3	4	5	6	7	8	9
1	3	1	1	3	0	2	2	0	1
2	1	2	1	1	0	2	1	0	2
3	1	1	2	1	0	2	0	0	1
4	3	1	1	3	0	2	2	0	1
5	0	0	0	0	0	0	0	0	0
6	2	2	2	2	0	3	1	0	2
7	2	1	0	2	0	1	2	0	1
8	0	0	0	0	0	0	0	0	0
9	1	2	1	1	0	2	1	0	2

Step 3 creates a sparse adjacency matrix from the earlier sparse group membership matrix. From the earlier figure, we see that **Users** 1 and 4 have three groups in common (groups 1, 2, and 3) and thus the elements (1, 4) and (4, 1) of the matrix have a 3 in them. The diagonal elements simply indicate the number of groups to which the corresponding users belong. User 1 belongs to three groups and hence (1, 1) has a 3. We only need the upper or lower triangle of the matrix, which we will take care of in a later step.

Step 4 creates an edge list from the sparse adjacency matrix. An edge list will have the following structure: (`user_id 1`, `users_id 2`, number of common groups). For the sample data in the preceding figure, the edge list will look like this (only 10 of the 47 edges are shown in the following figure). Once again, we need only the upper or lower triangle of this:

i	j	x
1	1	3
2	1	1
3	1	1
4	1	3
6	1	2
7	1	2
9	1	1
1	2	1
2	2	2
3	2	1
...	...	...

We have a symmetric network. Saying that users A and B have *n* groups in common is the same thing as saying that users B and A have *n* groups in common. Thus, we do not need to represent both of these in the adjacency matrix or edge list. We also do not need any edges connecting users to themselves and thus do not need the diagonal elements in the sparse matrix or elements with the same value for **i** and **j** in the edge list.

Step 5 eliminates the redundant edges and the edges that connect a user to themselves.

Step 6 saves the sparse network for possible future use.

We now created both a sparse adjacency matrix and an edge list representation of the social network of users in our chosen Meetup groups. We can use these representations for social network analyses.

See also

- *Downloading social network data using public APIs* in this chapter

Plotting social network data

This recipe covers the features in the `igraph` package to create graph objects, plot them, and extract network information from `graph` objects.

Getting ready

If you have not already installed the `igraph` package, do it now using the following code:

```
> install.packages("igraph")
```

Also, download the `users_edgelist_upper.Rdata` file from the book's data files to your R working directory. Alternately, if you worked through the previous recipe, *Creating adjacency matrices and edge lists*, you will have created the file and ensured that it is in your R working directory.

How to do it...

To plot social network data using `igraph`, follow these steps:

1. Load the data. The following code will restore, from the saved file, a data frame called `users.edgelist.upper`:

```
> load("users_edgelist_upper.Rdata")
```

2. The data file that we have provided `users.edgelist.upper` should now have 1,953 rows of data. Plotting such a network will take too much time--even worse, we will get too dense a plot to get any meaningful information. Just for convenience, we will create a much smaller network by filtering our edge list. We will consider as connected only users who have more than 16 common group memberships and create a far smaller network for illustration only:

```
> edgelist.filtered <- users.edgelist.upper[users.edgelist.upper$x
> 16,]

> edgelist.filtered  # Your results could differ

                   i        j  x
34364988     2073657  3823125 17
41804209     2073657  4379102 18
53937250     2073657  5590181 17
62598651     3823125  6629901 18
190318039    5286367 13657677 17
190321739    8417076 13657677 17
205800861    5054895 14423171 18
252063744    5054895 33434002 18
252064197    5590181 33434002 17
252064967    6629901 33434002 18
252071701   10973799 33434002 17
252076384   13657677 33434002 17
254937514    5227777 34617262 17
282621070    5590181 46801552 19
282621870    6629901 46801552 18
282639752   33434002 46801552 20
307874358   33434002 56882992 17
335204492   33434002 69087262 17
486425803   33434002 147010712 17

> nrow(edgelist.filtered)

[1] 19
```

3. Renumber the users. As we filtered the graph significantly, we have only 18 unique users left, but they retain their original user IDs. We will find it convenient to sequence them with unique numbers from 1 through 18. This step is not strictly needed, but will make the social network graph look cleaner:

```
> uids <- unique(c(edgelist.filtered$i, edgelist.filtered$j))
> i <- match(edgelist.filtered$i, uids)
> j <- match(edgelist.filtered$j, uids)
> nw.new <- data.frame(i, j, x = edgelist.filtered$x)
```

4. Create the `graph` object and plot the network:

```
> library(igraph)
> g <- graph.data.frame(nw.new, directed=FALSE)
> g
IGRAPH UN-- 18 19 --
+ attr: name (v/c), x (e/n)
> # Save the graph for use in later recipes:
> save(g, file = "undirected-graph.Rdata")
> plot.igraph(g, vertex.size = 20)
```

Your plot may look different in terms of layout, but if you look carefully, you will see that the nodes and edges are identical:

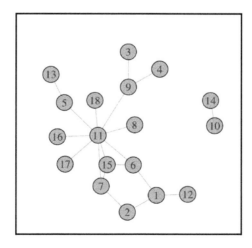

5. Plot the `graph` object with a different layout:

```
> plot.igraph(g,layout=layout.circle, vertex.size = 20)
```

The following graph is the output of the preceding command:

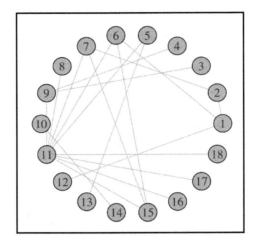

6. Plot the `graph` object using colors for the vertices and edges:

```
> plot.igraph(g,edge.curved=TRUE,vertex.color="pink",
edge.color="black")
```

Again, your plot may be laid out differently, but should be functionally identical to the following plot:

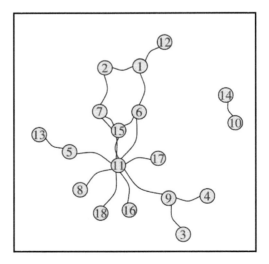

7. Plot the graph with node size proportional to node degree:

```
> V(g)$size=degree(g) * 4
> plot.igraph(g,edge.curved=TRUE,vertex.color="pink",
edge.color="black")
```

The output is similar to the following plot:

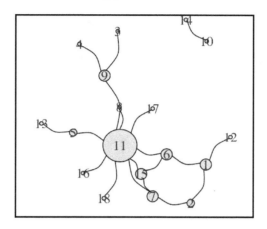

8. Plot the graph with the node `size` and `color` based on `degree`:

```
> color <- ifelse(degree(g) > 5,"red","blue")
> size <- degree(g)*4
> plot.igraph(g,vertex.label=NA,layout=
layout.fruchterman.reingold,vertex.color=color,vertex.size=size)
```

A plot identical to the following will be obtained:

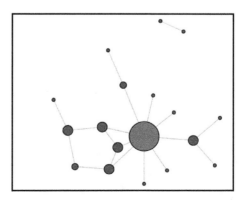

9. Plot the graph with the edge thickness proportional to edge weights:

```
> E(g)$x

[1] 17 18 17 18 17 17 18 18 17 18 17 17 17 19 18 20 17 17 17

> plot.igraph(g,edge.curved=TRUE,edge.color="black",
edge.width=E(g)$x/5)
```

The output is similar to the following plot:

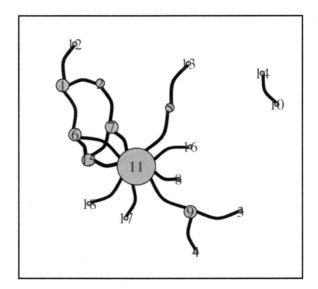

How it works...

Step 1 loads the saved network data in the form of an edge list.

With so much data, we will not find a plot to be a useful visual aid because it will be too cramped. Thus, for illustration, we redefine two users (nodes) to be related (connected in the social network) only if they have more than 16 group memberships in common.

Step 2 filters the edge list and retains only edges that meet the preceding criterion.

Although we have filtered the data, users still retain their original IDs, which are big numbers. Having user numbers in sequence starting with 1 might be nice.

Step 3 does this conversion.

Step 4 uses the `graph.data.frame` function from the `igraph` package to create a `graph` object. This function treats the first two columns of the `nw.new` data frame argument as the edge list and treats the rest of the columns as edge attributes.

We created an undirected graph by specifying `directed=FALSE`. Specifying `directed=TRUE` (or omitting this argument altogether as `TRUE` is the default) will create a directed graph.

Here, `g` is an undirected named graph represented by `UN`. A graph is treated as named if the vertex has a `name` attribute. The third letter indicates if the graph is weighted (`W`), and the fourth letter indicates if it is a bipartite (`B`) graph. The two numbers indicate the number of vertices and number of edges. The second line `+attr:name(v/c),x(e/n)` gives details about the attributes. The `name` attribute represents the vertex, and the `x` attribute represents the edge.

The step then uses the `plot.igraph` function from the `igraph` package to plot it.

We specified the `vertex.size` argument to ensure that the node circles were large enough to fit the node numbers.

Step 5 plots the very same graph but with the nodes laid out on the circumference of a circle.

Step 6 shows other options, which should be self-explanatory.

In step 7, we set the node (or vertex) size. We use `V(g)` to access each vertex in the `graph` object and use the `$` operator to extract attributes, for example, `V(g)$size`. Similarly, we can use `E(g)` to access the edges.

Step 8 goes further by assigning node color and size based on a node's degree. It also shows the use of the `layout` option.

There's more...

We can do much more with the `graph` object that the `graph.data.frame` function of the `igraph` package creates.

Specifying plotting preferences

We showed only a few options to control the look of the plot. You have many more options to control the look of the edges, nodes, and other aspects. The documentation of plot.igraph mentions these options. When using them, remember to prefix the node options with (vertex.) and edge options with (edge.).

Plotting directed graphs

In step 4 of the main recipe, we created an undirected graph. Here, we create a directed graph object, dg:

```
> dg <- graph.data.frame(nw.new)
> # save for later use
> save(dg, file = "directed-graph.Rdata")
> plot.igraph(dg,edge.curved=TRUE,edge.color="black",
edge.width=E(dg)$x/10,vertex.label.cex=.6)
```

On plotting the preceding graph, we get the following output:

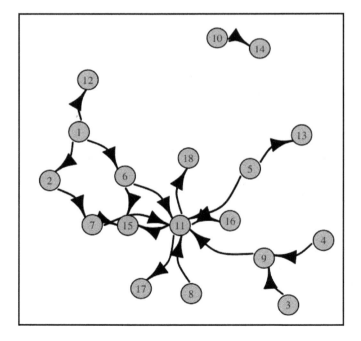

Creating a graph object with weights

If the name of the third column in the edge list passed to `graph.data.frame` is called `weight`, it creates a weighted graph. Hence, we can rename the third column from `x` to `weight` and redraw the graph:

```
> nw.weights <- nw.new
> names(nw.weights) <- c("i","j","weight")
> g.weights <- graph.data.frame(nw.weights, directed=FALSE)
> g.weights
IGRAPH UNW- 18 19 --
+ attr: name (v/c), weight (e/n)
```

When we check the graph properties, we see `W` in the third position of `UNW-`.

Extracting the network as an adjacency matrix from the graph object

Earlier, we created an edge list from a sparse adjacency matrix. Here, we show how to get the sparse adjacency matrix from the graph object that we created in step 4 of the main recipe. In the following, we use `type="upper"` to get the upper triangular matrix. Other options are `lower` and `both`.

```
> get.adjacency(g,type="upper")

18 x 18 sparse Matrix of class "dgCMatrix"
   [[ suppressing 18 column names '1', '2', '3' ... ]]

1  . 1 . . . 1 . . . . . 1 . . . . . .
2  . . . . . 1 . . . . . . . . . . . .
3  . . . . . . . 1 . . . . . . . . . .
4  . . . . . . . 1 . . . . . . . . . .
5  . . . . . . . . 1 . 1 . . . . . . .
6  . . . . . . . . 1 . . . 1 . . . . .
7  . . . . . . . . 1 . . . 1 . . . . .
8  . . . . . . . . 1 . . . . . . . . .
9  . . . . . . . . 1 . . . . . . . . .
10 . . . . . . . . . . . 1 . . . . . .
11 . . . . . . . . . . . 1 1 1 1 . . .
12 . . . . . . . . . . . . . . . . . .
13 . . . . . . . . . . . . . . . . . .
14 . . . . . . . . . . . . . . . . . .
15 . . . . . . . . . . . . . . . . . .
16 . . . . . . . . . . . . . . . . . .
17 . . . . . . . . . . . . . . . . . .
18 . . . . . . . . . . . . . . . . . .
```

In the preceding code, we did not get back the weights and got back a 0-1 sparse matrix instead.

If we want the weights, we can implement the following techniques.

Extracting an adjacency matrix with weights

The `graph.data.frame` function from the `igraph` package treats the first two columns of the data frame supplied as making up the edge list and the rest of the columns as edge attributes. By default, the `get.adjacency` function does not return any edge attributes and instead returns a simple 0-1 sparse matrix of connections.

However, you can pass the `attr` argument to tell the function which of the remaining attributes you want as the elements of the sparse matrix (and hence the edge weight). In our situation, this attribute will be `x`, representing the number of common group memberships between two users. In the following, we have specified `type="lower"` to get the lower triangular matrix. Other options are `upper` and `both`.

```
> get.adjacency(g, type = "lower", attr = "x")

18 x 18 sparse Matrix of class "dgCMatrix"
   [[ suppressing 18 column names '1', '2', '3' ... ]]

1   .  .  .  .  .  .  .  .  .  .  .  .  .  .  .  .  .  .
2  17  .  .  .  .  .  .  .  .  .  .  .  .  .  .  .  .  .
3   .  .  .  .  .  .  .  .  .  .  .  .  .  .  .  .  .  .
4   .  .  .  .  .  .  .  .  .  .  .  .  .  .  .  .  .  .
5   .  .  .  .  .  .  .  .  .  .  .  .  .  .  .  .  .  .
6  17  .  .  .  .  .  .  .  .  .  .  .  .  .  .  .  .  .
7   . 18  .  .  .  .  .  .  .  .  .  .  .  .  .  .  .  .
8   .  .  .  .  .  .  .  .  .  .  .  .  .  .  .  .  .  .
9   . 17 17  .  .  .  .  .  .  .  .  .  .  .  .  .  .  .
10  .  .  .  .  .  .  .  .  .  .  .  .  .  .  .  .  .  .
11  .  .  . 18 17 18 17 17  .  .  .  .  .  .  .  .  .  .
12 18  .  .  .  .  .  .  .  .  .  .  .  .  .  .  .  .  .
13  .  .  . 18  .  .  .  .  .  .  .  .  .  .  .  .  .  .
14  .  .  .  .  .  .  . 17  .  .  .  .  .  .  .  .  .  .
15  .  .  . 19 18  .  . 20  .  .  .  .  .  .  .  .  .  .
16  .  .  .  .  .  .  . 17  .  .  .  .  .  .  .  .  .  .
17  .  .  .  .  .  .  . 17  .  .  .  .  .  .  .  .  .  .
18  .  .  .  .  .  .  . 17  .  .  .  .  .  .  .  .  .  .
```

Extracting an edge list from a graph object

You can use the `get.data.frame` on an `igraph` object to get the edge list:

```
> y <- get.data.frame(g)
```

Use this to get only the `vertices`:

```
> y <- get.data.frame(g,"vertices")
```

Creating a bipartite network graph

Let's say we have a set of groups and a set of users with each user belonging to several groups and each group potentially has several members.

We can represent this information as a bipartite graph with the groups forming one set, the users forming the other, and edges linking members of one set to the other. You can use the `graph.incidence` function from the `igraph` package to create and visualize this network:

```
> set.seed(2015)
> g1 <- rbinom(10,1,.5)
> g2 <- rbinom(10,1,.5)
> g3 <- rbinom(10,1,.5)
> g4 <- rbinom(10,1,.5)
> membership <- data.frame(g1, g2, g3, g4)
> names(membership)

[1] "g1" "g2" "g3" "g4"

> rownames(membership) = c("u1", "u2", "u3", "u4", "u5", "u6", "u7", "u8",
"u9", "u10")

> rownames(membership)

 [1] "u1"  "u2"  "u3"  "u4"  "u5"  "u6"  "u7"  "u8"
 [9] "u9"  "u10"

> # Create the bipartite graph through the
> # graph.incidence function
> bg <- graph.incidence(membership)
> bg

IGRAPH UN-B 14 17 --
+ attr: type (v/l), name (v/c)

> # The B above tells us that this is a bipartite graph
```

```
> # Explore bg
> V(bg)$type

[1] FALSE FALSE FALSE FALSE FALSE FALSE FALSE FALSE
 [9] FALSE FALSE  TRUE   TRUE   TRUE   TRUE

> # FALSE represents the users and TRUE represents the groups
> # See node names
> V(bg)$name

[1] "u1"   "u2"   "u3"   "u4"   "u5"   "u6"   "u7"   "u8"
[9] "u9"   "u10"  "g1"   "g2"   "g3"   "g4"

> # create a layout
> lay <- layout.bipartite(bg)
> # plot it
> plot(bg, layout=lay, vertex.size = 20)
> # save for later use
> save(bg, file = "bipartite-graph.Rdata")
```

We created a random network of four groups and ten users that, when plotted, appears as follows:

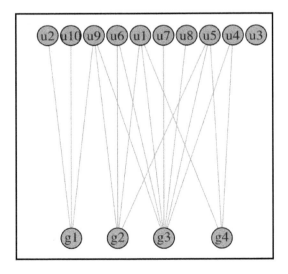

Generating projections of a bipartite network

Very often, we need to extract adjacency information about one or both types of nodes in a bipartite network. In the preceding example, with users and groups, we may want to consider two users as related or connected if they have a common group membership and create a graph only of the users. Analogously, we may consider two groups as connected if they have at least one user in common. Use the `bipartite.projection` function to achieve this:

```
> # Generate the two projections
> p <- bipartite.projection(bg)
> p

$proj1
IGRAPH UNW- 10 24 --
+ attr: name (v/c), weight (e/n)

$proj2
IGRAPH UNW- 4 5 --
+ attr: name (v/c), weight (e/n)

> plot(p$proj1, vertex.size = 20)
> plot(p$proj2, vertex.size = 20)
```

The first projection is plotted as follows:

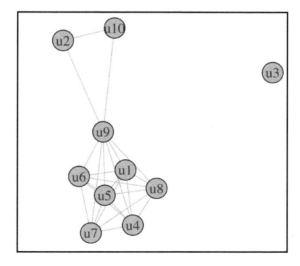

The next projection is generated as follows:

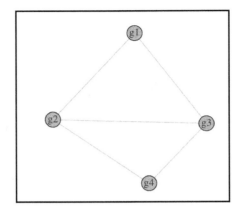

Computing important network metrics

This recipe covers the methods used to compute some of the common metrics used on social networks.

Getting ready

If you have not yet installed the igraph package, do it now. If you worked through the earlier recipes in this chapter, you should have the data files, directed-graph.Rdata, undirected-graph.Rdata, and bipartite-graph.Rdata, and should ensure that they are in your R working directory. If not, you should download these data files and place them in your R working directory.

How to do it...

To compute important network metrics, follow these steps:

1. Load the data files:

```
> load("undirected-graph.Rdata")
> load("directed-graph.Rdata")
> load("bipartite-graph.Rdata")
```

2. The `degree` centrality can be measured as follows:

```
> degree(dg)

 1  2  3  4  5  6  7  8  9 10 11 12 13 14 15 16 17 18
 3  2  1  1  2  3  3  1  3  1  9  1  1  1  3  1  1  1

> degree(g)

 1  2  3  4  5  6  7  8  9 10 11 12 13 14 15 16 17 18
 3  2  1  1  2  3  3  1  3  1  9  1  1  1  3  1  1  1

> degree(dg, "7")

7
3

> degree(dg, 9, mode = "in")

9
2

> degree(dg, 9, mode = "out")

9
1

> # Proportion of vertices with degree 0, 1, 2, etc.
> options(digits=3)
> degree.distribution(bg)

[1] 0.0714 0.2857 0.1429 0.3571
[5] 0.0714 0.0000 0.0000 0.0714
```

3. The `betweenness` centrality can be measured as follows:

```
> betweenness(dg)

 1  2  3  4  5  6  7  8  9 10 11 12 13 14 15 16 17 18
 0  1  0  0  0  5  5  0 10  0 32  0  0  0  0  0  0  0

> betweenness(g)

    1     2     3     4     5     6     7     8     9    10    11    12
 15.0   2.0   0.0   0.0  14.0  22.0  11.0   0.0  27.0   0.0  86.5   0.0
   13    14    15    16    17    18
  0.0   0.0   0.5   0.0   0.0   0.0
```

```
> betweenness(dg, 5)

5
0

> edge.betweenness(dg)

 [1]  2  1  6  7  6  6  1  5  8  8  5 15  1  2  2  6 10 10
10

> edge.betweenness(dg,10)

[1]  8
```

4. The `closeness` centrality can be measured as follows:

```
> options(digits=3)
> closeness(dg,mode="in")

      1       2       3       4       5       6
0.00327 0.00346 0.00327 0.00327 0.00327 0.00346
      7       8       9      10      11      12
0.00366 0.00327 0.00368 0.00327 0.00637 0.00346
     13      14      15      16      17      18
0.00346 0.00346 0.00690 0.00671 0.00671 0.00671

> closeness(dg,mode="out")

      1       2       3       4       5       6
0.00617 0.00472 0.00469 0.00469 0.00481 0.00446
      7       8       9      10      11      12
0.00446 0.00444 0.00444 0.00346 0.00420 0.00327
     13      14      15      16      17      18
0.00327 0.00327 0.00327 0.00327 0.00327 0.00327

> closeness(dg,mode="all")

      1       2       3       4       5       6
0.01333 0.01316 0.01220 0.01220 0.01429 0.01515
      7       8       9      10      11      12
0.01493 0.01389 0.01471 0.00346 0.01724 0.01124
     13      14      15      16      17      18
0.01190 0.00346 0.01493 0.01389 0.01389 0.01389

> closeness(dg)

      1       2       3       4       5       6
0.00617 0.00472 0.00469 0.00469 0.00481 0.00446
```

```
       7         8         9        10        11        12
 0.00446   0.00444   0.00444   0.00346   0.00420   0.00327
      13        14        15        16        17        18
 0.00327   0.00327   0.00327   0.00327   0.00327   0.00327
```

How it works...

Step 1 computes various metrics dealing with the degree of the vertices in a graph. **Degree** measures the number of edges connected to a vertex or node. Degree distribution provides the frequency of all degree measures up to the maximum degree. For an undirected graph, the degree is always the total adjacent edges. However, for a directed graph, the degree depends on the mode argument passed. Mode can be out, in, all, or total. Both all and total return the total degree of that node or vertex. You should be able to verify some of the numbers from the plots provided earlier.

Centrality determines how individual nodes fit within a network. High centrality nodes are influencers: positive and negative. There are different types of centrality, and we will discuss a few important ones here.

Step 2 computes betweenness, which quantifies the number of times a node falls in the shortest path between two other nodes. Nodes with high betweenness sit between two different clusters. To travel from any node in one cluster to any other node in the second cluster, one will likely need to travel through this particular node.

Edge betweenness computes the number of shortest paths through a particular edge. If a graph includes the weight attribute, then it is used by default. In our example, we have an attribute x. You will get different results if you rename the column to weight.

Step 3 computes **closeness**, which quantifies the extent to which a node is close to other nodes. It is a measure of the total distance from a node to all others. A node with high closeness has easy access to many other nodes. In a directed graph, if mode is not specified, then out is the default. In an undirected graph, mode does not play any role and is ignored.

Closeness measures the extent of access a node has to others and betweenness measures the extent to which a node acts as an intermediary.

There's more...

We show a few additional options to work on the graph objects.

Getting edge sequences

You can look at the edges--the connections--in the figure showing the directed graph in *Plotting directed graphs*. You can identify edges as E(1) to E(19):

```
> E(dg)
Edge sequence:
[1]   1  -> 2
[2]   1  -> 12
[3]   1  -> 6
[4]   2  -> 7
[5]   3  -> 9
[6]   4  -> 9
[7]   5  -> 13
[8]   5  -> 11
[9]   6  -> 11
[10]  7  -> 11
[11]  8  -> 11
[12]  9  -> 11
[13]  10 -> 14
[14]  6  -> 15
[15]  7  -> 15
[16]  11 -> 15
[17]  11 -> 16
[18]  11 -> 17
[19]  11 -> 18
```

Getting immediate and distant neighbors

The neighbors function lists the neighbors of a given node (excluding itself):

```
> neighbors(g, 1)
[1]   2   6 12
> neighbors(bg, "u1")
[1] 12 13 14
> # for a bipartite graph, refer to nodes by node name and
> # get results also as node names
> V(bg)$name[neighbors(bg,"g1")]
[1] "u2"  "u9"  "u10"
```

The `neighborhood` function gets the list of neighbors lying at most a specified distance from a given node or a set of nodes. The node in question is always included in the list as it is of distance 0 from itself:

```
> #immediate neighbors of node 1
> neighborhood(dg, 1, 1)
[[1]]
[1]  1  2  6 12

> neighborhood(dg, 2, 1)
[[1]]
 [1]  1  2  6 12  7 11 15
```

Adding vertices or nodes

We can add nodes to an existing `graph` object:

```
> #Add a new vertex
> g.new <- g + vertex(19)
> # Add 2 new vertices
> g.new <- g + vertices(19, 20)
```

Adding edges

If we need to add a new relationship between nodes 15 and 20, we can do the following:

```
> g.new <- g.new + edge(15, 20)
```

Deleting isolates from a graph

Isolated nodes have no connections or edges and therefore have degree 0. We can use this to select vertices that have 0 degree and delete them using `delete.vertices` as follows:

```
> g.new <- delete.vertices(g.new, V(g.new)[ degree(g.new)==0 ])
```

We can also use `delete.vertices` to delete a specific vertex. This function creates a new graph. If the vertex does not exist in the graph, you will see an error message `Invalid vertex names`. Plot the new graph to check whether the isolated vertex has been removed:

```
> g.new <- delete.vertices(g.new,12)
```

Deletion reassigns the vertex IDs even in some cases when edges are deleted. Hence, if you are using IDs instead of vertex names, exercise caution as the IDs may change.

Creating subgraphs

You can create new graphs by selecting the vertices you are interested in, using the following code:

```
> g.sub <- induced.subgraph(g, c(5, 10, 13, 14, 17, 11, 7))
```

You can also create new graphs by selecting the edges you are interested in, using the following code:

```
> E(dg)

Edge sequence:
[1]   1  -> 2
[2]   1  -> 12
[3]   1  -> 6
[4]   2  -> 7
[5]   3  -> 9
[6]   4  -> 9
[7]   5  -> 13
[8]   5  -> 11
[9]   6  -> 11
[10]  7  -> 11
[11]  8  -> 11
[12]  9  -> 11
[13]  10 -> 14
[14]  6  -> 15
[15]  7  -> 15
[16]  11 -> 15
[17]  11 -> 16
[18]  11 -> 17
[19]  11 -> 18

> eids <- c(1:2, 9:15)
> dg.sub <- subgraph.edges(dg, eids)
```

Cluster analysis

In this recipe, we will cover real-time Twitter Network Analysis based on tweets and retweets of topic.

Getting ready

First, sign up a Twitter developer account (`https://apps.twitter.com`) and create a sample application to generate (API keys and credentials) under the **Keys and Access Token** tab, which we will require later to fetch real-time data from Twitter. Additionally, make sure that you have the following packages installed:

```
install.packages(c("twitteR","igraph","dplyr"))
```

How to do it...

To compute important network metrics, follow these steps:

1. Load the following packages:

   ```
   > library(twitteR)
   > library(igraph)
   > library(dplyr)
   ```

2. Set your API keys and secret keys information from the Twitter app and then authenticate using the `twitter_oauth` method :

   ```
   > api_key <- <your consumer or api key>
   > api_secret <- <your api key secret>
   > access_token <- <your access token>
   > access_token_secret <- < your access token secret>

   > setup_twitter_oauth(api_key, api_secret, access_token,
   access_token_secret)
   [1] "Using direct authentication"
   ```

3. Now, we will search Twitter based on the keyword, "`demonetization`", and convert the tweets to a data frame object. Then we will use only the first 500 tweets for demonstration to avoid heavy computation:

   ```
   > alltweets <- searchTwitter("demonetization", n = 1500)
   > alltweets <- twListToDF(alltweets)
   > tweets <- alltweets[1:500,]
   ```

4. Now split the tweet data into two sets--one for retweet network and the other for original tweet network. Then create an edge list for retweet network:

   ```
   > split_point = split(tweets, tweets$isRetweet)
   ```

```
> reTweets = mutate(split_point[['TRUE']], sender = substr(text, 5,
regexpr(':', text) - 1))

> edge_list = as.data.frame(cbind(sender =
tolower(reTweets$sender), receiver = tolower(reTweets$screenName)))
> edge_list = count(edge_list, sender, receiver)
> edge_list[1:5,]
# A tibble: 5 x 3
        sender receiver n
        <fctr>  <fctr> <int>
1 _anujsinghal anurag29 1
2 _anujsinghal avi_saxena 1
3 _anujsinghal bhavadasnkm 1
4 _anujsinghal chandrav09 1
5 _anujsinghal crazydiode 1
```

5. Finally, create a retweet network using the edge list:

```
> reTweets_graph <- graph_from_data_frame(d=edge_list, directed=T)
> save(reTweets_graph, file = "retweet-graph.Rdata")

> par(bg="white", mar=c(1,1,1,1))
> plot(reTweets_graph, layout=layout.fruchterman.reingold,
    vertex.color="blue",
    vertex.size=(degree(reTweets_graph, mode = "in")), #sized by
in-degree centrality
    vertex.label = NA,
    edge.arrow.size=0.8,
    edge.arrow.width=0.5,
    edge.width=edge_attr(reTweets_graph)$n/10, #sized by edge
weight
    edge.color=hsv(h=.95, s=1, v=.7, alpha=0.5))
title("Retweet Network", cex.main=1, col.main="black")
```

The following plot demonstrates the **Retweet Network** based on real-time twitter tweets:

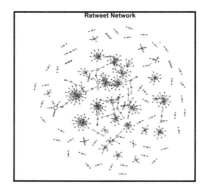

How it works...

First, we fetch real-time twitter tweets data using authentication keys and tokens and then convert it to a data frame using the `twListToDF()` method from the `twitterR` package. Afterward, we use the first 500 tweets as network analysis and visualization is computationally intensive and split it into `tweets` and `reTweets` datasets.

Next, we add sender information to the `reTweets` data frame with the `mutate()` function from `dplyr` and use the sender information to create an edge list of the `reTweet` network.

Then we create the `reTweet` graph data from the `reTweet` data frame using the `graph_from_data_frame()` method from the `igraph` package, and finally plot the `reTweet` graph using the `plot` function. The `vertex.size` attribute of the `plot` function is set to in-degree centrality of the vertex.

Force layout

In this recipe, we will use the `retweet-graph.Rdata` from the previous recipe and plot it using force layouts.

Getting ready

If you have not yet installed the `igraph` package, do it now. If you worked through the earlier recipes in this chapter, you should have the data file, `retweet-graph.Rdata`, and ensure that it is in your R working directory.

How to do it...

Perform the following steps to use force layout:

1. Load the data file:

```
> library(igraph)
> load("retweet-graph.Rdata")
```

2. Now we will plot the `reTweet` graph data using `Force Layout`:

```
> plot(reTweets_graph, layout=layout.fruchterman.reingold,
    vertex.color="blue",
    vertex.size=(degree(reTweets_graph, mode = "in")), #sized by
```

```
in-degree centrality
      vertex.label = NA,
      edge.arrow.size=0.8,
      edge.arrow.width=0.5,
      edge.width=edge_attr(reTweets_graph)$n/10, #sized by edge
weight
      edge.color=hsv(h=.95, s=1, v=.7, alpha=0.5))
title("Retweet Network using Force Layout", cex.main=1,
col.main="black")
```

The following plot illustrates the force directed algorithm layout:

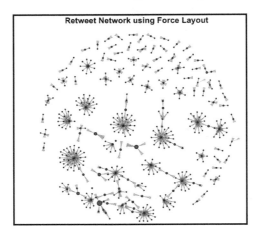

How it works...

We have use force-directed layout named `Fruchterman-Reingold` algorithm to plot the retweet network graph data. The idea of this force-directed layout algorithm is to consider a force between any two nodes and determines which direction a node should move based on the sum of the force vectors.

There's more...

We show another popular force-directed algorithm suitable for large networks that reduce the the computation complexity compared to a general force algorithm.

Force Atlas 2

Force Atlas 2 is another algorithm in the set of force-directed algorithms and it attempts to resolve the shortcomings of the Force algorithm by making a balance between the quality of the final layout and the speed of the computation algorithm. Its performance for large networks is much better when compared to the Force Atlas layout algorithm.

The speedup that is achieved in Force Atlas 2 is primarily due to the replacement of direct sum simulation used in Force Atlas with Barnes-Hut simulation.

Install and load the following package:

```
> install.packages("devtools")
> library(devtools)
> devtools::install_github("analyxcompany/ForceAtlas2")
> library(ForceAtlas2)
```

Next, define Force Atlas 2 layout with the number of iteration attribute (iterations) and how often a plot of the positions should be generated (plotstep). This is particularly useful to evaluate the convergence of the algorithm. Set plotstep=0 to suppress intermediate plots:

```
> load("retweet-graph.Rdata")
> layout <- layout.forceatlas2(reTweets_graph, iterations=2000,
plotstep=100)
```

Finally, use the preceding layout created to plot the reTweet graph data:

```
> plot(g, layout=layout)
```

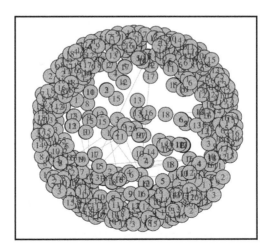

YiFan Hu layout

The Yifan Hu layout algorithm belongs to the category of force-directed algorithms, which includes the Force Atlas and Fruchterman Reingold algorithms. This algorithm is faster than the Force Atlas algorithm because of the way it optimizes the overall internode repulsions in the network.

Getting ready

If you worked through the previous recipes in this chapter, you should have the data file, `retweet-graph.Rdata`, and ensure that it is in your R working directory. If not, you should download these data files and place them in your R working directory. As of now, R doesn't provide any package that supports the `yifan hu` algorithm, so we will use the graph data from R and leverage `Gephi` (a popular graph visualization tool) to apply YiFan Hu layout over the data.

Make sure to download and install Gephi (`https://gephi.org/users/download/`) on your system.

How to do it...

To compute important network metrics, follow these steps:

1. Load the `reTweet` graph data and save it in the `graphml` format (which we will use to import in Gephi):

```
> load("retweet-graph.Rdata")
> write.graph(reTweets_graph, "reTweet_graph.graphml",
format="graphml")
```

2. Next, load the `reTweet_graph.graphml` file in Gephi, **File** | **Open...**:

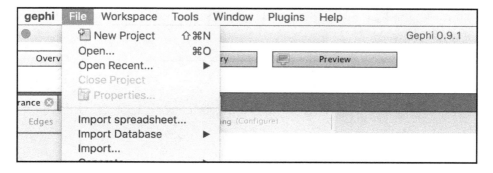

3. Now the `reTweet` graph data will be loaded in the graph panel of Gephi:

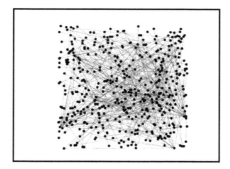

4. In the Layout panel, click on the drop-down menu that says **Choose a layout**, and from the drop-down menu, select **Yifan Hu**:

5. Now hit the **Run** button. The restructured graph will appear in the following Graph panel:

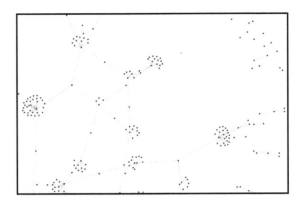

How it works...

The Yifan Hu layout algorithm uses the same concept as Force Atlas to compute the new layout of the network by optimizing the overall internode repulsions. The difference lies in the pair of nodes that are taken into consideration for the computation of repulsive forces. In the Yifan Hu layout algorithm, only pairs of adjacent nodes are taken into consideration. This is different from the Force Atlas algorithm in which every pair of nodes is considered for the computation of forces. This leads to reduced complexity in the Yifan Hu layout algorithm and hence the new layout is computed much faster.

There's more...

Here are some settings that you can change for the Yifan Hu layout algorithm to come up with the best possible layout for the graph under consideration:

- **Quadtree Max Level**: This defines the maximum level for the quadtree representation. A quadtree is a tree where each non-leaf node has exactly four children. The quadtree representation essentially places each node of the tree in a matrix, with four neighbors being its children. A higher value of this parameter results in higher accuracy and vice versa.
- **Theta**: This defines the approximation coefficient for the Barnes-Hut algorithm. A small value of theta would mean high accuracy.

- **Optimal Distance**: The edges in the graph in the Yifan Hu algorithm are visualized and assumed to be springs. This parameter defines the length of these springs. To get the nodes further apart from each other, use a large value for this parameter. To obtain a denser graph, use a small value.
- **Relative Strength**: This defines the ratio between the repulsive forces and the attraction forces in the graph.
- **Initial Step Size**: This is the initial step size that the algorithm will use in its integration phase. As prescribed in Gephi, a meaningful value, which is usually 10 percent of the optimal distance, should be chosen for this parameter.
- **Step ratio**: This is the ratio that will be used to recompute and update the step size during the execution of the layout algorithm.
- **Adaptive cooling**: This option is to choose the adaptive cooling scheme to configure the step size.
- **Convergence threshold**: This defines the threshold energy convergence levels for the algorithm to stop its execution. A high threshold will result in low accuracy and a low threshold in high accuracy in the resulting layout.

10
Put Your Best Foot Forward - Document and Present Your Analysis

In this chapter, we will cover the following topics:

- Generating reports of your data analysis with R Markdown and knitr
- Creating interactive web applications with shiny
- Creating PDF presentations of your analysis with R presentation
- Generating dynamic reports

Introduction

Other than helping us analyze data, R has libraries that help you with professional presentations as well. You can perform the following tasks:

- Create professional web pages that showcase your analysis and allow others to actively experiment with the underlying data
- Generate PDF reports of your analysis; your report can include embedded R commands for the system to execute and fill live data and charts so that, when the data changes, you can regenerate the report with a single button click
- Generate PDF presentations of your analysis

This chapter provides recipes for you to exploit all of these capabilities.

Generating reports of your data analysis with R Markdown and knitr

R Markdown provides you with a simple syntax to define analysis reports. Based on such a report definition, `knitr` can generate reports in HTML, PDF, Microsoft Word format, and several presentation formats. R Markdown documents contain regular text, embedded R code chunks, and inline R code. `knitr` parses the markdown document and inserts the results of executing the R code at specified locations within regular text to produce a well-formatted report.

R Markdown extends the regular markdown format to enable us to embed R code.

We can create R Markdown documents either in RStudio or directly in R using the markdown package. In this recipe, we will describe the RStudio approach.

Getting ready

If you have not already downloaded the files for this chapter, do so now and place the `auto-mpg.csv` and `knitr.Rmd` files in a known location. (This need not necessarily be the working directory of your R installation.)

Install the latest version of the `knitr` and `rmarkdown` packages:

```
> install.packages("knitr")
> install.packages("rmarkdown")
```

How to do it...

To generate reports using `rmarkdown` and `knitr`, follow these steps:

1. Open RStudio.
2. Create a new R Markdown document as follows:

    1. Select the menu option by navigating to **File | New File | R Markdown**.
    2. Enter the title as `Introduction`, leave the other defaults as is, and click on **OK**.

This generates a sample R Markdown document that we can edit to suit our needs. The sample document resembles the following screenshot:

Introduction

Kuntal Ganguly

August 15, 2017

R Markdown

This is an R Markdown document. Markdown is a simple formatting syntax for authoring HTML, PDF, and MS Word documents. For more details on using R Markdown see http://rmarkdown.rstudio.com.

When you click the **Knit** button a document will be generated that includes both content as well as the output of any embedded R code chunks within the document. You can embed an R code chunk like this:

```
summary(cars)
```

```
##      speed          dist
##  Min.   : 4.0   Min.   :  2.00
##  1st Qu.:12.0   1st Qu.: 26.00
##  Median :15.0   Median : 36.00
##  Mean   :15.4   Mean   : 42.98
##  3rd Qu.:19.0   3rd Qu.: 56.00
##  Max.   :25.0   Max.   :120.00
```

3. Take a quick look at the document. You do not need to understand everything in it. In this step, we are just trying to get an overview.

4. Generate an HTML document based on the markdown file. Depending on the width of your editing pane, you may either see just the `knitr` icon (a blue bale of wool and a knitting needle) with a downward-facing arrow or the icon and the text **Knit HTML** beside it. If you only see the icon, click on the downward arrow beside the icon and select **Knit HTML**. If you see the text in addition to the icon, just click on **Knit HTML** to generate the HTML document. RStudio may render the report in a separate window or in the top pane on the right side. The menu that you used to generate HTML has options to control where RStudio will render the report--choose either **View in pane** or **View in window**.

5. With the same file, you can generate a PDF or Word document by invoking the appropriate menu option. To generate a Word document, you need to have Microsoft Word installed on your system and to generate a PDF, you need to have the Latex PDF generator *pdflatex* installed. Note that the output item in the metadata changes according to the output format you choose from the menu.

6. Now that you have an idea of the process, use the menu option by navigating to **File | Open file** to open the `knitr.Rmd` file. Before proceeding further, edit line 40 of the file and change the `root.dir` location to wherever you downloaded the files for this chapter. For ease of discussion, we will show the output incrementally.

7. The metadata section is between two lines, each with just three hyphens (---), as follows:

```
---
title: "Markdown Document"
author: "Kuntal Ganguly"
date: "August 15, 2017"
output:
  html_document:
    theme: cosmo
    toc: yes
---
```

This is also seen in the following screenshot:

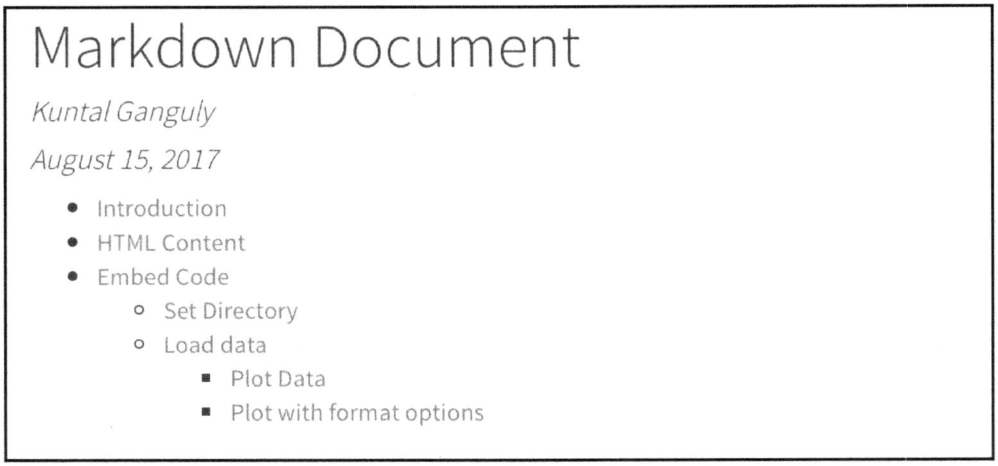

Markdown Document

Kuntal Ganguly

August 15, 2017

- Introduction
- HTML Content
- Embed Code
  - Set Directory
  - Load data
    - Plot Data
    - Plot with format options

8. The introduction section of the R Markdown document appears as follows:

```
* * *
# Introduction
This is an *R Markdown document*. Markdown is a simple formatting
syntax for authoring HTML, PDF, and MS Word documents. For more
details on using R Markdown see <http://rmarkdown.rstudio.com>.
```

When you click the **Knit** button a document will be generated that includes both content as well as the output of any embedded R code chunks within the document.

This is also seen in the following screenshot:

Introduction

This is an *R Markdown document*. Markdown is a simple formatting syntax for authoring HTML, PDF, and MS Word documents. For more details on using R Markdown see http://rmarkdown.rstudio.com.

When you click the **Knit** button a document will be generated that includes both content as well as the output of any embedded R code chunks within the document.

9. The HTML content of the document is as follows:

```
#HTML Content
<p> This is a new paragraph written with the HTML tag
<table border=1>
<th> Pros </th>
<th> Cons </td>
<tr>
<td>Easy to use</td>
<td>Need to Plan ahead </td>
<tr>
</table>
<hr/>
```

In the document, it appears as follows:

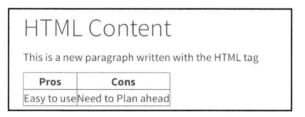

10. Embed the R Code. Change the following `root.dir` path to the folder where you stored the `auto-mpg.csv` and `knitr.Rmd` files:

```
# Embed Code
## Set Directory
You can embed any R code chunk within 3 ticks. If you add
echo=FALSE the code chunk is not displayed in the document. We can
set knitr options either globally or within a code segment. The
```

```
options set globally are used throughout the document.

We set the root.dir before loading any files. By enabling
cache=TRUE, a code chunk is executed only when there is a change
from the prior execution. This enhances knitr performance.

```{r setup, echo=FALSE, message=FALSE, warning=FALSE}
knitr::opts_chunk$set(cache=TRUE)
knitr::opts_knit$set(root.dir =
"/Users/kuntalg/projects/RCookbook/chapter8/")
```
```

This can be seen in the following screenshot:

Embed Code

Set Directory

You can embed any R code chunk within 3 ticks. If you add echo=FALSE the code chunk is not displayed in the document. We can set knitr options either globally or within a code segment. The options set globally are used throughout the document.

We set the root.dir before loading any files. By enabling cache=TRUE, a code chunk is executed only when there is a change from the prior execution. This enhances knitr performance.

Following codes are part of the `knitr.Rmd` file located at `root.dir` path specified in the Embed preceding code:

1. Load the data:

```
##Load Data
```{r loadData, echo=FALSE}
auto <- read.csv("auto-mpg.csv")
```
```

2. Plot the data:

```
```{r plotData }
plot(auto$mpg~auto$weight)
```
```

The output of the preceding command can be seen here:

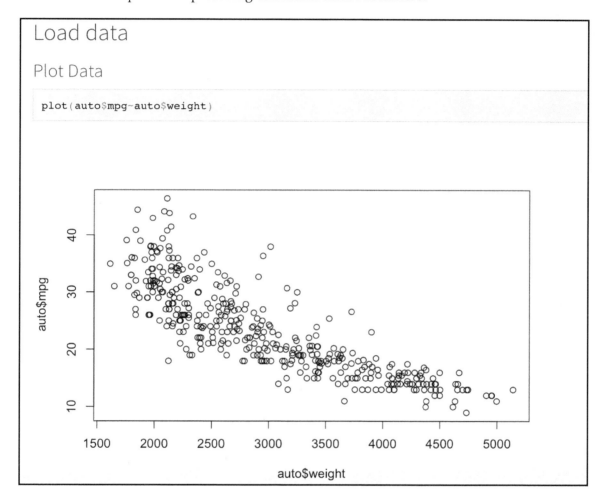

3. Plot with the format options:

```
```{r plotFormatData, echo=FALSE, fig.height=4, fig.width=8}
plot(auto$mpg~auto$weight)
str(auto)
```
```

The following screenshot shows the plotted output:

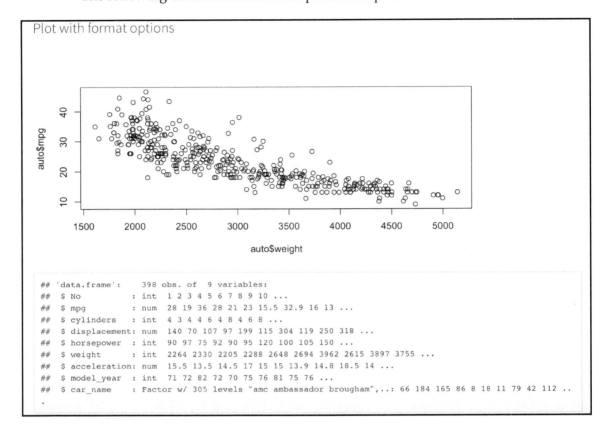

4. Embed the code within a sentence:

```
There are `r nrow(auto)` cars in the auto data set.
```

Here's the output of the preceding command:

There are 398 cars in the auto data set.

How it works...

Step 1 opens RStudio.

Step 2 creates a new R Markdown document. A new document includes a default metadata section between lines containing three dashes.

This metadata section includes the title and output sections and can, optionally, also specify the author and date.

Step 4 shows you how to generate the HTML document. If running in RStudio, you can indicate the desired output format by selecting the appropriate menu option. However, it is possible to run `knitr` within a standard R environment; in this case, the output specified in the markdown document determines the format of the output document.

Step 5 shows you how to generate a PDF or Word document based on the markdown document.

Step 6 opens a precreated document that illustrates many of the important features of `knitr`. We will explain the code in parts here.

Step 7 contains the metadata of the document:

- There are three output types: Word, PDF, and HTML
- The initial three hyphens indicate the start of the metadata section
- `toc:TRUE` causes the table of contents to be generated based on the headings in the document, which is explained in the next section
- The final three hyphens end the metadata section

Step 8 contains the Introduction section of our sample document:

- The three asterisks on a line by itself cause a horizontal line to be output.
- Lines starting with a single # signify a first-level heading and, if `toc:TRUE` is set in the metadata, it is added to the table of contents. Lines starting with ## signify second-level headings.
- Text surrounded by a single asterisk displays as italic and text surrounded by double asterisks displays as bold.
- Text starting with `<http` and ending with `>` is displayed as a URL.
- Checkout the *There's more...* section in this recipe for the most commonly used syntax.

Step 9 includes the HTML content of our sample document:

- Regular HTML coding can be embedded in an R Markdown document. `knitr` will only properly display the HTML if the output format is set in `HTML`; you must leave an empty line before starting the HTML code.
- In this segment, we used the HTML table syntax to produce a table.

Step 10 shows you how to embed R code in a markdown document:

- R code fragments or chunks begin on new lines with three back quotes (```) at the start. These chunks end with a line containing just three back quotes. The text of the R code segment starts with `r` followed by an optional name for the chunk (we can choose any unique name).
- We recommend that you do not mix the code for `knitr` settings with regular R code in a single chunk. Keep them in separate chunks. In this step, we set `cache=TRUE` and also set the home directory for `knitr`. The `knitr` options set here apply to the whole document. Thus, `cache` is enabled for each R code chunk that follows this setting.
- We set up display options for the current code chunk. If `echo=FALSE`, then the code chunk is not displayed in the document. Similarly, `message=FALSE` and `warning=FALSE` suppress any R messages and warnings in the document.

Next in the `knitr.Rmd` file we loads data from a csv file:

- We show a code chunk named `loadData` to read a `.csv` file into a variable. This code chunk does not appear in the report because we have chosen `echo=FALSE`.
- The location of the file is taken from the directory that we set in the earlier step. As we have enabled `cache`, the file will not read each time the document is generated.

And then plot data:

- We create a code chunk called `plotData`. The R code appears in the report because the default value for `echo` is `TRUE`. If an R code chunk produces any output, `knitr` automatically includes this output in the generated report.

Finally embed R code in line:

- We enclose the R code between a set of single back quotes. `knitr` substitutes the output of the R command in place of the inline R code.
- Thus, `nrow(auto)` returns the number of autos and is included in the generated document.

There's more...

The following is a list of the most commonly used markdown syntax elements. See `https://www.rstudio.com/wp-content/uploads/2016/03/rmarkdown-cheatsheet-2.0.pdf` for a complete list of markdown syntax elements:

Option	Syntax	Remarks
Italics	*text*	
Bold	**text**	
New Paragraph	Leave 2 spaces after the end of the line	
Header1-6	`# text`, `## text`, `### text`, and so on	Headers display the word in an appropriate font
Horizontal Rule `<hr>`	***	Draws a horizontal line
Unordered List (*, +, and –)	* List Item 1	Note that the space between * and the list item + and – can also be used
Unordered SubItem	+ sub item 1	Use an indented + to create a sublist or an indented – or an indented * to create sublists
Ordered list	1. List item 1. Another List item	Even for the ordered list, the indented + is used to create subitems

The following table shows the various display options in a code chunk:

Option	Description	Possible values
eval	Evaluate the code in the code chunk	`TRUE, FALSE`; default: `TRUE`

echo	Display code along with the output	TRUE, FALSE; default: TRUE
warning	Display warning messages	TRUE, FALSE; default: TRUE
error	Display errors	TRUE, FALSE; default: FALSE
message	Display R messages	TRUE, FALSE; default: TRUE
results	Display results	markup, asis, hold, hide; default: markup
cache	Cache the results	TRUE, FALSE; default: FALSE

Using the render function

In RStudio, document output can be generated using `knitr` by clicking on the `knit` button. You can also directly enter a command in the R command line. If you leave out the second argument, then the output specification in the markdown document determines the output format:

```
rmarkdown::render("introduction.Rmd","pdf_document").
```

To create the output in all formats mentioned in the markdown document, use the following command:

```
rmarkdown::render("introduction.Rmd","all")
```

Adding output options

The following output options can be added:

- Type of output document to build:
  - output:html_document
  - output:pdf_document
  - output:beamer_presentation
  - output:ioslides_presentation
  - output:word_document
- Number the section headings. If the sections are not named, then they are incrementally numbered:
  - number_sections = TRUE

- The `fig_width` and `fig_height` options are the default width and height in inches:
    - figures: `fig_width=7, fig_height=5`
- Theme: Visual theme; pass `null` to use custom CSS
- CSS: Include filename

Creating interactive web applications with shiny

The `shiny` package helps in building interactive web applications using R. This recipe illustrates the main components of a `shiny` application through examples.

Getting ready

Download the files for this chapter and store them in your R working directory. The code for this chapter contains files in various subfolders (named `DummyApp`, `SimpleApp`, `TabApp`, `ConditionalApp`, and `SingleFileApp`). Copy these folders to your R working directory.

Install and load the `shiny` package as follows:

```
> install.packages("shiny")
```

Restart RStudio after installing `shiny`.

How to do it...

To create interactive web applications with `shiny`, perform the following steps:

1. Get a feel for `shiny` by examining a dummy application with no functionality. The folder called `DummyApp` in your R working directory contains the `ui.R` and `server.R` files with the following code:

```
# ui.R
library(shiny)
shinyUI(pageWithSidebar(
    headerPanel("Dummy Application"),
    sidebarPanel(    h3('Sidebar text')   ),
    mainPanel(      h3('Main Panel text')   ) ))
```

```
#server.R
library(shiny)
shinyServer(function(input,output) { } )
```

2. Run the application using `runApp("DummyApp")`. If you have the files loaded in the code pane in RStudio, click on **Run App**.

3. The `SimpleApp` directory in your R working directory contains the `ui.R` and `server.R` files with the following code:

```
# ui.R
library(shiny)
shinyUI(fluidPage(
  titlePanel("Simple Shiny Application"),
  sidebarLayout(
    sidebarPanel(
      p("Create plots using the auto data"),
      selectInput("x", "Select X axis",
      choices = c("weight","cylinders","acceleration"))
    ),
    mainPanel(
        h4(textOutput("outputString")),
        plotOutput("autoplot"))    )
  ))
))
```

```
# server.R
auto <- read.csv("auto-mpg.csv")
shinyServer(function(input, output) {
    output$outputString <- renderText(paste("mpg ~",
        input$x))
    output$autoplot <- renderPlot(
        plot(as.formula(paste("mpg ~",input$x)),data=auto))
})
```

4. Enter the `runApp("SimpleApp")` command or, if the preceding files are loaded in the code pane, click on **Run App** to run the `shiny` application in the RStudio environment. The application opens in a separate window. When the application is running, RStudio cannot execute any command. Either close the application window or press the **Esc** key in RStudio to exit the application.

How it works...

A `shiny` application typically includes a folder with the `ui.R` and `server.R` files. The code in `ui.R` controls the user interface, and `server.R` controls the data that the application renders on the user interface, as well as how the application responds to user actions on the interface.

In step 1, the dummy application presents a simple static user interface with no scope for user interaction.

The `shinyUI` function of `ui.R` constructs the user interface. In `DummyApp`, the function constructs the user interface with three static elements. It uses the `pageWithSidebar` function to create a page with static text in `headerPanel`, `sidebarPanel`, and `mainPanel`.

The `shinyServer` function in the `server.R` file controls how the application responds to user actions. This function represents the listeners on the server side. For every user action, the `shinyServer` function gets the relevant values from the user interface. The relevant parts of the server's listener get executed and send the output back to the user interface, which then updates the screen with the new values. The reactivity of the `shiny` package is explained as follows. As `DummyApp` has no elements with which a user can actually interact and also has an empty `shinyServer` function, it cannot respond to user actions.

Step 2 builds a simple application in the `SimpleApp` folder. This application showcases the elements of a reactive application--one where the application truly reacts to user actions on the user interface. `shiny` has functions to generate static `html` as well as `html` code for user interface widgets, such as buttons, checkboxes, and drop-down lists, among others. The `ui.R` file in `SimpleApp` shows the use of the `p` function to add an HTML paragraph, the `selectInput` function to create a drop-down `listbox`, the `textOutput` and `h4` functions to create a level 4 heading text, and the `plotOutput` function to plot the output image from the server.

`shiny` has several layout options to customize the look and feel of the user interface. In this recipe, we used `fluidPage` with three panels: `titlePanel`, `sidebarPanel`, and `mainPanel`.

`shiny` uses reactive-programming. A user input, such as the user entering text, selecting an item from a list, or clicking on a button, is a reactive source. A server output, such as a plot or data table, is a reactive endpoint that appears in the user's browser window. Whenever a reactive source changes, the reactive endpoint that uses the source is notified to re-execute. In this recipe, both `renderText` and `renderPlot` are reactive. `renderText` depends on input x, which means that `renderText()` is executed each time the user selects a different x. `renderPlot` depends on both x and the color and, hence, any change to either of these two input values causes `renderPlot` to be invoked.

When you run the application, the preceding statements `shinyServer(function(input, output)` in `server.R` are executed just once during the first application load. After this, only the relevant portions of the `listener` function execute for each change in the user interface.

We loaded the `auto-mpg.csv` data file here once for the application. We typically load packages, data, and dependent R source files once during the initial load of the application.

There's more...

For a complete tutorial on `Shiny`, refer to `http://shiny.rstudio.com/tutorial`. We provide a few key additions relating to building `shiny` web applications here.

Adding images

To add images to the user interface, save the image file in the `www` directory under the application folder. Include the saved image file in `ui.R` with height and width in pixels as follows:

```
img(src = "myappimage.png", height = 72, width = 72)
```

The `css`, `javascript`, and `jquery` files are all stored in the `www` folder.

Adding HTML

`shiny` provides R functions for several HTML markup tags. We have seen a sample of the R function `h3("text here")` in our first dummy application. Similarly, there are R functions such as `p()` and `h1()` to include paragraph, header 1, and so on in a `shiny` application.

Adding tab sets

Tabs are created by the `tabPanel()` function and each tab can hold its own output UI components. The `TabApp` folder has the `ui.R` and `server.R` files for a tabbed user interface. We give the main excerpts from each in the following code:

```
# Excerpt from ui.R
mainPanel(
    tabsetPanel(
      tabPanel("Plot", textOutput("outputString"),
              plotOutput("plot")),
      tabPanel("Summary", verbatimTextOutput("summary")),
      tabPanel("Table", tableOutput("table")),
      tabPanel("DataTable", dataTableOutput("datatable"))
    )
  )
```

Add functionality to `server.R` to get the summary, table, and the `data.table` output:

```
# Excerpt from server.R to generate a summary of the data
output$summary <- renderPrint({
  summary(auto)
})

# Generate an HTML table view of the data
output$table <- renderTable({
  data.frame(x=auto)
})
# Generate an HTML table view of the data
output$datatable <- renderDataTable({
  auto
}, options = list(aLengthMenu = c(5, 25, 50), iDisplayLength = 5))
})
```

The options argument in `renderDataTable` expects a list. The preceding code specifies the items in the list and the number of items to display in the drop-down box.

Run the application with `runApp("TabApp")` to see the tabs and tab contents. If not all items are visible in the "`table`" tab, increase the size of the browser window.

Adding a dynamic UI

You can create dynamic user interfaces in two different ways: using `conditionalPanel` or `renderUI`. We show an example of each in this section.

We use `conditionalPanel` to show or hide a UI component based on a condition. In this sample, we draw a histogram or scatterplot of `mpg` based on user selection. For the scatterplot, we fix `mpg` on the *y* axis and allow the user to pick a variable for the *x* axis. Hence, we need to show the list of possible variables for the *x* axis only when the user chooses the scatterplot option. In `ui.R`, we check for the condition with `input.plotType != 'hist'` and then display the list of choices to the user:

```
sidebarPanel(
  selectInput("plotType", "Plot Type",
    c("Scatter plot" = "scatter", Histogram = "hist")),
  conditionalPanel(condition="input.plotType != 'hist'",
    selectInput("xaxis","X Axis Variable",
      choices = c(Weight="wt", Cylinders="cyl", "Horse Power"="hp"))
  )),
mainPanel( plotOutput("plot"))
```

To check how `conditionalPanel` works, execute `runApp("conditionalApp")` in your R environment and select the plot type. You will see `X Axis Variable` only when you choose scatterplot. In the case of `conditionalPanel`, the entire work is done in `ui.R` and is executed by the client.

In the preceding example, we had a fixed set of choices for the variables and hence we could build `selectInput` with these choices. What if this list is not known and is dependent on the user's selection of a dataset? The application in the `renderUIApp` folder illustrates this. In this application, the server builds the list of variable names dynamically based on the dataset chosen.

In the UI component, we need a placeholder, `uiOutput("var")`, to display the list that will be populated by the server every time a different dataset is chosen in the user interface.

In the server component, we use the `renderUI` function call to populate `output$var` using the variable names of the chosen dataset. In this sample, we also use a reactive expression as given here:

```
datasetInput <- reactive({
  switch(input$dataset,
    "rock" = rock,
    "mtcars" = mtcars)
})
```

A reactive expression reads input and returns an output. It regenerates the output only when the input it depends on changes. Every time it generates the output, it caches the output and uses it until the input changes. The reactive expression can be called from another reactive expression or from a `render*` function.

Creating a single-file web application

In R 3.0.0 version or higher, a `shiny` application can include just a single `app.R` file in a separate folder along with any needed data files and dependent R source code files. Create a new `SingleFileApp` folder and save the downloaded `app.R` here. Take a look at the downloaded `app.R` file and start the application by entering the `runApp("SingleFileApp")` command.

In `app.R`, the `shinyApp(ui = ui, server = server)` line is executed first by R. This `shinyApp` function returns an object of the `shiny.appobj` class to the console. When this object is printed, the shiny app is launched in a separate window.

It is possible to create a single-file Shiny application without a specific application directory and with a filename other than `app.R`. There should be a call to the `shinyApp` function, which is what tells R that it is a `shiny` application. We can then run `print(source("appfilename"))` to launch the application. The caveat if you run with a different name is that, when you modify the file, the application is not automatically relaunched.

Dynamic integration of Shiny with knitr

In `IntegrationApp`, we will illustrate the strategy to dynamically integrate the Shiny app into the `Rmd` file using `knitr` and `webshot` screenshot functionality to share R code of a Shiny application, while also documenting that code and showing a screenshot of the resulting app. Each time you make changes to your shiny app code, it will automatically get updated in the `Rmd` file along with a new screenshot without any manual intervention. First, make sure that you have the `shiny` and `knitr` packages installed. Next, install the `webshot` package:

```
install.packages("webshot")
webshot::install_phantomjs()
```

The `read_chunk()` function from the `knitr` package gets the code from R files (`ui.R` and `server.R`) into a code chunk in an `Rmd` file:

```
knitr::read_chunk("app/ui.R")
knitr::read_chunk("app/server.R")
```

The `appshot()` function from the `webshot` package programmatically takes a screenshot of a Shiny app. We can simply use this function in the `include_graphics()` function of the `knitr` package to capture and insert the screenshot in a single step :

```
appshot(app = "app/", file = "app.png", vheight = 300)
  knitr::include_graphics("app.png")
```

Voila, job done!

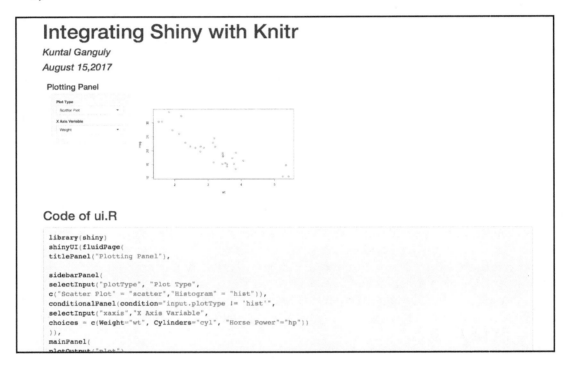

Just by updating the source files, the code in the `Rmd` file and the screenshot of the app will automatically get updated whenever you `knit()` the `Rmd` file.

Creating PDF presentations of your analysis with R presentation

`Rpres`, built into RStudio, enables you to create PDF slide presentations of your data analysis. In this recipe, we will develop a small application that showcases the important `Rpres` features.

Getting ready

Download the files for this chapter and store the `sample-image.png` and `Introduction.Rpres` files in your R working directory.

How to do it...

Open RStudio and create a new R Presentation document using the following steps:

1. Navigate to **File | New File** and click on **R Presentation**.
2. Enter the filename as `RPresentation` and save it in your R working directory.
3. RStudio creates a file with the extension, `Rpres`. This file includes a default title slide (the very first slide) and a few other sample slides. Creating this file also results in a preview being displayed in the upper right of the RStudio environment.
4. Fill in `author` and `date` and click on **Preview**.
5. By default, the preview appears in RStudio itself. However, to see all features properly, drop down the menu on the top right of the tab where the presentation appears and select **View in browser**.
6. Click on the arrow button at the bottom right to navigate through the slides.
7. Open the R Presentation document that you downloaded earlier.
8. Navigate to **File | Open File**.
9. Open the `Introduction.Rpres` file.
10. To embed an image, use the following code:

    ```
    Slide with image
    ===============
    ![Sample Image](sample-image.png)
    ```

11. To create a two-column layout, perform the following steps.
    The two columns are separated by `***` on a separate line. Add the following slide:

    ```
    Two Columns
    ===============
    left:40%

    **ColumnOne**
    -   this slide has two columns
    -       the first column has text
    -       the second column has an image
    ```

```
***
**ColumnTwo**

![Sample Image](sample-image.png)Two Columns
```

12. To add a transition to the slides--global transition setting:

```
Introduction
==========================================================
author: Kuntal Ganguly
date: 16 Aug 2017
transition:rotate
transition-speed:slow
```

13. To add incremental displays, add the following to the first slide:

```
Incremental Display
==========================================================
transition: concave
incremental: true
```

How it works...

In steps 1 and 2, a simple presentation is created.

In step 3, an R presentation file is opened. When a text is followed by a set of = characters (at least three on a line by itself), it is taken as the slide title.

In step 4, an image is added with the standard markdown syntax of the exclamation mark followed in square brackets by the alt text, followed by the image file's name in parentheses. The image occupies the entire slide if it is the only content on that slide.

In step 5, a two-column slide is created. The two columns are separated by three * characters. This time, the image occupies the entire column to which it is added.

The double asterisks signify a column. By default, the two columns occupy 50% of the slide width. In a two-column layout, each column by default occupies 50% of the slide width. Use left or right to change this. We used left: 40%.

A transition effect can be applied to all slides within a presentation or, specifically, for each slide. The default transition is linear. To apply to all slides, add it to the title slide as in step 6.

By default, all elements on the slide appear when `RPres` shows the slide. We can change this by setting `incremental = TRUE`. With this setting, list items, code blocks, and paragraphs are displayed incrementally with a mouse click. The first paragraph in a slide is immediately displayed and the increment rule is applied to the subsequent content. In step 7, we see this behavior in the display of bullet points.

There's more...

We will now describe additional options to control the display.

Using hyperlinks

External or internal links can be added to an R presentation. External links use the same R Markdown syntax. For internal links, we first need to add an `id` to a slide and then create a link using it, as the following code shows:

```
Two Columns
========
id: twocols

First Slide
========
[Go to Slide](#/twocols)
```

Controlling the display

The default size of an R presentation is 960 x 700 pixels. However, adding a specific width or height to a slide can change its default size:

```
Slide with plot
========================================================
title: false
```{r renderplot,echo=FALSE,out.width="1920px"}
plot(cars)
```
```

If the entire plot is not displayed in the slide when viewed in a browser, you can include `fig.width` and `fig.height` as follows:

```
Slide with plot
========================================================
title: false
```

```
```{r renderplot,echo=FALSE, fig.width=8,fig.height=4,
out.width="1920px"}
plot(cars)
```
```

Enhancing the look of the presentation

You can set the font in the title slide, after which the font is applied to all the slides. This global font can also be overridden in specific slides:

```
Introduction
=========================================================
author: Kuntal Ganguly
date: 16 Aug 2017
font-family: Arial
```

You can include a .css file in the title slide and use the styles defined in the .css file in the slides as follows:

```
Introduction
=========================================================
author: Kuntal Ganguly
date: 16 Aug 2017
css: custom.css

Two Columns
===============
class: highlight
left:70%
```

Generating dynamic reports

So far we have been playing with shiny, knitr, and markdown files to develop interactive applications and reproducible reports. In this recipe, you will learn how to generate a report with knitr and rmarkdown dynamically, and download at the click of a button from the Shiny app.

Getting ready

Download the files for this chapter, navigate to the `DynamicReport` folder, and set it as your R working directory. The `DynamicReport` folder has three files:

- `app.R`: This is the simple Shiny app file containing both `ui` and server code
- `report.Rmd`: This is the markdown file to generate downloadable dynamic reports based on the parameter passed from the Shiny app
- `auto-mpg.csv`: This data will be used to generate plots in the report file

How to do it...

1. Open RStudio and load the `app.R` file from **File | Open File**. The `app.R` file contains Shiny `ui` code to select the *x* axis value of the plot that will be embedded in the dynamic report. The parameter values from the `selectInput` widget will be passed to the shiny server code:

```
ui = fluidPage(
  selectInput("select", "Select X axis",
            choices = c("weight","cylinders","acceleration")),
  downloadButton("report", "Generate report")
)
```

2. The following shiny server code takes the selected input values of the `ui` panel. It then passes this parameter value along with the R markdown filename to the `rmarkdown::render()` function to generate downloadable dynamic reports based on the parameter passed, and saves the output in either `.html` or `.pdf` format:

```
server = function(input, output) {
  output$report <- downloadHandler(
    # For PDF output, change filename to "report.pdf"
    filename = "report.html",

    content = function(file) {
     report <- file.path("report.Rmd")

      # Set up parameters to pass to Rmd document
      params <- list(n = input$select)

  # Passing the `params` list, and evaluate it in child of the
  #global environment
```

```
          rmarkdown::render(report, output_file = file,
                            params = params,
                            envir = new.env(parent = globalenv())
          )
      }
  )
}
```

3. Run the shiny app.R file from Rstudio by clicking on the **Run App** button:

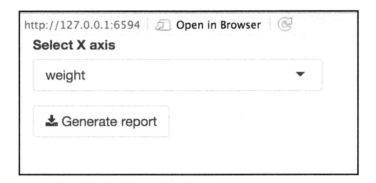

4. The report.Rmd files takes the parameter from the shiny server code to generate a dynamic scatterplot of the auto-mpg data:

```
---
title: "Download report"
author: "Kuntal Ganguly"
output: html_document
params:
  n: NA
---
```{r}
auto <- read.csv("auto-mpg.csv")
str(auto)
```

```{r}
# Plot the data
plot(as.formula(paste(params$n, "~mpg")), data=auto)
```
```

The following image shows the result of our commands:

Download report

Kuntal Ganguly

```
auto <- read.csv("auto-mpg.csv")
str(auto)

## 'data.frame':    398 obs. of  9 variables:
## $ No          : int  1 2 3 4 5 6 7 8 9 10 ...
## $ mpg         : num  28 19 36 28 21 23 15.5 32.9 16 13 ...
## $ cylinders   : int  4 3 4 4 6 4 8 4 6 8 ...
## $ displacement: num  140 70 107 97 199 115 304 119 250 318 ...
## $ horsepower  : int  90 97 75 92 90 95 120 100 105 150 ...
## $ weight      : int  2264 2330 2205 2288 2648 2694 3962 2615 3897 3755 ...
## $ acceleration: num  15.5 13.5 14.5 17 15 15 13.9 14.8 18.5 14 ...
## $ model_year  : int  71 72 82 72 70 75 76 81 75 76 ...
## $ car_name    : Factor w/ 305 levels "amc ambassador brougham",..: 66 184 165 86 8 18 11 79 42 112 ...

# Plot the data
plot(as.formula(paste(params$n,"~mpg")),data=auto)
```

How it works...

The Shiny app server code consists of two main parts.

A `downloadHandler()` function is used to knit the document on demand and passes parameter values to the R markdown document (which is parameterized).

By default, `rmarkdown::render()` will generate an HTML file that will have all plots and other images embedded directly in the HTML, so you can simply publish or send across the HTML file without any need to handle image files separately. However, you can also generate PDF output using the `rmarkdown::render()` function just by changing the filename argument of `downloadHandler()` to `"report.pdf"`. The `rmarkdown::render()` function has a lot of options to control the processing and output.

More information on this can be found at `https://www.rdocumentation.org/packages/rmarkdown/versions/1.6/topics/render`.

11
Work Smarter, Not Harder - Efficient and Elegant R Code

In this chapter, we will cover recipes for doing the following without explicit iteration:

- Exploiting vectorized operations
- Processing entire rows or columns using the apply function
- Applying a function to all elements of a collection with lapply and sapply
- Applying functions to subsets of a vector
- Using the split-apply-combine strategy with plyr
- Slicing, dicing, and combining data with data tables

Introduction

The R programming language, being procedural, provides looping control structures. Most people, therefore, tend to automatically use these control structures in their own code and end up with performance issues, as R handles loops very inefficiently. Serious number crunching and handling large datasets in R require us to exploit powerful, alternative ways to write succinct, elegant, and efficient code, as follows:

- Vectorized operations process collections as a whole, instead of operating element by element
- The apply family of functions processes rows, columns, or lists as a whole, without the need for explicit iteration
- The plyr package provides a wide range of **ply functions with additional functionalities, including parallel processing

- The `data.table` package provides helpful functions to manipulate data easily and efficiently

This chapter provides recipes using all these features.

Exploiting vectorized operations

Some R functions can operate on vectors as a whole. The function can either be a built-in R function or a custom function. In your own code, before you resort to a loop to process all elements of a vector, see whether you can exploit an existing vectorized function.

Getting ready

If you have not already downloaded the files for this chapter, do it now and ensure that the `auto-mpg.csv` file is in your R working directory.

How to do it...

To exploit vectorized operations, follow these steps:

1. Operate on all elements of vectors without explicit iteration (vectorized operations):

```
> first.name <- c("John", "Jane", "Tom", "Zach")
> last.name <- c("Doe", "Smith", "Glock", "Green")
> # The paste function below operates on vectors
> paste(first.name,last.name)

[1] "John Doe"   "Jane Smith" "Tom Glock"  "Zach Green"

> # This works even with different sized vectors
> new.last.name <- c("Dalton")
> paste(first.name,new.last.name)

[1] "John Dalton"  "Jane Dalton"  "Tom Dalton"  "Zach  Dalton"
```

2. Use vectorized operations within your own functions:

```
> username <- function(first, last) {
    tolower(paste0(last, substr(first,1,1)))
  }

> username(first.name,last.name)

[1] "doej"   "smithj"  "glockt" "greenz"
```

3. Apply an arithmetic operation implicitly on all the elements of a vector:

```
> auto <- read.csv("auto-mpg.csv")
> auto$kmpg <- auto$mpg*1.6
```

How it works...

By operating on entire vectors at a time, vectorized operations eliminate the need for explicit loops. R processes loops inefficiently, because it interprets the statements in a loop over and over again. Thus, loops with much iteration tend to perform poorly. Vectorized operations help us to get around this bottleneck, while at the same time making our code compact and more elegant.

Several built-in functions are vectorized and step 1 illustrates this with the `paste` function that concatenates strings.

The later part of step 1 shows that, if the vectors have unequal lengths, then the shorter vector recycles the list of vectors as needed. The `new.last.name` vector of size 1 repeats itself to match the size of the `first.name` vector. Hence, the last name `Dalton` is pasted to each element of `first.name`.

Vector operations work for built-in functions, custom functions, and arithmetic operations. A custom function to generate usernames using the two vectors `first.name` and `last.name` is seen in step 2.

Vector operations work even when we combine vectors and scalars in arithmetic operations. A new variable is created in step 3 in the `auto` data frame to represent fuel efficiency in **kilometers per gallon (kmpg)**, using a simple formula combining a vector and a scalar.

There's more...

R functions such as `sum`, `min`, `max`, `range`, and `prod` combine their arguments into vectors:

```
> sum(1,2,3,4,5)

[1] 15
```

On the contrary, beware of functions such as `mean` and `median` that do not combine arguments into vectors and yield misleading results:

```
> mean(1,2,3,4,5)

[1] 1
> mean(c(1,2,3,4,5))

[1] 3
```

Processing entire rows or columns using the apply function

The `apply` function can apply a user-specified function to all the rows or columns of a matrix and return an appropriate collection with the results.

Getting ready

This recipe uses no external objects or resources.

How to do it...

To process entire rows or columns using the `apply` function, follow these steps:

1. Calculate row minimums for the matrix:

```
> m <- matrix(seq(1,16), 4, 4)
> m

     [,1] [,2] [,3] [,4]
[1,]    1    5    9   13
[2,]    2    6   10   14
```

```
[3,]    3    7   11    15
[4,]    4    8   12    16

> apply(m, 1, min)

[1] 1 2 3 4
```

2. Calculate column maximums for the matrix:

```
> apply(m, 2, max)

[1]   4   8  12  16
```

3. Create a new matrix by squaring every element of the given matrix:

```
> apply(m,c(1,2),function(x) x^2)

     [,1] [,2] [,3] [,4]
[1,]    1   25   81  169
[2,]    4   36  100  196
[3,]    9   49  121  225
[4,]   16   64  144  256
```

4. Apply a function to every row and pass an argument to the function:

```
> apply(m, 1, quantile, probs=c(.4,.8))
      [,1] [,2] [,3] [,4]
40%    5.8  6.8  7.8  8.8
80%   10.6 11.6 12.6 13.6
```

How it works...

Step 1, creates a matrix and generates the row minimums for it:

- The first argument for `apply` is a matrix or array.
- The second argument (called `margin`) specifies how we want to split the matrix or array into pieces. For a two-dimensional structure, we can operate on rows as 1, columns as 2, or elements as c(1,2). For matrices of more than two dimensions, `margin` can be more than two and specify the dimension(s) of interest (see the *There's more...* section).
- The third argument is a built-in or custom function. In fact, we can even specify an unnamed function in-line, as step 3 shows.

The `apply` function invokes the specified function with each row, column, or element of the matrix, depending on the second argument.

The return value from `apply` depends on `margin` and the type of return value from the user-specified function.

If we supply more than three arguments to `apply`, it passes these along to the specified function. The `probs` argument in step 4 serves as an example. In step 4, `apply` passes along the `probs` vector to the `quantile` function.

> To calculate row/column means or sums for a `matrix`, use the highly optimized `colMeans`, `rowMeans`, `colSums`, and `rowSums` functions instead of `apply`.

There's more...

The `apply` function can use an array of any dimension as input. Also, you can use `apply` on a data frame after converting it into a matrix using `as.matrix`.

Using apply on a three-dimensional array

1. Create a three-dimensional array:

```
> array.3d <- array( seq(100,69), dim = c(4,4,2))
> array.3d

, , 1

     [,1] [,2] [,3] [,4]
[1,]  100   96   92   88
[2,]   99   95   91   87
[3,]   98   94   90   86
[4,]   97   93   89   85

, , 2

     [,1] [,2] [,3] [,4]
[1,]   84   80   76   72
[2,]   83   79   75   71
[3,]   82   78   74   70
[4,]   81   77   73   69
```

2. Calculate the sum across the first and second dimensions. We get a one-dimensional array with two elements:

```
> apply(array.3d, 3, sum)
[1] 1480 1224

> # verify
> sum(85:100)
[1] 1480
```

3. Calculate the sum across the third dimension. We get a two-dimensional array:

```
> apply(array.3d,c(1,2),sum)
     [,1] [,2] [,3] [,4]
[1,]  184  176  168  160
[2,]  182  174  166  158
[3,]  180  172  164  156
[4,]  178  170  162  154
```

Applying a function to all elements of a collection with lapply and sapply

The `lapply` function works on objects of types vector, list, or data frame. It applies a user-specified function to each element of the passed-in object and returns a list of the results.

Getting ready

Download the files for this chapter and store the `auto-mpg.csv` file in your R working directory. Read the data:

```
> auto <- read.csv("auto-mpg.csv", stringsAsFactors=FALSE)
```

How to do it...

To apply a function to all elements of a collection with `lapply` and `sapply`, follow these instructions:

1. Operate on a simple vector:

```
> lapply(c(1,2,3), sqrt)

[[1]]
[1] 1

[[2]]
[1] 1.414214

[[3]]
[1] 1.732051
```

2. Use `lapply` and `sapply` to calculate the means of a list of collections:

```
> x <- list(a = 1:10, b = c(1,10,100,1000),    c=seq(5,50,by=5))
> lapply(x, mean)

$a
[1] 5.5
$b
[1] 277.75
$c
[1] 27.5

> class(lapply(x,mean))
[1] "list"

> sapply(x, mean)

     a      b      c
  5.50 277.75  27.50

> class(sapply(x,mean))

[1] "numeric"
```

3. Calculate the minimum value for each variable in the `auto` data frame:

```
> sapply(auto[,2:8], min)
         mpg     cylinders displacement    horsepower
           9             3           68            46
      weight  acceleration   model_year
        1613             8           70
```

How it works...

The `lapply` function accepts three arguments: the first argument is the object, the second is the user-specified function, and the optional third argument specifies the additional arguments to the user-specified function. The `lapply` function always returns a list, irrespective of the type of the first argument.

In step 1, the `lapply` function is used to apply `sqrt` to each element of a vector. The `lapply` function always returns a list.

In step 2, a list with three elements is involved, each of which is a vector. It calculates the mean of these vectors. The `lapply` function returns a list while `sapply` returns a vector in this case.

In step 3, `sapply` is used to apply a function to columns of a data frame. For obvious reasons, we pass only the numeric columns.

There's more...

The `sapply` function returns a vector if every element of the result is of length 1. If every element of the result list is a vector of the same length, then `sapply` returns a matrix. However, if we specify `simplify=F`, then `sapply` always returns a list. The default is `simplify=T`.

Dynamic output

In the next two examples, `sapply` returns a matrix. If the function that it executes has row and column names defined, then `sapply` uses them for the matrix:

```
> sapply(auto[,2:6], summary)

       mpg cylinders displacement horsepower weight
Min.  9.00     3.000         68.0       46.0   1613
```

```
1st Qu.  17.50      4.000       104.2       76.0   2224
Median   23.00      4.000       148.5       92.0   2804
Mean     23.51      5.455       193.4      104.1   2970
3rd Qu.  29.00      8.000       262.0      125.0   3608
Max.     46.60      8.000       455.0      230.0   5140

> sapply(auto[,2:6], range)

     mpg cylinders displacement horsepower weight
[1,]  9.0         3           68         46   1613
[2,] 46.6         8          455        230   5140
```

One caution

As we mentioned earlier, the output type of sapply depends on the input object. However, because of how R operates with data frames, it is possible to get an unexpected output:

```
> sapply(auto[,2:6], min)

     mpg    cylinders displacement   horsepower      weight
       9            3           68           46        1613
```

In the preceding example, auto[,2:6] returns a data frame, and hence the input to sapply is a data frame object. Each variable (or column) of the data frame is passed as an input to the min function, and we get the output as a vector with column names taken from the input object. Try this:

```
> sapply(auto[,2], min)

 [1] 28.0 19.0 36.0 28.0 21.0 23.0 15.5 32.9 16.0 13.0 12.0 30.7
[13] 13.0 27.9 13.0 23.8 29.0 14.0 14.0 29.0 20.5 26.6 20.0 20.0
[25] 26.4 16.0 40.8 15.0 18.0 35.0 26.5 13.0 25.8 39.1 25.0 14.0
[37] 19.4 30.0 32.0 26.0 20.6 17.5 18.0 14.0 27.0 25.1 14.0 19.1
[49] 17.0 23.5 21.5 19.0 22.0 19.4 20.0 32.0 30.9 29.0 14.0 14.0
[61] .......
```

This happened because R treats auto[,2:6] as a data frame, but auto[,2] as just a vector. Hence, in the former case, sapply operated on each column separately, and, in the latter case, it operated on each element of a vector.

We can fix the preceding code by coercing the auto[,2] vector to a data frame and then passing this data frame object as an input to the min function:

```
> sapply(as.data.frame(auto[,2]), min)
auto[, 2]
        9
```

In the following example, we add `simplify=F` to force the return value to a list:

```
> sapply(as.data.frame(auto[,2]), min, simplify=F)
$`auto[, 2]`
[1] 9
```

Applying functions to subsets of a vector

The `tapply` function applies a function to each partition of the dataset. Hence, when we need to evaluate a function over subsets of a vector defined by a factor, `tapply` comes in handy.

Getting ready

Download the files for this chapter and store the `auto-mpg.csv` file in your R working directory. Read the data and create factors for the `cylinders` variable:

```
> auto <- read.csv("auto-mpg.csv", stringsAsFactors=FALSE)
> auto$cylinders <- factor(auto$cylinders, levels = c(3,4,5,6,8),
labels = c("3cyl", "4cyl", "5cyl", "6cyl", "8cyl"))
```

How to do it...

To apply functions to subsets of a vector, follow these steps:

1. Calculate mean `mpg` for each cylinder type:

   ```
   > tapply(auto$mpg,auto$cylinders,mean)

      3cyl     4cyl     5cyl     6cyl     8cyl
   20.55000 29.28676 27.36667 19.98571 14.96311
   ```

2. We can even specify multiple factors as a list. The following example shows only one factor, since the out file has only one, but it serves as a template that you can adapt:

   ```
   > tapply(auto$mpg,list(cyl=auto$cylinders),mean)

   cyl
      3cyl     4cyl     5cyl     6cyl     8cyl
   20.55000 29.28676 27.36667 19.98571 14.96311
   ```

How it works...

In step 1, the `mean` function is applied to the `auto$mpg` vector, grouped according to the `auto$cylinders` vector. The grouping factor should be of the same length as the input vector, so that each element of the first vector can be associated with a group.

The `tapply` function creates groups of the first argument based on each element's group affiliation as defined by the second argument, and passes each group to the user-specified function.

Step 2 shows that we can actually group by several factors specified as a list. In this case, `tapply` applies the function to each unique combination of the specified factors.

There's more...

The `by` function is similar to `tapply` and applies the function to a group of rows in a dataset, but by passing in the entire data frame. The following examples clarify this.

Applying a function on groups from a data frame

In the following example, we find the correlation between `mpg` and `weight` for each cylinder type:

```
> by(auto, auto$cylinders, function(x) cor(x$mpg, x$weight))
auto$cylinders: 3cyl
[1] 0.6191685
------------------------------------------------
auto$cylinders: 4cyl
[1] -0.5430774
------------------------------------------------
auto$cylinders: 5cyl
[1] -0.04750808
------------------------------------------------
auto$cylinders: 6cyl
[1] -0.4634435
------------------------------------------------
auto$cylinders: 8cyl
[1] -0.5569099
```

Using the split-apply-combine strategy with plyr

A common analytical pattern is to split data into pieces, apply some function to each piece, and then combine the results back together. The `plyr` package provides simple functions to apply this pattern, while simplifying the specification of the object types through systematic naming of the functions.

The `plyr` function name has three parts, `XYply`, where X specifies what sort of input you're giving , Y specifies the sort of output you want and ply part is common to all function names. X and Y represent one of the following options:

- **a** = array
- **d** = data.frame
- **l** = list
- _ = no output; only valid for Y; for example, useful when you're operating on a list purely for the side effects, making a plot, or sending output to screen/file

`ddply` has its input and output as data frames, and `ldply` takes a list as input and produces a data frame as output. Sometimes, we apply functions only for their side effects (such as plots) and do not want the output objects at all. In such cases, we can use _ for the second part. Therefore, `d_ply` takes a data frame as input and produces no output; only the side effects of the function application occur.

Getting ready

Download the files for this chapter and store the `auto-mpg.csv` file in your R working directory. Read the data and create factors for `auto$cylinders`:

```
> auto <- read.csv("auto-mpg.csv", stringsAsFactors=FALSE)
> auto$cylinders <- factor(auto$cylinders, levels = c(3,4,5,6,8),
labels = c("3cyl", "4cyl", "5cyl", "6cyl", "8cyl"))
```

Install the `plyr` package in your R environment if you do not have it already. This can be done using the following commands:

```
> install.packages("plyr")
> library(plyr)
```

How to do it...

To use the split-apply-combine strategy for data analysis with `plyr`, follow these steps:

1. Calculate mean `mpg` for each cylinder type (two versions):

```
> ddply(auto, "cylinders", function(df) mean(df$mpg))
> ddply(auto, ~ cylinders, function(df) mean(df$mpg))
cylinders     V1
1      3cyl 20.55000
2      4cyl 29.28676
3      5cyl 27.36667
4      6cyl 19.98571
5      8cyl 14.96311
```

2. Calculate the mean, minimum, and maximum `mpg` for each cylinder type and model year:

```
> ddply(auto, c("cylinders","model_year"),        function(df)
c(mean=mean(df$mpg),      min=min(df$mpg), max=max(df$mpg)))
> ddply(auto, ~ cylinders + model_year, function(df)
c(mean=mean(df$mpg), min=min(df$mpg), max=max(df$mpg)))

   cylinders model_year      mean   min   max
1      3cyl         72 19.00000  19.0  19.0
2      3cyl         73 18.00000  18.0  18.0
3      3cyl         77 21.50000  21.5  21.5
4      3cyl         80 23.70000  23.7  23.7
5      4cyl         70 25.28571  24.0  27.0
6      4cyl         71 27.46154  22.0  35.0
7      4cyl         72 23.42857  18.0  28.0
8      4cyl         73 22.72727  19.0  29.0
9      4cyl         74 27.80000  24.0  32.0
10     4cyl         75 25.25000  22.0  33.0
11     4cyl         76 26.76667  19.0  33.0
12     4cyl         77 29.10714  21.5  36.0
13     4cyl         78 29.57647  21.1  43.1
14     4cyl         79 31.52500  22.3  37.3
15     4cyl         80 34.61200  23.6  46.6
16     4cyl         81 32.81429  25.8  39.1
17     4cyl         82 32.07143  23.0  44.0
18     5cyl         78 20.30000  20.3  20.3
19     5cyl         79 25.40000  25.4  25.4
20     5cyl         80 36.40000  36.4  36.4
21     6cyl         70 20.50000  18.0  22.0
22     6cyl         71 18.00000  16.0  19.0
23     6cyl         73 19.00000  16.0  23.0
```

```
24    6cyl        74 17.85714 15.0 21.0
25    6cyl        75 17.58333 15.0 21.0
26    6cyl        76 20.00000 16.5 24.0
27    6cyl        77 19.50000 17.5 22.0
28    6cyl        78 19.06667 16.2 20.8
29    6cyl        79 22.95000 19.8 28.8
30    6cyl        80 25.90000 19.1 32.7
31    6cyl        81 23.42857 17.6 30.7
32    6cyl        82 28.33333 22.0 38.0
33    8cyl        70 14.11111  9.0 18.0
34    8cyl        71 13.42857 12.0 14.0
35    8cyl        72 13.61538 11.0 17.0
36    8cyl        73 13.20000 11.0 16.0
37    8cyl        74 14.20000 13.0 16.0
38    8cyl        75 15.66667 13.0 20.0
39    8cyl        76 14.66667 13.0 17.5
40    8cyl        77 16.00000 15.0 17.5
41    8cyl        78 19.05000 17.5 20.2
42    8cyl        79 18.63000 15.5 23.9
43    8cyl        81 26.60000 26.6 26.6
```

How it works...

In step 1, `ddply` is used. This function takes a data frame as input and produces a data frame as output. The first argument is the `auto` data frame. The second argument, `cylinders`, describes the way to split the data. The third argument is the function to perform on the resulting components. We can add additional arguments if the function needs arguments. We can specify the splitting factor using the formula interface ~ `cylinders`, as the second option of step 1 shows.

Step 2 shows how data splitting can occur across multiple variables as well. We use the `c("cylinders", "model_year")` vector format to split the data using two variables. We also name the variables as `mean`, `min`, and `max`, instead of the default `V1`, `V2`, and so on. The second option here also shows the use of the formula interface.

There's more...

In this section, we discuss the `transform` and `summarize` functions, as well as the identity function `I`.

Adding a new column using transform or mutate

Suppose you want to add a new column to reflect each auto's deviation from the mean `mpg` of the cylinder group to which it belongs:

```
> auto <- ddply(auto, .(cylinders), transform, mpg.deviation = round(mpg -
mean(mpg),2))
> auto <- ddply(auto, .(cylinders), mutate, mpg.deviation = round(mpg -
mean(mpg),2))
```

Using summarize along with the plyr function

We calculate the number of rows and the mean `mpg` of the data frame grouped by cylinders. The following command shows the output when `summarize` is used:

```
> ddply(auto, .(cylinders), summarize, freq=length(cylinders),
meanmpg=mean(mpg))
  cylinders freq  meanmpg
1      3cyl    4 20.55000
2      4cyl  204 29.28676
3      5cyl    3 27.36667
4      6cyl   84 19.98571
5      8cyl  103 14.96311
```

The following command creates histograms of `mpg` for each cylinder:

```
> par(mfrow = c(1,2))

> d_ply(auto,"cylinders",summarise,
    hist(mpg,xlab="Miles per Gallon",main="Histogram of Miles per
    Gallon",breaks=5))
```

The following plot is the output of preceding command:

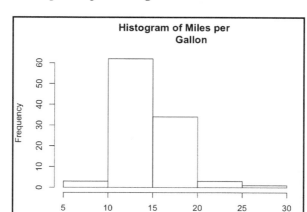

Concatenating the list of data frames into a big data frame

Run the following commands:

```
> autos <- list(auto, auto)
> big.df <- ldply(autos, I)
```

The `ldply` function takes a list input and spits out a data frame output. The identity function `I` returns the input as is. If the input is a list, then there is no split by argument; each list element is passed as an argument to the function.

Common grouping functions in plyr

Some of the commonly used grouping function in `plyr` is listed following with simple example:

- `apply` - It is used to apply a function to the rows or columns of a matrix, but not generally advisable for data frames as it will coerce to a matrix first.

    ```
    # Two dimensional matrix
    mat <- matrix(seq(1,9), 3, 3)
    # apply min to rows
    apply(mat, 1, min)
    ```

- `lapply` - It is used to apply a function to each element of a list, then get a list back and is the workhorse of other `ply` functions underneath the code.

  ```
  x <- list(a = 1, b = 1:3, c = 10:50)
  lapply(x, FUN = length)
  ```

- `sapply` - It is used to apply a function to each element of a list in turn, but get a vector back instead of a list.

  ```
  x <- list(a = 1, b = 1:3, c = 10:50)
  sapply(x, FUN = length)
  ```

- `mapply` - When you have several data structures (example, vectors, lists), then it is used to apply a function to the 1st elements of each data structures, and then the 2nd elements of each data structures, and so on, and finally coercing the result to a vector/array as in `sapply`.

  ```
  mapply(sum, 1:5, 1:5, 1:5)
  ```

- `tapply` - It is used to apply a function to subsets of a vector and the subsets are defined by some other vector, usually a factor. It is similar to other split-apply-combine functions available in R such as aggregate, `ddply`, by, and so on.

  ```
  # A vector
  x <- 1:20

  # A factor defining groups:
  y <- factor(rep(letters[1:5], each = 4))

  # Add up the values in x within each subgroup defined by y
  tapply(x, y, sum)
  ```

Split-apply-combine with dplyr

`plyr` can be slow with very large datasets that involve a lot of subsetting. `dplyr` is a package for data manipulation and it provides easy-to-use functions that are very handy when performing data analysis and manipulation with large datasets. The `dplyr` functions are similar to SQL, shown as follows:

dplyr Function	Description	Equivalent SQL Function
select()	Select columns (variables)	SELECT
filter()	Filter (subset) rows	WHERE

group_by()	Group the data	GROUP BY
summarise()	Summarise (or aggregate) data	-
arrange()	Sort the data	ORDER BY
join()	Joining data frames (tables)	JOIN
mutate()	Creating New Variables	COLUMN ALIAS

To install the `dplyr` package, type the following command:

```
install.packages("dplyr")
```

To load `dplyr` package, type the following command:

```
library(dplyr)
```

The following command will `select` a set of columns, `mpg` and `horsepower`:

```
> subsetData <- select(auto, mpg, horsepower)
> head(subsetData)
  mpg horsepower
1 19.0 97
2 18.0 90
3 23.7 100
4 21.5 110
5 28.0 90
6 36.0 75
```

The `filter` function will return all the rows that satisfy the following condition:

```
> filter(auto,model_year>80)
```

The `mutate` function is used to add new variables to the data, shown as follows:

```
> mutate(auto, mpg.deviation = round(mpg - mean(mpg),2))
```

The following command calculates the mean `mpg` of the data frame grouped by cylinders:

```
> summarise(group_by(auto,cylinders),mean(mpg))
```

The `pipe` operator, represented by `%>%`, is very useful for chaining code together. The following commands will show say we want to remove all the data corresponding to model_year < 80, group the data by month, and then find the mean of the `mpg` for each cylinders.

```
> auto %>%
    filter(model_year<80) %>%
    group_by(cylinders) %>%
    summarise(mean(mpg))
```

Slicing, dicing, and combining data with data tables

R provides several packages to do data analysis and data manipulation. Over and above the `apply` family of functions, the most commonly used packages are `plyr`, `reshape`, `dplyr`, and `data.table`. In this recipe, we will cover `data.table`, which processes large amounts of data very efficiently, without our having to write detailed procedural code.

Getting ready

Download the files for this chapter and store the `auto-mpg.csv`, `employees.csv`, and `departments.csv` files in your R working directory. Read the data and create factors for cylinders in `auto-mpg.csv`:

```
> auto <- read.csv("auto-mpg.csv", stringsAsFactors=FALSE)
> auto$cylinders <- factor(auto$cylinders, levels = c(3,4,5,6,8), labels =
c("3cyl", "4cyl", "5cyl", "6cyl", "8cyl"))
```

Install the `data.table` package in your R environment, as follows:

```
> install.packages("data.table")
> library(data.table)
> autoDT <- data.table(auto)
```

How to do it...

In this recipe, we cover `data.table`, which processes large amounts of data very efficiently, without our having to write detailed procedural code. To do this, follow these steps:

1. Select columns from the dataset:

```
> autoDT[,.(mpg)] #selecting single column
> autoDT[,.(mpg,horsepower,cylinders)] #selecting multiple column
```

2. Filter all `autoDT` whose `cylinders` can either be in `3cyl` or `4cyl`:

```
> autoDT[cylinders %in% c("3cyl","4cyl")]
>  #Filtering based on multiple condition
> autoDT[cylinders=="3cyl" & horsepower>90]
> autoDT[car_name %like% "chevrolet"] #Like operator for filtering
```

3. Calculate the mean `mpg` for each cylinder type:

```
> autoDT[, mean(mpg), by=cylinders]

      cylinders        V1
1:       4cyl 29.28676
2:       3cyl 20.55000
3:       6cyl 19.98571
4:       8cyl 14.96311
5:       5cyl 27.36667
```

4. Add a column for the mean `mpg` for each cylinder type:

```
> autoDT[, meanmpg := mean(mpg), by=cylinders]

> autoDT[1:5,c(1:3,9:10), with=FALSE]

   No mpg cylinders            car_name   meanmpg
1:  1  28      4cyl chevrolet vega 2300 29.28676
2:  2  19      3cyl     mazda rx2 coupe 20.55000
3:  3  36      4cyl        honda accord 29.28676
4:  4  28      4cyl     datsun 510 (sw) 29.28676
5:  5  21      6cyl         amc gremlin 19.98571
```

5. Add multiple columns of mean `mpg` and its deviation from mean:

```
> autoDT[, c("mean_mpg","mpg_deviation"):=list(mean(mpg),
  round(mpg - mean(mpg),2)), by=cylinders]
> autoDT[1:5,c(1:3,10:12), with=FALSE]

   No mpg cylinders meanmpg mean_mpg mpg_deviation
1:  1  28      4cyl 29.28676 29.28676         -1.29
2:  2  19      3cyl 20.55000 20.55000         -1.55
3:  3  36      4cyl 29.28676 29.28676          6.71
4:  4  28      4cyl 29.28676 29.28676         -1.29
5:  5  21      6cyl 19.98571 19.98571          1.01
```

6. Calculate summary statistics for a larger list of variables:

```
> autoDT[,lapply(.SD, mean), .SDcols = c("mpg", "horsepower")]
     mpg horsepower
1: 23.51457   104.1281
```

7. Create an index of cylinders by defining a key:

```
> setkey(autoDT,cylinders)

> tables()

      NAME   NROW NCOL MB
[1,] autoDT  398   10  1
      COLS
[1,]
No,mpg,cylinders,displacement,horsepower,weight,acceleration,model_
year,car_name
      KEY
[1,] cylinders
Total: 1MB

> autoDT["4cyl",c(1:3,9:10),with=FALSE]

No   mpg cylinders                 car_name  meanmpg
  1:   1  28.0      4cyl    chevrolet vega 2300 29.28676
  2:   3  36.0      4cyl           honda accord 29.28676
  3:   4  28.0      4cyl          datsun 510 (sw) 29.28676
  4:   6  23.0      4cyl              audi 100ls 29.28676
  5:   8  32.9      4cyl            datsun 200sx 29.28676
 ---
200: 391  32.1      4cyl     chevrolet chevette 29.28676
201: 392  23.9      4cyl           datsun 200-sx 29.28676
202: 395  34.5      4cyl  plymouth horizon tc3 29.28676
203: 396  38.1      4cyl toyota corolla tercel 29.28676
```

```
204: 397 30.5       4cyl      chevrolet chevette 29.28676
```

8. Calculate mean, min, and max mpg, grouped by cylinder type:

```
> autoDT[, list(meanmpg=mean(mpg), minmpg=min(mpg),
maxmpg=max(mpg)), by=cylinders]

   cylinders  meanmpg minmpg maxmpg
1:      3cyl 20.55000   18.0   23.7
2:      4cyl 29.28676   18.0   46.6
3:      5cyl 27.36667   20.3   36.4
4:      6cyl 19.98571   15.0   38.0
5:      8cyl 14.96311    9.0   26.6
```

How it works...

Data tables in the data.table package outperform the *apply family of functions and the **ply functions. The simple data.table syntax is DT[i,j,by], where the data table DT is the subset using rows in i to calculate j grouped by by.

In step 1, mean(mpg) is calculated, grouped by cylinders for all rows of the data table; omitting i causes all rows of the data table to be included.

To create a new column for the calculated j, just add :=, as in step 2. Here, we added a new column, meanmpg, to the data table to store mean(mpg) for each cylinder type.

By default, with is set to TRUE and j is evaluated for subsets of the data frame. However, if we do not need any computation and just want to retrieve data, then we can specify with=FALSE. In such a case, data tables behave just like data frames.

Unlike data frames, data tables do not have row names. Instead, we can define keys and use these keys for row indexing. Step 3 defines cylinders as the key, and then uses autoDT["4cyl",c(1:3,9:10),with=FALSE] to extract data for the key-column value, 4cyl.

We can define multiple keys using setkeyv(DT, c("col1", "col2")), where DT is the data table and col1 and col2 are the two columns in the data table. In step 3, if multiple keys are defined, then the syntax to extract the data is autoDT[.("4cyl"),c(1:3,9:10),with=FALSE].

If, in DT[i, j, by], i is itself a data.table, then R joins the two data tables on keys. If keys are not defined, then an error is displayed. However, for by, keys are not required.

There's more...

We see some advanced techniques using `data.table`.

Adding multiple aggregated columns

In step 4, we added one calculated column `meanmpg`. The `:=` syntax computes the variable and merges it into the original data:

```
> # calculate median and sd of mpg grouped by cylinders
> autoDT[,c("medianmpg","sdmpg") := list(median(mpg),sd(mpg)),
by=cylinders]
> # Display selected columns of autoDT table for the first 5 rows
> autoDT[1:5,c(3,9:12), with=FALSE]
   cylinders          car_name  meanmpg medianmpg     sdmpg
1:      3cyl    mazda rx2 coupe 20.55000     20.25  2.564501
2:      3cyl          maxda rx3 20.55000     20.25  2.564501
3:      3cyl       mazda rx-7 gs 20.55000    20.25  2.564501
4:      3cyl         mazda rx-4 20.55000     20.25  2.564501
5:      4cyl chevrolet vega 2300 29.28676    28.25  5.710156
```

Counting groups

We can easily count the number of rows in each group, as follows:

```
> autoDT[,.N ,by=cylinders]
   cylinders   N
1:      3cyl    4
2:      4cyl  204
3:      5cyl    3
4:      6cyl   84
5:      8cyl  103
```

We can also count after subsetting, as follows:

```
> autoDT["4cyl",.N]
[1] 204
```

Deleting a column

We can easily delete a column by setting it to `NULL`, as follows:

```
> autoDT[,medianmpg:=NULL]
```

Joining data tables

We can define one or more keys on data tables and use them for joins. Suppose a data table DT has a key defined. Then, if in DT[i, j, by], i is also a data table, R outer joins the two data tables on the key of DT. It joins the first key field of DT with the first column of i, the second key field of DT with the second column of i, and so on. If no keys are defined in DT, then R returns an error:

```
> emp <- read.csv("employees.csv", stringsAsFactors=FALSE)
> dept <- read.csv("departments-1.csv", stringsAsFactors=FALSE)
> empDT <- data.table(emp)
> deptDT <- data.table(dept)
> setkey(empDT,"DeptId")
```

At this point, we have two data tables, empDT and deptDT, and a key field in empDT. The department ID in deptDT also happens to be the first column. We can now join the two tables on department ID by the following code. Note that the column name in deptDT does not have to match the name of the key field in empDT; only the column position matters.

```
> combine <- empDT[deptDT]
> combine[,.N]
[1] 100
```

To prevent inadvertently creating large result sets, the data table's join operation checks to see if the result set has become larger than the size of either table and stops with an error immediately. Unfortunately, this check results in an error in some perfectly valid situations.

For example, if there were two departments in the deptDT table that did not appear in the empDT table, then the outer join operation will yield 102 rows and not 100. Since the number of resultant rows is more than the larger of the two tables, the preceding check results in an error message. The following code illustrates this:

```
> dept <- read.csv("departments-2.csv", stringsAsFactors=FALSE)
> deptDT <- data.table(dept)
> # The following line gives an error
> combine <- empDT[deptDT]
Error in vecseq(f__, len__, if (allow.cartesian) NULL else
as.integer(max(nrow(x),  : Join results in 102 rows; more than 100 =
max(nrow(x),nrow(i)) ... (error message truncated)
```

If we know for sure that what we are doing is correct, we can force R to perform the join by using allow.cartesian=TRUE:

```
combine <- empDT[deptDT, allow.cartesian=TRUE]
combine[,.N]
102
```

We get 102 rows because of the two departments that had no employees. The default outer join added two extra rows for these two departments. We can force an inner join by passing `nomatch=0`, as follows:

```
> mash <- empDT[deptDT, nomatch=0]
> mash[,.N]
[1] 100
```

Merging two datasets, `empDT` and `deptDT`, using inner, left, right, and full join:

```
> merge(empDT,deptDT, by="DeptId") #Inner join
> merge(empDT,deptDT, by="DeptId",all.x = TRUE) #Left join
> merge(empDT,deptDT, by="DeptId",all.y = TRUE) #Right join
> merge(empDT,deptDT, by="DeptId", all=TRUE) #Full join
```

Using symbols

We can use special symbols, such as `.SD`, `.EACHI`, `.N`, `.I`, and `.BY` in `data.table`, to enhance the functionality. We already saw some examples of `.N`, which represents the number of rows or the last row.

The `.SD` symbol holds all columns except the columns in `by`, and can be used only in the `j` evaluation part of `data.table`. The `.SDcols` symbol is used along with `.SD` and has columns to be included or excluded in the `j` part of `data.table`.

The `.EACHI` symbol is used in the `by` grouping to group each subset of the groups in `i`. This needs a key to be defined. If there is no key, R throws an error.

In the following example, we calculate the maximum salary in each department. If we omit `.SDcols="Salary"`, then R will try to find the max for all columns, since by default, `.SD` includes all columns. In such a case, R will throw an error, since there are columns with textual values in the `empDT` data table:

```
> empDT[deptDT, max(.SD), by=.EACHI, .SDcols="Salary"]

    DeptId    V1
1:       1 99211
2:       2 98291
3:       3 70655
4:       4    NA
5:       5 99397
6:       6 92429
7:       7    NA
```

In the following example, we calculate the average salary in each department. We give the name AvgSalary to this calculated column. We can either use list or the .() notation in the j evaluation part:

```
> empDT[,.(AvgSalary = lapply(.SD, mean)),
by="DeptId",.SDcols="Salary"]

   DeptId AvgSalary
1:      1  63208.02
2:      2  59668.06
3:      3  47603.64
4:      5  59448.24
5:      6  51957.44
```

In the following example, we calculate the average salary in each department. We also include the department name, DeptName, by joining empDT with deptDT:

```
> empDT[deptDT,list(DeptName, AvgSalary = lapply(.SD, mean)),
by=.EACHI,.SDcols="Salary"]
   DeptId    DeptName AvgSalary
1:      1     Finance  63208.02
2:      2          HR  59668.06
3:      3   Marketing  47603.64
4:      4       Sales        NA
5:      5          IT  59448.24
6:      6     Service  51957.44
7:      7  Facilities        NA
```

12
Where in the World? Geospatial Analysis

In this chapter, we will cover the following recipes:

- Downloading and plotting a Google map of an area
- Overlaying data on the downloaded Google map
- Importing ESRI shape files to R
- Using the sp package to plot geographic data
- Getting maps from the maps package
- Creating spatial data frames from regular data frames containing spatial and other data
- Creating spatial data frames by combining regular data frames with spatial objects
- Adding variables to an existing spatial data frame
- Spatial data analysis with R and QGIS

Introduction

A **geographic information system** (**GIS**) is the go-to technology that allows us to visualize, question, analyze, and interpret geospatial data to understand relationships, patterns, and trends in order to make better decisions about location such as real estate site selection, route selection, evacuation planning, natural resource extraction, and many more. With the recent growth of location-aware devices, it's increasingly easy to add spatial information to other data based on the address and related information.

In this chapter, we will cover recipes to perform some common operations with geospatial data using R packages such as sp, rgdal, RgoogleMaps, and ggmap along with a popular open source software--QGIS.

Downloading and plotting a Google map of an area

You can use the RgoogleMaps package to get and plot Google maps of specific areas based on latitude and longitude. This approach offers tremendous ease of use. However, we do not gain much control over the map elements and how we plot the maps. For finer control, you can use some of the later recipes in this chapter.

Getting ready

Install the RgoogleMaps package using the following command:

```
install.packages("RgoogleMaps")
```

How to do it...

To download and use Google maps of an area, follow these steps:

1. Load the RgoogleMaps package:

   ```
   > library(RgoogleMaps)
   ```

2. Determine the latitude and longitude of the location for which you need a map. In this recipe, you will get the map for the neighborhood of Seton Hall University in New Jersey, USA. The location is (lat, long) = (40.742634, -74.246215).

3. Get the static map from Google Maps and then plot it as follows. The output of the map is shown after the code:

   ```
   > shu.map <- GetMap(center = c(40.742634, -74.246215),      zoom=17)
   > PlotOnStaticMap(shu.map)
   ```

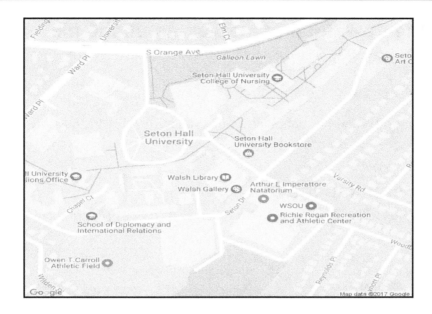

How it works...

First, we load the `RgoogleMaps` package. Then we determine the latitude and longitude of the location for which we want a map. Next, we use the `GetMap` function to acquire and store the map in an R variable called `shu.map`. The zoom option controls the zoom level of the returned map. The `zoom=1` option gives the whole world, and `zoom=17` covers a square area approximately a quarter of a mile on each side. Finally, we plot the map using the `PlotOnStaticMap` function.

There's more...

In the main recipe, we acquired and stored the map in an R variable. However, we can store it as an image file as well. We also have several options for the kind of map that we can download.

Saving the downloaded map as an image file

Use the `destfile` option to save the downloaded map as an image file:

```
> shu.map = GetMap(center = c(40.742634, -74.246215), zoom=16, destfile =
"shu.jpeg", format = "jpeg")
```

`GetMap` also supports other formats such as `.png` and `.gif`. See the help file for more details.

Getting a satellite image

By default, `GetMap` returns a road map. You can use the `maptype` argument to control what is returned:

```
> shu.map = GetMap(center = c(40.742634, -74.246215), zoom=16,       destfile
= "shu.jpeg", format = "jpeg", maptype = "satellite")
> PlotOnStaticMap(shu.map)
```

`GetMap` supports other map types such as `roadmap` and `terrain`. See the help file for details.

Overlaying data on the downloaded Google map

Spatial plotting capabilities are useful for those running data analytics in certain actuarial science industries such as finance or insurance. In this recipe, we will use the wage and crime datasets having spatial data points to overlay on a plotted Google map using the `RgoogleMaps` and `ggmap` packages.

Getting ready

Install the `RgoogleMaps` package. If you have not already downloaded the `nj-wages.csv` file, do so now and ensure that it is in your R working directory. The file contains information about the New Jersey Department of Education mashed up with latitude and longitude information downloaded from `http://federalgovernmentzipcodes.us`.

How to do it...

To overlay data on the downloaded Google map, follow these steps:

1. Load `RgoogleMaps` and read the data file:

    ```
    > library(RgoogleMaps)
    > wages <- read.csv("nj-wages.csv")
    ```

2. Convert `wages` to quantiles for ease of plotting:

    ```
    > wages$wgclass <- cut(wages$Avgwg, quantile(wages$Avgwg,
    probs=seq(0,1,0.2)), labels=FALSE, include.lowest=TRUE)
    ```

3. Create a color `palette`:

    ```
    > pal <- palette(rainbow(5))
    ```

4. Attach the data frame:

    ```
    > attach(wages)
    ```

5. Get the Google map for the area covered by the data:

    ```
    > MyMap <- MapBackground(lat=Lat, lon=Long)
    ```

```
[1]
"http://maps.google.com/maps/api/staticmap?center=40.115,-74.715&zo
om=8&size=640x640&maptype=mobile&format=png32&sensor=true"
center, zoom:  40.115 -74.715 8
```

6. Plot the map with the average wages overlaid with color and size proportional to the quantile:

```
> PlotOnStaticMap(MyMap, Lat, Long, pch=21, cex =
sqrt(wgclass),bg=pal[wgclass])
```

7. Add a `legend`:

```
> legend("bottomright", legend=paste("<=",round(tapply(Avgwg,
wgclass, max))), pch=21, pt.bg=pal,pt.cex=1.0, bg="gray",
title="Avg wgs")
```

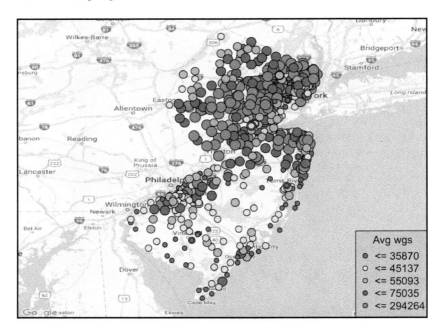

How it works...

First, the `RgoogleMaps` package is loaded and the data file is read. The file has geographic and other data for several school districts in New Jersey. We aim to show a Google map of the general area and overlay the average wages for each school district on the map.

Next, the `cut` function is used on the `Avgwg` column to create a new column called `wgclass`. This column represents the quantile to which a school district belongs. Then we create a color palette with five colors--one for each quantile. Next, the `MapBackground` function is used to get the static Google map for the general area and pass all the latitudes and longitudes to determine the overall extent of the map.

Finally, the `PlotOnStaticMap` function is used to plot the map along with the individual points because the call passes the latitudes and longitudes as the second and third arguments to the call. The other arguments play the following roles:

- `pch`: This determines the character used to plot each point
- `cex`: This determines the size of each point based on its quantile
- `bg`: This determines the background color of each point based on its quantile

Then we add a legend by calling the `legend` function. The arguments work as follows:

- The first argument determines the position of the legend.
- The `legend` function provides the vector of text for the legend. It creates the vector by finding the maximum `Avgwg` value for each `wage` class.
- As before, `pch` determines the character used to plot each point.
- The `pt.bg` argument determines the palette applied to the background color for the legend points.
- The `pt.cex` argument determines the size of the legend points.
- The `bg` argument determines the background color for the legend as a whole.
- The `title` argument specifies the title for the legend.

There's more...

The `RgoogleMaps` package offers tremendous ease of use but does not allow you control over the map elements and the type of layout. So we will look at another R package, `ggmap`, powered by the popular `ggplot2` package, to overlay data points over the map. In this section, we will analyze the Chicago crime dataset downloaded from `https://data.cityofchicago.org/` and simplified for this example:

1. Install and load `ggmap` and `maps` and read the data, `chicago-crime.csv`:

```
> install.packages(c("ggmap", "maps"))
> library(maps)
> library(ggmap)
```

```
> crimes <- read.csv("chicago-crime.csv")
```

2. Format the `Date` column into `Date` object:

```
> crimes$Date = strptime(crimes$Date, format = "%m/%d/%y %H:%M")
```

3. Get the map of Chicago using the `get_map` function and overlay some of the data points (for example, 100) on the map of `chicago`:

```
> chicago = get_map(location = "chicago", zoom = 11)
> ggmap(chicago)
> ggmap(chicago) + geom_point(data = crimes[1:100,], aes(x =
Longitude, y = Latitude))
```

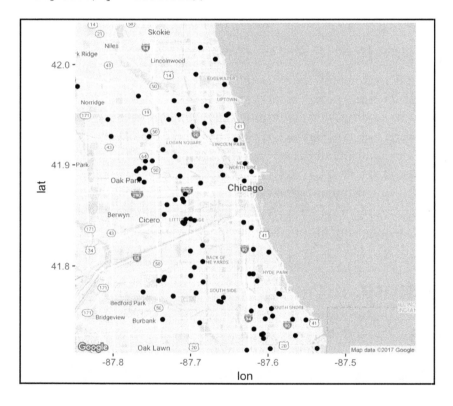

4. Now we will calculate the frequency of crime based on Latitude and Longitude and visualize this through a heat map:

```
> LatLonCounts = as.data.frame(table(round(crimes$Longitude, 2),
round(crimes$Latitude,2)))
> LatLonCounts$Lon = as.numeric(as.character(LatLonCounts$Var1))
> LatLonCounts$Lat = as.numeric(as.character(LatLonCounts$Var2))

> ggmap(chicago) + geom_tile(data = LatLonCounts, aes(x = Lon, y =
Lat, alpha = Freq), fill = "red")
```

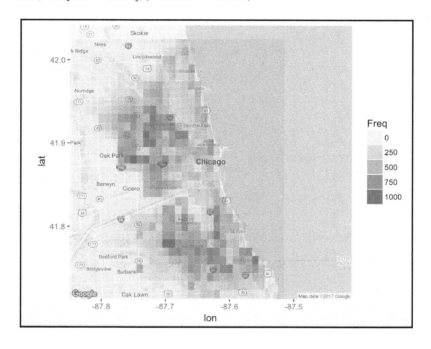

Importing ESRI shape files to R

Several organizations make **Environmental Systems Research Institute (ESRI)** shape files freely available and you can adapt them for your purposes. Using RgoogleMaps is easy, and we have seen that it offers very little control over map elements and plotting. Importing shape files, on the other hand, gives us total control. We should prefer this approach when we need fine control over the rendering of individual elements rather than just plotting a map image as a whole. The rgdal package offers the functionality to download shape files into R in a format that the sp package can handle.

Getting ready

Install the `rgdal` and `sp` packages. At the time of writing, installing `rgdal` on macOS X is tricky. Binary packages are unavailable and different versions of the OS require us to do different things. You will need to research this on the web and get it installed.

Copy the following files to your R working directory:

- `ne_50m_admin_0_countries.shp`
- `ne_50m_admin_0_countries.prj`
- `ne_50m_admin_0_countries.shx`
- `ne_50m_admin_0_countries.VERSION.txt`
- `ne_50m_airports.shp`
- `ne_50m_airports.prj`
- `ne_50m_airports.shx`
- `ne_50m_airports.VERSION.txt`

We obtained these files from `http://www.naturalearthdata.com/`.

How to do it...

To import ESRI shape files to R, follow these steps:

1. Load the `sp` and `rgdal` packages:

   ```
   > library(sp)
   > library(rgdal)
   ```

2. Read the ESRI file of `countries`:

   ```
   > countries_sp <- readOGR(".", "ne_50m_admin_0_countries")

   OGR data source with driver: ESRI Shapefile
   Source: ".", layer: "ne_50m_admin_0_countries"
   with 241 features and 63 fields
   Feature type: wkbPolygon with 2 dimensions

   > class(countries_sp)

   [1] "SpatialPolygonsDataFrame"
   attr(,"package")
   [1] "sp"
   ```

3. Read the ESRI file of `airports`:

```
> airports_sp <- readOGR(".", "ne_50m_airports")

OGR data source with driver: ESRI Shapefile
Source: ".", layer: "ne_50m_airports"
with 281 features and 10 fields
Feature type: wkbPoint with 2 dimensions

> class(airports_sp)

[1] "SpatialPointsDataFrame"
attr(,"package")
[1] "sp"
```

How it works...

In step 1, the `sp` and `rgdal` packages are loaded.

In step 2, the `readOGR` function from the `rgdal` package is used to read the `ne_50m_admin_0_countries.shp` shape file layer. An ESRI shape file comes in layers with all files in a layer having the same filename and different filename extensions. Each file contains some information about the map in a layer. The first argument to the `readOGR` function specifies the **data source name (DSN)**, or a directory containing the layer, and the second argument specifies the layer to be read.

The result of step 2 shows that `readOGR` returns an object of the `SpatialPolygonsDataFrame` class. The `sp` package defines several spatial classes including `SpatialPolygonsDataFrame`. This class stores spatial information for each country as a `polygon` and additionally has non-spatial attributes for each country stored in a slot called `data`. Effectively, a `SpatialPolygonsDataFrame` object is a spatial object (a collection of polygons) embellished with non-spatial attributes.

Step 3 uses the `readOGR` function to read another layer called `ne_50m_airports`. Examining the class of this object reveals it to be a `SpatialPointsDataFrame` object. Like `SpatialPolygonsDataFrame`, a `SpatialPointsDataFrame` object is also a spatial object (a collection of points) embellished with non-spatial attributes.

Using the sp package to plot geographic data

The sp package has the necessary features to store and plot geographic data. In this recipe, we will use the sp package to plot imported shape files.

Getting ready

Install the packages rgdal and sp. If you have issues installing the rgdal package on Mac or Linux, refer to the earlier recipe for details.

Copy the following files to your R working directory:

- ne_50m_admin_0_countries.shp
- ne_50m_admin_0_countries.prj
- ne_50m_admin_0_countries.shx
- ne_50m_admin_0_countries.VERSION.txt
- ne_50m_airports.shp
- ne_50m_airports.prj
- ne_50m_airports.shx
- ne_50m_airports.VERSION.txt

We obtained these files from http://www.naturalearthdata.com/.

How to do it...

To plot geographic data using the sp package, follow these steps:

1. Load the sp and rgdal packages:

```
> library(sp)
> library(rgdal)
```

2. Read the data:

```
> countries_sp <- readOGR(".", "ne_50m_admin_0_countries")
> airports_sp <- readOGR(".", "ne_50m_airports")
```

3. Plot the countries without color:

```
> # without color
> plot(countries_sp)
```

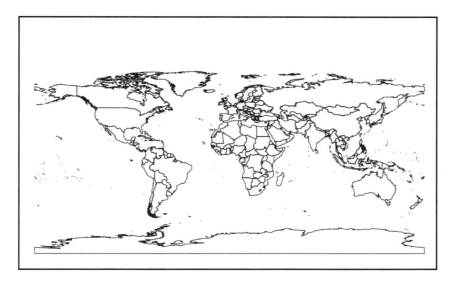

4. Plot the countries with color:

```
> # with color
> plot(countries_sp, col = countries_sp@data$admin)
```

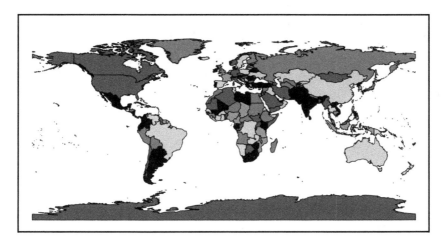

5. Add the airports. Do not close the previous plot:

```
> plot(airports_sp, add=TRUE)
```

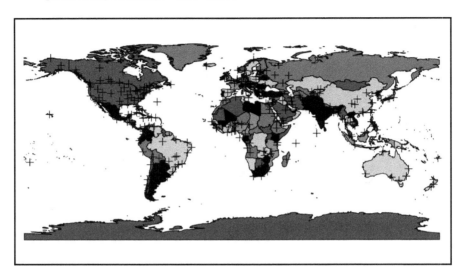

6. Plot the economic level (factor):

```
spplot(countries_sp, c("economy"))
```

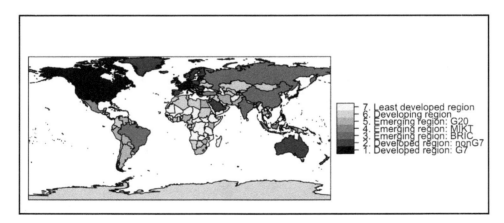

7. Plot the population (numeric):

```
spplot(countries_sp, c("pop_est"))
```

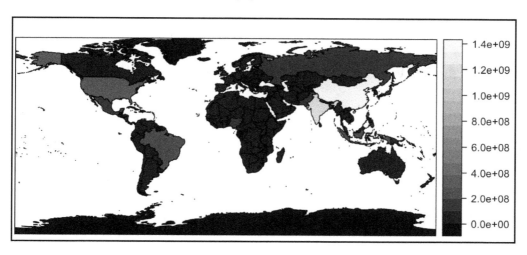

How it works...

If you have not already done so, you should read the *Importing ESRI shape files to R* recipe from this chapter.

In step 1, the sp and rgdal packages are loaded.

In step 2, readOGR is used to read the ESRI shape files of countries and airports.

Step 3 shows you how to plot the countries without color using the plot function. The plot function plots several polygon objects in countries_sp.

Step 4, similar to step 3, plots countries but adds color to them.

Step 5 adds the airport information using the plot function with the add=TRUE option. The airports_sp object contains several points and the plot function plots each point with specified properties such as plot character and size.

In steps 6 and 7, the use of the spplot function is demonstrated, which exploits the lattice plotting features. These steps show that spplot can handle both factors and numeric values.

Getting maps from the maps package

The maps package has several prebuilt maps that we can download and adapt. This recipe demonstrates the capabilities of these maps.

Getting ready

Install the maps package.

How to do it...

To get maps from the maps package, follow these steps:

1. Load the maps package:

   ```
   > library(maps)
   ```

2. Plot the world map:

   ```
   > # with country boundaries
   > map("world")
   > # without country boundaries
   > map("world", interior=FALSE)
   ```

3. Plot the world map with colors:

   ```
   > map("world", fill=TRUE, col=palette(rainbow(7)))
   ```

4. Plot the map of a country:

   ```
   > # for most countries, we access the map as a region on the world map
   > map("world", "tanzania")
   > # some countries (Italy, France, USA) have dedicated maps that we can directly access by name
   > map("france")
   > map("italy")
   ```

5. Plot a map of the USA:

```
> # with state boundaries
> map("state")
> # without state boundaries
> map("state", interior = FALSE)
> # with county boundaries
> map("county")
```

6. Plot a map of a state in the USA:

```
> # only state boundary
> map("state", "new jersey")
> # state with county boundaries
> map("county", "new jersey")
```

How it works...

The fact that the maps package has several prebuilt geographical databases, has enabled us to access the map of various countries as a region on the world map and even for some countries , it can be accessed directly by their names such as (Italy, France, USA).

Creating spatial data frames from regular data frames containing spatial and other data

When you have a regular data frame that has spatial attributes in addition to other attributes, processing the regular data frame becomes easier if you convert them to full-fledged spatial objects. This recipe shows you how to accomplish this.

Getting ready

Install the sp package. Download the nj-wages.csv file and ensure that it is in your R working directory.

How to do it...

To process a a regular data frame with spatial attributes, follow these steps:

1. Load the `sp` package:

    ```
    > library(sp)
    ```

2. Read the data:

    ```
    > nj <- read.csv("nj-wages.csv")
    > class(nj)
    [1] "data.frame"
    ```

3. Convert `nj` to a spatial object:

    ```
    > coordinates(nj) <- c("Long", "Lat")
    > class(nj)

    [1] "SpatialPointsDataFrame"
    attr(,"package")
    [1] "sp"
    ```

4. Plot the points:

    ```
    plot(nj)
    ```

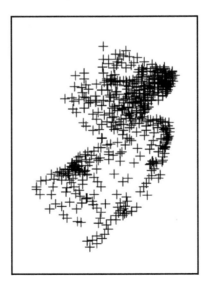

5. Convert the points to `Lines` and `plot` them:

```
nj.lines <- SpatialLines(list(Lines(list(Line(coordinates(nj))),
"linenj")))
> plot(nj.lines)
```

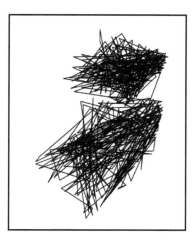

How it works...

In step 1, the `sp` package is loaded.

In step 2, the data file is read, showing that `nj` is now a regular data frame object.

In step 3, the `Lat` and `Long` variables are identified from the `nj` data frame as spatial coordinates through the `coordinates` function. We see that `nj` has now been transformed into a `SpatialPointsDataFrame` object--a full-fledged spatial object.

Creating spatial data frames by combining regular data frames with spatial objects

Often we have data that has some geographical aspect to it (such as postal codes) but does not have sufficient geographic coordinate information to plot. In order to display such information on a map representation, we will need to embellish the basic data with enough geographic coordinate information to plot.

The sp package has several SpatialXXXDataFrame classes to represent geographic information along with additional descriptive data. This recipe shows you how we can create and plot such objects. In this recipe, we demonstrate how to get a map from the maps package and convert it to a SpatialPolygons object. We then add data from a normal data frame to create a SpatialPolygonsDataFrame object, which we then plot.

Getting ready

Install the sp, maps, and maptools packages. Download the nj-county-data.csv file into your R working directory.

How to do it...

In this recipe, we demonstrate how to get a map from the maps package, convert it to a SpatialPolygons object, and then add data from a normal data frame to create a SpatialPolygonsDataFrame object, which we then plot. To do this, follow these steps:

1. Load the packages needed:

   ```
   > library(maps)
   > library(maptools) # this also loads the sp package
   ```

2. Get the county map of New Jersey:

   ```
   > nj.map <- map("county", "new jersey", fill=TRUE,      plot=FALSE)
   > str(nj.map)

   List of 4
    $ x    : num [1:774] -75 -74.9 -74.9 -74.7 -74.7 ...
    $ y    : num [1:774] 39.5 39.6 39.6 39.7 39.7 ...
    $ range: num [1:4] -75.6 -73.9 38.9 41.4
    $ names: chr [1:21] "new jersey,atlantic" "new jersey,bergen" "new
   ```

```
jersey,burlington" "new jersey,camden" ...
 - attr(*, "class")= chr "map"
```

3. Extract the county names:

```
> county_names <- sapply(strsplit(nj.map$names, ","),
function(x) x[2])
```

4. Convert the map to `SpatialPolygon`:

```
> nj.sp <- map2SpatialPolygons(nj.map, IDs = county_names,
proj4string = CRS("+proj=longlat +ellps=WGS84"))
> class(nj.sp)

[1] "SpatialPolygons"
attr(,"package")
[1] "sp"
```

5. Create a regular data frame from the file:

```
> nj.dat <- read.csv("nj-county-data.csv")
```

6. Create row names to match those in the map:

```
> rownames(nj.dat) <- nj.dat$name
```

7. Create `SpatialPolygonsDataFrame`:

```
> nj.spdf <- SpatialPolygonsDataFrame(nj.sp, nj.dat)
> class(nj.spdf)

[1] "SpatialPolygonsDataFrame"
attr(,"package")
[1] "sp"
```

8. Plot the map:

```
# plain plot of the object
> plot(nj.spdf)
> # Plot of population:
> spplot(nj.spdf, "population", main = "Population")
```

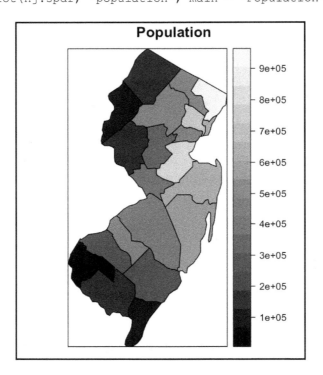

9. Based on incomes, a comparison can be obtained between `per_capita_income` and `median_family_income`:

```
spplot(nj.spdf,c("per_capita_income","median_family_income"),
main = "Incomes")
```

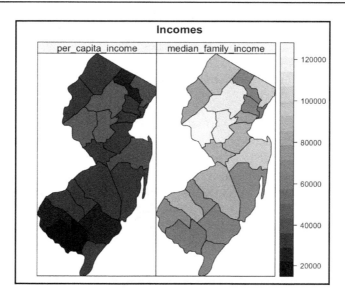

How it works...

In step 1, the maps, maptools, and sp packages are loaded.

In step 2, the map function in the maps package is used to get the county map of New Jersey.

From the maps package, we can get maps as lines or polygons. To color regions (such as countries on a world map or states or counties on country maps) based on their data values, we need to have the regions represented as polygons. The fill parameter controls whether or not we get a map as lines or polygons. We used the fill = TRUE option to get the map as polygons.

We will first convert the map to a SpatialPolygons object and then add nonspatial attribute values to make it a SpatialPolygonsDataFrame object.

Every polygon in a SpatialPolygons object must have a unique ID. From the output generated by step 2, we see that the individual regions (polygons, corresponding to the counties) in the map have names such as new jersey, atlantic.

In step 3, just the county names from the region names in the map are extracted by applying the `strsplit` function to each of the region names. We use the extracted county names as identifiers for the polygons. To combine spatial data with normal data frames, identifiers of polygons are matched with the row names of regular data frames. This is why we need to assign identifiers for the polygons.

In step 4, the `map2SpatialPolygons` function from the `maptools` package is used to generate a `SpatialPolygons` object, `nj.sp`, from the map, `nj.map`. This function uses the `IDs` argument supplied to name the polygons in the resultant `SpatialPolygons` object. If the length of the `IDs` argument does not match the number of polygons, then the function generates an error. At this point, we have a spatial object without any `nonspatial` attributes. Map files have geographic coordinate information in many different formats. The `proj4string` argument indicates the kind of coordinate information by creating a **Coordinate Reference System (CRS)** object.

In the current example, we indicate that the coordinates are represented as longitudes and latitudes and that the **World Geodetic System 1984 (WGS84)** standard is used. Depending on the coordinates in the map, other CRS objects may need to be created.

In step 5, data on the counties in New Jersey is read from a file and a normal data frame `nj.dat` is created. This data frame has no spatial attributes. We want to add the attributes from this data frame to the `SpatialPolygonsnj.sp` to create a `SpatialPolygonsDataFrame` object.

In step 6, the county names are assigned as the row names for the data frame. We will shortly see why.

In step 7, the `SpatialPolygonsDataFrame` function is used to combine spatial and non-spatial information into a single `SpatialPolygonsDataFrame` object. The function uses the `SpatialPolygons` object `nj.sp` as well as the `nj.dat` data frame. It matches both objects by matching the row names in the data frame with the polygon `IDs` in the `SpatialPolygon` objects. This is why we assigned the county names as row names in step 6 and also generated the county names in step 3. At this point, we have a `SpatialPointsDataFrame` object `nj.spdf` that contains both spatial and non-spatial information.

Step 8 shows that a regular plot of the `SpatialPointsDataFrame` object with the `plot` function displays only spatial information.

In step 9, the `spplot` function is used to plot the data and color each county based on its population. The last plot from step 9 clearly shows that `spplot` is based on the `lattice` package.

Adding variables to an existing spatial data frame

This recipe shows how you can add variables to spatial data frame objects. One approach (see the *Creating spatial data frames by combining regular data frames with spatial objects* recipe earlier in this chapter) will be to create all the necessary variables before creating the spatial data frame object. However, this might not always be feasible. This recipe shows how you can add non-spatial variables to an existing spatial data frame object.

Getting ready

Install the `sp`, `maps`, and `maptools` packages. Download and place the `nj-county-data.csv` file in your R working directory.

How to do it...

To add variables to an existing spatial data frame, follow these steps:

1. Perform the following steps shown (from the *Creating spatial data frames by combining regular data frames with spatial objects* recipe in this chapter):

```
> library(maps)
> library(maptools)
> nj.map <- map("county", "new jersey", fill=T, plot=FALSE)
> county_names <- sapply(strsplit(nj.map$names, ","),
function(x) x[2])
> nj.sp <- map2SpatialPolygons(nj.map, IDs = county_names,
proj4string = CRS("+proj=longlat +ellps=WGS84"))
> nj.dat <- read.csv("nj-county-data.csv")
> rownames(nj.dat) <- nj.dat$name
> nj.spdf <- SpatialPolygonsDataFrame(nj.sp, nj.dat)
```

2. Compute the population density for each county:

```
> pop_density <- nj.spdf@data$population/nj.spdf@data$area_sq_mi
```

3. Add a new variable to `nj.spdf`:

```
> nj.spdf <- spCbind(nj.spdf, pop_density)
> names(nj.spdf@data)

[1] "name"                    "per_capita_income"
[3] "median_household_income" "median_family_income"
[5] "population"              "no_households"
[7] "area_sq_mi"              "pop_density"
```

4. Plot the data:

```
spplot(nj.spdf, "pop_density")
```

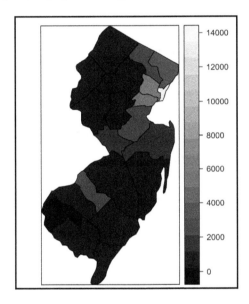

How it works...

In step 1, the code from the *Creating spatial data frames by combining regular data frames with spatial objects* recipe is repeated to create the `SpatialPointsDataFrame` object of New Jersey with county-level data.

In step 2, the underlying data frame is accessed through the `nj.spdf@data` variable and computes the population density based on the `population` and `area_sq_mi` variables.

In step 3, the `maptools` package method, `spCbind`, is used to add the new variable to the underlying data frame in the `SpatialpointsDataFrame` object, `nj.spdf`.

In step 4, the new variable is then plotted.

Spatial data analysis with R and QGIS

`QGIS` is a cross-platform, free, open source software that has become one of the leading GIS tools in the market in recent years. In this recipe, you will learn the integration between R and QGIS to perform spatial data analysis by executing an external R algorithm from the QGIS processing toolbox.

Getting ready

In order to execute an R algorithm in QGIS, we have to activate R in QGIS and indicate the location of R binaries. In the QGIS interface, go to the **Processing** | **Options...** | **Providers** menu. Then, go to **R scripts** and mark the checkbox next to **Activate**, and in the **R folder** option, browse and select the folder where R is installed in your machine. Finally, click on **OK**:

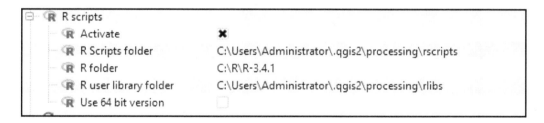

Note that the code for this recipe is under the `R-Qgis` folder located within the code of this chapter.

How to do it...

Perform the following steps to analyze spatial data with R and QGIS:

1. Load the airport data in the QGIS interface by navigating to **Layer** | **Add Layer** | **Add Vector Layer...** and browse the `airport.dbf` file:

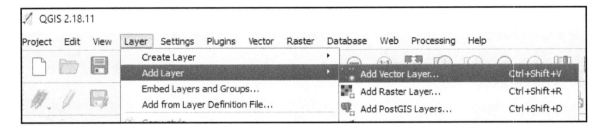

2. Now we can visualize the airport data:

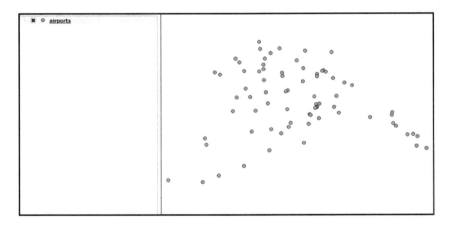

3. Check the attributes by right-clicking over the `airports` file and then click on **Open Attribute Table** from the QGIS layer panel:

	ID	fk_region	ELEV	NAME	USE
1	1	18	78.000	NOATAK	Other
2	2	18	264.000	AMBLER	Other
3	3	26	585.000	BETTLES	Other
4	4	18	9.000	RALPH WIEN MEM	Civilian/Public
5	5	18	21.000	SELAWIK	Other
6	6	26	1113.000	INDIAN MOUNTA...	Other
7	7	18	21.000	BUCKLAND	Other
8	8	16	243.000	TIN CITY LRRS	Other
9	9	16	1329.000	GRANITE MOUNT...	Other
10	10	16	9.000	PORT CLARENCE...	Other
11	11	26	207.000	RALPH M CALHO...	Other
12	12	16	108.000	KOYUK	Other
13	13	26	138.000	EDWARD G PITK...	Joint Military/Civil...
14	14	16	12.000	MOSES POINT	Other
15	15	16	33.000	NOME	Civilian/Public
16	16	26	1461.000	KALAKAKET CRE...	Military

airports :: Features total: 76, filtered: 76, selected: 0

4. Navigate to the processing toolbox panel and click on **R scripts** | **Tools** | **Create new R script**. Let's now generate a scatter plot of the spatial data using the `ggplot` package in the `Plot.rsx` script file, as shown in the following code:

```
##Point-pattern-analysis=group
##showplots
##Layer=vector
##X=Field Layer
##Y=Field Layer
##Group=Field Layer
require(ggplot2)
```

```
ggplot()+
geom_point(aes(x=Layer[[X]],y=Layer[[Y]],
color=as.factor(Layer[[Group]])))+
theme(legend.title = element_blank())+
xlab(X)+
ylab(Y)
```

5. Now execute the script by entering the required input parameters as follows:

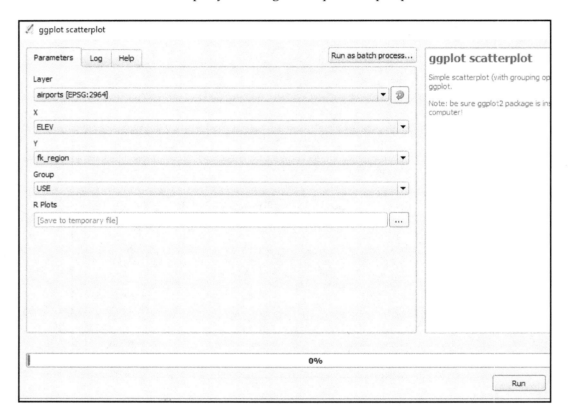

6. Next, click on the **Run** button to run the R algorithm within the QGIS toolbox to generate the plot:

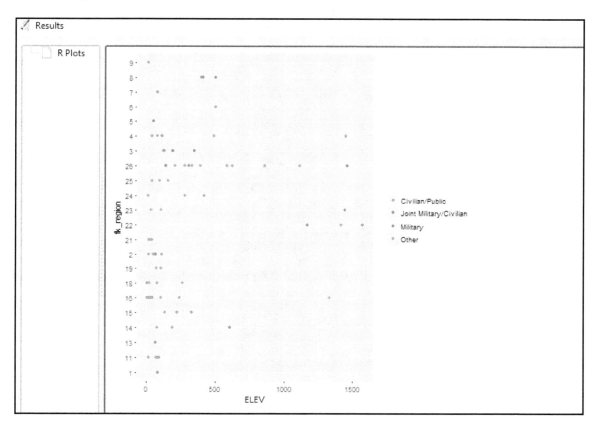

7. Next, we will do random sampling on the airport spatial data points. Create a new R script, RandomSampling.rsx, to perform random sampling from airport data points:

```
##Point-pattern-analysis=group
##Layer=vector
##Size=number 10
##Output= output vector
pts=spsample(Layer,Size,type="random")
Output=SpatialPointsDataFrame(pts, as.data.frame(pts))
```

8. Run the preceding script to generate the following output:

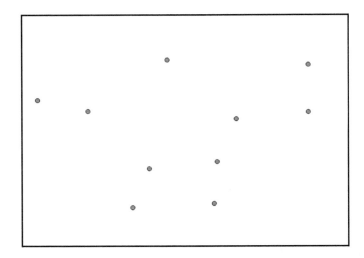

9. Finally, we will apply the `Ripley-Rasson` algorithm to estimate the spatial domain from which the airport spatial data points came. Now create a new R script, `Ripley-Rasson.rsx`, with the following code:

```
##Point-pattern-analysis=group
##Layer=vector
##Output=output vector
library("spatstat")
library("maptools")
proj4string(Layer)->crs
spatpoints = as(Layer,"SpatialPoints")
ripras=ripras(as(spatpoints,"ppp"))
polyg=as(ripras,"SpatialPolygons")
Output1= SpatialPolygonsDataFrame(polyg, data.frame(1))
proj4string(Output1)<-crs
Output<-Output1
```

Run the preceding `Ripley-Rasson.rsx` script to generate the following distribution:

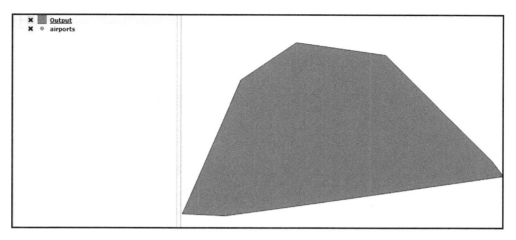

How it works...

In the R script earlier, the line starting with the double pound sign (##) informs QGIS about the inputs and outputs of the algorithm to create the graphic user interface. This information creates the corresponding R variables to be used later as input for R commands. The first line of the script, `Point-pattern-analysis=group`, indicate, the name of the group in which you want to put your script.

For example, in the `Plot.rsx` script, we are defining an input called `Layer` of the `vector` type and other inputs called `X`, `Y`, and `Group` of type `field` that take value from the vector map table of airport data. Once we define the input and output in the script, we define the R algorithm for data handling and visualization. The `showplots` command informs QGIS processing that we want to display a plot.

In `RandomSampling.rsx`, we create a sample of random data points from the actual airport spatial data points using the `spsample()` function of the `sp` package. The `type` parameter defines different categories of sampling logic (such as `stratified`, `regular`, `clustered`, and so on) to apply on the input data.

13
Playing Nice - Connecting to Other Systems

In this chapter, we will cover the following recipes to connect to other systems:

- Using Java objects in R
- Using JRI to call R functions from Java
- Using Rserve to call R functions from Java
- Executing R scripts from Java
- Using the xlsx package to connect to Excel
- Reading data from relational databases--MySQL
- Reading data from NoSQL databases--MongoDB
- Working with in-memory data processing with Apache Spark

Introduction

R is a popular statistical programming language with wide range of extensions/packages that support data processing and machine learning tasks. However, data analysis in R is often limited by two main factors:

- **Single threaded runtime environment**: This often increasing the processing and makes your data analysis slow.
- **Limitation of single machine's memory**: When accessing data stored in a data.frame or CSV file or any other format in R, the entire data must all fit in memory and this becomes a bottleneck when using a large dataset.

In this chapter, we will discuss how to overcome the two major pain points of R stated earlier by accessing data from datastore (**MySql** and **MongoDB**) or running analysis on distributed system with Apache Spark or even leveraging other multi threaded environment such as **Java**.

Datastore such as MongoDB or MySql are more efficient at storing and accessing data than CSVs due to compression and indexing and organize data into tables or collections and are better at handling large datasets.

SparkR is an R package that provides an R front-end to **Apache Spark**'s distributed computation engine to run large scale data analysis from the R shell.

The **rJava** package allows us to create and access Java objects using **Java Native Interface** (**JNI**) from within R. The Java-R Interface (JRI) and `Rserve` packages allow us to do the reverse by invoking R from within Java programs. We also discuss various ways to work on Excel files directly from R.

Using Java objects in R

Sometimes, we develop parts of an application in Java and need to access them from R. The `rJava` package allows us to access Java objects directly from within R.

Getting ready

If you have not already downloaded the files for this chapter, do it now and ensure that these files are in your R working directory:

1. Create a folder called `javasamples`, and move all the files with extension `.java` or `.class` into this folder under your working directory.
2. Install `rJava` using the `install.packages("rJava")` command.
3. Load the package using the `library(rJava)` command.
4. For `rJava` to work in your environment, the JDK version should be identical for the following, and we explain how to get them in sync for Mac OS X:

   - The environment JDK version: Execute `java -version` in your command line to get the installed version of Java. You will be using this version to create the `.jar` files or to compile Java programs.

- The JDK version in R: After you install and load the `rJava` package, check the JVM version in the R environment. We execute the commands to check this in the previous step. This should match with the response you get in the `java -version` command.

If there is a mismatch in the versions and you are using Mac OS X, do the following to install the latest version of `rJava` from the source:

1. Download the latest `rJava` source `rJava_0.9-7.tar.gz` from `http://www.rforge.net/rJava/files/`. The filename can be different with each new version of `rJava`:

   ```
   sudo R CMD javareconf
   ```

2. Include the following lines in your shell profile file (`.bash_profile` in bash, `.profile` in csh, and so forth); make sure to change the following folders as per your environment:

   ```
   export
   JAVA_HOME="/Library/Java/JavaVirtualMachines/jdk1.8.0_25.jdk/Conten
   ts/Home/
   export LD_LIBRARY_PATH=$JAVA_HOME/jre/lib/server
   export MAKEFLAGS="LDFLAGS=-Wl,-rpath $JAVA_HOME/lib/server"
   ```

3. Close your terminal window, and reopen it so that the profile settings take effect.
4. Install the downloaded `rJava` package, and make sure to change the filename:

   ```
   sudo R CMD INSTALL rJava_0.9-7.tar.gz
   ```

5. Close R or RStudio session, whichever you are using, and reopen it from the same terminal window by executing `open -a R` or `open -a RStudio`.
6. Load the library again using `library(rJava)`.
7. Check the JVM version using step 1:

   1. Download the three JAR files `JRI.jar`, `REngine.jar`, and `JRIEngine.jar` from `http://www.rforge.net/JRI/files/`; download the `RserveEngine.jar` files from `http://www.rforge.net/Rserve/files/`. Copy the four downloaded JAR files to the `lib` folder under your R working directory.

2. You can either use the class files provided or compile the Java code. These class files are created with `JDK 1.8.0_25`, and, if your JDK version is different, follow the next step to compile all the Java programs.

3. To compile the downloaded Java programs, go to the `javasamples` folder and execute the `javac -cp .:../lib/* *java` command. You should see files with the `class` extensions for each of the downloaded Java programs.

How to do it...

To use Java objects in R, follow these steps:

1. From within R, start the JVM, check the Java version, and set classpath:

```
> .jinit()

> .jcall("java/lang/System", "S", "getProperty",
"java.runtime.version")
[1] "1.8.0_25-b17"

> .jaddClassPath(getwd())

> .jclassPath()
[1]
"/Library/Frameworks/R.framework/Versions/3.1/Resources/library/rJa
va/java"
[2] "/Users/sv/book/Chapter11"  => my working directory
```

2. Perform these Java string operations in R:

```
> s <- .jnew("java/lang/String", "Hello World!")
> print(s)
 [1] "Java-Object{Hello World!}"

> .jstrVal(s)
[1] "Hello World!"

> .jcall(s,"S","toLowerCase")
[1] "hello world!"

> .jcall(s,"S","replaceAll","World","SV")
[1] "Hello SV!"
```

3. Perform these Java vector operations:

```
> javaVector <- .jnew("java/util/Vector")
> months <- month.abb

> sapply(months, javaVector$add)
 Jan  Feb  Mar  Apr  May  Jun  Jul  Aug  Sep  Oct  Nov  Dec
TRUE TRUE TRUE TRUE TRUE TRUE TRUE TRUE TRUE TRUE TRUE TRUE

> javaVector$size()
[1] 12

> javaVector$toString()
[1] "[Jan, Feb, Mar, Apr, May, Jun, Jul, Aug, Sep, Oct, Nov, Dec]"
```

4. Perform these Java array operations:

```
> monthsArray <- .jarray(month.abb)
> yearsArray <- .jarray(as.numeric(2010:2015))
> calArray <- .jarray(list(monthsArray,yearsArray))

> print(monthsArray)
[1] "Java-Array-
Object[Ljava/lang/String;:[Ljava.lang.String;@1ff4689e"

> .jevalArray(monthsArray)
 [1] "Jan" "Feb" "Mar" "Apr" "May" "Jun" "Jul" "Aug" "Sep" "Oct"
"Nov" "Dec"

> print(l <- .jevalArray(calArray))
[[1]]
[1] "Java-Object{[Ljava.lang.String;@30f7f540}"

[[2]]
[1] "Java-Object{[D@670655dd}"

> lapply(l, .jevalArray)
[[1]]
 [1] "Jan" "Feb" "Mar" "Apr" "May" "Jun" "Jul" "Aug" "Sep" "Oct"
"Nov" "Dec"

[[2]]
[1] 2010 2011 2012 2013 2014 2015
```

5. Insert this simple Java class `HelloWorld`:

```
> hw <- .jnew("javasamples.HelloWorld")
> hello <- .jcall(hw,"S", "getString")
> hello
[1] "Hello World"
```

6. Insert this simple Java class `Greeting` with a method that accepts an argument:

```
> greet <- .jnew("javasamples.Greeting")
> print(greet)
[1] "Java-Object{Hi World!}"

> g <- .jcall(greet, "S", "getString", "Kuntal")
> print(g)
[1] "Hello Kuntal"

> .jstrVal(g)
[1] "Hello Kuntal"
```

How it works...

The `.jinit()` function initializes the **Java Virtual Machine** (**JVM**) and needs to be executed before invoking any of the rJava functions. If you encounter errors at this point, **the issue is usually a lack of sufficient memory**. Close unwanted processes or programs, including R, and retry.

For rJava to work, we need to sync up the Java version in the system environment with the rJava version. We used the `.jcall("java/lang/System", "S", "getProperty", "java.runtime.version")` command to get the Java version within the R environment.

After making sure that the Java versions are identical, the first thing we need to do, to access any Java object, is to set up `classpath`. We do this using `.jaddClassPath`. We pass the R working directory since our Java classes reside here. However, if you have the Java class files in a different location or you created a `.jar` file, include that location instead. Once `classpath` is set using `.jaddClassPath`, you can verify it by executing `.jclassPath()`.

Step 2 illustrates string operations. We use `.jnew` to instantiate any Java object. The class name is separated by /. Hence, we refer to the string class as `java/lang/String` instead of `java.lang.string`.

The `jstrVal` function emits the equivalent of `toString()` for any Java object. In our example, we get the content of string `s`.

We use `.jcall` to execute any method on a Java object. In `jcall(s, "S", "toLowerCase")`, we are invoking the `toLowerCase` method on the string object `s`. The `"S"` variable in the call specifies the return type of the method invocation. In `.jcall(s, "S", "replaceAll", "World", "SV")`, we invoke the `replaceAll` method and get a new replaced string back.

We list the possible return types in the following table:

Return Type	Java Type	Remarks
I	int	
D	double	
J	long	
F	float	
V	void	
Z	boolean	
C	char	
B	byte (raw)	
L <class>	Java object of class <class>	Ljava/awt/Component
S	java.lang.String	S is special for Ljava/long/object
[<type>	array of objects of <type>	[D for array of doubles

Step 3 illustrates vector operations in Java from R. We first create a Java vector object using `javaVector <- .jnew("java/util/Vector")`. We then use the `add` method to add elements to this vector. Earlier in step 2, we used the `.jcall` function to invoke a method on an object, but now we use a shortcut that closely resembles what we typically do in Java. In Java, to call a method, we use the `"."` operator, and in R, we use the `$` operator. Thus, we use `javaVector$add` to invoke the `add` method on the `javaVector` object.

Step 4 illustrates Java array operations. The two key functions are `.jarray` to create an array object and `.jevalArray` to return an array object. We create three array objects-- `monthsArray`, `yearsArray`, and `calArray` using the `.jarray` function. When we print the array object using `print(monthsArray)`, we get the object type of each of the array elements. However, when we execute `.jevalArray(monthsArray)`, we get the contents of the array. The `calArray` object is a list of two Java array objects, and we also see how to extract array elements in this step.

Step 5 shows how to instantiate a custom Java object and invoke methods on it. If you have not already compiled the Java code, refer to the *Getting Ready* section at the beginning of this recipe for the instructions. We used `.jnew` to instantiate a `HelloWorld` object called `hw`. We always pass the class name along with the package to the `.jnew` function. Once the object is created, we can invoke methods. An example of invoking the `getString` method is shown in Step 6.

Step 6 shows the instantiation of another custom object `Greeting` and the invocation of a method. The arguments to the method follow the method name, as in `.jcall(greet,"S", "getString", "Shanthi")`. Here, the string `Shanthi` is an argument passed to the `getString` method.

There's more...

The following are a few key additional useful commands to invoke Java objects from the R environment.

Checking JVM properties

You may want to check the JVM properties, if you encounter issues in executing Java commands in the R console:

```
> jvm = .jnew("java.lang.System")
> jvm.props = jvm$getProperties()$toString()
> jvm.props <- strsplit(gsub("\\{(.*)}", "\\1", jvm.props), ",   ")[[1]]
> jvm.props
 [1] "java.runtime.name=Java(TM) SE Runtime Environment"
 [2]
"sun.boot.library.path=/System/Library/Java/JavaVirtualMachines/1.6.0.jdk/C
ontents/Libraries"
 [3] "java.vm.version=20.65-b04-462"
 [4] "awt.nativeDoubleBuffering=true"
 [5] "gopherProxySet=false"
 [6] "mrj.build=11M4609"
```

```
 [7] "java.vm.vendor=Apple Inc."
 [8] "java.vendor.url=http://www.apple.com/"
 [9] "path.separator=:"
[10] "java.vm.name=Java HotSpot(TM) 64-Bit Server VM"
..........
```

Displaying available methods

The following commands are useful to get a list of available methods, or to get the method signature:

```
> .jmethods(s,"trim")
[1] "public java.lang.String java.lang.String.trim()"
```

The preceding command indicates that the `trim` method can be invoked on a `String` object, and it returns a `String` object:

```
> # To get the list of available methods for an object
> .jmethods(s)
 [1] "public boolean java.lang.String.equals(java.lang.Object)"
 [2] "public java.lang.String java.lang.String.toString()"
 [3] "public int java.lang.String.hashCode()"
 [4] "public int java.lang.String.compareTo(java.lang.String)"
 [5] "public int java.lang.String.compareTo(java.lang.Object)"
 [6] "public int java.lang.String.indexOf(int)"
.....
```

Using JRI to call R functions from Java

The JRI allows you to execute R commands inside Java applications as a single thread. JRI loads R libraries into Java and, thus, provides a Java API to R functions.

Getting ready

Make sure all the steps in the earlier recipe *Using Java objects in R*, are completed.

How to do it...

To use JRI to call R functions from Java, follow these steps:

1. Set up environment variables `R_HOME` to where R has been installed, and add the R `bin` directory to the environment variable `PATH`.

2. Open a new terminal window (on OS X and Linux systems), or open a command prompt window on Windows. Make sure to change the values according to your environment. The following commands help to set up environment variables on OS X and Linux systems. Make sure to change your directory location:

```
export R_HOME=/Library/Frameworks/R.framework/Resources

export  PATH=$PATH:/Library/Frameworks/R.framework/Resources/bin/
```

3. Execute the Java command as follows from the `javasamples` directory. Make sure to change the values according to your environment. Also, there is **no space** between `-D` and `java.library.path`:

```
cd javasamples
java -
Djava.library.path=/Library/Frameworks/R.framework/Resources/librar
y/rJava/jri -cp ..:../lib/* javasamples.SimpleJRIStat

1520.15
```

How it works...

In step 1, we set up the environment variables `R_HOME` to where `R` has been installed and add the `R` bin directory to the environment variable `PATH`. If these environment variables are not set, you will see the following error message:

```
"R_HOME is not set. Please set all required environment variables before
running this program.
Unable to start R."
```

In step 2, we run the `SimpleJRIStat` Java program. Open the `SimpleJRIStat.java` code:

- In the main method, we first create an instance of `Rengine` to begin an R session.
- We check to make sure that the R session is active with the `waitForR` method.

- We create an array of doubles in Java and assign it to a variable called `values`. The `values` variable exists in the R environment and not in our Java environment.
- The `eval` method of `Rengine` is equivalent to executing commands in the R console. The output from the `eval` method is an `org.rosuda.JRI.REXP` object. Depending on the content of `REXP`, methods such as `asString()` and `asDouble()` can be executed to extract the result returned by R. In our Java code, we use the R function `mean` to calculate the average of the array and assign it to a Java `REXP` variable `mean`.
- We then use the `asDouble` method to get the value from `mean`, and print it out.
- We finally close the R session by calling the `end` method.

To execute the Java code, we need to add the `-Djava.library.path` switch (there is no space between `-D` and `java.library.path`) and point to the `rJava` location. To use `REngine` from Java, we add the appropriate JAR files to `classpath`. Since we are executing the command from the `javasamples` folder, we add `..` to `classpath` to refer to the parent folder where our library files are located under the `lib` folder.

There's more...

It is possible to create graphs using R from a Java program. Let's look at `SimplePlot.java`:

- In the main method, first we create an `Rengine` instance and check whether the R session is created successfully.
- We set the working directory in R, either from the last argument that was passed while executing the command, or from the current user directory from where the Java command was executed. The `args.length == 0` array indicates that no argument is passed during the execution of the code, and hence, we use the user directory as the R working directory.
- We use the `read.csv` function to read the file in R and load it into an R variable, `auto`.
- We use the `nrow` function to get the number of rows in `auto`, and print the value.
- We set `.png` as device and use `auto.png` as the filename to be created.
- We then use the plot function to plot `weight` vs `mpg`.
- We turn the device off to flush the file contents.
- We finally end the R session.

To execute the Java code, use the following command. Change the argument to the call to reflect your R working directory where the `auto-mpg.csv` file resides:

```
java -
Djava.library.path=/Library/Frameworks/R.framework/Resources/library/rJava/
jri/ -cp ..:../lib/* javasamples.SimplePlot /Users/sv/book/Chapter11
```

Using Rserve to call R functions from Java

The `Rserve` package is a TCP/IP server that accepts requests from clients. It allows other technologies to access R. Every connection has a separate workspace and working directory.

Getting ready

If you have not already downloaded the files for this chapter, do so now and ensure that the files are in your R working directory:

1. Create a `javasamples` folder, and move all the files with extension `Java` and `class` into this folder under your working directory.
2. Install `Rserve` using `install.packages('Rserve')`.
3. Load the package using `library(Rserve)`.
4. Download the three JAR files, `JRI.jar`, `REngine.jar`, and `JRIEngine.jar` from `http://www.rforge.net/JRI/files/` and the `RserveEngine.jar` files from `http://www.rforge.net/Rserve/files/`. Copy the four downloaded JAR files to the `lib` folder under your R working directory.
5. You can either use the class files provided or compile the Java code. These class files are created with JDK version 1.8.0_25, and, if your JDK version is different, follow the next step to compile all the Java programs.
6. To compile the downloaded Java programs, go to the `javasamples` folder, and execute the `javac -cp ..:../lib/* *java` command. You should see files with the `class` extensions for each of the downloaded Java programs.

How to do it...

To use `Rserve` to call R functions from Java, follow these steps:

1. Start the `Rserve` server to accept client connections:

   ```
   > Rserve(args="--no-save")  - On Mac and Linux
   > Rserve() - on windows
   Rserv started in daemon mode.
   ```

2. Execute the Java program to draw `ggplot` in R and display the image. Change the argument to the call to reflect your R working directory where the `auto-mpg.csv` file resides:

   ```
   java -cp ..:../lib/* javasamples.SimpleGGPlot
   /Users/sv/book/Chapter11
   ```

How it works...

In step 1, we start the `RServe` server from R. If the server is already up and running, you will see the : `##> SOCK_ERROR: bind error #48(address already in use)` message.

You can remove the current `RServe` process by killing it at the OS level. We can also start `Rserve` as a daemon process from the command line by executing `R CMD Rserve`.

`Rserve` can run locally or on a remote server accessible by multiple clients. To access the remote `Rserve` server, provide the hostname or the `IP` address of the server while creating the `RConnection`.

In step 2, we run the `SimpleGGPlot` Java program. To connect to `RServe` from Java, we add the appropriate `jars` to `classpath`. Since we are executing the command from the `javasamples` folder, we add `..` to `classpath` to refer to the parent folder where our library files are located under the `lib` folder. We also pass the folder name where the `auto-mpg.csv` file resides since that folder is our R working directory.

Open the `SimpleGGPlot.java` code as follows:

- In the main method, we first create an `RConnection` object.
- We invoke the `eval` method on the `RConnection` object to execute commands in R.

- The `RConnection` object throws `REngineException`, and hence, we add the `try` and `catch` blocks to catch the exception.
- We evaluate the following functions in R from Java:
    - We first load the `ggplot2` package in R.
    - We set the working directory in `R` using the argument passed. If no argument is passed, then the user's current directory is used to set the `R` working directory.
    - We read the contents of the `auto-mpg.csv` file using `read.csv`.
    - We create a device to save the graph and then generate `ggplot` for `weight vs mpg`.
    - We close the device to flush out the contents to the file.
    - We then read the binary content of the file.
    - The output of the `eval` or `parseAndEval` method are the `org.rosuda.REngine.REXP` objects, and, depending on the content of the `REXP` methods such as `asString()`, `asBytes()` can be executed to extract the result returned by R. In our Java code, we read the binary content of the file from the `REXP` object `xp` using `asBytes()`.
        - We close the connection after the user closes the `JFrame` image window
        - If `RServe` is not running, you will see a message:

```
Exception in thread "main"
org.rosuda.REngine.Rserve.RserveException: Cannot
connect: Connection refused".
```

There's more...

- In the *Using JRI to call R functions from Java* recipe, we showed how to execute a function in R and retrieve the value from R in Java. Here, we show how to retrieve an array from R into Java.

Retrieving an array from R

The following steps help in retrieving an array from R:

- Open the Java program, `SimpleRservStat.java`:
    - We instantiate a new `RConnection` object

- We assign a Java array of doubles to an R variable
- We calculate the mean of this array in R and print it in Java
- We then calculate the range, and since range is an array, we invoke the `asDoubles()` method on the `REXP` object that is returned from the `eval` method
- We then print the array of doubles after converting it into a string:
  - Execute the following Java code command line from the `javasamples` directory; be sure to pass your own R working directory in place of the last part of the command:

```
java -cp ..:../lib/* javasamples.SimpleRservStat
/Users/sv/book/Chapter11
```

Executing R scripts from Java

In earlier recipes, we executed R functions from within Java. In this recipe, we execute an R script from Java and read the results from R into Java for further processing.

Getting ready

Make sure all the steps in the first recipe, *Using Java objects in R*, in this chapter are completed. Also make sure the `auto-mpg.csv` and `corr.R` files are in your R working directory.

How to do it...

Execute the Java program from your command prompt to invoke an R script from a Java program. Be sure to change the last part to reflect your R working directory:

```
java -
Djava.library.path=/Library/Frameworks/R.framework/Resources/library/rJava/
jri/ -cp ..:../lib/* javasamples.InvokeRScript mpg weight
/Users/sv/book/Chapter11
```

How it works...

We execute the Java program, `InvokeScript` with three arguments. The first two arguments mention the columns of the `auto` table for which correlation is computed, and the optional third argument is the working directory, where the `auto-mpg.csv` file and the R script reside.

Let's look at the `InvokeScript.java` code:

- In the main method, first we create an `Rengine` instance and check whether the R session is created successfully.
- We check whether there are at least two arguments passed to the `InvokeScript` Java program. If not, we display an error message:

  ```
  To execute, please provide 2 variable names from auto-mpg dataset.
  ```

- If the length of the arguments array, `args.length`, is equal to 2, we know that the user did not provide the R working directory; take the user's current directory as the working directory, and set it in R.
- We set two variables, `var1` and `var2` from the arguments using the method assign. These variables are created in the R environment.
- We then invoke the `eval` method to source the R script file `corr.R`.
- We get the result into a `REXP` object.
- We print the value by invoking the `asDouble` method on the `REXP` object.
- Finally, we close the `Rengine` object to release the R session.

Let's look at the R script `corr.R`:

- Load the contents of the `auto-mpg.csv` file into an R object auto.
- Execute the `cor` function to calculate the correlation between the two variables that were passed as an argument to the Java program, `InvokeScript`.

Using the xlsx package to connect to Excel

There are multiple packages to connect Excel with R; in this recipe, we discuss the `xlsx` package. Other commonly used packages are `RExcel` and `XLConnect`.

Getting ready

If you have not already downloaded the files for this chapter, do it now and ensure that the files are in your R working directory:

- Install `xlsx` using `install.packages("xlsx")`.
- Load the library using `library(xlsx)`.
- Read the data:

```
> auto <- read.csv("auto-mpg.csv", stringsAsFactors=FALSE)
```

How to do it...

To connect to Excel using the `xlsx` package, follow the steps:

1. Save a data frame to an Excel workbook:

```
> write.xlsx(auto, file = "auto.xlsx", sheetName =    "autobase",
row.names = FALSE)
```

2. Add two new columns to the auto data frame:

```
> auto$kmpg <- auto$mpg * 1.6
> auto$mpg_deviation <- (auto$mpg -    mean(auto$mpg))/auto$mpg
```

3. Create Excel objects such as workbooks, worksheets, rows, and cells:

```
> auto.wb <- createWorkbook()
> sheet1 <- createSheet(auto.wb,"auto1")
> rows <- createRow(sheet1, rowIndex=1)
> cell.1 <- createCell(rows, colIndex=1)[[1,1]]
> setCellValue(cell.1, "Hello Auto Data!")
> addDataFrame(auto, sheet1, startRow=3, row.names=FALSE)
```

4. Assign styles to cells:

```
> cs <- CellStyle(auto.wb) +    Font(auto.wb, isBold=TRUE,
color="red")
> setCellStyle(cell.1, cs)
> saveWorkbook(auto.wb, "auto_wb.xlsx")
```

5. Add another sheet to an Excel workbook:

```
> wb <- loadWorkbook("auto_wb.xlsx")
> sheet2 <- createSheet(auto.wb,"auto2")
> addDataFrame(auto[,1:9], sheet2, row.names=FALSE)
> saveWorkbook(auto.wb, "auto_wb.xlsx")
```

6. Add columns to a worksheet, and save the workbook:

```
> wb <- loadWorkbook("auto_wb.xlsx")
> sheets <- getSheets(wb)
> sheet <- sheets[[2]]
> addDataFrame(auto[,10:11], sheet, startColumn=10,
row.names=FALSE)
> saveWorkbook(wb, "newauto.xlsx")
```

7. Read from an Excel workbook:

```
> new.auto <- read.xlsx("newauto.xlsx", sheetIndex=2)
> head(new.auto)
> new.auto <- read.xlsx("newauto.xlsx", sheetName="auto2")
```

8. Read a specific region from an Excel workbook:

```
> sub.auto <- read.xlsx("newauto.xlsx",  sheetName="autobase",
rowIndex=1:4, colIndex=1:9
```

How it works...

There are multiple options for reading and saving a worksheet. Let's look at a few examples.

Step 1 saves the auto data frame to a new worksheet called autobase and creates the Excel file. If we do not include row.names=FALSE, the row numbers are displayed as the first column in the spreadsheet.

Step 2 adds two additional columns to the auto data frame. The first column kmpg is kilometers per gallon, and the second new column is the mean mpg deviation. We used vector operations to compute the columns.

Step 3 shows the following functions to create workbooks, worksheets, rows, and cells:

- `createWorkbook`: This creates a workbook object and returns a reference to the object.
- `createSheet`: This creates a worksheet and gives it the name passed in. If a sheet name is not provided, a default sheet name `sheetx` is used.
- `createRow`: This creates a row within the sheet. `rowIndex` specifies the row number.
- `createCell`: This creates a cell in the given row at a specific column index.
- `setCellValue`: This assigns a value to the specified cell.
- `addDataFrame`: This includes a data frame to the specified sheet. By default, `row.names` are included, and the starting row and column is 1. However, these can be passed as an argument to specify a different row and column index. In our example, we used `startRow=3`, since we manually created the first row to hold the heading followed by an empty row. We defaulted the column to 1.

Step 4 shows how styles can be added to a cell. We can add styles while creating the row, column, or adding a data frame. Whatever you can do in Excel by way of styling can be done within R. Here, we see an example of adding a color and font to our heading row cell.

Step 5 shows the addition of a new sheet. We use `addDataFrame` to add a data frame. Once again, we use `row.names=FALSE` so as not to include the row numbers as a column. Since we did not specify the `startRow`, it is taken as 1. We save the workbook with the two new sheets as `auto_wb.xlsx`.

Step 6 uses the `addDataFrame` function to add a data frame to a worksheet. We first read the previously saved workbook file `auto.xlsx` using `loadWorkbook` and save it in a variable `wb`. We then call the `getSheets` function to get all the worksheets in this workbook. The `getSheets` function returns an array, and we can get a specific sheet by mentioning its index. Hence, `sheets[[2]]` returns the second sheet in the workbook.

We add the two new columns that we created in step 2 to the sheet. Finally, we save the workbook.

Step 7 shows how to read directly from an Excel file using `read.xlsx`. We can refer to a specific sheet either using `sheetIndex` or `sheetName`. The `sheetIndex` attribute starts from 1.

Step 8 shows how to load a specific region from an Excel sheet. The `rowIndex` attribute is set to `1:4` and extracts the header row and the first three data rows.

Reading data from relational databases - MySQL

You can connect to relational databases using several different approaches.

The `RODBC` package provides access to most relational databases through the **ODBC** (**Open Database Connectivity**) interface. The `RJDBC` package provides access to databases through the JDBC interface and, hence, needs a Java environment.

There are database packages such as `ROracle`, `RMySQL`, and so on to provide connectivity to the specific relational databases.

Each of the aforementioned options performs differently and has different requirements. You should benchmark and select the package that performs best for your specific needs. In general, `RJDBC` performs poorly, and hence, you will likely choose `RODBC` or your database-specific R package. In this recipe, we describe the steps to work with the MySQL database and build the foundation to create a `recommendation` system for the final recipe of the book.

Getting ready

First create a data frame to work with as follows:

```
> customer <- c("John", "Peter", "Jane")
> orddt <- as.Date(c('2014-10-1','2014-1-2','2014-7-6'))
> ordamt <- c(280, 100.50, 40.25)
> order <- data.frame(customer,orddt,ordamt)
```

Then install the `MySQL` server, and create in it a database called `Customer`.

To use the `RODBC` package, perform the following steps:

1. Download and install MySQL Connector/ODBC for your operating system.
2. Create a DSN in the ODBC Configuration Manager by selecting the correct driver for your platform.
3. In R, execute `install.packages("RODBC")`.

To use the `RJDBC` package, perform the following steps:

1. Download and install MySQL Connector/J for your operating system.
2. Install Java Runtime, and set the `JAVA_HOME` environment variable accordingly.
3. In R, execute `install.packages("RJDBC")`.

To use the `RMySQL` package, perform the following steps:

1. Download and install MySQL Connector/J for your operating system.
2. Create an environment variable `MYSQL_HOME` pointing to the folder where MySQL is installed.
3. Only on Windows, copy `libmysql.dll` from the `lib` directory of your MySQL installation to the bin directory.
4. In R, execute `install.packages("RMySQL")`.

To load the `.csv` files in MySQL and later read it using `RMySQL`, do the following:

1. Make sure you have the `rating.csv` and `accommodation.csv` files in the working directory.
2. Create database and tables in MySQL:
    1. Log in to your MySQL console or MySQL client (change your hostname/IP, username, and password credentials with the attributes `-h` , `-u`, and `-p` respectively) `mysql -h localhost -u root -p` as shown in the following screenshot:

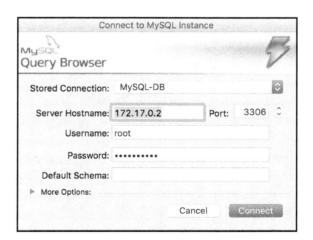

You can also use MySQL graphical browser to create database and tables:

```
CREATE DATABASE IF NOT EXISTS recommendation;
USE recommendation;
CREATE TABLE IF NOT EXISTS rating
(
 userId int,
 movieId int,
 rating int
);
CREATE TABLE IF NOT EXISTS accommodation
(
  id varchar(255),
  title varchar(255),
  location varchar(255),
  price int,
  rooms int,
  rating float,
  type varchar(255)
  PRIMARY KEY (ID)
);
```

2. Load the `.csv` files into MySQL tables either from the MySQL console/browser or through the `mysqlimport` utilities.

```
load data local infile 'rating.csv' into table rating;
> mysqlimport --fields-terminated-by=, --verbose --
local -u root -p recommendation rating.csv
```

3. Verify the data in the tables from the MySQL console/browser:

```
mysql> select * from rating limit 5;
+--------+---------+--------+
| userId | movieId | rating |
+--------+---------+--------+
|      1 |    1193 |      5 |
|      1 |     661 |      3 |
|      1 |     914 |      3 |
|      1 |    3408 |      4 |
|      1 |    2355 |      5 |
+--------+---------+--------+
5 rows in set (0.00 sec)
```

How to do it...

We will show how to use each of the preceding packages to connect to the database.

Using RODBC

To use the RODBC package to connect to the database, follow these steps:

1. Load the RODBC library, and create a connection object:

```
> library(RODBC)
> con <- odbcConnect("order_dsn", uid="user", pwd="pwd")
```

2. Save the order object into a table in the database:

```
> sqlSave(con,order, "orders",append=FALSE)
```

3. Get all orders from the database table:

```
> custData <- sqlQuery(con, "select * from orders")
```

4. Close the connection object:

```
> close(con)
```

Using RMySQL

To use the RMySQL package, follow these steps:

1. Load the RMySQL library, and create a connection object:

```
> library(RMySQL)
> con <- dbConnect(MySQL(), dbname="recommendation",
host="127.0.0.1", port=3306, username="root",     password="root")
```

2. Save the order object into a table in the database:

```
> dbWriteTable(con,"orders", order)
```

3. Get all accommodations from the database table:

```
> # Get all rows/data using dbReadTable
> dbReadTable(con,"accomodation")
> # Get rows based on query using dbGetQuery
```

```
> dbGetQuery(con,"select * from accommodation limit 5")
```

4. Get the accommodations grouped by location, based on their price, from the database table using a loop:

```
> rs <- dbSendQuery(con, "select location, max(price) from
accommodation group by location order by max(price) desc")
> while(!dbHasCompleted(rs)) {
  fetch(rs,n=2)
  }
> dbClearResult(rs)
> dbDisconnect(con)
> dbListConnections(dbDriver("MySQL"))
```

Using RJDBC

To use the RJDBC package, follow these steps:

1. Load the RJDBC library, and create a connection object. Make sure to point to the correct location of the downloaded .jar file:

```
> library(RJDBC)
> driver <- JDBC("com.mysql.jdbc.Driver",     classpath=
"/etc/jdbc/mysql-connector-java-5.1.34-bin.jar", "'")
> con <- dbConnect(driver, "jdbc:mysql://host:port/Customer"     ,
"username","password")
```

2. The remaining operations are identical to those in the *Using RMySQL* section.

How it works...

The preceding code first creates a data frame called order with three rows. It then connects to a MySQL database using different methods and reads data from it.

Using RODBC

In this method, we execute the following command:

```
> con <- odbcConnect("cust_dsn", uid="user", pwd="pwd")
```

The con variable now has a connection to the database associated with the DSN. All subsequent database calls use this connection object. When all database operations are done, we close the connection.

Although we will typically not create tables or insert data from R, we have shown the code for this just for illustration. The sqlSave function saves the data in the R data object to the specified table. We used append=FALSE because the table does not already exist, and, hence, we will want R to create the table first and then insert the data. If the table already exists, you can use append=TRUE.

The sqlQuery function executes the supplied query and returns the result set as a data frame.

Using RMySQL

The RMySQL package uses the MYSQL_HOME environment variable to get to the needed libraries:

```
> dbWriteTable(con, "orders", order)
```

The dbWriteTable function inserts records into the table. If the table does not exist, it creates the table. By default, row.names of the data frame is added as a column to the table; if it is not needed, remember to set it to FALSE:

```
> dbReadTable(con, "accomodation")
```

The dbReadTable function reads the table and creates a data frame:

```
> dbGetQuery(con,"select * from accomodation limit 5")
```

The dbGetQuery function executes the query and returns all the results as a data frame. When the table is large, it is better to use the dbSendQuery and fetch results as needed:

```
> rs <- dbSendQuery(con, "select * from accomodation")
> while(!dbHasCompleted(rs)) {
+     fetch(rs,n=2)
+ }
> dbClearResult(rs)
> dbDisconnect(con)
```

The dbSendQuery function returns rs, a result set object. When you fetch rows with this object, since n=2, two records are returned from the database. While using dbSendQuery, it is a good idea to use a loop until dbHasCompleted is TRUE. Remember to clear the pointer with dbClearResult, and close the connection using dbDisconnect:

```
> dbListConnections(dbDriver("MySQL"))
```

The `dbListConnections` function lists all the open connections.

Using RJDBC

With JDBC, we can connect to any database. Hence, we need to tell R which driver to use. Once the driver is assigned in R, we use this later to create a connection to the database using the appropriate `.jar` files.

When connecting to a MySQL database, all the statements after getting the connection object are identical to those in the RMySQL scenario.

There's more...

The database-specific packages provide a lot of functionality, and pretty much most of what can be done within a SQL client can also be done from within an R environment. We show a few examples as follows.

Fetching all rows

The following command is used to fetch all rows:

```
> fetch(rs,n=-1)
```

Use `n=-1` to fetch all rows.

When the SQL query is long

When the SQL query is long, it becomes unwieldy to specify the whole query as one long string spanning several lines. Use the `paste()` function to break the query over multiple lines and make it more readable:

```
> dbSendQuery(con, statement=paste(
    "select ordernumber, orderdate, customername",
    "from orders o, customers c",
    "where o.customer = c.customer",
    "and c.state = 'NJ'",
    "ORDER BY ordernumber"))
```

Note the use of the single quotes to specify a string literal.

Reading data from NoSQL databases - MongoDB

In the previous recipe, we showed that R connects very well with relational and SQL databases. However, recently, a new range of NoSQL databases have emerged rapidly in response to the growing ecosystem of applications that collect and process different types of data, with schema-less designs having more flexibility. We will illustrate this with MongoDB using the `rmongodb` and `mongolite` packages.

Getting ready

Prepare the environment by following these steps:

1. Download and install MongoDB.
2. Start `mongod` as a background process.
3. Make sure the `Chicago_Crimes_2012_to_2017.csv` file is in the working directory of R.
4. Install the `rmongodb`, `mongolite`, `ggplot2`, `ggmap`, `data.table`, `dplyr` packages for this recipe:

   ```
   install.packages(c("rmongodb", "mongolite", "ggplot2", "ggmap",
   "data.table", "dplyr"))
   ```

How to do it...

To read data from MongoDB, follow these steps:

1. Load the Chicago crime dataset with a data table. This dataset is taken from `Kaggle` and modified for this recipe:

   ```
   > library(data.table)
   > crimes=data.table::fread("Chicago_Crimes_2012-2017.csv")
   ```

2. Load `rmongodb` and `mongolite`:

```
> library(rmongodb)
> library(mongolite)
```

3. Create the MongoDB crime collection, and insert data into it:

```
> crime_collection = mongo(collection = "crimes", db = "Chicago")
> crime_collection$insert(crimes)
```

4. Verify the MongoDB crime collection:

```
> # Using mongolite
> crime_collection$count()
> crime_collection$iterate()$one()

> using rmongodb
> mongo <- mongo.create(host = "localhost")
> mongo.is.connected(mongo)
> mongo.get.database.collections(mongo,"Chicago")
> mongo.find.one(mongo, ns="Chicago.crimes")
```

5. Find total assaults in the collection:

```
> crime_collection$count('{"PrimaryType" : "ASSAULT" }')
[1] 182578
```

6. Find the top five most common types of crime:

```
> library(dplyr)

> crimes<-crime_collection$find('{}', fields = '{"_id":0,
"PrimaryType":1,"Year":1}')

>crimes%>%group_by(PrimaryType)%>%summarize(Count=n())%>%arrange(de
sc(Count))%>%head(5)

# A tibble: 5 x 2
 PrimaryType Count
 <chr> <int>
1 <NA> 878049
2 THEFT 658920
3 BATTERY 527400
4 CRIMINAL DAMAGE 310910
5 NARCOTICS 270480
```

How it works...

The `fread()` function is similar to `read.table` and reads data from the `.csv` file in a fast and efficient way.

The `mongo` function creates a mongo connection with a database and a collection name. Then we use the insert function on that connection object to load data into the collection.

The `count()` function is used to count the total number of documents (that is, the number of rows inserted) in the collection. The `iterate()one()` function returns the first documents in the collection.

The `find()` function automatically simplifies the collection into a data frame. The empty query `{}` attribute means select all data. The `fields` attribute is used to filter specific columns from the output.

The `mongo_create` function creates a mongo session. If no argument is passed, it connects to the localhost at the default port `27017`, where `mongod` is running.

Ensure that R has a valid mongo session using `mongo.is.connected(mongo)`.

The `mongo.get.database.collections` function lists all the collections in that database.

The `mongo.find.all` function lists all the rows in that collection. By passing in a valid JSON object, the query results are limited by the search condition specified in the JSON object. If a JSON object is not passed, all rows are returned. R creates a data frame with the returned result.

There's more...

The fluidity of the NoSQL environment and the newness of MongoDB mean that the `rmongodb` and `mongolite` packages change frequently. You should update the `rmongodb` and `mongolite` packages to get the latest enhancements into your R environment. The API of `mongolite` is elegant and resembles the actual MongoDB style operation compared to `rmongodb`; hence, most code in this recipe uses it.

Find most severe crime zone

The `aggregate()` function allows you to run an aggregation pipeline. For example the following pipeline calculates the total crimes per location and then shows it using a horizontal bar plot which is shown in the graph after the code:

```
> library(ggplot2)
> crime_collection$aggregate('[{"$group":{"_id":"$LocationDescription",
"Count": {"$sum":1}}}]')%>%na.omit()%>%
arrange(desc(Count))%>%head(10)%>%
ggplot(aes(x=reorder(`_id`,Count),y=Count))+
geom_bar(stat="identity",fill='#c37600')+geom_text(aes(label = Count),
color = "blue") +coord_flip()+xlab("Location Description")
```

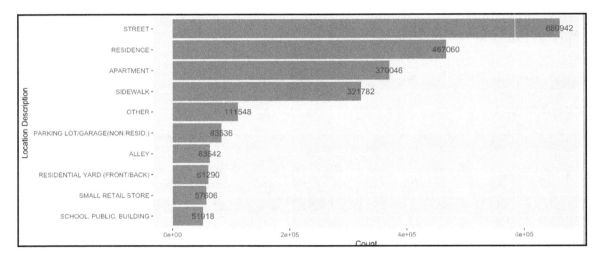

Plotting the crimes on the Chicago map

We can use the `ggmap` function to plot crime data points on the Chicago map using the latitude and longitude values provided for each crime activity:

```
> library(maps)
> library(ggmap)
> query= crime_collection$find('{}', fields = '{"_id":0, "Latitude":1,
"Longitude":1,"Year":1}')
> LatLonCounts=as.data.frame(table(round(query$Longitude,2),
round(query$Latitude,2)))

> # Convert the Longitude and Latitude variable to numbers:
> LatLonCounts$Long = as.numeric(as.character(LatLonCounts$Var1))
```

```
> LatLonCounts$Lat = as.numeric(as.character(LatLonCounts$Var2))

> ggmap(chicago)+geom_tile(data = LatLonCounts, aes(x = Long, y = Lat,
alpha = Freq), fill="red")+ggtitle("Crime
Distribution")+labs(alpha="Count")+theme(plot.title =
element_text(color="blue",hjust=0.5))
```

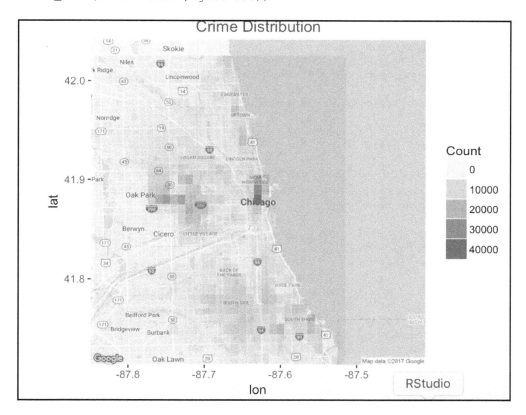

Working with in-memory data processing with Apache Spark

Apache Spark is a fast, general-purpose, fault-tolerant framework for interactive and iterative computations on large, distributed datasets. It supports a wide variety of data sources as well as storage layers.

It provides unified data access to combine different data formats, `streaming data`, and defining complex operations using high-level, composable operators. You can develop your applications interactively using Scala, Python, or R shell. In this recipe, you will learn various way of interacting with Apache Spark through R for data handling, along with predictive analysis on datasets.

Getting ready

There are different ways of installing Apache Spark with R:

- Install directly from a GitHub repository:

```
if (!require('devtools')) install.packages('devtools')
  devtools::install_github('apache/spark@v2.1.1', subdir='R/pkg')
```

- Install from a downloaded binary Apache Spark package: R library is in an `R/lib/SparkR` subdirectory. It can be used to install SparkR directly using the following commands:

```
$ export SPARK_HOME=/path/to/spark/directory
$ cd $SPARK_HOME/R/lib/SparkR/
$ R -e "devtools::install('.')"
```

- Load the `library` SparkR:

```
> library(SparkR)
> Sys.setenv(SPARK_HOME='/path/to/spark/directory')
 .libPaths(c(file.path(Sys.getenv('SPARK_HOME'), 'R', 'lib'),
.libPaths()))
```

How to do it...

1. Initialize SparkSession object:

```
> sparkR.session() # From your R console or RStudio

# Alternatively, you may launch sparkR shell which comes with
predefined SparkSession.
> bin/sparkR
```

2. Create Spark DataFrame:

```
> irisDF <- createDataFrame(iris) //Create a Spark DataFrame
> showDF(irisDF,4) //Print the contents of the Spark DataFrame
+-----------+-----------+-----------+-----------+-------+
|Sepal_Length|Sepal_Width|Petal_Length|Petal_Width|Species|
+-----------+-----------+-----------+-----------+-------+
|      5.1|        3.5|         1.4|        0.2| setosa|
|      4.9|        3.0|         1.4|        0.2| setosa|
|      4.7|        3.2|         1.3|        0.2| setosa|
|      4.6|        3.1|         1.5|        0.2| setosa|
+-----------+-----------+-----------+-----------+-------+
only showing top 4 rows
```

3. The following is a subsetting data example:

```
> subIrisDF <- select(irisDF, c("Sepal_Length","Petal_Length"))
> showDF(subIrisDF,5)
+-----------+-----------+
|Sepal_Length|Petal_Length|
+-----------+-----------+
|      5.1|        1.4|
|      4.9|        1.4|
|      4.7|        1.3|
|      4.6|        1.5|
|      5.0|        1.4|
+-----------+-----------+
only showing top 5 rows
```

4. The following shows grouping and aggregation on DataFrame:

```
> library(magrittr)
> aggrIrishDF <- irisDF %>% groupBy("Species") %>%
avg("Sepal_Length") %>%
withColumnRenamed("avg(Sepal_Length)","avg_sepal_len") %>%
orderBy ("Species")
> #Format the computed double column
>aggrIrishDF$avg_sepal_len <-
format_number(aggrIrishDF$avg_sepal_len,2)
> #This shows group wise average sepal length sorted by species
name.
> showDF(aggrIrishDF)
+----------+-------------+
| Species|avg_sepal_len|
+----------+-------------+
|    setosa|         5.01|
|versicolor|         5.94|
| virginica|         6.59|
```

```
+----------+------------+
```

5. This shows an SQL operation on DataFrame:

```
> #Create a view of the DataFrame to run SQL over the data
> createOrReplaceTempView(irisDF,"iris_vw")
> collect(sql("SELECT * FROM iris_tbl LIMIT 5"))
> collect(sql("SELECT Species, avg(Sepal_Length)
avg_sepal_length, avg(Sepal_Width) avg_sepal_width FROM iris_tbl
GROUP BY Species ORDER BY avg_sepal_length desc")
```

The following output is generated by preceding commands:

```
> collect(sql("SELECT * FROM iris_vw LIMIT 5"))
  Sepal_Length Sepal_Width Petal_Length Petal_Width Species
1          5.1         3.5          1.4         0.2  setosa
2          4.9         3.0          1.4         0.2  setosa
3          4.7         3.2          1.3         0.2  setosa
4          4.6         3.1          1.5         0.2  setosa
5          5.0         3.6          1.4         0.2  setosa
>
> collect(sql("SELECT Species, avg(Sepal_Length)
+ avg_sepal_length, avg(Sepal_Width) avg_sepal_width FROM iris_vw
+          GROUP BY Species ORDER BY avg_sepal_length desc"))
      Species avg_sepal_length avg_sepal_width
1   virginica            6.588           2.974
2  versicolor            5.936           2.770
3      setosa            5.006           3.428
>
```

How it works...

The entry point to SparkR is the `SparkSession` object, which represents the connection to the Spark cluster. The node on which R is running becomes the driver. Any objects created by the R program reside on this node. At the moment, R cannot be used to manipulate the RDDs of Spark directly. Therefore, for all practical purposes, the R API for Spark only has access to Spark SQL abstractions.

There's more...

The entry point to SparkR is the `SparkSession` object, which represents the connection to the Spark cluster. The node on which R is running becomes the driver. Any objects created by the R program reside on this node. At the moment, R cannot be used to manipulate the RDDs of Spark directly. So for all practical purposes, the R API for Spark has access to only Spark SQL abstractions.

Classification with SparkR

Download the data files for this chapter from the book's website, and place the `boston-housing-logistic.csv` file in your R working directory:

```
> df <- read.df("boston-housing-logistic.csv", "csv", header = "true",
inferSchema = "true", na.strings = "NA")
> traindata <- sample(df,FALSE,0.8)
> testdata <- except(df,traindata)

> model <- glm(CLASS ~ NOX+DIS+RAD+TAX+PTRATIO,data = traindata, family =
"binomial")
> predictions <- predict(model, newData = testdata)
> head(predictions)
  NOX DIS RAD TAX PTRATIO B CLASS label prediction
1 0.538 4.2579 4 307 21.0 386.75 0 0 0.10200645
2 0.437 4.2515 5 398 18.7 394.92 1 1 0.77829571
3 0.871 1.4191 5 403 14.7 172.91 0 0 0.03680177
4 0.464 4.4290 3 223 18.6 396.90 1 1 0.87503152
5 0.585 2.3817 6 391 19.2 396.90 1 1 0.21772395
6 0.458 6.0622 3 222 18.7 394.12 1 1 0.81264607
```

Movie lens recommendation system with SparkR

In the earlier recipe with R and MySQL, we set up a `recommendation` database with a `rating` table containing movie-lens data. We will fetch the data from MySQL using the SparkR `read.jdbc()` function, then use the **Alternating Least Square** (**ALS**) recommendation algorithm on the data examples to generate a predictive model:

```
> jdbcUrl="jdbc:mysql://localhost:3306/recommendation"
> dfRates = read.jdbc(jdbcUrl, "recommendation.rating", user = "root",
password = "root")
> df_list <- randomSplit(dfRates, c(7,3), 2)
> recommendDF <- df_list[[1]]
> recommendTestDF <- df_list[[2]]
```

```
># Fit a recommendation model using ALS with spark.als
> model <- spark.als(recommendDF, maxIter = 5, regParam = 0.01, userCol =
"userId",itemCol = "movieId", ratingCol = "rating")

> summary(model) # Model summary
> predictions <- predict(model, recommendTestDF)
> head(predictions)
userId movieId rating prediction
1 53 148 5 4.774571
2 3184 148 4 2.228373
3 4387 148 1 3.740824
4 1242 148 3 4.478038
5 216 148 2 2.066219
6 3829 148 2 3.492133
```

If you get an error while running the preceding invokeJava or RBackendHandler
Error code, run the following code first:

```
> Sys.setenv(SPARK_HOME="/path/spark/home")
 > Sys.setenv('SPARKR_SUBMIT_ARGS'='"--packages" "com.databricks:spark-
csv_2.11:1.2.0" "sparkr-shell"')
 > library(SparkR)
 > sparkR.session(master = "local[*]")
```

Index

selecting 312, 313
grid
  multiple plots, generating 77, 80
groups
  combining 446

H

heatmap
  creating 283, 284, 285
  plotting, over geospatial data 286, 287
hierarchical clustering
  used, for performing cluster analysis 188, 189, 190
hist3D() function
  attributes 311
histogram plot
  creating 273
  generating 272
histograms
  density plot, overlay 73, 74
  generating 64, 65, 66
  working 72, 73
Holt-Winters method
  used, for forecasting 250, 252, 253
  used, for smoothing 250, 252, 253
HTML table data
  extracting, from web page 14
hybrid systems
  building 330, 331, 332
hyperlinks
  using, in R presentations 417

I

image classification system
  developing, pretrained deep neural networks used 336, 337
image segmentation
  with mini-batch K-means 197, 198, 199
interactive web applications
  creating, with shiny 407, 409
internal clustering validation 204
intervals
  creating, automatically 32
item-based collaborative filtering (IBCF) 317

J

Java Native Interface (JNI) 486
Java objects
  using, in R 486, 487, 488, 489, 490, 491, 492
Java program
  graphs, creating with R 495
Java Virtual Machine (JVM) 490
Java
  about 486
  available methods, displaying 493
  JRI, used for calling R functions 493, 494
  R scripts, executing from 499
  Rserve, used for calling R functions 496, 497
JavaScript Object Notation (JSON) 9
JRI
  used, for calling R functions 494
JSON data
  extracting 16
  reading 15
json formatter
  URL 358
JVM properties
  checking 492

K

k-fold cross-validation
  performing 181, 182
k-means clustering 194
k-medoids clustering 200
knitr
  dynamic integration of shiny 413
  used, for generating reports of data analysis 396, 397, 398, 403, 404
KNN classification
  about 124
  caret, used for selecting appropriate values of k 125
  KNN, used for computing raw probabilities instead of classification 127
  process of running KNN, automating for k values 125
KNN for multiple k values
  running, convenience function used 151
KNN models

building, for regression 145, 146, 147, 148
KNN
   running, convenience function used 150
   running, with cross-validation 149

L

labels
   adding 291
lapply function
   used, for applying functions to elements of
     collections 429, 431
lattice package
   used, for plots creating 80, 81, 82, 83, 84
lattice plot command
   annotations 81
   data 81
   formula 81
   graph type 81
lda function 130
leave-one-out cross-validation
   performing, to limit overfitting 184, 185
legend
   adding 291, 293
   moving 294
line graph
   creating 264, 266
   used, for visualizing plot 311
linear discriminant function (LDF) 131
linear discriminant function analysis
   using, for classification 130, 131, 132
linear models
   options, using in formula expression 158
linear regression
   performing 152, 153, 155, 156
   variable selection, performing in 159, 160
list of data frames
   concatenating, into big data frame 439
lm function
   forcing, to use specific factor level as reference
     157
loaded packages
   datasets, listing in 20
logistic regression
   using, for classification 133

M

maps package
   used, for obtaining maps 466, 467
markdown syntax elements
   reference 405
MASS package 130
Mean absolute error (MAE) 344
Mean squared error (MSE) 344
mean/median imputation
   outliers, treating with 48
mean
   used, for replacing missing values 23
measures, for data analysis
   asymmetry measures 55
   center measures 54
   spread measures 55
Meetup API
   URL 356
mice() function
   parameters 44
min-max range
   variable, rescaling to 26
mini-batch K-means
   using, in image segmentation 197, 198, 199
Missing at Random (MAR) 44
missing data
   handling 34, 35, 36, 37
missing values
   cases, removing with 20, 21
   replacing, with mean 23
ML algorithms
   applications 335
ml-100k dataset, MovieLens website
   reference 325
model-based clustering
   with EM algorithm 213, 214, 215, 216
models
   suitable model, identifying 345, 346
MongoDB
   about 511
   data, reading from 511, 512
mosaic graphs
   creating 274, 275
movie lens recommendation system

principal component analysis
  dimensionality, reducing with 217, 218, 219, 220
principal components (PCs) 99
public APIs
  used, for downloading social network data 356, 357, 358, 360, 361

Q

QGIS
  and R, used for spatial data analysis 477, 478, 479, 481, 482, 483
qplot
  used, for creating graph 264

R

R data files
  attaching, to environment 20
  detaching, from environment 20
R files
  data, reading from 18
R functions
  calling, JRI used 493, 494
  calling, Rserve used 496, 497
R libraries
  data, reading from 18
R Markdown
  used, for generating reports of data analysis 396, 397, 398, 403, 404
R presentation of analysis
  display, controlling 417
  hyperlinks, using 417
  look, enhancing 418
R presentation
  PDF presentations of analysis, creating with 414, 415, 416
R scripts
  executing, from Java 499
R
  about 485
  and QGIS, used for spatial data analysis 477, 478, 479, 481, 482, 483
  array, retrieving from 498
  ESRI shape files, importing 459, 461
  Java objects, using in 486, 487, 488, 489, 490,

random data partitions
  case 60, 61
  convenience function, using 62
  creating 60, 62
  set of values, sampling from 63
random forest models
  building, for regression 171, 172, 173, 176
  using, for classification 111, 112, 113
random values sampled
  imputing, from non-missing values 24
randomForest package 111
rating matrix
  visualizing 320, 321, 322
read.csv() function
  about 10
  column delimiters, handling 11
  column headers, handling 11
  data, reading from website 12
  missing values, handling 12
  strings, reading as characters 12
  variable names, handling 11
read.fwf() function
  about 17
  columns, excluding from data 18
  files with headers 17
receiver operating characteristic (ROC)
  about 101
  arbitrary class labels, using 104
receiver operating characteristic charts
  generating 101, 103
recommendation model
  parameters, optimizing 347
recommender models
  evaluating 338, 340, 342, 344
Recommender System 315
recommender systems 315
recommenderlab package 320
regression analysis 143
regression trees
  building 162, 163, 164, 165, 167, 168
  generating, ensemble method used 170
regression
  KNN models, building for 145, 146, 147, 148
  neural networks, using for 177, 178, 179, 180

World Geodetic System 1984 (WGS84) standard
474

XML data
reading 12, 13

www.ingramcontent.com/pod-product-compliance
Lightning Source LLC
LaVergne TN
LVHW081507050326
832903LV00025B/1409